THE AMERICAN MIND

An Interpretation of American

Thought and Character Since the 1880's

BY HENRY STEELE COMMAGER

New Haven & London · Yale University Press

For E.A.C.

XXXVIII

. . . . .

O, give thyself the thanks, if aught in me
Worthy perusal stand against thy sight.
For who's so dumb that cannot write to thee,
When thou thyself dost give invention light?
Be thou the tenth Muse, ten times more in worth
Than those old nine which rhymers invocate;
And he that calls on thee, let him bring forth
Eternal numbers to outlive long date.
   If my slight Muse do please these curious days,
   The pain be mine, but thine shall be the praise.

"To be an American is of itself almost a moral condition, an education, and a career."

Santayana, *Character and Opinion in the United States*

Preface

I F EIGHTEENTH-CENTURY titles were still fashionable, I would call this book Prolegomenon to an Interpretation of Some Aspects of American Thought and Character from the 1880's to the 1940's. That title would have the merit of accuracy. For two things will be at once apparent to the reader of this book: first, that it is an interpretation rather than a detailed chronicle; and second, that it does not pretend to cover the whole of that vast and amorphous subject embraced in the phrase "American Mind." For these two limitations —I will not call them shortcomings—I submit no apologies. There are histories enough—of philosophy, religion, literature, politics, and the social sciences—and the gaps that remain will doubtless be filled by competent scholars. Nor do I feel any sense of compunction for my failure to discuss at length such things as art, education, criticism, psychology, anthropology, business, science, technology, and a dozen other manifestations of American culture that doubtless require attention in any thoroughgoing evaluation of the American mind and character. My reasons for omitting all but incidental references to these subjects are very simple: I do not know enough about them, or I have not been able to make up my mind about them.

What I have been concerned with throughout this book is that elusive thing which I have called the American mind. The far from inarticulate major premise of my investigation is that there is a distinctively American way of thought, character, and conduct. I have tried to discover and to interpret this American way in some of its most revealing manifestations. I do not for a moment suppose that those which I have discussed are the only manifestations, nor am I sure that they are its most dramatic or most significant. They are merely those which seem to me significant and which I feel some competence in interpreting.

It should be unnecessary to add that I do not attempt in these pages a substantive history of even those manifestations of thought and conduct which I attempt to interpret. I am not concerned here with abbreviated histories of American philosophy or religion, sociology or economics, politics or law, but with ideas that illuminate the American mind and ways of using ideas that illustrate the American character. This means, of course, that my interpretation is both selective and subjective. It means, too, that I have discussed only those aspects of American thought which did seem to me revealing, and discussed them only in relation to my theme. Those accustomed to neat and artificial divisions in the humanities and the social sciences may find this a bit upsetting. Thus because I am not, here, interested in literature as such but in literature as philosophical expression, I have allowed men of letters to speak when and where they would— at one time on the social transition, at another on determinism, at still another on economy and politics. And, as many writers whom I cherish—Elinor Wylie, for instance, or Robert Frost—have little to say that is germane to my subject, I have respected their independence and not tried to force them to testify.

I have chosen the period from the mid-eighties to the present because it seems to me that the mid-eighties and the nineties constituted something of a watershed in American history and thought and that the period since that time has a certain unity: the reasons for these conclusions are set forth in the text. But I do not subscribe to any catastrophic interpretation of history, and I think that readers who compare my interpretation of the nineteenth- and the twentieth-century American will admit that I have not neglected the force of inheritance or the factor of continuity. And though I have been concerned throughout with the evaluation of what is characteristically American, I have not, I hope, been insensitive to the central consideration that most of the currents of thought which I have traced flowed through the western world. Indeed it is precisely because American thought owes so much to English and European thought that I have attempted to distinguish what are its American forms, characteristics, idioms, and idiosyncrasies. In a sense this book is a study in comparative cultural history.

My debts are many and, in part, intangible. I owe something, for example, to the Foundation which a quarter of a century ago enabled me to study Scandinavian character and institutions at first hand. I owe a great deal to the generous authorities of Cambridge University whose invitation to teach at that ancient and enchanting seat of learning gave me the opportunity to compare English with American civilization. I owe much to the officials of the Office of War Information and the United States Army who at one time and another sent me abroad. My deepest intellectual debt is to Vernon Louis Parrington whose great study of American thought has long been an inspiration and whose disciple I gladly acknowledge myself. My deepest personal debt, aside from that so inadequately acknowledged in the dedication, is to my friend and colleague Allan Nevins whose unfailing erudition, acumen, sagacity, and kindness has sustained me throughout the writing of this book. Nor would it be seemly to forget those neglected scholars and collaborators without whose assistance this book could not have been written: the librarians of Columbia University, who have borne patiently with my demands, and Miss Marcia Dalphin of the Rye Free Library. To all these and to the many others who have helped me unwittingly—to Geoffrey Bruun and Ross Hoffman, to Marquis James and Jacques Barzun and Frank Tannenbaum, to Guy Chapman and Denis Brogan—I give my thanks.

H. S. C.

Rye, New York
December 1, 1949

Contents

PART I

PART II

Contents

PART I

CHAPTER I

The Nineteenth-Century American

I

O VER A PERIOD of two and a half centuries, marked by such adventures as few other people had known, Americans had created an American character and formulated an American philosophy. That character all but eludes description and that philosophy definition, yet both were unmistakable. Certainly the hundreds of foreign visitors who swarmed over America and embarked so glibly upon interpretation had no difficulty in distinguishing American from Old World character, and, though the details which they recorded changed from decade to decade, the basic pattern which they celebrated or deprecated persisted. To Crèvecoeur's famous question, "What then is the American?" Crèvecoeur himself, Tocqueville, and Bryce, each separated by half a century, returned much the same answer. It required almost a new vocabulary to do justice to the changes in material circumstances which each successive generation of interpreters discerned, but for the analysis of character the old vocabulary sufficed. Nor did those Americans of 1900 who read Henry Adams' description of their ancestors of 1800 hesitate to claim legitimate descent: the lineaments, the accent, the character were all familiar.

The American character was the product of an interplay of inheritance and environment, both varied and complex. For the inheritance was not only British but European, not only of the seventeenth and eighteenth centuries but of two thousand years. That America was the offspring of Britain was acknowledged; that the roots of her culture and her institutions traced back to Greece and Rome and Palestine was not to be forgotten; and the basic institutions of state, church, and family which Americans maintained and the fundamental values which they cherished advertised the origin and the relationship.

But the inheritance was highly selective and the impact of environment uneven. Institutions—notably those of a political and juridical character—suffered only minor modifications, but the modification of social organization was so profound as to suggest a departure from the normal course of evolution, while the psychological modification was nothing less than revolutionary. Every American in Britain in the 1940's recognized as familiar such political institutions as the representative system, parties, and civil rights, but few felt themselves at home socially in the Mother Country, while Americans removed but one generation from Italy, France, and Germany experienced in those countries a profound sense of alienation. Nothing was more astonishing than the feebleness of hereditary loyalties unless it was the strength of newly acquired antipathies, and that people who best represented a cross section of Europe found it most difficult to understand or to sympathize with the Old World.

That so heterogeneous an inheritance should result in so homogeneous a character suggests that environment was decisive. The environment, to be sure, was scarcely less diverse than the inheritance, for, as every politician and student of sectionalism knew, the American continent disclosed a multiformity comparable to that of all Europe. Yet geographical differences were no more effective than racial mixtures in producing profound social diversity: what emerged was rather an amalgam which was distinctively national. The differences between a Yankee, a Southerner, and a Plainsman were insignificant compared with the differences that separated Germans, Frenchmen, Italians, and Poles; and for that matter, Vermonters and Texans could understand each other's language rather better than Yorkshiremen and Cornishmen. Certainly Americans from the cotton fields of the South or the prairies of the Middle Border managed to proclaim their love for rocks and rills, for woods and templed hills, without the slightest sense of incongruity. Local attachments persisted, especially in the rural areas, but the rise of the local-color school and the literary celebration of idiom and idiosyncrasy were testimony rather to their decline than to their vitality; in time, manifestations of provincialism, like Currier and Ives prints, were to become collectors' items.

It was not, in short, particular environments that determined the American character or created the American type but the whole of the American environment—the sense of spaciousness, the invitation to mobility, the atmosphere of independence, the encouragement to enterprise and to optimism. Whereas in Europe, with its age-old traditions of feudalism and nationalism, the particular triumphed over the general, in America, which came to maturity during the industrial revolution and acknowledged few traditions of strong local loyalties with which it had to break, the general triumphed over the particular. That people, which displayed the most diverse racial stocks and the most variegated climates and soils, achieved a distinctive and stable national character with an ease that confounded not only the expectations of her critics but all history and experience.

What then was the American of the nineteenth century? What qualities did he inherit from the eighteenth century; what did he take with him into the twentieth? What characteristics persisted from the Old World, what were modified by the New, what emerged from the impact of environment and the influence of heterogeneity to create an American type? What were the fundamental rather than fortuitous, the general rather than local, qualities that distinguished that type?

2

Nothing in all history had ever succeeded like America, and every American knew it. Nowhere else on the globe had nature been at once so rich and so generous, and her riches were available to all who had the enterprise to take them and the good fortune to be white. As nature and experience justified optimism, the American was incurably optimistic. Collectively, he had never known defeat, grinding poverty, or oppression, and he thought these misfortunes peculiar to the Old World. Progress was not, to him, a philosophical idea but a commonplace of experience: he saw it daily in the transformation of wilderness into farm land, in the growth of villages into cities, in the steady rise of community and nation to wealth and power.

To the disgust of Europeans, who lived so much in the past, he lived in the future, caring little for what the day might bring but much for the dreams—and profits—of the morrow. He planned ambitiously and was used to seeing even his most visionary plans surpassed; he came at last to believe that nothing was beyond his power and to be impatient with any success that was less than triumph. He had little sense of the past or concern for it, was not historical minded, and relegated interest in genealogy to spinsters who could have no legitimate interest in the future. Even the recent past became speedily legendary; children whose parents had heard the war whoop of the Indians and seen vast herds of buffalo cover the plains played at Indians much as English children played at King Arthur. The American saw the present with the eye of the future: saw not the straggling, dusty town but the shining city, not the shabby shop but the throbbing factory, not the rutted roads but gleaming rails. In every barefoot boy he saw a future president or millionaire, and as the future belonged to his children, he lived in them, worked for them, and pampered them.

With optimism went a sense of power and of vast reserves of energy. The American had spacious ideas, his imagination roamed a continent, and he was impatient with petty transactions, hesitations, and timidities. To carve out a farm of a square mile or a ranch of a hundred square miles, to educate millions of children, to feed the western world with his wheat and his corn, did not appear to him remarkable. His very folklore was on a large scale—the Paul Bunyans and Mike Finks—and the empire builders so closely approximated the folklore type that it was easy to confuse real and legendary characters: Daniel Boone, Davy Crockett, and Sam Houston belonged to mythology as well as to history. Because his imagination was constantly challenged by the realities of geography and history, he was receptive to large plans and heroic speculations. Crevecoeur had observed of the newcomer that "two hundred miles formerly appeared a very great distance, now it is but a trifle; he no sooner breathes our air than he forms schemes, and embarks on designs he never would have thought of in his own country," and what was true of the immigrant was even more true of the hardened American.

His culture, too, was material: he took comfort for granted and regarded with condescension people who failed to come up to his standards. Those standards were exalted. If the American had not yet attained the luxury in which the Old World aristocracy could indulge, he had achieved a general well-being higher than that which obtained elsewhere in the world. Nowhere was the workingman's or the farmer's table more lavishly provisioned, nowhere did the average man and woman dress better, nowhere could women and children be more readily excused from hard labor. The American had always met hardship with fortitude, partly because he was so sure that fortitude, together with industry, shrewdness, and a little luck, was bound to be rewarded in the end. He preached the gospel of hard work and regarded shiftlessness as a vice more pernicious than immorality. He liked solid evidence of wealth but distrusted ostentation; women whose position and wealth anywhere else would have justified servants did their own housework. He was accustomed to prosperity, resented anything that interfered with it, and regarded any prolonged lapse from it as an outrage against nature. The worst misfortune that could befall a political party was a depression, and the worst that could be said against a law was that it was harmful to business. Whatever promised to increase wealth was automatically regarded as good, and the American was tolerant, therefore, of speculation, advertising, deforestation, and the exploitation of natural resources, and bore patiently with the worst manifestations of industrialism.

All this tended to give a quantitative cast to his thinking and inclined him to place a quantitative valuation upon almost everything. When he asked what was a man worth, he meant material worth, and he was impatient of any but the normal yardstick. His solution for most problems was therefore quantitative—and education, democracy, and war all yielded to the sovereign remedy of numbers. Foreigners who thought this vulgar had no conception of its origin or its connection with the realities of American life, and this because it was so hard for the foreign imagination to conceive of power and quantity in American terms. To describe America indeed required a new vocabulary and almost a new arithmetic. Hence the American passion for population statistics, skyscrapers, railroad mileage, production records, school and college enrollment figures; hence the pleasure in sheer size—in the Great Lakes, the Mississippi River, Niagara Falls, Texas; hence the toleration of trusts, combines, and giant corporations; hence, perhaps, the cheerful acquiescence in majority decisions.

This quantitative cast of American thought was an indication of an intense practicality which extended to most, though by no means to all, matters. Often romantic about business, the American was practical about politics, religion, culture, and science. He was endlessly ingenious and resourceful, always ready to improvise new tools or techniques to meet new conditions. "A plaine souldier that can use a pick-axe and a spade," Captain John Smith had discovered, "is better than five knights," and on every successive frontier that discovery was the price of survival. The American borrowed readily from Indian or immigrant and naturalized what he borrowed; he improvised jauntily, had little respect for custom, and was willing to try anything. His reaction to most situations was a practical one, and he was happiest when he could find a mechanical solution to problems: the cotton gin, the steamboat, the harvester, the six-shooter, the sewing machine, vulcanized rubber, the telegraph and telephone, barbed-wire fencing, the typewriter, and a thousand other inventions anticipated the day when the American was to be notorious for his passion for gadgets. He was among the first to concede to technology a place in higher education, and West Point Academy trained engineers as well as soldiers. That the British were the greatest maritime people in the world, no one would deny; yet it was Nathaniel Bowditch whose *Practical Navigator* became the seaman's bible, and Matthew Maury who explored the physical geography of the sea. The Prussians and the French were the acknowledged masters of the military art, but balloons, wire entanglements, trench warfare, and underseas projectiles were first used effectively in the American Civil War; and no one who pondered the inexhaustible resourcefulness of Union and Confederate soldiers could doubt that a comparable resourcefulness in a later generation would spell disaster to any foreign enemy.

Theories and speculations disturbed the American, and he avoided abstruse philosophies of government or conduct as healthy men avoid medicines. Benjamin Franklin was his philosopher, not Jonathan Edwards, and when he took Emerson to heart it was for his emphasis on self-reliance rather than for his idealism. No philosophy that got much beyond common sense commanded his interest, and he ruthlessly transformed even the most abstract metaphysics into practical ethics. Transcendentalism in Germany and England led to an abdication from public affairs, but in America to an incessant concern with affairs public and private. Even when he rejected the religious implications of Utilitarianism, the American was incurably utilitarian, and it was appropriate that the one philosophy which might be called original with him was that of instrumentalism. If he failed to explore those higher reaches of philosophical thought which German and English philosophers had penetrated, it was rather because he saw no necessity for such exploration than because he was incapable of undertaking it; he felt instinctively that philosophy was the resort of the unhappy and the bewildered and knew that he was neither.

His religion, too, notwithstanding its Calvinistic antecedents, was practical. He was religious rather than devout, and with him the term "pious" came to be one of disparagement, just as later the term "Puritan" came into disrepute. Saintliness was not the most conspicuous quality in his religious leaders, and to the doctrine of salvation by grace he stubbornly opposed an instinctive faith in salvation by works. Sundays, he was troubled by a suspicion of sin—his womenfolk, more often—but he had no racking sense of evil, and his philosophy persisted in ignoring the one problem which had challenged philosophers from the beginning of time. He did not believe in the Devil or believed in him only as a bogey with which to scare naughty children and drunkards. Denominations multiplied but rather as organizations than as dogmas, and the average American was no more capable of distinguishing between Methodist and Presbyterian theologies than between Republican and Democratic principles—an incapacity which neither embarrassed him nor qualified his zeal. The most significant aspects of his two most original religions—Mormonism and Christian Science—were the practical ones.

In politics, too, he profoundly mistrusted the abstract and the doctrinaire. To the charge that he had no political philosophy he was cheerfully indifferent, for he regarded his freedom from the exactions of political theory as good fortune rather than misfortune. No party whose appeal was primarily intellectual could command his support, and his inability to differentiate philosophically between the two major parties abated his party loyalties not a whit. Because his parties were organizations to which he could attach miscellaneous principles rather than principles around which he had to build organizations, he was able to avoid the multiparty system which had bedeviled the continental nations of the Old World and make two parties serve his needs.

Yet, notwithstanding his youthfulness and his incurable amateurishness, the American was politically mature. That maturity was not conceded abroad where government was associated with dynasties and ruling classes, but that the average American had longer and larger experience in government than the average Englishman, Frenchman, or German was simply a historical fact. He early displayed a natural talent for politics. His political instruments were as ingenious as his mechanical contrivances: the federal system, the constitutional convention, and judicial review were the products of sophistication and art, and he brought the political party to its highest development. His greatest literary achievements, too, were political and historical, and statesmen of older nations could read *The Federalist* with profit, while they confessed that the Declaration of Independence was as influential in their own lands as any local product. In his politics, as in his agriculture and his fighting, the amateur spirit produced results that might well excite the envy of professionals. Few of his presidents had fallen below mediocrity, none of his statesmen had been wicked and few dangerous, and, notwithstanding the great aberration of 1860, the general level of his political leadership was appreciably higher than that of most other countries.

The American's attitude toward culture was at once suspicious and indulgent. Where it interfered with more important activities, he distrusted it; where it was the recreation of his leisure hours or of his womenfolk, he tolerated it. For the most part, he required that culture serve some useful purpose. He wanted poetry that he could recite, music that he could sing, paintings that told a story. Stephen Foster was his most beloved composer, and Currier and Ives his favorite artists. Art was something that had happened in the past, and when he could afford it he bought the paintings of artists long dead, listened to lectures on French cathedrals, and built museums to look iike mausoleums. Education was his religion, and to it he paid the tribute both of his money and his affection; yet, as he expected his religion to be practical and pay dividends, he expected education to prepare for life—by which he meant, increasingly, jobs and professions. His attitude toward higher education was something of a paradox. Nowhere else in the western world did colleges multiply and flourish as in America, yet not until Eliot reformed Harvard and Gilman built The Johns Hopkins did he have a real university. No people was more avid of college degrees, yet nowhere else were intellectuals held in such contempt or relegated to so inferior a position; and in America alone the professor—invariably long haired and absent minded—was an object of humor.

Completely committed to his life in the New World and enraptured with its riches and rewards, the American cherished an uncritical and unquestioning conviction that his was the best of all countries, and every emigrant who crossed the Atlantic westward—few went the other way—confirmed him in his assumption that this fact was every-where acknowledged. To the American, his wilderness was indeed paradise enough; he did not so much disparage other peoples and countries as ignore them. Back in the 1790's the Duc de Liancourt discovered the American belief that "no one has any brains, except in America; that the wit, the imagination, the genius of Europe are already in decrepitude," and a century and a half later British and French hosts to American soldiers and sailors rediscovered this as-sumption of incontestable superiority. Schoolbooks gave formal sup-port to the popular belief. Geographies spoke with contempt of the peoples of the East and with pity of those of the Old World. Histories dismissed ten centuries of Europe as the Dark Ages. Greece and Rome furnished heroes to compare with Washington, but no modern nation did so, and Blenheim and Waterloo ranked well below Saratoga and Yorktown.

The moral superiority of his country was equally axiomatic to the American. The assumption of superiority was accompanied by a sense of destiny and mission. Even in the eighteenth century every Ameri-can knew that it was westward the course of empire took its way and could recite—"with rapture," John Adams said—

> The eastern nations sink, their glory ends,
> And empires rise where the sun descends.

Jefferson called his country the world's best hope, and Lincoln, the last best hope of earth, and those who did not read presidential mes-sages could quote:

> A world is thy realm; for a world be thy laws,
> Enlarged as thine empire, and just as thy cause.

Or, better yet:

> Humanity with all its fears,
> With all the hopes of future years,
> Is hanging breathless on thy fate.

Successive generations were equally eager to spread the American idea over the globe and exasperated that foreign ideas should ever intrude themselves into America, and the legal term, alien, carried almost invariably a connotation of repugnancy.

Even when Americans had believed in the doctrine of predestination, they had not accepted it fatalistically or logically abandoned efforts to merit salvation. Nor did confidence in the future, no matter how justified by experience, now encourage fatalism. Rather it stimulated energy and efforts—stimulated them all the more as every white American felt that he had a personal stake in that future and that its realization would be personally profitable. Industry brought tangible rewards, and the American was industrious; thrift was a slow and prosaic way to success compared with speculation in land or business, and the American, while he did not cease to exalt thrift, was by nature a speculator. Since every village might become a Chicago, every mine a Comstock or a Mesabi, lack of faith was a species of treason; braggartism became a virtue and criticism a vice.

The inclination to experiment was deeply ingrained in the American character and fortified by American experience. America itself had been the greatest of experiments, one renewed by each generation of pioneers and each wave of immigrants, and, where every community was a gamble and an opportunity, the American was a gambler and an opportunist. He had few local attachments, pulled up stakes without compunction, and settled easily into new communities; where few regions or professions were overcrowded and every newcomer added to the wealth and the drawing power, he was sure of a welcome. He was always ready to do old things in new ways, or for that matter, to do things which had not been done before. Except in law, tradition and precedent discouraged him, and whatever was novel was a challenge. Pioneering had put a premium upon ingenuity and handiness, and where each man turned readily to farming, building, and trading, it seemed natural that he should turn with equal readiness to preaching, lawing, or doctoring, or combine these with other trades and professions. The distrust of the expert, rationalized into a democratic axiom during the Jacksonian era, was deeply ingrained in the American character and persisted long after its original justification had passed. With opportunism went inventiveness, which was similarly invited by circumstances. Americans who recorded at the patent office in Washington more inventions than were recorded in all the Old World nations together likewise found more new roads to heaven than had ever before been imagined, while their schools multiplied the seven liberal arts tenfold. Denominationalism and the inflated curriculum were monuments to the passion for experiment and inventiveness as well as to theological and secular learning.

Circumstances opened the way to talent or to luck, and the American had no use for caste or class. He was democratic and equalitarian, but his democracy was social and political rather than economic, and, as he himself expected economic success next year or the year after, he had little envy of those who achieved it this year. Where shrewdness in speculation had been elevated to a public service, he was not inclined to look too critically at the means whereby success was achieved. He tolerated with mere ceremonial protests the looting of the public domain or the evasion of taxes or the corruption of legislatures, so long as these things brought visible profits, and resented government interference with private enterprise far more than private interference with government enterprise. The self-made man, not the heir, was the hero, and by "made" the American meant enriched.

<h1 style="text-align:center">3</h1>

Throughout the nineteenth century, the sense of equality permeated the American's life and thought, his conduct, work, and play, his language and literature, his religion and his politics, and it conditioned all the relationships of his life. Except on the Fourth of July, he said little about it, since he took it for granted like his right to say what he pleased or to worship where he pleased; nothing was more characteristic, or more exasperating to foreigners, than the palpable sincerity with which even Southerners confessed their faith in equality while rejecting its practice. It was imposed by circumstances rather than by logic: where so few started with anything but their strength and character and where success was so easy, artificial advantages counted for little. Where all men were equal in the sight of God, it was difficult not to admit equality in the eyes of men; and where all men were equal at the ballot box, it was impolitic to encourage privilege.

Yet equality was not primarily political, and those who celebrated it as such missed its significance. In America it antedated universal suffrage; in time other countries attained a comparable political equality without any perceptible effect on existing class distinctions or class consciousness. It was social, it was cultural, it was psychological. It was, even with the extremes of wealth and poverty, in a curious sense economic; though economic inequality was, more and more, the fact, economic equality was the assumption, and the poor took for granted their right to luxuries and privileges elsewhere the prerogative of the rich. It was chiefly the absence of class distinctions rather than the triumph over them. Wherever men and women met in typical gatherings—camp meetings, militia drill, Grange picnics, political conventions, church sociables, Chautauqua assemblies—they met on a basis of equality. Leadership fluctuated and was dictated by the situation itself rather than by antecedent social position. Education mirrored society, and the public school was the great leveler. The playing field, which was equally important, had its own standards. Like the frontier, it placed a premium on ingenuity and physical prowess, and like the frontier and the school, it was leveling. Baseball had as much claim to be called the national American game as cricket the English, and it was characteristic that it could be played by almost any number with almost any apparatus in almost any place; the English game was far more exacting in its requirements and depended far more for its effects on ritual and ceremony.

The sense of equality introduced an ease and sincerity into social relationships not to be found elsewhere. Love had always found a way to penetrate the barriers of class; in America it could direct its shafts against more formidable barriers. Talent had always been able to break through class distinctions; in America it could conserve its energy for the tasks before it. Accent and pronunciation were refused their ancient prerogatives; family and even wealth their customary advantages; and, as these artificial insignia of authority were at a discount, the importance of power was exaggerated: the unwillingness of the rich to retire and enjoy their wealth, the absence of a leisure class, was a logical result. Where the poor felt no burden of inequality, they were relieved from the aggressive assertion of their rights and displayed no such self-conscious pretensions as in the Old World; where wealth could not in itself command acknowledgment of social superiority, it was relieved, in turn, from the compulsions of ostentatious display. Few outward signs of rank were tolerated. The poor did not flourish forelocks, nor did those who performed ordinary services accept tips. The rich lived much as their neighbors and had not yet learned to flaunt butlers, thumb a Social Register, or order their meals in French. Even before the end of the century, all this had changed for the worse.

Nowhere did the sense of equality manifest itself more ostentatiously than in the American's manners. Those manners were the despair of European aristocrats and the delight of European democrats, for more flagrantly than almost anything else they advertised the American's satisfaction in a classless society. Every American was convinced that man made manners rather than manners man, and if the conviction encouraged social eccentricity, the price was not too high. With no court to establish and no upper classes to practice social formalities, Americans conducted themselves pretty much as their instincts dictated, and those instincts were for the most part kindly and generous. Where European manners were rigid and punctilious, American were flexible and careless; where every English gentleman knew what was due him as a gentleman, the American was on the whole more conscious of what was due his fellow men as men. Though etiquette books poured from the presses by the score, they failed to impose upon the American either uniformity or convention. There was formality, to be sure, and the drawing rooms of Boston or Charleston saw as much courtliness as could be found in English country houses, but more and more the leveling standards of the frontier, spontaneous and unpretentious, came to permeate the whole country. As, outside the South, Americans recognized neither superiors nor inferiors, the special codes which had been elaborated to lubricate the relations of classes were superfluous, and social intercourse, freed of such restraints, was natural and genial.

As the English influence waned, the terms "Gentleman" and "Esquire," evaporated. The term "Lady" had never achieved its Old World meaning, and it was suggestive that the one calculated *Portrait of a Lady* was drawn by an expatriate author and that the most successful of society painters, John S. Sargent, was another expatriate. Yet Americans had a passion for titles. Honorary colonels littered the landscape even outside Kentucky, and family pride recalled no privates in Union or Confederate armies. In country towns every druggist was called doctor and every teacher professor, and American law early dispensed with the lowly solicitor and elevated every magistrate to judge. Perhaps the most interesting thing about these titles was their availability, and their uselessness: they were as much an expression of carelessness, good nature, and humor as of respect for position or yearning for status. Such yearning for status as there was fluttered the bosoms of women; it was the women who filled home-town papers with stories of their presentation at the Court of St. James's, and every novelist who wrote of social climbing described the phenomenon largely, if not exclusively, in feminine terms.

In politics especially there was more equality than democracy. Nothing was more fatal to political success than the appearance of superiority. William Henry Harrison was as rich as Martin Van Buren, but when it was established that Harrison drank hard cider from a jug and Van Buren sipped foreign wines from golden goblets, the triumph of Harrison was inevitable. Although present wealth was tolerated as proof of native talent, it behooved every ambitious politician to have himself born in a log cabin or a sod house, and if he could manage to work his way through college so much the better. The hard work of political organization was left to those whose ostentatious mediocrity could not be gainsaid; if Americans sometimes permitted their statesmen to wear a toga, their political bosses were required to dress just like everybody else.

No military caste dominated the almost nonexistent army, and except in time of war no social advantage attached to the uniform. Except occasionally in the ante-bellum South, leading families did not naturally earmark one son for the law, one for the church, and one for the army or the navy. The Society of the Cincinnati, which was limited to Revolutionary officers and their descendants, was impotent; the Grand Army of the Republic, which embraced privates, was a powerful organization. The principle that the civilian was superior to the soldier was as much an expression of the suspicion of military standards as of the fear of military usurpation. Lee, whose credentials to such aristocracy as existed were unimpeachable, not only held himself rigidly subordinate to President Davis, but after the war marched ostentatiously out of step with soldiers on parade.

The American was good natured, generous, hospitable, and sociable, and he reversed the whole history of language to make the term "stranger" one of welcome. There were pioneers who could not stand the sight of a neighbor's smoke, but for the most part the American was gregarious, and he became increasingly so with the passing years: the front porch was an American invention. He had as yet formulated few of those rules and developed few of those habits designed to transform a crowd into a society, and perhaps for this reason he embraced with peculiar enthusiasm those fraternal organizations that gave him an artificial sense of security and companionship. His generosity and hospitality were careless rather than calculated, flowed from a consciousness of abundance and a pleasure in society rather than from adherence to moral or social precepts. The tithe had never been popular in America, but voluntary contributions to religion were customary, and nowhere was private philanthropy more extravagant. Social relationships, too, were charitable, and the standards for admission to fraternal organizations, clubs, and schools were lax, yet society easily withstood what would elsewhere have been the shock of promiscuity. Indeed, to the abhorrence of Old World observers, extravagance and carelessness flourished from generation to generation, and both were explained by the same good fortune, for in a country so richly endowed there was no need for parsimony, and in a country so open and free from tradition, circumspection and caution were profitless.

Carelessness was perhaps the most pervasive and persistent quality in the American. He was careless about himself, his speech, his dress, his food, even his manners; those who did not know him thought him slovenly and rude. His attitude toward the English language pained the traditionalists, but he brought to language and grammar something of the same vitality and ingenuity that he brought to his work or his religion, and they served his needs and reflected his character. He was careless about rank and class, about tradition and precedent, about the rights and prerogatives of others and about his own rights and prerogatives. He tolerated in others minor infractions of law or custom and expected to be similarly indulged in his own transgressions: hence his vast patience with noise, litter, the invasion of privacy, and sharp practices. Although he had, as it were, invented time, he did not, like his English cousins, make a fetish of punctuality, nor did he celebrate the hours with such ritual as tea or dressing for dinner. He was careless about his work and his trade, and, preferring to have machines work for him, he regarded with equanimity the decline of inherited traditions of craftsmanship. While the products of his machines could compete anywhere in the world market, the products of his handicraft could not.

The American took, in fact, little pride in a finished job, prizing versatility above thoroughness. He was the world's most successful farmer, but his cultivation was gargantuan rather than intensive, and scientific agriculture lagged a generation or more behind that of Europe while, after the eighteenth century, landscape gardening was regarded as a European rather than an American art. The construction of the transcontinentals was one of the greatest engineering feats of modern history, but the American's railway tracks, like his roads, had to be rebuilt every few years. Every town and city confessed the same characteristic—whole sections only half built, houses falling down a decade after they had been put up, ambitious plans unfulfilled. A ragged, unfinished quality characterized much of his culture. He undertook the most gigantic educational program in history, but it was the universal opinion that American education was eclectic rather than thorough. His speech revealed his impatience: he slurred over his words, left his sentences unfinished, and developed to the full the possibilities of slang. Neither Transcendentalism nor pragmatism, the two ways of thinking that can properly be designated American, had a systematic quality, and it was suggestive that his most characteristic form of philosophy, pragmatism, should emphasize the unfinished nature of the universe. Many Americans preferred their preachers untrained, and most of them distrusted the professional soldier.

The explanation was obvious and not wholly discreditable. The American rarely expected to stay put and had little interest in building for the future. It was easier to skim the cream off the soil, the forests, the mines—or business investments—and go on to something new, especially when new was so often synonymous with better. He had, besides, boundless confidence in the ability of the next generation to look after itself, and where both land and resources appeared inexhaustible, that faith seemed well founded. Familiar with the marvels of science and invention, he was reluctant to make commitments for future generations, to bind them to any place, any career, any policy, or technique which might speedily be outmoded or unprofitable. For this self-indulgence he paid a high price, and his descendants a higher. Dazzled by the concept of infinity, prodigal of the resources of nature and of his own resources, greedy and reckless, he did more damage in a century than nature could repair in a thousand years. From Maine to Oregon he left forests in ruins; instead of cultivating, he mined the soil; he killed off bison and pigeon, polluted streams, wasted coal, oil, and gas. His habits of waste he transmitted to a generation that could no longer afford them; his refusal to think beyond the present encouraged a hostility to planning that was to prove almost disastrous.

The American's attitude toward authority, rules, and regulations was the despair of bureaucrats and disciplinarians. Nowhere did he differ more sharply from his English cousins than in his attitude toward rules, for where the Englishman regarded the observance of a rule as a positive pleasure, to the American a rule was at once an affront and a challenge. His schools were almost without discipline, yet they were not on the whole disorderly, and the young girls and spinsters who taught them were rarely embarrassed. This absence of discipline in the schools reflected absence of discipline in the home. Parents were notoriously indulgent of their children and children notoriously disrespectful of parents, yet family life was on the whole happy, and most children grew up to be good parents and good citizens. The laxity of discipline in his armies was a scandal tolerated only because they somehow fought well and won battles. It seemed entirely natural that during the Civil War privates should elect their officers and that the greatest of the generals should so often see his plans miscarry because he hesitated to give firm orders to his subordinates or to insist upon obedience. If Lincoln did not pardon quite so many sleeping sentinels as folklore relates, it was characteristic that folklore should celebrate as a virtue a gesture so disruptive to all discipline.

Almost the only rules which the American took seriously were those which regulated his games. His sense of sportsmanship was keen, and, though he was tolerant enough of a little cheating in politics or business, he would not tolerate it in amateur sport. The distinction was a nice one and, on the whole, creditable to the American character, for it suggested a scale of values in which material profits were not the most important. Sport was still confined pretty much to organized games and was predominantly amateur. The American hunted and fished chiefly for food and had not yet arrived at that stage of sophistication which regarded mountain climbing as a diversion or held it dishonorable to fish for trout with bait.

His attitude toward law was a curiosity. It was the universal observation that few people were more lawless than the American, and statistics seemed to confirm this. Quite aside from crime that was recorded in statistics, minor infractions of law were universal. Yet if the American displayed a cavalier disrespect for law and an abiding suspicion of lawyers, he venerated Law. It was his pride that every American was equal before the Law, that no one—not even the highest official—was immune from the operation of the Law. In his country alone, the Constitution was supreme law; here alone the judiciary could nullify acts of all legislative bodies. Certainly nowhere else in the world was law more assiduously studied; nowhere else did lawyers play so important a role in politics or in daily affairs. The American lawyer was a leading citizen at a time when his English colleague was but a minor clerk, and throughout the century lawyers dominated the legislature of even the farming states. Whatever the ordinary standards of politics, judicial standards were invariably high, even where judges were elective, and while the American indulged recklessly in the most scurrilous criticism of his president or his Congress, he would scarcely tolerate criticism of his Supreme Court.

This paradox was more apparent than real. The American was at once intelligent and conservative, independent and reliable. Rules represented tradition, and discipline authority; he knew that his country had become great by flouting both and that in a land where everything was yet to be done and where the future was in his hands he could continue to flout both with impunity. At the same time he thought his government and his Constitution the best in the world, credited them with a large measure of the success of his experiment, and would not tolerate any attack upon their integrity. It was suggestive that in 1776 the American rebels claimed to be the real champions of the British Constitution and that in 1861 Southerners justified secession not on the right of revolution but on constitutional grounds. Certainly to those who accepted the legend of American lawlessness it was puzzling that the United States had never known revolution; that in a society allegedly anarchical, government was stable, most elections orderly, and property safe; and that a democracy should be able to boast the oldest written constitution in the world.

His disrespectful attitude toward authority and his complacent confidence in the superiority of his institutions combined with prosperity and well-being to make the American lenient toward dissent and nonconformity. He knew that America had been founded in dissent, that the Republic had been born of dissent, that every pioneer who pulled up stakes and headed for the frontier registered—along with a vote of confidence in the future—a vote of dissent from the past. Individualism, too, required nonconformity and paid dividends:

the American was always taking a short cut to freedom, a short cut to fortune, a short cut to learning, and a short cut to heaven. A society which had not had time to nourish its own traditions invited nonconformity. Indeed, had the American wished to be a traditionalist, he would have found it difficult to determine what tradition he should honor, and after the middle of the century a Supreme Court justice observed that western judges commonly pronounced good law because they were so ignorant of the precedents.

Nature, too, conspired with history to justify heterodoxy, for where heretics could indulge their heresies in the wilderness, it was easy to tolerate them. Certainly the Mormons had less trouble in Utah than in Illinois. While America was still rural, every village boasted its eccentric, but as the country became more thickly settled and its economy more tightly knit, eccentricity declined and conformity became a virtue. By the close of the century, even the West had caught the infection of orthodoxy. Oklahoma became impatient with Jesse James and Dakota bored with Calamity Jane; only in the South, where the tradition of individualism was strongest and where an inferior class indulged its masters, were idiosyncrasies encouraged. The triumph of standardization over individualism was a memorial to the passing of the old America.

Yet even in the nineteenth century, and increasingly as that century wore on, nonconformity was indulged out of good nature rather than respected out of principle, allowed in conduct rather than in doctrine. Confident of the superiority of his own institutions, the American could suffer almost any individual misconduct, but he was inclined to regard criticism of those institutions as an outrage, and ideas or practices that challenged the fundamental tenets of his faith excited an obloquy that would have pained Thomas Jefferson. The Mormons were, after all, hounded out of Missouri and Illinois; the South, for all its individualism, was implacably intolerant on the Negro question; and what seemed to be attacks upon the economic or constitutional order—strikes, for example, or populism—aroused a shrill and vindictive bigotry.

The American was not lacking in a sense of discipline, but it was a discipline imposed by circumstances rather than by the state. It was imposed, to be sure, by school and church but more rigorously by a way of life close to nature and subject to nature's iron laws—by the endless chores required of every boy and girl, by the care of animals required on every farm and in most village homes, by the responsibility of large families, by the lack of servants in the North and the care of Negroes in the South, by the inescapable obligations of membership in self-governing and self-regulating communities. That dissipation of social responsibility which came with urbanization, and of economic responsibility which came with the corporation, was still in the future.

For all his individualism, the American was much given to co-operative undertakings and to joining. Nowhere else except in Britain did men associate so readily for common purposes; nowhere else were private associations so numerous or so efficacious. On the European continent, establishment of a church, a college, a hospital, a mission, waited on the pleasure of the crown or the state. In America, as in Britain, they waited on the interest of the individual or the group, and it was not customary to look to the state for permission, guidance, or aid. In a state of nature it was natural that men should create their own institutions, and Americans had experienced that state of nature which Old World philosophers could but imagine. They had discovered that men could come together and make a church, and their churches were voluntary organizations. They had discovered that men could come together and make a state, and the constitutional convention was their most original political contribution. As the American had created his church and his state, he took for granted his capacity to create all lesser institutions and associations.

A thousand organizations sprang up—organizations to do good, to prosper business, to influence politics, to recollect the past, to mold the future, to conquer culture. In time everyone organized: boys and girls in schools, businessmen and scholars, friends and neighbors, old settlers and newcomers, vegetarians and teetotalers, those who survived a blizzard and those who grew roses and those who collected stamps, and, finally, with the organization of Nationalist Clubs, even those who had read a book—Bellamy's *Looking Backwards*. It was an effort to give an appearance of stability to an unstable society, to create order out of disorder, to substitute new loyalties for those which had been dissipated and new conventions for those which had been lost, to enlarge horizons and inflate opportunities. It was an expression of faith in the efficacy of common enterprise, in the ability of men to make their own institutions, in the power of fraternity and democracy.

In one realm the American was a conformist, and that was the realm of morals. Although he did not always observe them, he accepted without question the moral standards of the Puritans, and if a later generation was to find him repressed and inhibited, there is little evidence that he was conscious of his sufferings. It was the testimony of foreign observers that nowhere else were morals more pure or female virtue more deeply respected, and the statistics of illegitimacy confirmed this impression. White women were safe anywhere; chastity was taken for granted before and fidelity after marriage. That violations of the moral code were common could not be denied by anyone familiar with the history of miscegenation in the South or of prostitution in the larger cities, yet these violations were surreptitious, not flagrant, and it was considered neither sophisticated nor aristocratic to keep a mistress. In a rural society men and women married early, reared large families, and lived as equals in the home and in the community. The social position of women was an elevated one; nowhere were they more honored and protected, nowhere more encouraged in their intellectual development, nowhere given wider scope for the employment of their talents and virtues. In all matters of church and school, women took the lead, and the experience of every boy with women teachers throughout his school days doubtless did much to confirm the respect with which he was taught to regard the opposite sex. Women not only controlled education and religion but largely dictated the standards of literature and art and clothed culture so ostentatiously in feminine garb that the term itself came to have connotations of effeminacy.

Conformity and conventionalism in matters of morals sometimes assumed aggressive form, and the willingness to resign control of the whole field of culture to women combined with the tradition of Puritanism to encourage intolerance and justify censorship. Language was emasculated, literature expurgated, art censored. Piano legs were draped with pantalets, words like belly and breast dropped from polite conversation, the discussion of sex confined to men and of obstetrics to women, while Shakespeare and Fielding joined French writers generally in disrepute. Early in the century a furor was raised when Hiram Powers exhibited his undraped "Greek Slave," and at the end of the century Thomas Eakins, perhaps the greatest of American painters, was driven from the Pennsylvania Academy when he used male models in mixed classes. Dancing, plays, and mixed bathing came under the ban. Censorship of art and literature slid easily into censorship of morals, especially those having to do with love and drinking; modesty degenerated into Comstockery and the temperance move‧ment into prohibition.

The romantic view of sex was by no means out of character, for in many matters the American was romantic and sentimental. His senti‧ment was spontaneous rather than introspective, an expression of the enthusiasm of his nature and the richness of his imagination rather than of bathos: it was closer to that of the Frenchman than to that of the German. He was sentimental about Nature in her grander aspects and liked rolling rhetoric in his orators. He thought the whole history of his country romantic and heroic and on every Fourth of July and Decoration Day indulged in orgies of sentiment. He felt no need for the picturesque anachronisms which provided the Old World with its romance—feudal castles and knights in armor and royal courts—and he applauded when his greatest humorist, who was him‧self the most sentimental of men, found them all faintly ridiculous. But he romanticized his own history—the Pilgrim and the Puritan; the backwoodsman and the Indian whom he fought; the cowboy, the miner, and the trapper; the ragged Continentals and the Blue‧jackets of 1812 and the Blue and the Gray. As he had always been on the winning side, he could indulge a sentimental affection for lost causes, and while the Confederacy was worsted on the battlefield, it was victorious in song and story and almost in the history books. Southerners, who had known the bitterness of defeat, could take some satisfaction in the reflection that it was "Dixie," after all, that became the national song.

Imagination and enthusiasm characterized the American's humor as well as his sentiment. Humor was not only a positive but a notorious national trait; as pervasive as optimism and carelessness—and closely allied with both—it cropped up in the most unexpected places and left few things untouched. It was entirely fitting that the most beloved of his national heroes should be cherished especially for his humor. It is difficult to imagine that trait in Victoria or in Bismarck, or enthu‧siasm for it among British or Germans had it existed. There were as many varieties of humor as there were regions: Yankees, Negroes, and cowboys all had their special dialects but all spoke a common lan‧guage.

From Franklin to Mark Twain, American humor tended to exag‧geration and extravagance; not until the next century was it to sour into sophistication and wit. It was fundamentally outrageous, and in this reflected the attitude toward authority and precedent. It celebrated the ludicrous and the grotesque with unruffled gravity: Franklin's story of the cod leaping Niagara Falls, Mark Twain's discovery of the Petrified Man, Bill Nye's gratification that the Navy was safe behind the brick walls of the Brooklyn Navy Yard, and Finley Peter Dunne's celebration of the Hay Fleet all had the authenticity of the American game of poker. It bore the impress of the frontier long after the frontier had passed. It was leisurely and conversational; the tall story was usually a long story and was designed to be heard rather than read. It was shrewd, racy, robust, and masculine, often vulgar but rarely gross. It was generous and good natured, malicious only when directed against vanity and pretense. It cultivated understatement, not, as with the British, as a sign of sophistication, but as an inverse exaggeration: Lincoln's dynamited cur whose usefulness, as a dog, was about over and Mark Twain's frog that had "no p'ints that's better'n any other frog" were as native as Paul Bunyan or Mike Fink. It was democratic and leveling, took the side of the underdog and ridiculed the great and the proud. The politician was its natural butt: if America developed no Daumier or Hogarth, her cartoonists were, on the whole, the best in the world, and they addressed their talent chiefly to politics. American humor recounted few comedies of manners, for these appeared where class distinctions were sharp and social climbing a passion, but many comedies of circumstance: where almost every man had, at one time or another, aimed too high, adventured too boldly, boasted too loudly, it was consoling to see him get his comeuppance. Nature played the part in American humor that social distinctions did in British: it was forever putting men in their place. Thus Mark Twain could find in the currents and snags of the Mississippi a proper foil for the vanity of man but confessed of Henry James's *The Bostonians,* which appeared cheek by jowl with *Huckleberry Finn* in the hospitable pages of the same magazine, that he would "rather be damned to John Bunyan's heaven than read that." The twentieth century seems to have concluded that James was a greater writer than Mark Twain, but the nineteenth entertained no such hothouse notion.

4

American philosophy—if so pretentious a term may be used for the things Americans believed in—was, like the American character, an amalgam of inheritance and experience; and if the inheritance is more obvious, the experience is more interesting. To confess that the formal corpus of philosophy was inherited tells us little, for the American was a free agent, and if the term inheritance suggests a passive role it is misleading. That the Declaration of Independence was a recapitulation of John Locke's *Second Treatise on Government* was wryly remarked by John Adams and has been monotonously reaffirmed, but it is pertinent to observe that Locke rationalized a revolution and Jefferson inspired one and that Locke is rather better known in the American translation than in the original. The important inquiry is why the American took what he did from the accumulated store of philosophy and what he did with what he took.

Puritanism, rationalism, and idealism were the three major sources of American philosophy; each was naturalized, and the naturalization was progressively more thorough. Freed from denominational sponsorship, Puritanism could permeate secular rather than merely theological thought; freed from the burden of nonconformity, it could serve as a philosophical instrument rather than a sectarian challenge. The Enlightenment, too, could perform its task of illumination without war or revolution, without setting class against class or past against future, and as there were no barriers of church or state to assail, no infamy to crush, it could forego the luxury of martyrdom. Whereas in France and Germany it was explosive, in America its alchemy was tranquil and pervasive. Opposites could fuse, and in a Franklin could be merged the virtues of Puritanism without its defects, the illumination of the Enlightenment without its heat; if politicians or churchmen asserted an incompatibility between morality and rationalism, the careers of Jefferson and John Quincy Adams suggested that such a conflict did not materialize in practice. For all practical purposes the warfare between Puritanism and the Enlightenment was as factitious in America as the later warfare between science and religion. Idealism was even more energetically Americanized, until in the end its spiritual ancestors could scarcely acknowledge its legitimacy. The American Transcendentalists subscribed sincerely to the metaphysics of Kant and Coleridge, but their busy emulation of the Utilitarians was a scandal.

It is this unmistakably American accent in which imported philosophy was expressed that is most instructive. Such philosophy, to be acceptable and useful, had to emancipate itself from its Old World rhetoric, conform to the realities of American experience, and reconcile itself to the idiosyncrasies of the American character. The American had found felicity in the New World, and his philosophy had to justify a genial view of Providence and Nature, a romantic concept of Man, and a sanguine interpretation of history. He had exercised freedom, and his philosophy had to permit nonconformity and exalt democracy. He had cultivated individualism, and his philosophy had to leave room for experimentation and chance. He was practical, and his philosophy had to serve utilitarian purposes. He was successful, and it had to leave room for free will and secular rewards. He was unsophisticated, and it had to avoid subtleties.

At the same time, philosophy, even in its American metamorphosis, was more than a mere transcript of experience or reflection of character. It was an active instrument, a stimulus and a provocation as well as a rationalization and a rule. It had work to do and was required to pay its way. It had to fortify the American for the experience that he was to embrace, justify his effort and his hazards, give meaning to his history, and guarantee his destiny. It had to prove that the happiness of man was dependent on virtue, enterprise, freedom, and the recognition of the sovereignty of moral law. Thus the Declaration of Independence was a document that made memorable a moment in history; it was a rationalization of an act and an inspiration of conduct; it was a continuing force in an illimitable future.

America, the sage Tocqueville observed, was "the country in the world where philosophy is least studied," and if the generalization grandly ignored some score ancient nations, it was nevertheless true that from Thomas Jefferson to William James the philosophical hall of fame could, without censure, dispense with any American figure except Emerson. Perhaps the only fact more remarkable than the failure of so intelligent a people to engage in philosophical speculations was their ability to neglect them without perceptible loss. That the American was not philosophical was reiterated with so monotonous an insistence as to imply that the fact constituted an affront. He embraced ideas without rigorous inquiry into their validity, abandoned them without proof of their invalidity. He looted the philosophical stores of the past, took what pleased him without reference to logical coherence, and fitted it all together into a pattern that had symmetry only in his eyes. Whatever of English, French, German, or even Oriental philosophical grist went into his mill came out as American as buckwheat flour. The American was the implacable enemy of metaphysical abstractions: even in politics, where he was most mature, his favorite argument was felicitously called Common Sense. As he distrusted authority in politics, he distrusted it in philosophy, and nowhere was Everyman more brashly his own philosopher or the cracker-box philosopher more indulged. From the point of view of the Old World, he vulgarized philosophy as he vulgarized grammar and manners.

Yet for all the reluctance of Americans to exalt formal philosophy or indulge in metaphysical speculation, they confessed, with impressive unanimity, to a common view of the cosmic processes and of their significance to man, articulated their institutions to the moral structure of the universe, and acknowledged in their daily lives the binding force of moral law. The view of the universe which they held, the moral axioms which they obeyed, the values which they cherished, can be stated briefly because their moral code, though by no means free of inconsistencies, was singularly wanting in qualifications or subtleties.

American thought, like the American character, was permeated with optimism, with the sense of a spacious universe, with confidence in the infinite possibilities of human development, and with reverence for a righteous God and a just moral code. Americans believed in a universe governed by laws which were immutable and unassailable but which left room, somehow, for the play of free will, and they were confident that their reason was sufficiently acute to discover these laws and their will sufficiently firm to observe them. Secular law they held to be but a transcription of the Law of Nature and of Nature's God, and accorded it appropriate vicarious respect. Acknowledging the sovereign efficacy of the Higher Law, they held human institutions valid only when in conformity to it. They worshiped a God who was just but benevolent and who "delighted in the happiness of man here and his greater happiness hereafter." They reveled in a Nature that was exacting but beneficent and found its generosity a sure sign of Providential favor. As nature and history conspired to confirm their belief that they held a title deed to good fortune, they regarded every qualification on their felicity—a drought, a depression, a military defeat—as an outrage.

Although Americans acknowledged the majesty of God, they did not embrace the corollary of man's insignificance, and though they never formally repudiated the tenets of Calvinism, they did not acquiesce in the doctrine of the depravity of man. They held rather that man was the child of God, the purpose and end of creation, that he had within him some portion of divinity, that he was capable of infinite moral improvement and was destined, ultimately, for perfection. Nothing in their experience suggested that this faith was without foundation. Although sin and the Devil persisted in formal confessions of faith, in fact both were banished from the popular consciousness, and from Jonathan Edwards to Josiah Royce no major philosopher faced squarely the problem of evil. Americans held all men to be equal in the sight of God and all white men in the eyes of the law, and the compulsion of that qualification confounded their logic and tortured their conscience. They accepted the political implications of democracy and the social implications of the brotherhood of man; their intelligence permitted them to practice self-government and their prosperity to indulge in humanitarianism and philanthropy. As they identified their own moral concepts with those of the cosmos, they were vastly concerned for the rights of mankind. They trusted their own conscience and practiced toleration, at first from necessity and eventually from choice. As they admitted no conflict between the claims of liberty and of law and found nothing in theology or philosophy to moderate their passion for freedom, they succeeded in making liberty under law the basis of their commonwealth, their social order, and their morality. Where their English cousins implored God to send some king victorious, happy and glorious, they invoked God as "author of liberty" to keep their land bright with freedom's holy light.

They believed passionately in themselves and their destiny, and their deep sense of gratitude to Providence did not preclude pride in what they had themselves accomplished. Born of geography, nourished by history, confirmed by philosophy, self-reliance was elevated to a philosophical creed, and in time individualism became synonymous with Americanism. As the rich and spacious continent had dazzled but not confounded their imagination, so their speedy conquest of it induced a sense of limitless power.

Have the elder races halted?
Do they droop and end their lesson,
Wearied over there beyond the seas?
We take up the task eternal

boasted Walt Whitman, and it was no idle boast. Their sense of material superiority graduated easily into a sense of moral superiority, and manifest destiny was not really fulfilled with the rounding out of the continent but persisted in both the material and spiritual realms.

5

This body of beliefs could not but have practical consequences, reflected in the habitual conduct of the American people. That there was a quantitative gap between the American creed and the American conduct could not be denied, but there was no qualitative difference. Even the popular manifestations of American philosophy were consistent with its cultivated formulation. If popular practice failed to live up to the principles of the American creed, it never repudiated them—not even where the Negro was involved. Every thoughtful foreigner remarked inconsistencies in that creed. But consistency was more striking than the inconsistencies, and certain principles, attitudes, and habits persisted through the century. These are to be discovered not in the formulas of philosophers but in the daily life of the people.

How, then, was the formal philosophy to which Americans subscribed translated into the vernacular? How did Sunday maxims weather weekday trials? What virtues did the nineteenth-century American extol, what vices condemn, what heroes exalt, what villains execrate? What history did he know, what stories did he treasure, what heroes and heroines of literature did he cherish, what songs did he sing, what poems recite, what maxims and aphorisms memorize? What were the standards of conduct, inculcated by parents, the school, the playground, and popular literature?

The American had a high sense of honor and would not tolerate acts dishonorable by his standards. Words like truth, justice, loyalty, reverence, virtue, and honor meant much to him and meant simply, for he had not yet learned to be confused by semantics, and he had no use for that sophistry which blurred the bright distinction between right and wrong. He admired industry, temperance, sportsmanship, and all the virtues which he thought stemmed from the Puritans. He recognized the sovereignty of the individual conscience, consulted it on most matters, and yielded the same privilege to others. He was inclined to bow to the majority even on matters of morals, rather because the existence of a majority opinion was itself a weighty argument than because of timidity. Religion, though not theology, was a very real part of his life, permeated his secular thought, and furnished him the maxims by which he judged conduct. The Bible was universally read; as its verses were familiar to all, it was the common storehouse of allusion, and public speech caught the contagion of its noble eloquence. Children read Bible stories in diluted form; their parents enjoyed *Ben Hur* and *Quo Vadis* as their grandparents had enjoyed *The Prince of the House of David;* and hundreds of hymns, familiar to all Protestants, broke down denominational barriers.

The American had a strong sense of fair play, even in war, and learned early that to be a bully was contemptible and to be a good loser admirable. In his personal affairs he was litigious rather than belligerent, insisted on his rights but granted equal rights to others; and he was usually a good neighbor, not by the English standard of respect for privacy but by the American standard of friendliness. He was not easily excited to war, but when war came he fought hard and, by such standards as obtained, fairly. He fought best when sure his cause was just, and only those who ignored the opposition to the War of 1812 and the Mexican War could pretend that he was easily persuaded. He was reluctant to take the offensive and loath to be maneuvered into the position of aggressor. On Lexington Common, Captain Parker held his fire: "If *they* mean to have a war," he said, "let it begin here," and that same day Major Buttrick, at Concord bridge, waited for the British Grenadiers to take the initiative. The Civil War could not begin until each side had satisfied itself that the other was the aggressor. President Polk went to extreme lengths to make it clear that American blood had been shed on American soil before recommending war with Mexico, and it was Lincoln who required him to indicate the spot. Later generations never forgave Polk the trick of his rationalization, and, though of all American presidents he was the most uniformly successful, he never achieved popularity but went down in history as "Polk the mendacious."

The American admired in the military those virtues he admired in civil life: he did not maintain a double standard of morality for war and for peace. Mere victory in battle gave no assurance of popular acclaim, nor defeat of odium. Washington was revered for other than soldierly qualities; Scott, victor in two wars, was never loved; and Lee was more nearly a national hero than Grant. The American preferred heroism to be personal: the tradition of the frontier scout was strong, and the bold sortie, the surprise attack, the dashing raid, appealed to him more than the well-ordered campaign. The victor of Saratoga was all but forgotten, but Mad Anthony Wayne and Francis Marion were immortalized; Jackson and Sheridan, for all their Draconian qualities, were more popular than Longstreet or Meade.

He tried to preserve some of the amenities of civilization even in war: when Pickett's baby was born, the Yankees lit bonfires, and when Meagher's Irish brigade charged up Marye's Heights to certain death, the Confederates cheered their gallantry. When he faced an opponent who did not know, or observe, the rules of the game in war as in sports, the American was confused and infuriated—which was one reason why Indian warfare was attended with such monstrous cruelty. When Southerners protested against the antics of Ben Butler in New Orleans, public opinion forced his removal; and even the march through Georgia, which to contemporaries seemed so outrageous, was conducted with what now seems relative propriety.

War did not furnish all his heroes, nor were the virtues of those it did furnish exclusively military. Whom did the American revere, whom did he condemn? Who were the models held up to the emulation of the young? Every child carried with him a number of images of the father of his country: the boy George with his hatchet—"Father, I cannot tell a lie"; the young Washington on Braddock's Field; Washington crossing the Delaware; kneeling in prayer at Valley Forge; adjusting his spectacles as he addresses his comrades-in-arms— "I have grown not only gray but almost blind in the service of my country"; retiring in the end to Mount Vernon. He was clearly first in war and first in peace, yet too remote and formidable to be first in the hearts of his countrymen. That place in the affections of Americans was long held rather by Benjamin Franklin, who was recalled more familiarly munching his loaf of bread, trundling his wheelbarrow through the streets of Philadelphia, flying his kite, compiling the homely aphorisms that adorned a hundred readers, and flaunting his fur cap at the Court of Versailles. When Poor Richard seemed too tame, there was the fiery Patrick Henry, and every schoolboy knew that Caesar had his Brutus, and echoed, with appropriate gestures, the invitation to "Give me liberty or give me death." Besides these, there was a splendid gallery of lesser heroes: John Smith saved by the beautiful Pocahontas; Roger Williams trekking through the snow to Narragansett Bay; Daniel Boone hewing out the Wilderness Trail; Paul Revere on his Midnight Ride; Jefferson penning the Declaration; Marion the Swamp Fox; Nathan Hale with but one life to lose for his country; Ethan Allen to whom profanity was permitted; John Paul Jones who had just begun to fight; Perry who met the enemy at Put-in-Bay; Decatur who burned the *Philadelphia* in Tripoli harbor; Jackson who went straight from New Orleans to the White House. All of them, in the end, made way for Lincoln, the very apotheosis of the American, too homely for idolatry, too inscrutable for mere history, a legend before the lilacs bloomed again. These were his heroes: a people could have worse.

Alas, he was hard up for villains: Benedict Arnold loomed up through history in lonely infamy. Aaron Burr, to be sure, had been tried for treason, but most Americans confessed a sneaking admiration for the man who had tried to carve out an empire for himself, particularly at the expense of the Spaniards. General Wilkinson, the most logical candidate for villainy, was forgotten. Obviously Calhoun could not qualify: a little wickedness, it was felt, might have relieved that tiresome rectitude. Simon Legree did well enough, for those north of the Ohio, and eventually they transferred their execration to the slave power. But the reality was less plausible than the fiction: no one could make a villain out of Jefferson Davis, or anything but a hero out of Robert E. Lee. Booth might have qualified, but Booth was mad. For a real villain the American had to go abroad, to the unhappy George III: victim of Henry's eloquence, foil of Franklin's wit, whipping boy of the great Declaration, he was assured an awful immortality. Nothing afforded better testimony to the innocence and good fortune of the American than this paucity of real villains, this willingness to be content with one luckless traitor, one character out of fiction, one mad actor, and one mad monarch: it was like the absence of evil in his philosophy, or of the Devil in his religion.

Literature, too, furnished heroes, scarcely less familiar or less loved than those of history, and the selection of these was far from fortuitous. No two people would agree upon the list, but every list must include Leatherstocking, Deerslayer, Uncle Tom, Huck Finn, Tom Sawyer, Jo March, and perhaps Silas Lapham, and each of these symbolized real or ideal qualities in the American character. It was, on the whole, a romantic group, and the society that it represented was clearly more innocent and more fortunate than that represented by the memorable characters of the next century: Cowperwood, Babbitt, Scarlett O'Hara, George Apley, and the Joads.

One quality these fictional heroes and heroines had in common: they were all countryfolk, even the luckless Silas Lapham. It was inevitable that the American should choose rural heroes, for his ideas and ideals were formed by country living; his poetry and song and mythology were unfailingly rural. Of all the writers whose countenances shone benignly on playing cards of "Authors" only Holmes could be called urban. No novel of city life caught the imagination of these generations, no poem or song that celebrated urban virtues or delights. Whitman, who embraced city and country alike in his warm enthusiasm, had to wait until the twentieth century for popular approval. While heroes and heroines were countryfolk, villains were often city slickers; not until the twentieth century did Americans adopt a hero whose origins and character were wholly urban, and not until then did literature occasionally concede the advantages of city life. No article of faith was more passionately held than that the farmer was the peculiarly beloved of God, and a thousand songs and poems recalled the felicities of the farm. It was the barefoot boy who was really blessed; it was back to the Old Kentucky Home or Old Virginny that everyone wanted to go; it was the old oaken bucket that aroused the most poignant nostalgia, and it was "when dreaming in throngful city ways, of winter joys his boyhood knew" that "the worldling's eyes gathered dew"; "Snowbound" was to Americans what the "Cotter's Saturday Night" was to the Scots; and Thanksgiving, the most American of all holidays, was ineradicably rural.

It was not so much the books he read as the poems he remembered and the songs he sang that reflected the American's sentiments and faiths. Longfellow and Whittier were his chosen poets; Dan Emmett, George Root, and above all, Stephen Foster, put his sentiments to music. Poets and composers alike expressed his delight in simple things, in the beauty of the countryside, the charm of rural life, the affection for the past, so long as it was American. As he had so little of pomp and circumstance in his own life, he made much of the homely joys. He knew that through pleasures and palaces though he might roam, be it ever so humble there was no place like home; he admired the village blacksmith who looked the world in the face; he invoked blessings on the little man, barefoot boy with cheek of tan.

Boyhood figured largely in his literature and in his recollections, and if America produced no Andersen, Grimm, or even Andrew Lang, it was not only that these were all available but also that the American experience was so fabulous that there was little need to take refuge in fairy tales. No other literature was so conscious of childhood or so indebted to it. *St. Nicholas* was the best of all children's magazines and its list of contributors was a veritable hall of fame. From Irving and Cooper to Howells and Crane, almost every major author wrote for children, and many of them mixed reminiscence with fiction to recreate, more authentically, the children's world. The list is long and impressive: *Little Women* and *Little Men, Tom Sawyer* and *Huck Finn,* Lucy Larcom's *New England Girlhood* and E. E. Hale's *New England Boyhood,* Aldrich's *Story of a Bad Boy,* Noah Brooks's *Boy Emigrants,* Warner's *Being a Boy,* Howells' *A Boy's Town,* White's *Court of Boyville,* and Hamlin Garland's *Boy Life on the Prairie.*

What do these volumes tell us of the American boy? What were the moral axioms and standards of conduct which he learned from other boys, from home, family, and school, and how did he translate them into his simple and forthright practices? The evidence is far from conclusive, for the recollections of adults, no matter how faithful, are sentimental and nostalgic and, in the nineteenth century, were prudish as well. The sentimentalism and the reticence can be discounted; they distorted the general picture no more violently, let us say, than the realism of James Farrell about his Studs Lonigan. The nostalgia was pervasive but not poignant: it was not because adult life was so bleak that Clemens, Aldrich, Howells, and others recalled childhood with such affection, and there was little reluctance to let children grow up.

A striking uniformity characterizes these recollections of boyhood. The setting was everywhere rural or small town, and almost all the families lived in respectable poverty. This alone furnished a common denominator, but the common denominator of morals, habits, and customs was even more marked. The code of the boy's town was everywhere the same, and it was one which mirrored faithfully enough the code of the adult world. Every boy was mischievous but few were vicious: the bully, the thief, the liar, the sneak were ostracized more effectively than among grownups. Every boy had his own high sense of honor and enforced it. He was brave, stood up for himself, fought for his rights and fought fairly, learned to take a dare and a risk, scorned a coward, a tattletale, a sissy, and a skulker. He was gregarious, played in gangs, was loyal to his playmates, and rarely cherished enmities. He was chivalrous toward women, respectful to grownups, indifferent toward girls until adolescence, and then romantic about them. He was thoughtless rather than unkind, collected pets indiscriminately, and unfailingly was attached to some dog. He had a lively imagination which found expression chiefly in games; lived in a world inhabited by Indians, cowboys, pirates, and smugglers; and learned much from the town ne'er-do-wells who told him tall tales but rarely corrupted him. He was superstitious but not religious, went to church because he had to, and disliked Sundays. He was fair in his dealings with others, a good loser in games, would not take too sharp an advantage, and scorned every form of meanness. He was simple and democratic, knew few distinctions of class or color, resented snobbery or affectation, made friends readily with the poor and the shiftless, and was uncomfortable in the presence of wealth.

Everyone about him worked hard, and he took for granted a heavy burden of chores and did them with varying degrees of faithfulness. He early learned to be responsible for a numerous brood of smaller brothers and sisters, and his unexpressed sense of loyalty to his family was strong. He lived close to nature; came early under the discipline of farm animals, crops, and weather; delighted especially in swimming, fishing, hunting, and skating; and knew few artificial pleasures except the circus. He took school for granted and, on the whole, enjoyed it; at home he found books and newspapers and was not excluded from grown-up talk about politics or crops or neighbors. He lived in a world of his own, yet was part of the adult world; morally and socially his world was not very different from that inhabited by his parents.

When the American read history, it was to find confirmation of the moral truths preached in the churches and taught in the schools. His historians arrived, almost by instinct, at the conclusion to which the great Lord Acton was later to come through prodigious erudition—that the significance of history was to be found in the struggle for freedom. The history of America vindicated this conclusion, as it did faith in progress, in the validity of democracy and equality, and in the ultimate triumph of right over wrong. This was what Bancroft told him early in the century, and Fiske half a century later, and what these titans affirmed, the textbooks of Peter Parley and the McGuffeys and their successors echoed. He knew little of the history of other lands or times, but some events were familiar enough—the story of Thermopylae, for example, of Arnold Winkelried, and of Robert Bruce—while, if Plutarch did not exercise the authority he had enjoyed in the eighteenth century, he was still a household word. The American preferred Macaulay's version of English history to any other and welcomed with enthusiasm Motley's demonstration of the "deep-laid conspiracy of Spain and Rome against human rights"; when his favorite novelist turned to history it was to sing the praises of the Maid of Orleans. For the rest, history was a story and a romance, a record of battles, of deeds of daring, and of mighty blows struck for freedom; it was a monument to the Pilgrim Fathers, the Indian fighters, the patriots of the Revolution, the Founding Fathers, the trailmakers and pioneers of the West. It was designed to point a moral and adorn a tale, and if the tale was sometimes exotic, the moral was always relevant to American experience.

His passion for material comforts could not be denied, but this was almost universal in the western world. What was unique—or shared only by the Scots—was his even greater passion for education. It was not to be forgotten that his school system was the oldest in the world and the most successful, that he was the first to establish public libraries, and he first to make the higher learning available to women. All his institutions advertised his lively concern for education and self-improvement. Every schoolhouse was a monument to this passion, every library, every lyceum and Grange and Chautauqua. The image of the young Lincoln studying by the flickering light of a log fire was not so much quaint as familiar. It was appropriate that his favorite philosopher should have founded a newspaper, a magazine, a library, and an academy and that his greatest democratic statesman should have thought the founding of the University of Virginia as sure a claim to immortality as the authorship of the Declaration of Independence. It was appropriate that his charter of government for the western states should provide that "religion, morality and knowledge being necessary to good government and the happiness of mankind, schools and the means of education shall forever be encouraged"; what other colonial charter contained a like admonition? Nowhere did newspapers flourish more immoderately or the art of printing justify itself more strikingly than in the land where illiteracy was held a disgrace. While children trudged miles along country lanes to country schools, their elders organized lyceums to which the great and learned gladly spoke. The catalogue of any lyceum over a period of years suggests not only catholicity of interest but a standard of popular intelligence that could not be matched elsewhere in the world and that was certainly far more rigorous than that imposed by the radio of the next century. Yet it was ominous that, quantitatively, education took on a sectional character: while lyceums flourished in the North, illiteracy flourished in the South; and that contrast which Hinton Helper observed in the mid-nineteenth century—and which he ascribed to slavery—persisted into the mid-twentieth.

Schools were not only an expression of American philosophy; they were the most effective agent in its formulation and dissemination. What lessons did the schools teach, what standards of morality did they sustain, what notions of patriotism did they implant? What, especially, was the philosophy distilled in the pages of the Webster *Spellers* and the McGuffey *Readers* which shared sovereignty over the juvenile mind? What children have learned in school is not to be taken too seriously as an index to their character, but it is an almost infallible guide to the moral system that adults approve, and when that approval persists for three generations, it attains almost constitutional dignity.

One note which recurred, insistently and harmoniously, was love of country and of freedom. Patriotism was inculcated on almost every page of the Readers, Spellers, and Histories that served American youth, and a common body of stories, hero tales, legends, and maxims gave unity to a people threatened by sectional differences, and tradition to a people without a common past. Throughout the century these were the things that every child knew, that every man remembered: God sifted a whole nation that he might send choice grain over into this wilderness; As for me, give me liberty or give me death; If they mean to have a war, let it begin here; We hold these truths to be self-evident . . . life liberty and the pursuit of happiness; Where liberty dwells, there is my country; My only regret is that I have but one life to lose for my country; Millions for defense, not one cent for tribute; Don't give up the ship; We have met the enemy, and they are ours; I shall never surrender nor retreat; Liberty and union, now and forever, one and inseparable; Damn the torpedoes, go ahead; Lee to the rear; Government of the people, for the people, by the people; Bury contention with the war; Malice toward none, charity for all. The phrases, too vital to be trite, entered into the very fibre of their being, gave them self-assurance and dignity.

Poetry, learned really by heart as well as head, exalted what history recalled: Let independence be your boast, ever mindful what it cost; Then conquer we must, for our cause it is just, and this be our motto, in God is our trust; Here once the embattled farmers stood, and fired the shot heard round the world; Ay, tear her tattered ensign down, long has it waved on high; We cross the prairies as of old the Pilgrims crossed the sea, to make the West, as they the East, the homestead of the Free; As He died to make men holy, let us die to make men free. It was all to seem naïve to a later generation, but it was not lacking in nobility of inspiration and it served its purpose.

The moral lessons which the Readers taught had to draw on imagination rather than history for reinforcement and were lacking in dignity though not in point. The Readers taught industry, obedience to parents, kindness to the old and to animals, temperance, generosity, promptness, and the inevitable triumph of the virtuous over the wicked. There was no scale of virtues, but all were indistinguishable, and consequently values were confused. They did not commend capital punishment for even the most heinous crimes, but the boy who loitered at play fell into the pond and was drowned. They did not promise an easy road to heaven, but the lad who shared his cake with an old man was overwhelmed with rewards. Promptness was rewarded as handsomely as charity, idleness punished as severely as malice; and it was no wonder if Americans sometimes lost their sense of proportion in their judgment of moral issues. The Readers insisted on the necessity and the virtue of work: He who would thrive, must rise at five, he who has thriven may lie till seven; Each morning sees some task begun, each evening sees its close; Count that day lost, whose low descending sun, views from thy hand no worthy action done. They maintained that life was real and earnest, and the Psalm of Life was almost the national poem. They promised that right would triumph in the end, for, Behind the great unknown, standeth God within the shadows, keeping watch above His own. Children may have revolted against these moral lessons, but each successive generation taught them to its children until they became as fixed in the popular consciousness as the Ten Commandments or the golden rule.

It was a naïve creed. To a sophisticated generation, it came to seem Arcadian in its simplicity. Yet it served its purpose, and it compares not unfavorably with the creed of rigorous Calvinism of the seventeenth century or the chaotic creedlessness of the twentieth. It sustained most Americans throughout the nineteenth century and some into the twentieth. Yet changes were under way even before the nineties, and after that decade those changes were sharp enough to suggest the coming of a new era.

By the close of the century, formal philosophy was at a low ebb. Emerson's Transcendentalism had lost its hold, and William James's pragmatism was still to come. The hard times of the nineties cast a shadow on the traditional American optimism, and much of the new literature was written in that shadow. The sense of destiny, as strong as ever, was soon confused with the white man's burden and stained with chauvinism; but William Jennings Bryan, the most eloquent political champion of the older ideals, was the unreconciled leader of anti-imperialism. The Spanish War was the most spectacularly successful of all American wars, but it satisfied the American pride rather than the American conscience, and though Admiral Dewey was acclaimed a greater John Paul Jones and an equal of Farragut, it is suggestive that he never joined them in the American hall of fame.

The new folklore celebrated business rather than adventure, the new heroes were captains of finance and titans of industry, and history itself abandoned temporarily the praise of famous men to record the impact on society of impersonal problems. As the poets of the transition years were too aloof or too precious to furnish a whole people lines they could quote or songs they could sing, Americans of the new generation continued to console themselves with Longfellow, Whittier, and Stephen Foster. *Little Women* had been sentimental, but the Elsie books, in their day as widely read, were saccharine; *Tom Sawyer* and *A Boy's Town* pictured a life that was crude, but the values explicit in the Alger books were vulgar. Vulgarity characterized politics as well, and it was difficult to know whether to prefer the monotony of presidents like Arthur, Harrison, and McKinley, who were honest but dull, or the diversion of politicians like Conkling, Quay, and Mark Hanna, who were picturesque but corrupt.

CHAPTER II

The Watershed of the Nineties

I

THE DECADE of the nineties is the watershed of American history. As with all watersheds the topography is blurred, but in the perspective of half a century the grand outlines emerge clearly. On the one side lies an America predominantly agricultural; concerned with domestic problems; conforming, intellectually at least, to the political, economic, and moral principles inherited from the seventeenth and eighteenth centuries—an America still in the making, physically and socially; an America on the whole self-confident, self-contained, self-reliant, and conscious of its unique character and of a unique destiny. On the other side lies the modern America, predominantly urban and industrial; inextricably involved in world economy and politics; troubled with the problems that had long been thought peculiar to the Old World; experiencing profound changes in population, social institutions, economy, and technology; and trying to accommodate its traditional institutions and habits of thought to conditions new and in part alien.

The process of adjustment was, to be sure, nothing novel in American experience. No people of modern times had ampler experience in adaptation or had proved more adaptable. Instability had characterized American society from the time the first settlers landed along the banks of the James and on the shores of Cape Cod down to the passing of the frontier almost three centuries later. The uprooting from the Old World—a phenomenon which persisted for three centuries—was the first and perhaps the most profound wrench, and as each successive generation pulled up stakes and moved west, the process of transplanting and accommodation to new physical and social conditions was repeated. Never had that process been more violent or complex than during the generation after the Civil War —a generation which saw the expansion of settlement from the

Missouri to the Pacific, the disruption of the plantation system and the redistribution of white and Negro population in the South, a revolution in agriculture, the rise of the modern industrial city, and the coming of the new immigration.

Yet throughout the nineteenth century this process of adjustment, for all the disorder with which it was attended, took place within an economic and social framework that was reasonably stable and a political and moral framework that was almost entirely so. Thus the institutions of property, family, school, church, and state, although subjected to continuous buffetings, were never seriously challenged. Thus, though men had to find new techniques of government, the fundamental practices of democracy were everywhere taken for granted. Thus the ethical standards to which men conformed were rarely questioned. In short, to the nineteenth-century American the cosmic scheme was familiar, the cosmic laws were regular. Even the processes of disintegration and reintegration followed a familiar pattern.

Certainly, though there was a continuous breaking up and reshaping of communities and even of institutions, there was no progressive deterioration from frontier to frontier or from country to city. Quite the contrary. The heritage of the past which pioneers took with them into the wilderness or which countryfolk brought to the cities, though it might be temporarily dissipated, was never lost, and the various processes of adaptation were material rather than moral. The traditions of western civilization were, after all, unbroken, and the American traditions, planted in the seventeenth and eighteenth centuries on the eastern seaboard, flourished without embarrassment over the whole continental expanse throughout the nineteenth century. If American society never achieved stability, neither did it suffer from stagnation or decay. If some of the amenities and even the achievements of civilization were sacrificed to change, something too was gained in new opportunities for the demonstration of energy, ingenuity, and independence.

With the closing years of the nineteenth century, this familiar pattern was distorted, and the rhythm of change became impetuous and erratic. Change itself became qualitative as well as quantitative. As a result, the demands made upon the integrity of the American character and the resourcefulness of the American mind at the end of the century were more complex and imperative than at any time in a hundred years. It was not only that Americans had to adjust themselves to changes in economy and society more abrupt and pervasive than ever before. It was rather that for the first time in their national experience they were confronted with a challenge to their philosophical assumptions. They were not unaccustomed to profound alterations in their physical surroundings; they were unprepared for the crumbling of their cosmic scheme. They were now to be required not only to articulate their economy to a new technology and adjust their society to new ways of life—that was a familiar task—but to make their politics and morals conform to new scientific and philosophical precepts. Under the impact of these new forces, the note of confidence which had long characterized the American accent gave way to doubt, self-assurance to bewilderment, and resolution to confusion.

2

By 1890 the Civil War era was drawing to a close—the era chiefly concerned with problems that grew out of war and Reconstruction. The men for whom the war had been the great and abiding experience—whose imaginations were fired by the recollection of Missionary Ridge and Little Round Top and the Bloody Angle, whose heroes were Grant and Lee, Sherman and Jackson—were passing from the scene. McKinley was the last Civil War general to be a candidate for the presidency, and it is suggestive that his opponent, Bryan, had been born in the year of secession. Already the war was becoming a romantic memory: its grand figures were writing their stately memoirs, and novelists were celebrating its heroic virtues; the most realistic story of the war came from Stephen Crane, born six years after Appomattox. The cruel wounds of war and the hateful wounds of Reconstruction were healing. Veterans in blue and gray could celebrate their reunions together, a magnanimous North returned Confederate battle flags, and Force Acts were abandoned, together with interest in the issues which had seemed to require them. The memory of the war did not fade, but memory of its causes and its issues did; except in the minds of professional rabble rousers and on the tongues of professional Southerners, ancient sectional antipathies were all but forgotten, and North and South traveled peacefully the road to reunion.

Even the more recent past seemed already remote and strange. Within a generation the Indian had been driven from his ancestral hunting grounds and cooped up in reservations; and Indian warfare, which for two and a half centuries had been a grim reality, became a game played by children who confused King Philip's War with Custer's Last Stand. The mining kingdom had flourished and declined and had been transformed into a business controlled by eastern corporations, and the desperadoes who once terrorized Alder Gulch and Bannock City were embalmed in dime novels. The Texas longhorns that had ranged the grasslands from the Rio Grande to the Yellowstone now grazed behind barbed wire, and the cowboy, most authentic of frontier types, prepared to move to dude ranches and Hollywood. All but one of the great transcontinental railroads whose construction had excited world-wide enthusiasm had been completed, and the builders had become objects of execration rather than of admiration. It had all happened only yesterday, as it were, yet already it was a ripe subject for romantic fiction and for legends. As early as 1883, Buffalo Bill had found it profitable to turn his career into a show; and less than ten years after Custer had been massacred on the banks of the Little Big Horn, a rising politician from New York City could capitalize on ranching in the Dakota country. By the end of the century the nostalgic stories of Owen Wister and the romantic drawings of Frederic Remington were thrilling thousands of city-folk to whom the Wild West was as distant and as exotic as Salem witchcraft.

With the decade of the nineties—or roughly from the mid-eighties to the Spanish War—the new America came in as on flood tide. These years witnessed the passing of the old West, the disappearance of the frontier line and of good, cheap farm land, the decline of the cattle kingdom, the completion of the transcontinentals, the admission of the Omnibus States, and the final territorial organization of the trans-Mississippi area. They revealed a dangerous acceleration of the exploitation of natural resources; the seizure of the best forest, mineral, range, and farm land by corporations; and the beginnings of the conservation and reclamation movement. They were marked by a profound and prolonged agricultural malaise and the transfer of the center of economic and political gravity from country to city. They saw the advent of the New South; an unprecedented concentration of control of the processes of manufacture, transportation, communication, and banking in trusts and monopolies; the rise of big business; the emergence of the successful businessman as hero; and the beginning of that process which was to be celebrated in President Coolidge's aphorism that "the business of America is business."

It was the period, too, of the shift from the "old" to the "new" immigration, of the coming of that

> wild motley throng,
> Men from the Volga and the Tartar steppes

whose influx caused such anguish to Thomas Bailey Aldrich and to labor leaders. This decade saw the decline of the idealistic Knights of Labor and the beginnings of the modern labor movement sponsored by the American Federation of Labor, the emergence of labor trouble as a constant in industry, the beginnings—with the Haymarket riot, the Homestead and the Pullman strikes—of class conflict in American society, and the fashioning of new legal and political weapons for that struggle.

And in this period came at last a full-throated recognition of the crowding problems of agriculture, urban life, slums, trusts, business and political corruption, race prejudice, and the maldistribution of wealth, and with it, convulsive efforts to adapt a federal political system to a centralized economy, and a laissez-faire philosophy to a program of social democracy. From the Interstate Commerce Act of 1887 and the Antitrust Act of 1890, we can conveniently date the beginnings of federal centralization; from Fuller's appointment to the Chief Justiceship in 1888, that revolutionary shift in the interpretation of the Fourteenth Amendment which did so much to nullify state action in the economic and social area; from the Populist platform of 1892, the formulation of that program of economic reform which in one way or another was to dominate politics for the next half-century. Under the impact of new problems the old parties seemed about to disintegrate, and new parties, the Populist and the Socialist, threatened to disrupt the traditional two-party system.

Society, always fluid in America, seemed in process of disintegration; the reintegration, though persistent and effective, was less obvious. The rapid growth of big cities, the torrential increase in immigration and the growing concentration of the newcomers in the cities of the Northeast, the decline of the planter class in the South and the assault upon the social citadels of the North by the new rich, the

emancipation of women and the decline in the birth rate, all contributed to the dislocation. The rise of the city was not merely a social
or an economic phenomenon; it was psychological as well. The shift
from "Snowbound" to "The Man with the Hoe," from Cooper's
Oak Openings to Garland's *Main Travelled Roads,* was not literary
merely. When the farmer ceased to

> reign like kings in fairy land,
> Lords of the soil . . .

and became, instead, a hayseed—or just a headache—a revolution had
occurred in American thought. Equally revolutionary was the emancipation of woman, ushered in by the typewriter, the telephone exchange, and a hundred labor-saving devices, dramatized by the vote,
and guaranteed by birth control. It was not that woman had heretofore been a slave even to domesticity; it was rather that her new status
and opportunities worked a profound change in the size of the family, the character of the home, and the nature of economy and culture.

There had always been some objection to immigrants; now the
problem of assimilation was accentuated by differences in racial origins, in cultural traditions, in skills, and in religion, that seemed qualitative. War and Reconstruction in the South, the eclipse of Beacon
Street and Gramercy Park by such fashionable suburbs as Brookline
and Tuxedo Park made an end of the only indigenous aristocracies
America had known, and by assuring everywhere the triumph of
the middle class, greatly accelerated the drift toward social uniformity, substituted crude for gracious social standards, and gave to class
antipathies an economic rather than a social slant.

It was a period of rising nationalism and national self-consciousness,
whipped up by the yellow journalism of Pulitzer, Hearst, and their
imitators and romanticized by a school of novelists who proved the
American past designed deliberately to enable ladies to while away
summer afternoons. Patriotism became not only filiopietistic but
self-conscious: the Colonial Dames and the Daughters of the American Revolution organized in 1890 to recreate the social distinctions
their ancestors had fled and defend the shibboleths their ancestors
had attacked. The nation abandoned such isolationism as it had enjoyed and became a world power; but while public opinion applauded policies designed to expand national influence and enhance
national wealth, it was not prepared to endorse policies enlarging

national responsibility. That dichotomy of political and economic imperialism and moral and psychological isolationism which was to confuse American politics for half a century was dramatized by the debate over imperialism and the enunciation of the Open Door policy. Cleveland, who was alarmed by the rough methods of American expansion into the Pacific, yet did not hesitate to reaffirm the Monroe Doctrine, and his secretary of state announced, with more truth than tact, that "the United States is practically sovereign on this continent and its fiat is law." Soon Roosevelt and Lodge were to add new corollaries to the famous doctrine and assert, even more arrogantly, American hegemony in the Western Hemisphere. The United States blundered into the Spanish War and emerged not only dominant in the Caribbean but, unexpectedly, a Pacific power. It took over Hawaii and the Philippines, proclaimed an open door but permitted other nations to hold the keys, began construction of an Isthmian canal designed to implement Captain Mahan's arguments regarding the importance of sea power, accepted the thankless role of conciliator between Russia and Japan, and asserted an interest in the politics of Europe and even of Africa. Josiah Strong made the white man's burden a Christian duty, Captain Mahan ransacked history to justify naval supremacy, John W. Burgess celebrated American nationalism as Treitschke did German, and Theodore Roosevelt brandished a big stick. The piercing protests of the anti-imperialists were drowned out by the thunder of manifest destiny.

Nor was it only in the arena of politics and economy that these were transition years. Not since the 1840's had there been such a ferment in the intellectual world; not since then had established institutions been subjected to so critical a scrutiny, or traditional philosophy to so sharp a challenge. The neat, orderly universe of the Enlightenment—a universe governed by laws whose nature could be discovered by man—was disintegrating under the blows of Darwinian evolution, the new physics, and the new biology; and philosophers, baffled or disillusioned in their search for universal laws, contented themselves with analyses of its fragmentary and fortuitous manifestations. That Henry Adams exaggerated the unity of the eighteenth century and the multiplicity of the twentieth could be doubted by no one who studied the careers of Aaron Burr and Woodrow Wilson, yet the decline of harmony and balance in the American character was notorious, and the transition from the age of confidence to the age of doubt manifested itself in many ways. That confusion and doubt rather than certitude and confidence should characterize the thought of a people at the height of their material prosperity and the maturity of their scientific development was surprising, but no more surprising than that the material prosperity should bring so little general contentment and the science solve so few fundamental problems.

If unity seemed lost, multiplicity had its virtues and rewards. American thought revealed a relentless curiosity, eager experimentation, generous catholicity, and unabashed secularism. The social took from the natural sciences the inductive method, and there was everywhere enthusiastic investigation and a search, if not for ultimate truth, then for useful facts and empirical understanding. Within little more than a decade—perhaps the most fruitful in the history of American scholarship—came James's *Psychology*, Veblen's *Theory of the Leisure Class*, Wine's *Report on Crime and Pauperism*, Turner's "Frontier in American History," Brooks Adams' *Law of Civilization and Decay*, Bliss's *Encyclopaedia of Social Reform*, Hall's *Adolescence*, Ostrogorski's *Democracy and the Organization of Political Parties*, Ward's *Psychic Factors in Civilization*, Wilson's *The State*, Mahan's *Influence of Sea Power upon History*, Boas's *Development of the Culture of North-West America*, Dewey's *The School and Society*, Henry Adams' *History of the United States*, and Royce's *The World and the Individual*. Never before had the anatomy of American society and economy been so scrupulously laid bare; never before, as Santayana was to observe, had men known so many facts and been masters of so few principles.

3

It was all part of the process of coming of age, a strenuous effort to come to terms with a new economic and philosophical order for which Americans were but inadequately prepared by experience or by instruction. The dominant impression at the turn of the century is not that of material development, splendid as that was, but of bewilderment and distraction. The safest thing that could be said of the vast display of economic, political, and intellectual energy was that it created as many problems as it solved, raised as many issues as it laid, contributed as much to discontent as to contentment.

The generation of the nineties should have been self-confident and triumphant, for the past was reassuring and the future dazzling. The continent had been subdued, the Republic extended to its farthest reaches—its stability established, its power acknowledged, its influence felt throughout the world. Liberty, enlightenment, and prosperity flourished, at least as vigorously as elsewhere in the world. Yet no previous generation had been more bedeviled by problems, and no earlier problems, except those of slavery, had seemed more vexatious. Instead of being exalted, thoughtful Americans were overwhelmed with a consciousness of questions unsolved, promises unfulfilled, and certitudes lost.

The problems which confronted the men of this transition generation were no longer the familiar ones, nor did they yield to the familiar solutions. They were for the most part new, at least in their philosophical implications, and their novelty created confusion and consternation. The old issues—tariff, money, banking, railroads, trusts, the Negro—persisted but rather as symptoms than as first causes, and men felt a growing conviction that the origins of these issues were moral rather than economic or political. More fundamental problems pressed for attention and solution, problems of a varied character that threatened the very foundations of the democratic order, tested the place of the individual in society, and challenged traditional morality. The mood of optimism, which had for so long inspired the conduct and stimulated the energies of men, was succeeded by a mood of scientific skepticism which inspired confusion and stimulated doubt.

There was the ethical problem which arose from the attempt to apply the individualistic moral code of the eighteenth and early nineteenth centuries—a moral code in which good and evil were significant terms, and responsibility personal—to the complex, impersonal practices of a twentieth-century economic order. There was the parallel difficulty of accommodating a government based on the eighteenth-century principle that government is a necessary evil to the felt necessities of a welfare state. There was the problem of salvaging the individual in an economy dominated by vast, impersonal, and largely incomprehensible forces and of justifying individual effort in a deterministic philosophy which offered less play for free will than had any previous system of thought to which Americans had subscribed. There was the problem of fulfilling the new role of the nation in world affairs, of adjusting emotional isolationism to the realities of economic and political internationalism.

Nor was there leisure in these troubled years to contemplate the nature of the changes that were hurrying men so breathlessly from their old moorings, to analyze the new problems that were vexing them, to make adjustments to changing conditions. The crowding events of the nineties gave, rather, a peculiar urgency to the task of readjustment and impressed upon the whole process a fragmentary and opportunistic character. The political readjustments of the Revolutionary era had been prepared for by generations of thought and training and a decade of high-minded discussion. The far-flung reform movements of the mid-nineteenth century were the logical product of the Enlightenment and Transcendentalism and derived from these coherence and direction. There was no comparable philosophical preparation for the effort to come to terms with the new world of science and technology that loomed up over the horizon in the closing years of the nineteenth century. Particular changes could not be fitted neatly into some familiar pattern; intellectual adjustments could not be articulated to some accepted philosophy. "How idle in our new situation," wrote Edward A. Ross, "to intone the old litanies." The philosophical presuppositions upon which the stable order of the past had rested, and from which American conduct had derived its justification and American institutions their validity, were themselves under attack. It was not only economy and society but morality that was being atomized under the impact of new forces astir in the world.

The transition from the stability of the nineteenth to the instability of the twentieth century was made against the background of economic disorder, panic, and depression. Never before, not even in the dark days of the seventies, had the outlook seemed so bleak. Every group, every interest was affected by the economic depression that struck the country in the late eighties: farmers, workingmen, the railroads, industries, banks. Only the sheltered or the willfully blind could think Ignatius Donnelly's preamble to the Populist platform of 1892 merely rhetorical:

We meet in the midst of a nation brought to the verge of moral, political, and material ruin . . . business prostrated, homes covered with mortgages, labor impoverished, and the land concentrating in the hands of capitalists. The urban workmen are denied the right to organize for self-protection, imported pauperized labor beats down their wages, a hireling standing army, unrecognized by our laws, is established to shoot them down, and they are rapidly degenerating into European conditions. The fruits of the toil of millions are boldly stolen to build up colossal fortunes for a few, unprecedented in the history of mankind; and the possessors of these, in turn, despize the Republic and endanger liberty. From the same prolific womb of governmental injustice we breed the two great classes—tramps and millionaires.

Hard times came to the plains with the great drought of 1887, a drought which held on, summer after summer, for five iron years. In the first four years of the nineties, more than eleven thousand farm mortgages were foreclosed in Kansas alone, and in fifteen counties of that state more than three quarters of the farm land fell to the mortgage companies, most of them owned in the East. Soon the pioneers who had followed "fair freedom's star . . . to the sunset regions" were plodding back east; on their wagons, once freighted with hope, the scrawl, "In God we trusted, in Kansas we busted." Elsewhere in the West, conditions were almost as bad. As wheat fell below fifty cents a bushel and corn to twenty-eight cents, counties and towns were bankrupted, schools and churches closed their doors. The great blizzard of 1886–87 all but wiped out the cattle on the open ranges, and as the men who had driven the longhorns up the Chisholm and Goodnight trails were ruined, the great cattle companies of the East moved in and took over. In the South, too, suffering was acute and prolonged. Concentration on cotton, the collapse of markets, the malign effect of the crop-lien system, brought universal hardship. Cotton fell to five cents a pound and tobacco to the lowest point in two decades, and share cropping spread like an epidemic. By 1900 one third of all American farmers were tenants, and the fear that Jefferson's "chosen people of God" would end up as peasants seemed not unfounded.

Labor suffered just as acutely, and if the average workingman had less to lose than the farmer, his very lack of resources exposed him more cruelly to the vicissitudes of the economic cycle. The great strike of 1886 collapsed, and the most hopeful and idealistic of American labor organizations, the Knights of Labor, went to pieces under the impact of hard times, incompetent leadership, and the Haymarket tragedy. A series of strikes, violently conducted and ruthlessly suppressed, brought home to Americans the reality of class conflict: the

McCormick Harvester strike and the Haymarket riot, which ended with the judicial murder of five alleged anarchists; the sanguinary Homestead strike of 1892, the great Pullman strike of 1894, and that same year, warfare along the Cripple Creek in Colorado. The panic of 1893 was the worst the country had ever experienced. Hundreds of banks closed their doors, thousands of factories and mines shut down, one fourth the railroads went into the hands of receivers, and over fifteen thousand commercial failures testified to the breakdown of the economic system. That winter, and the next, millions of working-men walked the streets in a vain search for jobs or shivered in long soup lines, for haphazard charity was the only answer that society had yet formulated to acts of God like panics and unemployment. "Society here, as well as in Europe, is shaking," wrote Henry Adams, and added that "men died like flies under the strain." He was think-ing of his Back Bay friends; the strain on the farmer, the working-man, the small shopkeeper, was heavier than even he could imagine.

Everything seemed to conspire against the victims of hard times: the weather, foreign markets, the business cycle, the unfathomable operations of the money system. Even the government seemed part of the conspiracy. With deflation spelling ruin to debtors, Congress demonetized silver and went on a gold standard. When the govern-ment found itself in desperate financial straits, it turned to the House of Morgan; and Wall Street and State Street, so long the objects of popular execration, could pose as saviors of the country. Tariff re-form, which promised some measure of relief from high prices and monopoly practices, was betrayed by a Congress more sensitive to pressure from lobbies than to the voice of the people. An income tax, which might have distributed more equitably the burden of taxation, was voided by a Supreme Court trembling before the specter of communism. The Interstate Commerce Act was sabotaged, the Sherman Antitrust Act betrayed by those pledged to enforce it, the injunction was used to break strikes, and the noble concept of free-dom of contract was perverted into a weapon to nullify social legis-lation. When Jacob Coxey led his shambling army of unemployed to Washington, the authorities could think of no better reception than to jail its leaders for walking on the grass; when captains of industry presented their petitions, they were accorded a different welcome.

Meantime the rich who, in the words of Frederick T. Martin "owned America," went their way undaunted. Andrew Carnegie, to be sure, preached a Gospel of Wealth and concluded that it was a disgrace to die rich, but with corporations to act for them the rich had never been more irresponsible. Darwin had taught them that they were the fittest to survive, and Spencer that their survival was part of the scheme of things; while here at home there was the unimpeachable authority of Bishop Lawrence to demonstrate that "Godliness is in league with riches." The rich grew steadily richer, and big business bigger. The process of consolidation, inaugurated in the eighties, suffered only a temporary setback by the panic of 1893 and, with the return of prosperity after 1896, went its way unembarrassed by state or federal antitrust laws. "What looks like a stone wall to a layman," observed Mr. Dooley, "is a triumphal arch to a corporation lawyer." The natural resources of the country drifted remorselessly into the control of giant corporations, and concentration of control progressed implacably in the fields of transportation, communication, and banking. Before the glacierlike advance of the great corporation, small businessmen and shopkeepers were ground out of existence or absorbed. The philosophy of individualism had never been more ardently praised, but free enterprise was threatened by those who invoked it, and the exercise of individualism restricted by those to whom the economic doctrine of laissez faire was a scientific law.

4

The decade of the nineties marked the end of an era; it heralded, even more unmistakably, the beginning of one. Not only economically and politically but intellectually and psychologically, it attached itself to the twentieth rather than to the nineteenth century. It fixed the pattern to which Americans of the next two generations were to conform, set the problems which they were required to solve. The American of 1950 felt at home with his parents and grandparents of the 1890's, as the Americans of that decade did not with an earlier generation. A half-century separates Theodore Parker's sermons on the *Perishing and Dangerous Classes of Boston, How the Other Half Lives,* and *Grapes of Wrath,* but it is clear that Jacob Riis is closer to Steinbeck than to Parker, just as it is clear that the *Theory of the Leisure Class* is closer to *Middletown* than to *Walden.* To the American of 1950 the political figures of the nineties seemed almost contemporary; move back but a decade or two and they become quaint and archaic. He could believe in Bryan, LaFollette, and Theodore Roosevelt, but he could accept Conkling and Blaine, Harrison and Arthur, only by an effort of the imagination—an effort which he seldom cared to make. He could and did read E. A. Robinson, Stephen Crane, and Frank Norris without feeling that they were dated; he relegated to the schoolbooks the poetry of E. C. Stedman, the stories of Bret Harte and Harriet Beecher Stowe.

The great issues of the nineties still commanded popular attention half a century later; the seminal minds of that decade still directed popular thought. Problems of isolation and internationalism, of laissez faire and government planning, of the causes and cures of panics, the contrasts of progress and poverty, the humanizing of urban life, the control of business and the rights of labor, the place of the Negro and the immigrant in society, the improvement of agriculture and the conservation of natural resources, the actualization of democracy into social security—all these things which had monopolized public interest in the nineties, seemed no less urgent in the 1930's and 1940's. The roots of the New Deal were in populism, the origins of world power in the Spanish War and the acquisition of Hawaii and the Philippines. Fifty years after their formulation the American was still exploring the economic ideas of Veblen, developing the sociological doctrines of Lester Ward, elaborating on the historical theories of Henry Adams and the historical interpretations of Frederick Jackson Turner, experimenting with the educational theories of John Dewey, amplifying the philosophy of William James, applying the artistic standards of Louis Sullivan and Thomas Eakins, accommodating political institutions to the teachings of Frank Goodnow and Woodrow Wilson, catching up with the juridical doctrines of Justice Holmes. Notwithstanding two world wars, enormous material growth, astonishing advances in technology, and revolutionary changes in science, the threescore years that came after 1890 possessed an unequivocal unity.

CHAPTER III

Transition Years in Literature and Journalism

I

IF THE POLITICAL and economic dividing line of the nineties seems sharp, the literary is nothing less than dramatic. Within a few years, most of the great figures who had long dominated American letters passed from the scene. Lanier, Emerson, Longfellow, Hayne, and Louisa May Alcott died in the eighties; Lowell, Melville, Bancroft, Parkman, Whitman, Whittier, and Holmes followed in the early nineties. Henry James and Bret Harte had found refuge in England, Lafcadio Hearn in Japan. Mark Twain and William Dean Howells lived on, but it was the disillusioned Mark Twain of *The Man That Corrupted Hadleyburg* and *The Mysterious Stranger,* the rebellious Howells of *A Traveler from Altruria* and *Through the Eye of a Needle.* Aldrich and Gilder, Stedman and Stoddard, to be sure, lingered on in the twilight of the past, writing their

> Triolets, villanelles, rondels, rondeaus,
> Ballades by the score with the same old thought

Although Barrett Wendell, dean of American critics, accorded them more respect than he gave Walt Whitman, their day was over, and there was poignancy in Aldrich's lament:

> The oldtime fire, the antique grace,
> You will not find them anywhere.
> Today we breathe a commonplace
> Polemic, scientific air.

The dying of the old-time fires, the passing of the antique grace, was not unique to America. The great Victorians, too, were withdrawing from the stage—Arnold and Ruskin, Tennyson and Browning, Trollope and Reade—and across the ocean there was the same lament, the same bewilderment, at the ascendancy of Oscar Wilde and Rudyard Kipling, the Fabians, and the *Yellow Book*. "A new generation that I know not and mainly prize not has taken universal possession," wrote Henry James, who was aggrieved over the rejection of time-tested standards.

The literature of the postwar years had been regional and romantic; that of the nineties was sociological and naturalistic. Where the literature of the earlier generation had celebrated the amenities of life and escaped from its vexations, that of the later magnified the vexations and repudiated the amenities. Like politics, it was weighted down with urgent problems, but where with Hawthorne or Melville these had been spiritual, with Norris and Crane, Garland and Dreiser, they were material. It could be justly said that the novelists and even the poets of the earlier generation had ignored their own society; it could not be denied that the writers of the nineties were overwhelmed by it. They were not so much philosophers as reporters, and so comprehensive and accurate were their transcriptions of the contemporary scene that, if the whole documentary record of this generation should be lost, we could reconstruct it faithfully from imaginative literature.

Romanticism, to be sure, did not die with Bayard Taylor nor realism begin with Stephen Crane. The cult of Stevenson flourished throughout the nineties and into the new century, and Virginia preferred the dashing historical novels of Mary Johnston to the sober pictures of social change by Ellen Glasgow. Nor did all the realists dedicate themselves to history or reform: Ambrose Bierce and Henry B. Fuller would confound that generalization. Yet the differences that distinguished most of the significant writers of this decade were of vocabulary and style rather than philosophy. Even the poets returned to the tradition of Whittier and Lowell and volunteered part of their talents to the clarification of those issues that troubled the pages of the *Congressional Record*. As early as 1875 the gentle Sidney Lanier had hurled poetic bolts against the standards of the market place:

O Trade! O Trade! would thou wert dead!
The Time needs heart—'tis tired of head. . . .

Yea, what avail the endless tale
Of gain by cunning and plus by sale?
Look up the land, look down the land,
The poor, the poor, the poor they stand
Wedged by the pressing of Trade's hand.

(*The Symphony*)

Yet Lanier's quarrel with Trade was chivalric rather than prole-
tarian. An American Pre-Raphaelite, he was more at home with King
Arthur's knights or the Elizabethans than with Karl Marx or Johan
Most, and his poetry did not echo labor's demand for shorter hours
and higher wages but its

Monstrous foul-air sigh
For the outside leagues of liberty,
Where Art, sweet lark, translates the sky
Into a heavenly melody.

William Vaughn Moody's protest, which came, significantly, a quarter of a century later, was more realistic:

I watched when the captains passed;
She were better captainless.
Men in the cabin, before the mast,
But some were reckless, and some aghast,
And some sat gorged at mess.

(*Gloucester Moors*)

Moody and his New England contemporary, Edwin Arlington Robinson, represented the mood of Victorian doubt: in Moody's *Gloucester Moors* we hear echoes of Matthew Arnold's *Dover Beach,* and in
Robinson's *Captain Craig* of Browning's *Pippa Passes;* in both there
is that moral earnestness, that search for lasting values, that assertion
of the ineradicable dignity of man in the face of misgivings about
the omnipotence of God or the benevolence of Nature, which we associate with the Victorians.

2

What Moody and Robinson, Santayana, Stephen Crane, and Edwin
Markham interpreted philosophically, the novelists grappled with
more passionately. Passion is not an emotion customarily associated

with the homely and humane William Dean Howells, but more fully than any other literary interpreter Howells revealed the impact of new social and economic forces upon the artist—all the more, perhaps, because he was concerned with the spiritual rather than the physical consequences of those forces. The younger rebels of 1890–1905—Garland, Norris, Crane, Dreiser—had no past; the older practitioners—Page, Stockton, Crawford, Bret Harte, Cable— were indifferent to the future. Howells embraced half a century and was more nearly national in scope than any other writer except Mark Twain. In more than half a hundred novels and stories he furnished the most faithful transcription of middle-class America that can be found in our literature, and Mr. Homo from Altruria could have reconstructed from the writings of his creator a substantial part of that American society about which he was so curious. In them he could have found genre paintings of the New England village and the Ohio town, sedate Boston and bustling New York, suburbia and even Bohemia; he could have met farmers and workingmen, doctors and clergymen, artists and writers, and—most frequently and intimately —the American woman. There, too, he could have familiarized himself with those superficial problems of social conduct that engaged so large a part of her attention and those profounder moral problems whose very existence testified to the comparative innocence of American society.

The dictator of literary Boston, Howells never forgot his frontier origins or abandoned his democratic simplicity; the historian of manners, and above all of feminine manners, he was rarely indifferent to the larger questions of social justice. His earlier novels, reflecting the "smiling aspects of American life," dealt often with trivia, but as he grew older he became steadily more serious and more radical, and after he moved to New York in 1886 he turned to issues "nobler and larger than those of the love affairs common to fiction."

It was not New York that gave Howells a new vision. Rather, that new vision persuaded him to abandon Brahmin Boston and "the miserable literary idolatries of the past" and cast in his lot with the bustling metropolis that was already the economic and soon to be the literary capital of the nation. The move was symbolic rather than controlling, as was the title of its first product: *A Hazard of New Fortunes.* For the gentle, old-maidenly gossip who had presided over the discreet pages of the *Atlantic,* who had written so tenderly of the American girl, who had avowed himself a disciple of Jane Austen and Alphonse Daudet, had fallen under the spell first of Turgenev, then of Tolstoy and Hardy, and now confessed himself a follower of Henry George and Edward Bellamy. "I feel sure," he said, "that I can never look at life in the same mean and sordid way that I did before I read Tolstoy"; and if the adjectives were less than fair to his earlier vision, they explain why his new vision placed "art forever below humanity."

Howells had always befriended young writers; now he championed Garland and Crane, Norris and Herrick, counted Bellamy the most influential of all American novelists, and hailed Thorstein Veblen's *Theory of the Leisure Class.* "I should hardly like to trust pen and ink with all the audacity of my social ideas," he wrote, "but after fifty years of optimistic content with civilization and its ability to come out all right in the end, I now abhor it, and feel that it is coming out all wrong in the end unless it bases itself on real equality." After the Haymarket riot in 1886 and the execution of five anarchists—"the thing forever damnable before God and abominable to civilized men," he called it—he seldom again indulged in optimistic contentment. His stories, for the next decade, have a somber note heretofore lacking; if the vocabulary is less violent than that of Stephen Crane or Jack London, the criticism is scarcely less fundamental. *The Minister's Charge, Annie Kilburn, The Quality of Mercy, The Son of Royal Langbrith,* and above all the two Utopian romances, *A Traveler from Altruria* and *Through the Eye of a Needle*—all but the last published between 1887 and 1897—portray a society harassed by the irresponsibility of acquisitive capitalism, the evils of industrialism, and the disintegration of traditional standards of morality. For all his timidity and quaint propriety, his almost feminine domesticity, no one better understood or presented the transition from the old America to the new than this dean of American letters who at the height of his fame and influence cast his lot in with the protestants and rebels of his generation.

Because Howells was content with familiar material and traditional themes and with a style that was classical and chaste, the full force of his originality and impact of his courage were not at once apparent. Though his dissent from the accepted practices and standards of his day was sharper than that of most of his contemporaries, he appeared less bold than some of his own disciples. His break with

the past was philosophical rather than material, it was less an uprooting than a transformation. He never permitted himself, except in
some of his private letters, a violent gesture or a raucous note, and
he voiced regrets more often than hopes. The gap that separated him
from, let us say, F. Marion Crawford or Thomas Bailey Aldrich was
just as deep as that which separated the spokesmen of agrarian revolt
or the recorders of urban growth or of political and social corruption
from their predecessors, but it was less ostentatious.

The ostentatious break was an achievement of the younger generation. First in the field were the spokesmen of agrarian discontent:
the mordant Ed Howe, whose Country Town was a Kansas Sodom;
Joseph Kirkland, who hoped to be the American Hardy but was not
even a lesser realist like Eden Philpotts; Hamlin Garland, the rebellious son of the Middle Border; the versatile Harold Frederic; and,
ablest of them all, Frank Norris, who wrote in the spirit of Zola.
These ardent young rebels reversed the tradition of "Sweet Auburn"
and "Snowbound" to record "the sweat, flies, heat, dust, and drudgery" of farming, the burden of life "under the lion's paw," the hopeless struggle with the railroads, the trusts, and the vagaries of weather,
the grinding poverty which led so often to spiritual and intellectual
impoverishment, the tragic futility of the high hopes of the pioneer.
They were the literary spokesmen of the Populists, the vanguard of
the muckrakers, dismally aware of the passing of the old America,
desperately eager to humanize the new.

Typical of them all, both for what he saw and for what he failed
to see, for the bitterness of his revolt and for its inconclusiveness, was
Hamlin Garland. From his boyhood he remembered beauty and adventure and abundance, his mother's songs and his uncle's music,
the Grange meetings and the picnics and the spelling bees in the
country schoolhouse, the teeming wild life of the prairie and the wav-
ing grain and the splendid sunsets; and nostalgia gave poignancy to
his later disillusionment. To a boy, the marching song of the Garlands,

> Then over the hills in legions, boys,
> Fair freedom's star
> Points to the sunset regions, boys,

had the clang of a battle hymn; he recalled it later as a hymn of
fugitives. Back east in Boston he had read Ibsen and Taine, Darwin
and Spencer, and had come under the influence of Henry George

and Whitman and Benjamin Flower, editor of *The Arena*. When he returned to his Dakota homestead, what he saw was not pastoral romance but poverty and hardship and defeat.

All the gilding of farm life melted away. The hard and bitter realities came back upon me in a flood. Nature was as beautiful as ever . . . but no splendor of cloud, no grace of sunset, could conceal the poverty of these people; on the contrary they brought out, with a more intolerable poignancy, the gracelessness of these homes and the sordid quality of the mechanical daily routine of these lives. . . . I perceived life without its glamor.

And it was life without glamor that he described along the *Main Travelled Roads*—life where every house had its message of sordid struggle and half-hidden despair, and all the good days were in the past; and he dedicated the collection to "my father and my mother, whose half century of pilgrimage on the main travelled roads of life has brought them only pain and weariness."

He enlisted in the Populist crusade, contributed a novel and a handful of stories, and supported *The Arena,* forgotten now, in its agitation for a more humane economic order. He envisioned a new cultural movement, more democratic and more American than had been known before, and in 1894 he issued a manifesto, *Crumbling Idols,* more remarkable for moderation than for iconoclasm. Soon he yielded to the lure of the Far West, soon the Middle Border came to take on a nimbus of romance, and eventually Whitman and Henry George were forgotten. In the end, Garland was himself one of the crumbling idols of the Middle Border.

The city, long neglected by literature, achieved a notoriety as unlovely as that of the frowzy country town or the dusty, main traveled roads. Novelists went slumming with Jacob Riis, searched out crime and vice with the Lexow Committee (which in 1894 exposed the vices of New York), learned about ward politics with young Cleveland and young Roosevelt, and traced with Frederick Townsend Martin the passing of the idle rich. Crane and Fuller, Herrick and Dreiser, Phillips and Poole, all novelists of the transition years, painted a varied gallery of characters, but with all of them it was the city that was both hero and villain—usually the latter. The city came to dominate literature as it dominated economy and society. It is suggestive that few American novelists came to terms with the city as Arnold Bennett came to terms with his Five Towns or H. G. Wells with London.

The most notable exception was one whose stories were most journalistic—O. Henry. The historian of "Bagdad-on-the-Hudson" went to New York in 1902, mastered with quick observation the external life of the city, and wrote with affection of his Four Million; but sometimes the affection seemed as calculated and as artificial as the style which expressed it. Humor became increasingly urban, tin-pan alley supplied the songs for the nation, and Horatio Alger supplanted Jacob Abbott of the Rollo books in furnishing moral guidance for the youth of the land.

Although politics had been for a century the consuming interest of the average American, literature had all but ignored it, and American letters boasted neither a Disraeli nor a Trollope. The student who attempted to reconstruct the pattern of American politics from imaginative literature would be equally puzzled by the paucity of his material before the 1880's and the monotony of the argument thereafter, for, from *The Gilded Age* on, politics was thought worthy of literary treatment only when ostentatiously unworthy. Honest politicians were not unknown to American history, but they were rare in American literature. Perhaps it was merely that corruption made better copy than probity, but it was difficult to escape the conclusion that the realistic novel recognized in the boss a more authentic figure than the statesman and that a literature which was achieving social consciousness addressed itself inevitably to that aspect of politics which most troubled the American conscience.

In 1880 Henry Adams fastidiously deplored a corruption which he identified with *Democracy,* foreshadowing that piercing disillusionment that vibrates through the pages of the *Education.* Almost twenty years later Booth Tarkington's *The Gentleman from Indiana* —a pure costume piece—portrayed political wickedness with a veracity sufficiently convincing to earn its author a reproof from Theodore Roosevelt. Winston Churchill's *Coniston* and *Mr. Crewe's Career* recounted in fiction the battles which the author lost in the hurlyburly of New Hampshire politics. *The Thirteenth District* owed much to Altgeld and "Golden Rule" Jones, but more to Brand Whitlock's own experience in Toledo ward politics. *Stratagems and Spoils* and the moving "Mercy of Death" partially answered the question which young William Allen White himself had asked: "What's the matter with Kansas?"; but their implications were more than local. And a long series of novels—*Joshua Craig, The Conflict,* and

George Helm—supplied the seamy background against which David Graham Phillips projected his study of the *Treason of the Senate*. All these novels sounded variations on the same theme—the disintegration of older integrities, or what were imagined to be older integrities, in the face of the complex temptations of the new economic order. Perhaps the most penetrating literary commentary on the changing nature of politics came not from any novelist but from Finley Peter Dunne, whose transcriptions of the wit and wisdom of "Mr. Dooley" pricked every political bubble and exposed every political fraud of these transition years.

The disintegration of social standards implicit in the assault of the new rich on the citadels of society was mirrored no less sharply in the pages of the novelists of these years. The process described by Hjalmar Boyesen, Robert Grant, Howells, and Edith Wharton—and eventually, with growing reverence, by Booth Tarkington—was not in itself one of disintegration but a symptom and a consequence of antecedent disintegration. What was significant was not that the social parapets of Boston and New York and Indianapolis should be breached but that men who had conquered a continent, reared great industrial empires, flung railroads across mountains should have thought they were worth breaching. What suggested the emergence of a new social consciousness was not the decline of Knickerbocker or Beacon Hill aristocracy—that had always been in process of decline and renewal—but the confusion of standards and values which persuaded the new rich that membership in that aristocracy was so important. Certainly the vast concern with social climbing between 1870 and 1910 was a new phenomenon, and it assumed the existence of a social ladder which had not heretofore been recognized. The seaboard cities, to be sure, had long maintained an aristocracy, but it had not been exclusively dependent on either money or genealogy; that membership in it had carried moral connotations was familiar to anyone who had studied the career of a Forbes in Boston or a Petigru in Charleston. It had been open, in the past, rather to talent and manners than to money or even family; the increasing emphasis on wealth, during the Gilded Age, made it both vulnerable and futile.

The triumph of new wealth over old was, after all, a subject for comedy rather than tragedy. Howells and Boyesen, who were not personally involved, dealt with it as such: the Ralstons of Howells'

Letters Home, the Buckleys of Boyesen's *Social Strugglers* are comic figures, and their ambitions, disappointments, and triumphs cannot be taken too seriously. Edith Wharton, who was very much involved in it all, viewed the whole process as a social revolution rather than a comedy of manners. That Undine Spragg should successfully exploit the Custom of the Country seemed to her more significant than that American society should have produced an Undine Spragg, and she shared while she scorned "the old New York way of taking life without effusion of blood; the way of people who dreaded scandal more than disease, who placed decency above courage, and who considered that nothing was more ill-bred than scenes, except the behaviour of those who gave rise to them." The society which she portrayed was already decadent, its defenses shaky and precarious; she did not inquire why anyone should want to join it but rather what was the effect upon it of the barbarian invasion. When the social world of Washington Square and Lenox crumbled, she fled to France Yet Mrs. Wharton was able to recollect her own country in tranquillity and—as *Ethan Frome* and *The Age of Innocence* testify—with no apparent diminution of powers.

Flight from America was to become a familiar gesture, but it was neither general nor very significant, and it was perverse of Matthew Josephson to name a canvas of expatriates *Portrait of the Artist as American.* Even Henry James's exile, which achieved a peculiar notoriety, was physical rather than intellectual, and the revival of James's popularity a quarter-century after his death suggests that he may have been mistaken in his notion that his own country could not understand him. The historical novelist, Marion Crawford, was not to be taken too seriously, nor Henry Harland who edited the *Yellow Book;* while getting and spending, Stephen Crane laid waste his powers in an alien land. Lafcadio Hearn was a special case. Unfitted by fate and his own character for security in any society, he found sorry compensation for physical and psychological inadequacies in Japan, and the most poignant tragedy of his life was his disillusionment with the country of his adoption. Perhaps the most significant thing about the migration of American artists to London or to the Left Bank was that it should have occasioned surprise and indignation. "An Englishmen," wrote one of the expatriates, Logan Pearsall Smith, or other European who settles in America incurs no kind of moral blame, either in the land he has deserted or in his new-adopted home. . . . But to desert America is somehow regarded as a kind of treachery, as if America were more than a country, were a sort of cause, and its Stars and Stripes the banner of a crusading army which it is dishonorable to desert. (*Unforgotten Years*)

After all, the migration of intellectuals from the Old World to the New was substantially larger than that which went in the other direction, and if emigration proved that the abandoned countries were cultural and spiritual deserts, the situation was most confusing for the American *émigrés*. "It is a wretched business, this quarrel of ours with our own country, this everlasting impatience to get out of it," wrote Henry James. But Henry Adams observed that "the American was to be met at every railway station in Europe, carefully explaining to every listener that the happiest day of his life would be the day he should land on the pier in New York"; and a whole series of novelists from Howells to Booth Tarkington and Sinclair Lewis confirmed the validity of the Adams rather than the James interpretation. Perhaps the most interesting thing about the international novels of James and Howells, as of those by Tarkington and Lewis, was their testimony that the Americans carried with them, so infallibly, their Americanism.

More illuminating than Edith Wharton's history of the decline and fall of the Knickerbocker aristocracy was Ellen Glasgow's chronicle of the social transformation of Virginia—and by implication, of the South—from the Civil War to the first World War. She pictured the transformation not only of a society but of a culture; she recorded the impact upon that culture not of wealth alone but of the Civil War and Reconstruction, of the rise of the farmer and the workingman and the industrialist, of new ideas and new values. "In the middle eighties," she wrote in the novel *Virginia*:

When Virginia grew to womanhood, the past order still lingered on as a state of mind; and the Southern woman, who had borne the heaviest burden of the old slavery, and the new freedom, was valued, in sentiment, chiefly as an ornament to civilization, and as restraining influence over the nature of man. But the next decade was scarcely over when one of those momentous revolutions of opinion, more drastic in the end than any revolution of facts or institutions, had already begun. Insurgent youth, hardened by the poverty and deprivation of the postwar years, had damaged though it had not as yet entirely broken through, the fixed pattern of custom. Even in the feminine sphere was self-assertion, somewhat gradually but beneficently displacing self-sacrifice. Sentimentality, both as a rule of conduct and as a habit of mind, was yielding to the more practical, and the more profitable, virtues of common sense.

It was the revolution of opinion that Miss Glasgow traced—especially of feminine opinion—and she did not think the opinion of the first families alone worth recording. The custom of her country was more deeply ingrained, more pervasive, than that of Knickerbocker New York, and, as the society of her Virginia Pendleton was never so dependent on money as that of the northern cities, it was not so vulnerable to the assaults of new wealth. Its transformation, therefore, was more a metamorphosis than a conquest, more a natural process than a drawing-room drama. Miss Glasgow's long career as a writer stretched from the days when McKinley was new in the White House down to Franklin D. Roosevelt's third term. She wrote not merely *The Sheltered Life* but *The Romance of a Plain Man;* she recorded not alone the antics of *The Romantic Comedians* but the *Voice of the People,* and one of her panels of Virginia history was called *Barren Ground.*

This last was a title that would have appealed to those intrepid realists, Rose Terry Cooke, Harriet Prescott Spofford, Mary E. Wilkins, and Sarah Orne Jewett. They painted the Indian summer of New England, and it is instructive that all of them were women and that women—mostly spinsters—were so often in the foreground of their quiet landscapes. The men who applied their brushes to these scenes —Howells, for example, or Aldrich—were inclined to touch up the reds and yellows in the foliage a bit too much. It was a changing New England that Miss Cooke and her successors described, and indeed "change and decay in all around I see" was the theme of most of their stories and novels. The young men had gone off to the West or to the cities, and the little villages, once so flourishing, seemed to be inhabited entirely by old men and women. The newcomers from Poland and Italy and Quebec whom Edna Ferber and Gladys Carroll were to welcome had not yet moved in to take the place of the Yankee farmers, nor, except along the North Shore and in the Berkshires, had summer folk come to restore the weather-beaten houses and call their former owners "natives." Everywhere were forsaken farmhouses and abandoned farms; the stone fences had tumbled down, and the firs marched boldly across the upland meadows and over the farms which had given up the unequal competition with the rich soils of Iowa and Minnesota. The whole region seemed icebound, and not only in the wintertime. Social life was cramped and ingrown; Puritanism had curdled into censoriousness, and the intellectual energy that had once found expression in lyceums or in political and religious radicalism contented itself now with the remembrance of things past. Many of the old places were haunted, and the inhabitants seemed almost to cherish their ghosts.

Yet no soil which nourished Mary E. Wilkins and Sarah Orne Jewett could be called barren, nor did these artists confine themselves to exercises in nostalgia. *A New England Nun* and *The Country of Pointed Firs* were not Hoosier whimsey or Kentucky moonshine translated to New England, nor did the recorders of the New England decline adopt that "local-color" pattern which cheapened its material by reliance on idiom and indulgence in quaintness. They were closer to Ed Howe, Hamlin Garland, and Joseph Kirkland than to James Lane Allen or John Fox. Miss Wilkins' *Pembroke* was almost as bleak as Ed Howe's *Country Town,* and her *Old Lady Pingree* might have lived along one of Hamlin Garland's *Main Travelled Roads,* while Miss Jewett's *Deephaven* had characters as mean as those who inhabited Joseph Kirkland's Spring County. Yet the angular spinsters and rough peddlers, the country doctors and parsons and schoolteachers who dwell in these cramped pages had somehow come to terms with their environment. That environment was mean and narrow, but they had kept their pride, their self-respect, and their integrity: they may have been frustrated and inhibited, but they cherished their frustrations, as it were, and respected their inhibitions. The line of literary succession, it is well to remember, leads from Miss Jewett and Miss Wilkins to Robert Frost rather than to Eugene O'Neill, to "Mending Wall," rather than to *Desire under the Elms.*

3

Journalism not only mirrored the transition from nineteenth- to twentieth-century America, but itself participated in and was subjected to the process. As in literature, the transition was gradual enough, and no sharp line of demarcation divides the old from the new; only in the perspective of half a century can we see how deep is the chasm that separates William Cullen Bryant from Col. R. R. McCormick, E. L. Godkin from William Randolph Hearst, the *North American Review* from the *Reader's Digest,* or the old *St. Nicholas* from the comic-strip magazines.

Samuel Bowles III, himself one of the ablest practitioners of the old journalism, noted the change as early as the seventies. "With the deaths of James Gordon Bennett and Horace Greeley," he wrote, "personal journalism also comes practically to an end." The obituary on personal journalism was premature: Pulitzer was just entering the field, Godkin was yet to take over the *Evening Post,* Grady the *Atlanta Constitution,* and Watterson the *Courier-Journal.* Even as Bowles wrote, young Joseph Pulitzer assumed charge of the *St. Louis Post-Dispatch;* though he did not represent the negation of personal journalism, neither was he an editor in the sense that Greeley and Bowles had been editors. The transition from the old to the new can be dated more accurately, however, from the mid-nineties—from the invasion of New York by William Randolph Hearst and Adolph S. Ochs in 1896, the death of Charles A. Dana in 1897, and the retirement, three years later, of the already legendary E. L. Godkin.

Godkin, whose journalistic career embraces the whole of the transition period, and who edited both a magazine and a newspaper, may be taken as a type, if a superior and special one, of the older journalism. Certainly, with him journalism was a personal affair: it was indeed something of an embarrassment that he was an editorial writer rather than an editor and never a newspaperman in the sense that the elder Bennett was, or the brilliant Dana. When he took over the old *Evening Post* in 1883, he regarded it much as he had for so long regarded *The Nation:* as a personal organ and, largely, a political one. He was not concerned with circulation, made no concessions either of editorial policy or of general journalistic appeal, maintained exalted literary and moral standards, took sides passionately on public issues, and thought himself the conscience of America—or at least of that element of America that frequented the Harvard and the Century clubs.

Godkin was a crusader but conducted his crusades with intellectual weapons, disdaining appeals to mob psychology; he was a partisan, but his partisanship was wrapped in the vestments of morality, and he was politically independent; he was a scholar and thought himself an economist—indeed, the high priest of the Manchester School of economic liberals; he was something of a philosopher, very much of a gentleman, and a marvelously incisive writer. It was not astonishing that he should be the one American editor to win Matthew Arnold's approval or that men like Charles Eliot Norton and James Russell Lowell should regard him as an oracle. He lived to see the advent of that "yellow" journalism, which he thought "the nearest approach to Hell in any Christian state," and of "a blackguard boy with several millions of dollars at his disposal" who presumed to dictate the policies of the nation; but he was too proud to follow where the Pulitzers and the Hearsts led. He retired at the turn of the century, somehow serene though defeated, seeing journalism vulgarized, the "chromo" civilization which he had once derided triumphant, and his adopted country embarked upon paths of conquest which he thought disastrous. His like was not seen again.

The passing of Godkin was important primarily as a symbol. By 1900 the day of the great editors was all but past—of Greeley, Bryant, and Dana in New York, of Bowles of the *Springfield Republican,* Horace White of the *Chicago Tribune,* Henry Grady of the *Atlanta Constitution,* Murat Halstead of the *Cincinnati Commercial,* and the many others who had for so long contributed color and leadership to the political scene. Two veterans, Henry Watterson of the *Louisville Courier-Journal* and William Rockhill Nelson of the *Kansas City Star,* survived rather bleakly into World War days. It was suggestive that Adolph S. Ochs who, in Charles Miller, inherited an able editor, deliberately fixed for the *New York Times* a policy of editorial anonymity.

Yet it would be misleading to record the transition in journalism in biographical terms: the passing of the great editors was symptomatic rather than consequential. In time the editorial writer was metamorphosed into a columnist, but most columnists were hired men, not policy makers. The transformation of the newspaper was, in fact, far more than editorial; it was physical, it was economic, it was psychological, it was moral. It was part of the transformation of America itself—of the process of mechanization, urbanization, and centralization, of the concentration of economic control, of the emancipation of women, the broadening of social interests, the standardization, democratization, and vulgarization of culture. It was conditioned by all these developments, it reflected them, and it contributed to them.

The basic factors in the transformation were doubtless scientific and economic. The introduction of linotype machinery, the octuple press, the folding machine, color processes, wireless reporting, news photography and photogravure, press associations such as the AP and the UP, telegraph and cable services, special features, syndicated columns, and Sunday supplements, the rising costs of reporting, labor, and transportation, all added enormously to the cost of acquiring and operating a newspaper. In Greeley's day, and Bennett's, it was possible to start a paper without capital, and as late as 1878 twenty-year-old Adolph S. Ochs took over the *Chattanooga Times* for 250 dollars, and Joseph Pulitzer the *St. Louis Post-Dispatch* for a few thousand. Forty years later Munsey paid four million for Bennett's *Herald* and Scripps a reported six million for the Pittsburgh *Press,* while by 1930 it cost Cyrus H. K. Curtis eighteen million to acquire the old *Philadelphia Inquirer*. The history of a single paper offers an even more striking illustration of the economic change. In 1880 Nelson bought the *Kansas City Star* for three thousand dollars; in 1929 his estate sold it for eleven million.

What this meant was that the burden of financing a newspaper came to be borne by advertising and that the business office, of necessity, supplanted the editorial. Already by the nineties, newspaper advertising brought in some ninety million dollars annually; by 1915 the figure was almost three hundred million, and by 1920 over six hundred million. The relation between advertising and circulation was obvious, and editors who failed to see it were replaced by others more perspicacious. It was not that under the new dispensation advertisers were in a position to dictate newspaper policy; quite the contrary. It was rather that, in a general way, advertising revenue was geared to circulation, and papers were continuously on the hunt for new circulation. The *Evening Post* had rarely sold over twenty-five thousand copies, but Hearst and Pulitzer were willing to help stir up a war with Spain in order to send the circulation of their papers over the half-million mark.

The press of the 1830's had discovered untapped strata of readers, and the press of the nineties, fortified for the task by improved technological processes and a wholly amoral philosophy, returned to the sensationalism that the elder Bennett had found so profitable. The fifteen years from the mid-eighties to the turn of the century saw the introduction of almost every editorial device or policy that we associate with modern journalism. Irving Bacheller, author of *Eben Holden,* and the enterprising Edward Bok began to experiment with the syndicated feature, and the "boiler-plating" of the future was on the way; Richard Outcault's "Yellow Kid," who gave his name to a whole school of journalism, made his bow, and the day of the comics dawned; Frank Munsey tried his hand at a tabloid—the ill-starred *Star;* Dorothy Dix and, hot on her trail, Beatrice Fairfax, began to give advice to the lovelorn, who proved insatiable; Eugene Field and Finley Peter Dunne inaugurated the modern column; the fabulous E. W. Scripps organized the first chain of newspapers, and Hearst forged a larger one in which every link was weak; sports sections became respectable and Sunday supplements essential; the *World* and the *Journal* embarked upon competing crusades more concerned with circulation than with reform; news photography was perfected in time to celebrate American victories over Spain; the Associated Press faced, and lost, its first suit as a monopoly.

The best and the worst of the new journalism appeared almost simultaneously in the mid-nineties, when the obscure young Ochs from Tennessee bought the enfeebled *New York Times* and the rich young Hearst from California the *New York Morning Journal.* Adolph S. Ochs was by no means the first journalist to acknowledge that a newspaper was a public institution, but more successfully than any of his predecessors he translated acknowledgment of responsibility into policy. He was astute enough to know that the sensationalism of Pulitzer would bring quicker returns than the respectability of Godkin, but the kind of newspaper he wanted to create was closer to the New York *Evening Post* than to the *World,* and he believed that he could make one that would sacrifice neither profits nor integrity. He set for his staff standards of accuracy, impartiality, dignity, clarity, and comprehensiveness never before achieved in American journalism, and he saw to it that they lived up to those standards. Refusing to exploit any of the usual techniques which assured prosperity to his rivals, eschewing sensationalism, sex, crime, comics, jingoism, or rabid partisanship, confining himself to "all the news that's fit to print," Ochs made the *New York Times* not only the best paper in the country but one of the ornaments of American civilization.

Those who were encouraged by the success of the *Times* were sobered when they contemplated the spectacular career of the *Journal,* for if Ochs and the *Times* represented all that was most admirable in modern journalism, Hearst and his chain represented all that was most sinister. Hearst had no conception of a newspaper as a public trust and in this was probably closer to the business standards of the nineties than was Ochs or even Pulitzer, whose ideals, at least, were high. Determined at all costs to win mammoth circulation, from the beginning Hearst prostituted his newspapers, resorting to tricks of sensationalism, pandering to morbid tastes, violating professional ethics. He indulged in the most extreme jingoism, exalted the most narrow nationalism, and opposed all genuine liberalism. Because he was sooner or later on both sides of most questions, and because for a time he entertained political ambitions, he managed to champion some popular issues; because he had almost limitless resources, he was able to buy some first-rate journalistic talent, to introduce some mechanical improvements, and to pioneer in some interesting journalistic experiments. But in the end he added nothing of value to American journalism, and his debauchery of the public taste worked incalculable harm.

The decade of the nineties saw the arrival in New York of another newspaperman whose influence, for the most part deplorable, was to be pervasive and lasting. Like Ochs and Hearst, Frank Munsey represented important new developments in American journalism and, for that matter, in American economy and culture. An entrepreneur who at one time owned more valuable newspaper properties than any one else in the country, Munsey knew nothing about journalism as a craft, had no ascertainable policies beyond an uncritical attachment to the status quo, and recognized no responsibility to the newspaper profession or to the public. To him journalism was a business, not very different from the grocery enterprise in which he was so profitably engaged. Shrewd, single-minded, and possessed by a driving energy, he was the Jay Gould of journalism; not a builder but a speculator, and one who cut his frequent losses with a jaunty disregard for the consequences. He bought newspapers and magazines as he bought real estate or stock in United States Steel, and sold them as callously. Those he did not sell he frequently killed off, for he thought that American journalism was overcompetitive and believed in strength through size.

Munsey owned, at one time or another, *Munsey's Magazine*, the *Argosy*, the New York *Press, Sun, Globe, Herald,* and *Telegram,* the *Baltimore American* and *News,* the *Philadelphia Times,* the *Washington Times,* and the *Boston Journal;* if it can be said that these journals were not, like Hearst's, a positive force for evil, it should be added that neither were they a power for good. "Frank Munsey," wrote his fellow journalist, William Allen White, in one of the bitterest of obituaries, "contributed to the journalism of his day the talent of a meat packer, the morals of a money changer, and the manners of an undertaker. He and his kind have about succeeded in transforming a once-noble profession into an eight per cent security."

At the same time Munsey was in many ways a symbol of what was happening in these transition years. Emerging from Maine a poor and ill-educated but fiercely ambitious lad, he was a Horatio Alger hero—appropriately enough, he began his publishing career with Alger's *Do and Dare;* and like so many Alger heroes he attached himself early to the forces of money and conservatism. He started the first tabloid; he combined newspaper and magazine publishing; he developed the newspaper chain and illustrated that policy of destroying competition by consolidation so characteristic of big business in this generation. He achieved a high degree of impersonality in journalism; as he had few opinions on public affairs, he contributed nothing himself, and as he was suspicious of talent, he smothered the contribution of others. His battle for Theodore Roosevelt in 1912 was his one great crusade, and it was somehow typical that his support did T. R. more harm than good. Even his philanthropy ran true to form. Although he had never shown the faintest interest in art, he left his large fortune to the Metropolitan Museum, and the rubble of a dozen once-proud newspapers and magazines went to build the foundations for new art collections.

The New York *Evening Post* and New York *World* also felt the crushing impact of the new transitional forces. After Godkin, the *Evening Post* was ably carried on for two decades and more by Horace White, Rollo Ogden, and Simeon Strunsky. Its staff in the time of Woodrow Wilson, whose main policies it staunchly supported, was probably the most brilliant ever boasted by an American newspaper. But rising costs were too much for an intellectual journal of low circulation, and in 1923 Cyrus H. K. Curtis swallowed it up. As for the *World,* a fighting liberal daily and the leader of the whole Democratic press, it achieved even greater distinction after Pulitzer's death (1911) than before. First under the gifted Frank Cobb and then under Walter Lippmann, it was admirably edited; and it too possessed a galaxy of famous writers. The competition of the tabloids, however, pressed it hard after 1920, while other factors were adverse. In 1931, amid manifestations of heartfelt public grief, it perished, leaving the *St. Louis Post-Dispatch* alone to carry on the family tradition.

4

The transformation of magazines followed that of the newspapers, and the modifications were, if anything, more extreme. Like the newspapers, magazines responded to technological changes, addressed themselves to a broader and less exacting audience, revealed a more alert social consciousness, or a readier eclecticism, acquiesced in specialization and departmentalization, became increasingly dependent on advertising, and accommodated themselves to those readers to whom the advertising was addressed. The gap that separates *Harper's* or *St. Nicholas* of the 1930's from their ancestors of the 1880's is deeper than that which separates the *New York Times* or *Washington Post* or *Chicago Tribune* of the two periods; and the advent in the twenties of picture magazines, digests, and comics introduced more far-reaching changes than the newspaper press experienced. Quantitatively, too, the change was impressive. Newspaper circulation increased substantially after the advent of Pulitzer and Hearst, but the increase in magazine circulation was incomparably greater; while the number of newspapers declined in proportion to the population, the number of magazines multiplied spectacularly and almost intolerably. In the half-century after Cyrus Curtis launched *The Ladies' Home Journal,* America became a nation of magazine readers.

In 1890 the magazine field was dominated by respectable monthlies like the *Atlantic, Harper's, Scribner's,* and *The Century,* by journals of opinion like *The Nation,* the *Independent,* and the *Harper's Weekly,* and by children's magazines like the *St. Nicholas* and the *Youth's Companion.* Content with a modest subscription list (one hundred thousand was regarded as praiseworthy) and devoted largely to fiction with a sprinkling of essays, travel narratives, historical and biographical studies, all embellished with the best illustrations that Americans have ever been privileged to enjoy, these magazines made few concessions to the contemporary scene and none to vulgar taste. They catered to the educated middle class, were designed for the home and the club, and observed the amenities imposed by such hospitality; where they discussed current events, it was with scholarly objectivity. In their handsome pages appeared the best works of American and—this was before the day of international copyright—of foreign authors. No magazine of the twentieth century, unless possibly *Poetry* or *Story* or *The New Yorker,* published as much enduring literature as each of the great nineteenth-century monthlies presented every decade.

By the late eighties the revolution was already under way. *The Forum* was established in 1886 for the discussion of controversial issues: a typical number in the early nineties included articles on venality in voting, the Homestead strike, socialized religion, the Negro, relations with China, the mine laborers of Pennsylvania, and popular education. Three years later Benjamin O. Flower, half crackpot, half genius, founded *The Arena,* the original muckraking magazine, its pages open to Populists and Socialists and heretics of all kinds. Then in quick succession came *Munsey's,* the *Cosmopolitan, McClure's, The Review of Reviews,* and, boldly in the year of the great panic, *The Outlook,* which according to Theodore Roosevelt, who was an expert in this field, "always stood for righteousness." Meantime, too, there were new weeklies to compete with *The Nation* and *The Independent: Collier's,* which was originally more concerned with current affairs than with fiction; the *Literary Digest,* which presented a symposium of press opinion on all controversial subjects; within a few years, a revitalized *Harper's Weekly;* and personal organs like Bryan's *Commoner* and *LaFollette's Weekly.*

The distinguishing marks of these new magazines were a lively interest in current problems, a sympathy with progressivism, and an inclination toward sensationalism. They prepared the way for the muckraking magazines of the next decade—*McClure's, Everybody's,* the *Cosmopolitan, The American Magazine, Pearson's, Hampton's,* and their imitators. There was little that was new about the muckraking formula that was served up by these magazines; it was merely a more skillfully blended and more plausibly advertised imitation of what *The Forum* and *The Arena* had been doing for a decade. What was new was the appearance of editors who appreciated its value--men like S. S. McClure, John Brisben Walker, and John O'Hara Cosgrave—and of a remarkable group of journalists able and eager to exploit it: Lincoln Steffens, Ida Tarbell, Burton J. Hendrick, Mark Sullivan, Charles E. Russell, and others. These managed, in the few years in which they had a free hand, to stir public opinion as it had never been stirred before by journalism and to increase the circulation of their magazines by the hundred thousands.

The picture of American life which the muckraking magazines drew was almost as one sided as that which had been painted by the sedate monthlies. If the earlier journals reflected the age of confidence, the new mirrored the age of doubt. Dedicated as they were to exposure and reform, they came to have almost a vested interest in corruption and concentrated on it to the exclusion of what Howells had called "the more smiling aspects of American life." They suffered, too, from the qualities which afflicted the whole protest movement for which they spoke, its opportunism, its sensationalism, and its philosophical superficiality. Certainly it was remarkable how short lived the whole phenomenon proved to be. Some of the muckraking magazines, like *McClure's* and *Everybody's,* were bought by the very interests they attacked; some, like *Hampton's,* were killed by the bankers; some, like *Collier's* and *The American Magazine,* were transformed into innocuous vehicles for light fiction, homely features, the adulation of business, and lavish advertising. That combination, which was in the end to boast far greater drawing and staying power than the muckrake formula, had already made its appearance in two magazines which Curtis of Philadelphia had projected, *The Ladies' Home Journal* and *The Saturday Evening Post.*

No periodical combined more felicitously the qualities of the older and the newer journalism than *The Ladies' Home Journal.* It was in 1889 that young Edward Bok—he was only twenty-six—took charge of the magazine that Mrs. Curtis had been editing, and during the thirty years that he directed it, he made it, if not the most influential, perhaps the most typical of all American magazines. His mixture of pleasant fiction, useful domestic departments, modest reforms, and easy culture proved irresistible. "Ruth Ashmore" conducted a column of Talks to Girls, who responded with a steady avalanche of letters; Dr. Coolidge advised on infant care; Dwight Moody dispensed spiritual comfort; and the editor himself directed campaigns to improve domestic architecture, interior decoration, and gardens, clean up the sore spots in towns and cities, and elevate the popular appreciation of art by the distribution of millions of reproductions of acknowledged masterpieces. Occasionally there were bolder gestures. A campaign for sex education cost seventy-five thousand subscriptions before it was dropped; a fight against the patent-medicine evil brought reforms, and agitation against the exploitation of Niagara Falls by greedy power companies paved the way for the enactment of the Burton Bill. As circulation mounted, Bok was able to engage the most popular authors, and Kipling, Conan Doyle, Anthony Hope, Mark Twain, Sarah Orne Jewett, and Joel Chandler Harris graced the pages of his magazine. Advertising, which was held to comparatively high standards, came to be increasingly important, for the day was already at hand when Americans would buy magazines for the advertising rather than the reading matter.

What Bok did for *The Ladies' Home Journal,* George Horace Lorimer did for *The Saturday Evening Post.* This struggling and obscure weekly which Curtis had picked up for one thousand dollars in 1898 became, under the gifted Lorimer, the most powerful and popular of all weekly magazines and the one which most faithfully catered to the interests and mirrored the sentiments of the upper income groups in American society. Lorimer, who had received his first business training from the packing-master, Philip Armour, early conceived an immense admiration for the businessman and an unshakable conviction that business was the stuff of romance, of government, of society—and of journalism. Himself the author of the fabulously popular *Letters of a Self-Made Merchant to his Son,* Lorimer directed his magazine to what he thought the interests and sentiments of the average businessman and his wife and children, filling it with glamorous fiction, histories of business and industry, biographies and autobiographies of self-made merchants, political commentary, and articles designed to celebrate the superiority of America over all other countries, of private over public enterprise, and of conservative over liberal politics.

It was as a medium for fiction that the *Post* made its greatest contribution and acquired its widest circulation—before the depression of the thirties, well over three million—and it was here that Lorimer displayed his greatness as an editor. From the beginning the *Post* opened its pages, and its coffers, liberally to the best American and

English writers as well as to the most popular, and for half a century after its rebirth in 1899 it furnished the fullest index to the literary taste of the American people generally. During Lorimer's editorship it published such novels as Frank Norris' *The Octopus* and *The Pit,* Owen Wister's *Lady Baltimore,* Jerome K. Jerome's *Passing of the Third Floor Back,* James B. Cabell's *The Eagle's Shadow,* Joseph Hergesheimer's *Java Head,* John P. Marquand's *The Late George Apley,* and many others no less notable. Willa Cather, Ellen Glasgow, Edith Wharton, Theodore Dreiser, Brand Whitlock, Thomas Beer, and Sinclair Lewis appeared in its hospitable pages, and from England came contributions by Joseph Conrad, Leonard Merrick, Rudyard Kipling, Rebecca West, and others of the great Edwardian and Georgian schools. Intellectuals who were inclined to think *The Saturday Evening Post* something invented by George Babbitt overlooked the distinguished quality of its fiction during the whole of the Lorimer era.

More typical of the *Post* under Lorimer, however, and more effective in boosting circulation, were the contributions of such familiar stand-bys as the popular novelists, Mary Roberts Rinehart, Edna Ferber, Fannie Hurst, Rupert Hughes, Ben Ames Williams, and Harry Leon Wilson, of humorists like P. G. Wodehouse and Octavus Roy Cohen and Irvin Cobb, of mystery-story writers like Earl Derr Biggers, Agatha Christie, and Mignon Eberhart, and of a group of illustrators of whom Norman Rockwell was easily the most popular. These writers and artists, and others like them, furnished week after week better entertainment than any other popular magazine could offer, interpreted amiably the surface of American life, and were careful not to offend against those canons of good taste approved by Emily Post, those standards of morality sustained by the YMCA, and those cultural interests represented by Chautauqua.

Lorimer himself was more interested in politics than in literature and fancied himself and his magazine a major force in public affairs. Yet he did not have the crusading instinct of Curtis' other editor, Bok, and he failed to connect the *Post* with any of the main currents of American political or economic life. He campaigned, sedately, for conservation and the development of national parks but was inclined to view with distrust crusades designed to reform social or economic ills, or even a recognition that such ills existed in America. His temper was conservative, and he imposed it upon his magazine.

Each week Samuel Blythe or Garet Garrett, or other commentators whose point of view was that of Lorimer himself, contributed some article deploring unrestricted immigration or labor unions or governmental extravagance or public invasion of private business or the menace of Bolshevism, celebrating isolation, the American home, and private enterprise, popularizing the work of some captain of industry or titan of finance or pillar of politics, skillfully blending a strong mixture of economic conservatism with a mild brand of social liberalism. Although Lorimer flirted, fleetingly, with Theodore Roosevelt and Albert Beveridge, his sympathies lay increasingly with the reactionary wing of the Republican party, and toward the end of his editorship he made the *Post* all but the unofficial organ of that party.

Lorimer was sure, throughout most of his journalistic life, that he spoke for the average American: it required the 1932 and 1936 elections to disillusion him, and his biographer records that after the second of these elections he seemed a broken man. What he represented, in fact, was upper middle-class opinion—the opinion of the Pullman car rather than of the day coach, of the commuter rather than the subway rider, of the country club rather than the corner drugstore or the crossroads general store. That he represented these more accurately and more fully than any other editor of his generation cannot be denied, and it was true, as Bernard De Voto observed, that the historian of the future could recover the surface of American life more fully and with less distortion from the pages of the *Post* than from the run of those novels and poems that never appeared in its golden pages. What he might find of that part of American life that lay beneath the surface was less clear.

The formula which Bok and Lorimer employed so successfully was soon emulated by a host of competing magazines—the *Woman's Home Companion, The Delineator, The Pictorial Review, Collier's, The Red Book, Cosmopolitan*—all packed with innocuous articles, with fiction that no one could remember from year to year, and with advertising, and all catering chiefly to women who, relieved from large families and household drudgery, found leisure something of a problem. If the magazines of the new day lacked distinction, they doubtless served the same purpose that the movies and the radio would shortly serve so well—that of killing time pleasantly. Even this much can scarcely be said for their rivals of the next generation, the digests and picture magazines. These, by appealing to the eye rather than to the mind, watering down all ideas, and simplifying all problems, cheapened the taste and enervated the mind of their reading public.

There was distinction in the journals of the new century, but it was to be found along the byroads rather than on the broad highways. The opening year of the century saw the establishment of *The World's Work,* under the editorship of the progressive and dynamic Walter Hines Page, who thus early revealed the awareness of American responsibility in world affairs that was to distinguish his subsequent diplomatic career. He had served an apprenticeship on the querulous *Forum* and the sedate *Atlantic* and was thus familiar with the best traditions of the older journalism and initiated into the practices of the newer. His own preference was for a liberalism that was lively without being sensational, an internationalism that was responsible but not imperialistic, and literary standards that were respectable without being formidable. For a decade he made *The World's Work* a force for enlightenment.

Such a force, too, were the *New Republic* and *The Dial*. The former was launched in 1914 under the editorship of Herbert Croly, who was already famous for his *Promise of American Life,* and of young Walter Lippmann, whose *Preface to Politics* and *Drift and Mastery* had marked him as one of the most distinguished publicists of his generation; the second was given a new lease on life when, in 1916, it moved from Chicago to New York. The *New Republic* was a "weekly journal of opinion," designed "less to inform or entertain its readers than to start little insurrections in the realm of their convictions." While it did not fail to be informative and even entertaining, its chief function was critical, and like the muckraking magazines of the preceding decade it rejoiced in exposing incompetence and chicanery, in pricking bubbles of complacency, and in provoking a healthy discontent. Launched at a time when most of the muckraking magazines had perished and when *The Nation* had lapsed into temporary conservative respectability, it filled a real void and revealed that the tradition of dissent could flourish—even during war and prosperity. Later it grew erratic and, as an isolationist organ belying the purpose of its founders, lost influence. *The Dial,* too, was critical and dissident, but in the literary and artistic arena rather than the political. With a board of editors scarcely less distinguished than that which had presided so uncertainly over the original *Dial* of the 1840's—Conrad Aiken, Harold Stearns, Van Wyck Brooks, and the brilliant Randolph Bourne, a legend even in his own lifetime—it published the best American and European literature and did not neglect the arts. Its demise in 1929 was an intellectual loss that the America of the depression years could ill afford.

Notwithstanding the increase in the tempo of life and the lowering of standards, sedate journalism, too, flourished as vigorously as in the preceding generation. The quarterlies held their own, and by any test *The Yale Review,* the *Virginia Quarterly Review,* and some of the smaller quarterlies were as good as their nineteenth-century predecessors. Trade journals like *Fortune,* established in 1930, set editorial and typographical standards higher than any heretofore reached, and if the *Commercial and Financial Chronicle* could not compete with the London *Economist,* it was superior to the old *Niles' Register* or *DeBow's Review.* Such scholarly magazines as the *Harvard Law Review* and *Foreign Affairs* were indubitably better than any of their type abroad, and hundreds of more specialized academic publications were generally well edited and not always cursed with pedantry. And in *The New Yorker,* launched in 1925, Americans could boast a magazine as liberal, lively, and intelligent as anything published in the western world, and as surely one of the glories of American civilization as the *New York Times,* or *The Atlantic Monthly.*

CHAPTER IV

John Fiske and the Evolutionary Philosophy

I

IN 1901 AMERICANS were able to read John Fiske's *The Life Everlasting* and, in translation, Ernst Haeckel's *Riddle of the Universe:* thus the epilogue of eighteenth- and the prologue of twentieth-century philosophy presented themselves in dramatic juxtaposition. To Haeckel the universe was a blank; if it had meaning or purpose, neither had been disclosed to man. To Fiske, with his confident assurance of progress, perfection, and immortality as scientific truths, it was no riddle; it meant intensely and meant good, and to find its meaning was his meat and drink.

Fiske had caught the first glimmer of that meaning forty years earlier when, in the same glorious spring, he had discovered both Darwin and Spencer. His adolescent years had been troubled by doubts and misgivings which the most exhausting study of science and theology had not quieted. Then, just as he turned eighteen, he recorded reading the latest works of the two great Cambridge antagonists, Louis Agassiz and Asa Gray and, in bold capitals, DARWIN'S "THE ORIGIN OF SPECIES." A few months later, browsing in Boston's Old Corner Bookshop, he came across *Social Statics,* together with a prospectus of the cosmic plan already elaborated by Herbert Spencer, and he knew that his perplexities were at an end. "My soul is on fire," he wrote, and as his duty to mankind, he promptly subscribed to the whole series that Spencer had so ambitiously projected. Under the elms of Petersham he read choice passages from the *First Principles* to his fiancée and felt that he was holding communion with Omniscience. Darwin and Spencer accompanied him on his courtship, his marriage, his ventures into law, anthropology, religion, and history, his ill-starred connection with Harvard College, and his glorious career as popularizer of science and history to the English-speaking world. In the end he made the findings of Darwin respectable even to the clergy and, in impersonal alliance with William Graham Sumner, conquered America for the doctrines of Spencer.

The impact of Darwin on religion was shattering; his impact on philosophy was revolutionary. Evolution banished the absolute, supplanted special design, challenged not only the Scriptural story of creation but creation itself, and revealed man not as the product of beneficent purpose but of a process of natural selection that, by defying the interposition of the Deity, confounded the concept of omnipotence. Yet it was a blow to Man rather than to God who, in any event, was better able to bear it, for if it relegated God to a dim first cause, it toppled Man from his exalted position as the end and purpose of creation, the crown of Nature, and the image of God, and classified him prosaically with the anthropoids. It repudiated the philosophical implications of the Newtonian system, substituted for the neat orderly universe governed by fixed laws a universe in constant flux whose beginnings were incomprehensible and whose ends were unimaginable, reduced man to a passive role, and by subjecting moral concepts to its implacable laws deprived them of that authority which had for so long furnished consolation and refuge to bewildered man. Every institution was required to yield to its sovereign claims: the church, the state, the family, property, law; every discipline was forced to adapt itself to its ineluctable pattern: history, economics, sociology, philology, art, literature, religion, ethics.

Fiske was too learned in science to doubt the validity of biological evolution, and the hostility of Agassiz only confirmed him in his contumacy; he was, for all his heterodoxy, too good a Christian to acquiesce in its irreverent implications; he was too abandoned to romanticism to admit for a moment that the findings of science could impair the dignity of man. He made it his business to reconcile not only religion but the whole of philosophy with evolution, and his success was spectacular.

He thought his mind rigorously scientific (had he not mastered Humboldt's *Kosmos* at the age of eighteen?) but his response to the doctrine of evolution was as subjective as any impulse to which Emerson had yielded in his most transcendental moments: thus he illustrated that combination of practicality and sentiment, that optimistic exploitation of the most impersonal scientific data, so characteristic of his countrymen. To the mere material view, the universe might appear a senseless bubble-play of Titan forces, with life, love, aspiration, and beauty brought forth only to be extinguished, but this view was vulgar and fallacious. For on warm June mornings, along green country lanes—so Fiske wrote—with sweet pine odors wafted in the breezes which sighed through the branches, and cloud shadows flitting over blue mountains, he felt that the profoundest answers which science vouchsafed to questions of the nature and purpose of life were but fragmentary and superficial. Evolution did not cancel faith but validated it, for it gave scientific support to the intuitions of men. It illuminated a process; it did not explain away a first cause. Far from eliminating God, it enhanced His glory; if it broke with the seventeenth-century, Calvinistic notion of an arbitrary God, it confirmed the eighteenth-century, enlightened notion of a rational God. That He was now required to conform to Darwin as well as to Newton was not felt to be too great an imposition upon His resourcefulness, nor to detract in the least from His majesty. For evolution revealed that "the things and events of the world do not exist or occur blindly or irrelevantly, but that all, from the beginning to the end of time, and throughout the farthest sweep of illimitable space, are connected together as the orderly manifestations of a Divine Power," and it asserted that "all the phenomena of the universe, whether they be what we call material or what we call spiritual, are manifestations of this infinite and eternal power."

Nor, rightly viewed, did the evolution of Man out of the primordial slime detract in the least from his dignity or from his assurance of immortality. On the contrary, evolution made clear that the perfecting of man was the chief object of the creative activity of the universe.

According to Darwinism, the creation of Man is still the goal towards which Nature tended from the beginning. Not the production of any higher creature, but the perfecting of Humanity, is to be the glorious consummation of Nature's long and tedious work. Thus we suddenly arrive at the conclusion that Man seems now, much more clearly than ever, the chief among God's creatures. On the primitive barbaric theory, which Mr. Darwin has swept away, Man was suddenly flung into the world by the miraculous act of some unseen and incalculable Power, acting from without; and whatever theology might suppose, no scientific reason could be alleged why the same incalculable Power might not at some future moment, by a similar miracle, thrust upon the scene some mightier creature in whose presence Man would become like a story beast of burden. But he who has mastered the Darwinian theory, he who recognizes the slow and subtle process of evolution as the way in which God makes things come to pass, must take a far higher view. He sees that in the deadly struggle for existence which has raged through aeons of time, the whole creation has been groaning and travailing together in order to bring forth that last consummate specimen of God's handiwork, the Human Soul.

As he pondered the findings of the evolutionists, Fiske was enraptured with the vision unfolded before his eyes. He, who was moved to tears by the fleecy clouds floating over Petersham or the mighty chords of Beethoven, was ravished now by a glimpse of the destiny of man nobler by far than any which the poor theology or the meager science of the past had permitted:

The future is lighted for us with radiant colors of hope. Strife and sorrow shall disappear. Peace and love shall reign supreme. The dream of poets, the lesson of the priest and the prophet, the inspiration of the great musician, is confirmed in the light of modern knowledge; and as we gird ourselves upward for the work of life, we may look forward to a time when in the truest sense the kingdoms of this world shall become the Kingdom of Christ.

Cosmic Philosophy (1874) and its successors secured God in that sovereignty which had been momentarily threatened by scientists who lacked vision and faith, reconciled evolution with immortality, and made it possible to be on the side of both apes and angels. But what of those laws of Nature which had regulated not only the circling stars and the changing seasons but the institutions and conduct of men and which had for so long given reassurance to the children of the Enlightenment?

2

To bring human society within the embrace of evolution was the task of Herbert Spencer, who completed the great work Darwin had commenced. This philosopher who boasted the most capacious intellect of all time, whose genius surpassed that of Aristotle and Newton as the telegraph surpassed the carrier pigeon, whose revelations were more effective than those from Sinai—the phrases are culled from the tributes of American contemporaries—brought all human phenomena within the framework of scientific laws and furnished scientific proof for that doctrine of progress which had heretofore rested upon faith. His great "System of Synthetic Philosophy" demonstrated that man had evolved socially and psychologically as well as biologically from the simple to the complex, from savagery to civilization, from chaos to order, from anarchy to law, and promised continued progress toward ultimate perfection in harmony with the immutable workings of cosmic forces. "Progress," he wrote, "is not an accident but a necessity. What we call evil and immorality must disappear. It is certain that man must become perfect. . . . Always towards perfection is the mighty movement—towards a complete development and a more unmixed good."

To Fiske, to E. L. Youmans, editor of the *Popular Science Monthly,* to Godkin, to Henry Holt, to a whole generation in search of scientific reassurance about the fate of man, this was a gospel of good cheer. For it appeared to solve a problem that was gravely troubling the most thoughtful men of that era—the problem of the sanctions behind those moral and religious teachings which for centuries had guided the footsteps of men along paths of righteousness to salvation. The philosophy of the Enlightenment, with its faith in Reason and in Law and its acceptance of absolutes, had been found wanting. The defects did not at first appear fatal, and they had been partially healed by Transcendentalism, with its assertion of the validity of truths that transcended reason and made scientific proof superfluous. That there was a basic harmony between the Enlightenment and Transcendentalism, in their American versions, every student of Jefferson and Emerson knew. Both philosophies assumed a universe governed by law and intelligible to reason; both taught that God, or Providence, was benevolent, Nature beneficent, Man and Society perfectible. To both, Man was the focus of the universe, and to both, the laws that controlled Nature and Society guaranteed, in the end, the infinite happiness of mankind.

Yet Transcendentalism, too, with its reliance upon a priori intuitions rather than sensational facts, became increasingly unacceptable to a generation whose idols were the machine and the laboratory. By the mid-nineteenth century it had lost respectability everywhere but in America; in America it was still respectable but largely ineffective. Yet the late nineteenth century seemed to offer nothing in the place of either the Enlightenment or Transcendentalism; neither the arid Common Sense philosophy disseminated from Princeton by James McCosh nor Hegelianism, curiously transplanted to St. Louis and explained by W. T. Harris in his *Journal of Speculative Philosophy,* could reassure Americans in their precarious faith in Man, Reason and Progress or stem the rising tide of materialism.

At this juncture, the evolutionary philosophies of Darwin and Spencer saved the day. They answered, almost miraculously, the needs of their generation. Although at first they seemed to threaten the very foundations of traditional belief, a more mature appreciation of their meaning—Fiske's, for example—discovered that the substitution of evolution for the Scriptures or for Reason derogated neither from the sovereignty of the Supreme Lawgiver nor from the majesty of the laws. The doctrines of evolution certified a universe governed by Law and the progressive destiny of Man, not on the basis of fallible Reason nor on mere intuition but by the irreproachable findings of science. Evolution outmoded rather than nullified the Enlightenment and Transcendentalism, for though its methods were profoundly different, its conclusions were much the same. Progress was no longer a mere conclusion of logic but a necessity of nature. Scientific determinism lost its terrors when it was seen to be benevolent, shaping Nature and Man for ends that could justly be called divine. Where the Enlightenment had built a Heavenly City and Transcendentalism a Utopia, evolution held out the dazzling prospect of a future more glorious than anything that either had imagined, and its promise carried conviction. Morality itself was furnished, for the first time, with a scientific foundation. Reason and intuition had wrestled vainly with the problem of evil in a universe logically or ideally good; evolution made the problem irrelevant, for evil, which was now seen to be but a maladjustment to nature, was destined inevitably to disappear in that larger harmony which was good.

Between them, Darwin and Spencer exercised such sovereignty over America as George III had never enjoyed. Fiske was their vice-regent. Breathless with enthusiasm, buoyant and cheerful and generous, an intellectual dynamo with a mind that raced like electricity and with an inexhaustible store of learning, prodigal of his talents, equally ready to edit an encyclopedia or preach a sermon or outline cosmic philosophy or survey all history, he devoted himself indefati-

gably to his self-appointed mission. Articles and books flowed ceaselessly from his unfailing pen, and when he was not writing he was
talking—to women's clubs, to universities, to churches, to the President and his Cabinet. He was a perambulating encyclopedia, a
peripatetic university, the most articulate and persuasive representative
of Victorian optimism of his generation. He was sure that he could
read the cosmic processes and that they promised well for man. He
thought the world good but knew that the best was yet to be, confessed faith in an eternity which confirmed the conception of an
hour. It never occurred to him that the implications of the gospel
which he spread made his own career superfluous if not irrelevant.

For evolution, operating remorselessly through cosmic laws, promised ultimate perfection, to be sure, but it was a perfection to which
man made and could make no independent contribution. Though
it seemed at first glance far from exacting in its demands, it imposed in the end a price higher than that required even by Calvinism—the logical abandonment of free will. For having pushed God
back to a first cause and denied Him the privilege, so carefully safeguarded by the Calvinists, of being arbitrary, it proceeded to remove
man from the controls, to reduce him to a passive element in nature
rather than an active agent in working out his own salvation. By
subjecting the destinies of man to the inexorable operations of natural
selection, it vetoed man's interposition and nullified his own efforts.
Progress was sure, but the price was submission and conformity.

Conformity to evolution had obvious attractions in the prosy realms
of business or law or politics, but it took on somber overtones in the
realms of ethics and morals. That far-off divine event to which the
whole creation moved could inspire philosophers and poets and those
who knew they were moving with creation. For the command to
accept things as they were, to acquiesce in the inscrutable operations
of evolution, natural selection, and the survival of the fittest, was
welcome enough to those whose lines had fallen in pleasant places
and who could point to their own survival as conclusive evidence
that they were in harmony with nature. It was scarcely acceptable
to those whom the inexorable operations of nature or society condemned to unfitness or destruction. And to those who still cherished
an old-fashioned faith in the ability of man to mold his own destiny
and to earn his own salvation, it was nothing less than revolting.

3

Did Americans really want a universe all carefully prearranged, an evolution immutably predetermined, a cosmic system which was self-starting and self-regulating, which coldly eliminated man, made his hopes and ambitions, his fortitude and his gallantry, his strivings and achievements, as well as his vices and failings and eccentricities, superfluous and irrelevant? Did they want it even in its immediate and secular manifestations, its rigid economic and social patterns? Did they want to settle back and let nature take its course, let all things work themselves out in some stupendous process, toward some unforeseeable end? Was a philosophy which presented a closed universe, its mechanics patented by Herbert Spencer, its distant promises underwritten by John Fiske, consistent with the American character, adaptable to the American tradition?

The full implications of the Spencerian version of Darwin took some time to filter down into the consciousness of the American people. That Spencer dominated the thought of the average American —especially the middle-class American—during the half-century after Appomattox is acknowledged: what is not fully appreciated is that it was the economic and political implications of his teaching rather than the psychological and philosophical that enlisted support and excited enthusiasm. It is suggestive that the book which was read longest and which exerted the greatest influence was *The Man versus the State:* as late as 1916 the most distinguished statesmen and educators in the country delighted to contribute enthusiastic introductions to every chapter. For here, as elsewhere in Spencer's voluminous works, the let-alone philosophy was so formulated as to appeal at once to the traditional individualism and the acquisitive instincts of Americans, who were able without too great inconsistency to regard whatever they did, individually, as in harmony with evolution and whatever government or society did, collectively, as contrary to natural law.

Yet Americans had never willingly let either history or nature alone, or even the universe, and if Margaret Fuller accepted it— which may be doubted in view of her subsequent activities—few other Americans did. They were, almost by instinct, tinkerers, and experience had taught them that they could change anything. They had always adhered to the Laws of Nature and Nature's God—but they had interpreted the laws, and their interpretation had confounded the theology, the philosophy, and the history of the past. They could gracefully subscribe to evolution, for the notion of change, of growth, of development from homogeneity to heterogeneity, was part of their experience. They could not consistently accept determinism, even the grand, age-long determinism of the Spencerian system. They could believe in progress: their own history was the most convincing proof of the validity of that concept; they were logically and psychologically precluded from believing in a progress to which they made no contribution and which was divorced from their control. The temporary usefulness of Spencer's social philosophy to the dominant interests in America is obvious and its popularity not incomprehensible, but any widespread and prolonged acquiescence in the Spencerian philosophical system must be counted an aberration.

CHAPTER V

William James and the Impact of Pragmatism

I

TO WILLIAM JAMES, who had first won fame in the new science of psychology, Spencerian determinism was an intellectual and moral affront. A son of Henry James the elder whose residence in New York had not estranged him from Concord, he had grown up in the atmosphere of Transcendentalism and, notwithstanding his repudiation of its loose logic and its easy absolutes, he never entirely freed his mind from its rich optimism, its faith in the spiritual resources of man, its hospitality to individual inspiration, its confidence that men could validate intuitive truths by effective action. From Emerson, from George Ripley, long-time familiars in his household, from Franklin B. Sanborn, the Plutarch of the Transcendentalist movement, from all those legendary and noble figures who lived on in the afterglow of the golden day, he had learned how practical and open minded idealism could be when shorn of its German metaphysics and translated into the American vernacular. His wonderful father, from whose character rather than convictions his own philosophy was to derive so much, had exposed him to Swedenborgianism, and though he rejected its mysticism he never entirely escaped its influence. Even before he had come to any definition of his own philosophy, his philosophical preconceptions were fixed: a suspicion of all absolutes, all rigidities, and all systems; an inclination to leave all questions open to reconsideration; an indulgence of eccentricity and nonconformity; a preference for what was artistically and emotionally as well as intellectually appealing; a compelling consciousness of moral obligation.

Neither his father nor the Transcendentalists had won William

James to their ways of thinking, and when he turned from painting, and then from medicine, to psychology and philosophy, he began with Spencer. He was just Fiske's age when he came across *First Principles,* and, like Fiske, he was "carried away with enthusiasm by the intellectual perspective which it seemed to open," and when his friend Charles Peirce attacked it, he confessed that he felt "spiritually wounded, as by the defacement of a sacred image." Yet a quarrel with Spencer was almost hereditary: had not the elder Henry James written that *"pace* Messrs. Darwin and Spencer . . . when we speak of human *nature,* we speak of what logically belongs to man alone, and therefore disconnect him with all lower existence," an anticipation of the argument Lester Ward was to advance. Within a few years James came around to Peirce's point of view and engaged cheerfully in iconoclasm. "My quarrel with Spencer," he wrote prophetically in 1878, "is not that he makes much of environment, but that he makes nothing of the glaring and patent fact of subjective interests which cooperate with the environment in moulding intelligence. These interests form a true spontaneity and justify the refusal of *a priori* schools to admit that mind was pure, passive receptivity."

This did not mean that James had gone over to the Idealists, to T. H. Green in England or William T. Harris in America, so busy repairing the damage the Transcendentalists had inflicted on the purity and integrity of Kant and Hegel. Hegel was no more acceptable to James than Spencer. As early as 1880 James was writing disparagingly of the "Hegelian wave which seems to me only another desperate attempt to make a short cut to paradise." His objection was as much emotional as rational: "The through-and-through philosophy, as it actually exists . . . seems too buttoned-up and white-chokered and clean-shaven a thing to speak for the vast, slow-breathing unconscious Kosmos with its dread abysses and its unknown tides." He was scarcely less impatient with Kant. "Pray contribute no farther," he advised one young disciple, "to philosophy's prison discipline of dragging Kant around like a cannonball tied to its ankle." His fundamental criticism of Hegel and Kant was not logical or even aesthetic but moral: he thought their acquiescence in absolutes, their tendency to see the world as good rather than to strive to make it good, paralyzed the will. The objection illuminates not only James's character, but the metamorphosis of Idealism in

America: it could scarcely have been relevant when the Transcendentalists were in the vanguard of every movement looking to the reformation of society.

Confronted with a choice between Spencerian naturalism and Hegelian idealism, between a "brute," tough-minded philosophy which banished idealism and mysticism in the name of science and a formal, tender-minded philosophy which banished science in the name of mysticism and idealism, with, in short, two absolutes, James refused resolutely to embrace either or even to admit that these were the only possible choices. He wanted, instead, a system that would combine the virtues of both without their paralyzing monism: a scientific loyalty to facts and confidence in human values, empiricism without inhumanity or irreligion, and rationalism that did not disdain the concrete or exclude human joys and sorrows. As no existing philosophical system offered this, he constructed his own, and the originality and audacity of pragmatism were not the least American charactcristics associated with his name. He took to himself the challenge of that verse from the *Greek Anthology:*

> A shipwrecked sailor, buried on this coast,
> Bids you set sail.
> Full many a gallant bark, when we were lost,
> Weathered the gale.

And if he never sailed his bark into quiet harbors, hc knew the joy of keeping it afloat in boisterous gales and turbulent seas.

Mark Twain once observed that he had never known a real seeker after truth: sooner or later everyone engaged in that search found what he was looking for and gave up the quest. It was a pity that he did not know William James. For James believed, passionately, that truth was not something that was found, once and for all, but was forever in the making, that it was not single and absolute but plural and contingent. It was not only that he was tolerant and hospitable to a degree heretofore unknown in modern philosophy but that tolerance and hospitality were an essential ingredient in his philosophical system. Philosophy had for him, as his colleague and critic, Santayana, observed, "a Polish constitution; so long as a single vote was cast against the majority, nothing could pass. . . . It would have depressed him," he added, "if he had had to confess that any important question was finally settled."

This was an exaggeration. One important question was settled, with irrevocable finality: the question of the relative validity of dogma and skepticism. For, almost from the beginning, James confronted all dogma with skepticism and made skepticism itself a dogma. He turned his countenance from all absolutes, causes, finalities, fixed principles, abstractions, and rigidities, and embraced instead pluralism, uncertainty, practicality, common sense, adventure, and flexibility. To the philosophy of first causes he opposed one of consequences; to the philosophy of ultimates he opposed one of expediency; to the philosophy of determinism he opposed one of free will. To the concept that truth could be found either by the exercise of pure reason or by the scientific observation of nature, he opposed the concept that truth was not in fact to be found but to be made, that it was not something that was inert and static but something that happened to an idea or a course of conduct:

The truth of an idea is not a stagnant property inherent in it. Truth *happens* to an idea. It *becomes* true, is *made* true by events: its verity *is* in fact an event, a process: the process namely of its verifying itself, its veri-*fication*. Its validity is the process of its valid-*ation*. . . . The true is the name of whatever proves itself to be good in the way of belief, and good, too, for definite assignable reasons.

To this attitude toward truth, James applied first the name "practicalism" and then pragmatism. Pragmatism was not in itself a philosophy but a philosophical method; to Giovanni Papini's observation that it was a method of doing without a philosophy, James made no objection, for he was willing enough to dispense with most of the formal philosophies of the past in so far as they required adherence to some established orthodoxy. As he could not reconcile the conflicting monisms of the reigning philosophical systems, he submitted pragmatism as "a method of settling metaphysical disputes that might otherwise be interminable." Confronted by questions which, for the most part, merely raised other and more profound questions, James asked instead what the practical consequences of any answer would be and accepted or rejected that answer as its consequences were profitable or unprofitable, useful or useless, good or bad:

Grant an idea or belief to be true, what concrete difference will its being true make in anyone's actual life? How will the truth be realized? What experiences will be different from those which would obtain if the belief were false? What, in short, is the truth's cash value in experiential terms? The moment pragmatism asks this question, it sees the answer. *True ideas are those that we can assimilate, validate, corroborate and verify. False ideas are those that we can not.* That is the practical difference it makes to us to have true ideas; that, therefore, is the meaning of truth, for it is all that truth is known as.

In short, "the true is only the expedient in the way of our thinking, just as 'the right' is only the expedient in the way of our behaving."

2

Pragmatism was a philosophy of expedience. It put ideas to work and judged them by their results. It accepted "any idea upon which we can ride" as "true instrumentally," and instrumentalism came to be its preferred name. It rejected theories and abstractions and established the single standard of workability. It was as practical as the patent office—or the Declaration of Independence. Its expediency was individual; it came, increasingly, to be social, to require that men work together to establish the truth of their hopes.

It was a democratic philosophy, held every man a philosopher, gave every man a vote, and counted the votes of the simple and the humble equal to those of the learned and the proud. It took its truths where it found them, sometimes in the unlikeliest places. It made philosophy a servant, not a master, an instrument, not an end. It assumed that men could direct their spiritual as they did their political destinies; it overthrew the tyranny of philosophical authoritarianism and substituted the democracy of popular representation.

It was an individualistic philosophy. It assigned to each individual, as it were, a leading role in the drama of salvation, gave him a share and a responsibility in making what he held good come true. It denied him the consolation of unconditional reliance on God or on Nature and decreed that he succeed or fail through his own efforts. It emphasized his uniqueness rather than his conformity, and it encouraged him to put his own faith to the test. It was voluntaristic and raised its armies by enlistment, not by conscription. It was impatient with authority—the authority of history or science or theology—and preferred the teachings of experience to the dictates of logic. It stood for home rule in the realm of ideas. It celebrated the perceptions of the average man rather than the subtleties of metaphysicians, for "it is only the minds debauched of learning," said James, "who have ever suspected common sense of not being absolutely true."

It was a humane and optimistic philosophy. It subscribed readily enough to the doctrine of progress, but made that doctrine contingent rather than absolute—contingent upon the contributions which men were willing to risk for its realization. It held that man's fate was not determined by mechanical powers but by man himself, and it insisted that man could create as well as succumb to environment. It accepted evolution, but emphasized its flexibility and submitted that the mind and spirit of man was as much a part of the evolutionary process as his body. It assured to every man the dignity of active participation in the drama of the cosmos. Because it taught that men held the future in their own hands, it was drenched with optimism.

It was an adventurous philosophy. It asserted that truth was prospective as well as retrospective. Rejecting any guarantee of ultimate salvation, it gambled instead on the virtue, the intelligence, and the courage of men. It was willing to try any hypothesis and would not discriminate against novelty, originality, or even eccentricity. It assumed that "the universe is still pursuing its adventures" and joined gaily in the pursuit. It repudiated any system of moral security and voted instead for free enterprise in the moral realm. The challenge was familiar:

Suppose that the world's author put the case to you before creation, saying: "I am going to make a world not certain to be saved, a world the perfection of which shall be conditional merely, the condition being that each several agent does its own level best. I offer you the chance of taking part in such a world. Its safety, you see, is unwarranted. It is a real adventure, with real danger, yet it may win through. It is a social scheme of cooperative work genuinely to be done. Will you join the procession? Will you trust yourself and trust the other agents enough to face the risk?"

That there was a risk was clear enough to James, for men might guess wrong, or the attempt might fail. Yet it was the effort, the fight, that exhilarated him. Nor did he, in fact, ever dream though right were worsted wrong would triumph; held we fall to rise, are baffled to fight better, sleep to wake.

That these qualities in pragmatism reflected qualities in the American character has been too often remarked to justify elaboration. Practical, democratic, individualistic, opportunistic, spontaneous, hopeful, pragmatism was wonderfully adapted to the temperament of the average American. It cleared away the jungle of theology and metaphysics and deterministic science and allowed the warm sun of common sense to quicken the American spirit as the pioneer cleared the forests and the underbrush and allowed the sun to quicken the soil of the American West. In a sense, the whole of American experience had prepared for it and now seemed to validate and justify it. For America had been a gamble that had paid off, an experiment that had succeeded; it had enlisted the average man, had required him to play his part in a common enterprise, and had rewarded his courage and audacity with boundless generosity. In practice, Americans had always been instrumentalists. They had assumed that their faiths were true and had so acted as to make them true. They had assumed the worth of democracy, of equality, of freedom, assessed the practical consequences of these assumptions, and committed themselves to their realization. When they had pledged their lives, their fortunes, and their sacred honor to the triumph of the doctrines of the Declaration, they had acted pragmatically. Every American knew that the world in which he lived was, in part, of his own making, that he had bent Nature to his will and won Providence over to his side, and the sublimation of this long experience to a philosophical theory could not startle him. Pragmatism's willingness to break with the past, reject traditional habits, try new methods, put beliefs to a vote, make a future to order, excited not only sympathy but a feeling of familiarity. No wonder that, despite the broadsides of more formidable philosophers, pragmatism caught on until it came to be almost the official philosophy of America. To Americans it seemed the common sense of the matter, and the average American rejoiced that the logicians and metaphysicians who had long plagued him were at last confounded.

Not only was pragmatism sympathetic to the American character, its implications and conclusions were no less harmonious with the most authentic American thought. For though James rejected the sentimentality and the monism of the Transcendentalists and accepted evolution, he was nevertheless closer to Emerson and the Transcendentalists than he ever admitted. "Why should we not also enjoy an original relation to the universe?" Emerson had asked, and James had but echoed the question. The methods of the two philosophies —if either can be called that—were dramatically different, but the inspiration and the consequences were much the same. Both expressed the optimism and the practical idealism of the American character; both were individualistic and democratic. The Transcendentalists, even with their faith in a priori truths, had the sporting instinct; they took a chance that the heart knew better than the head, they gambled on what their intuitions told them was good, even against the findings of the laboratory, and labored heroically to make that good come true. Nor, on the other hand, was pragmatism without its intuitive elements. James, who had been trained in the laboratory, revered the factual, the concrete, statistical evidence and sensational proof, but his faith in an open universe, in a pluralistic cosmos, in the notion that truth could be tested by its consequences, was no less an assumption than the faith of the Transcendentalists that their intuitions would lead them to God was an assumption. By any pragmatic test, too, these different ways of thinking had much in common, for they led to much the same consequences—to a tender interest in the underprivileged, a deep respect for the integrity of the individual, a fighting confidence in the possibility of reform. Between Thoreau's opposition to the Mexican and James's to the Philippine War there was not much to choose, nor in their open-mindedness toward social and political experiments. The comparison must not be pressed too far. Pragmatism expressed the individualism of the pioneer who felled the forests of Indiana rather than of the visionaries who ploughed the fields of Brook Farm; it was closer to the opportunism of the Progressive movement than to the fanaticism of the abolitionist crusade.

3

Certainly this was true of pragmatism as formulated by William James. It was perhaps less true of instrumentalism as formulated by James's illustrious successor, John Dewey. For though Dewey confessed small indebtedness and some hostility to Transcendentalism, he had an ungrudging respect for the kind of cooperative enterprise symbolized by Brook Farm. His individual was not the individual celebrated by James—wrestling with his soul, fighting his way to some course of conduct, some decisive action, which would reveal the meaning of truth. He was rather an individual operating within a network of associations, seeking, in common with his fellow men, some truth that had meaning to the community. That community, to be sure, was not Josiah Royce's community: it was more secular than spiritual, more concerned with immediate and particular than with ultimate and universal ends.

The metamorphosis of pragmatism in the mind of Dewey was illustrated by the difference between James and Dewey themselves. Both were liberals, but James's liberalism looked backwards to the nineteenth, Dewey's forward to the twentieth century. It is almost equally difficult to imagine Dewey dedicating a book to John Stuart Mill or James sympathizing with the Soviet experiment. While James enlisted in few causes, those in which he did enlist were by preference lost causes: he was attracted to them, one felt, as humane old women are attracted to stray cats, not because they were meritorious but because they were unfortunate. He preferred gallantry to victory, individual combat with the outcome uncertain to scientific warfare with triumph sure. Dewey's zeal for social amelioration had none of this quixotic character. He was too serious minded to enjoy a battle for its own sake: the issues of the crusades which he fought were too pressing, the stakes too high. He would fight readily enough on the side of minorities but not just because they were minorities: it is difficult to imagine his joining James in opposition to the licensing of physicians on the ground that the requirement would exclude Christian Science practitioners, mental therapists, and faith healers!

More fully than any other philosopher of modern times, Dewey put philosophy to the service of society. More, he formed a whole network of alliances—with science, with politics, with education, with aesthetics, all directed toward advancing the happiness of mankind. His quarrel with the Transcendentalists was not merely that their system of truth was absolute but that it encouraged atomistic individualism; his quarrel with the determinists not merely that they reduced the individual to insignificance but that they did not respect experience. The ends he sought were public, not private. Truth was, to him, not merely what worked for the individual but what worked for the group, and it was to be achieved by cooperative action. Morality was social, not individual. The elimination of the abstract arguments which had engaged philosophers of the past, he wrote, would permit philosophy to devote itself to a more fruitful and more needed task. It would encourage philosophy to face the great social and moral defects and troubles from which humanity suffers, to concentrate its attention upon clearing up the causes and exact nature of those evils and upon developing a clear idea of better social possibilities; in short, upon projecting an idea or ideal which, instead of expressing the notion of another world or some far-away unrealizable goal, would be used as a method of understanding and rectifying specific social ills.

The task of philosophy was, in short, "to clarify men's ideas as to the social and moral strifes of their own day."

So faithfully did Dewey live up to his own philosophical creed that he became the guide, the mentor, and the conscience of the American people: it is scarcely an exaggeration to say that for a generation no major issue was clarified until Dewey had spoken. Pioneer in educational reform, organizer of political parties, counselor to statesmen, champion of labor, of woman's rights, of peace, of civil liberties, interpreter of America abroad and of Russia, Japan, China, and Germany to the American people, he was the spearhead of a dozen movements, the leader of a score of crusades, the advocate of a hundred reforms. He illustrated in his own career how effective philosophy could be in that reconstruction of society which was his preoccupation and its responsibility.

This shift in the emphasis of philosophy from the salvation of the individual to the reconstruction of society reflected a comparable shift in society itself. For notwithstanding the achievements of medicine and humanitarianism in saving lives, the twentieth century was remarkable for the decline of the significance of the individual. Literature neglected heroes and villains and had recourse to social description. Social history triumphed over political or military, and biographers became iconoclasts. The study of economic man fell into disrepute and the study of business cycles rose to favor. Almost everything became socialized: medicine, religion, architecture, education, law, charity, recreation, reading, war. It was scarcely remarkable that philosophy should accommodate itself to this pattern.

4

Of all the philosophies to which Americans have subscribed, pragmatism lent itself most unavoidably to vulgarization. The translation of Spencerian evolution into an apology for the practices and malpractices of the business community suggests an analogy, but it was, after all, difficult to vulgarize further what was intrinsically tawdry: Andrew Carnegie's career, one feels, did not so much caricature Spencer's ideas as dramatize them. But pragmatism was affluent, magnanimous, heroic; it enlisted all those sentiments we have come to consider generous and noble in the battle for salvation. That it should have been equated with a success philosophy, watered down to an acquiescence in cash values or a justification of business efficiency, associated with a series of shabby compromises and concessions, translated into a cunning technique for outwitting Providence, was discreditable. Yet the transition from the principle that truth is to be discovered in the practical consequences of conduct to the notion that whatever works is necessarily truth was dangerously easy. Soon critics were speaking wittily of the will-to-make-believe or of the philosophical anesthetic or of the pragmatic acquiescence.

As pragmatism was a public affair, directed to and enlisting the common man, it not only exposed itself to but invited vulgarization. "The pragmatism that lives inside of me," James burst out, "is so different from that of which I succeed in wakening the idea inside of other people, that theirs makes me feel like cursing God and dying"; but his reaction was wry rather than desperate, and he could read Mr. Dooley's version of pragmatism with equanimity. For popularization was, after all, a sign of vitality: there was little danger that the labored mysticism of Royce or the exquisite aestheticism of Santayana would suffer from such vandalism. When philosophy spoke the language of the people, connected itself with their experience, addressed itself to their interests, illuminated their problems, it was natural that they should seize upon it and fashion it to their purposes.

The charge of vulgarization can be ignored, then, not as untrue but as irrelevant, except to note that a philosophy sponsored by democracy suffered the consequences of that sponsorship. More serious was the charge that pragmatism was inherently anti-intellectual, that it appealed to the arbitrary, the fortuitous, and the irrational, encouraged illusions and eccentricities, destroyed authority and discipline, and played into the hands of those who exploited the emotions. Santayana recalled that the irrationality of pragmatism "gave me a rude shock. I could not stomach that way of speaking about truth;

and the continual substitution of human psychology—normal madness, in my view—for the universe, in which man is but one distracted and befuddled animal, seemed to me a confused remnant of idealism, and not serious."

That pragmatism challenged authority, dissolved institutions, destroyed security, cannot be denied, for James himself admitted that he was "willing that there should be real losses and real losers, and no total preservation of all that is." It provided a convenient rationalization, if not the inspiration, for the attack on the State, the Law, Sovereignty, and many other concepts which had enjoyed the finality of Euclidian axioms and which had served to foreclose rather than provoke inquiry. It was, later, to give comfort to those who wished to substitute their personal absolutes, or anarchies, for the absolutes of the past.

James himself might have found some cause for gratification in the charge that pragmatism was anti-intellectual, for he waged a life-long war against that intellectualism which was abstract, refined, and artificial. That was the game he was after, and he hung its skins on the walls of his study. In its place, however, he submitted not irrationality but reason that was organic and evolutionary, that adjusted itself to the whole range of human experience, that regarded the intellect not as a thing apart but as an agent in the creation of truth. His pragmatism was not irrational but gave reason a function and a dignity it had not theretofore enjoyed.

It is perhaps fair to ask whether, in the great crisis of the twentieth century which tested the efficacy of all philosophies, that people who most fully subscribed to pragmatism or that people who clung to the traditions of Hegelian idealism conducted themselves more rationally. It would be a bold student who, comparing America and Germany in the generation after James's death, could have concluded that it was the pragmatists who had abandoned themselves to emotionalism and their souls to anarchy, who had displayed contempt for reason or for law or for morality. It has been noted, to be sure, that the tyrant Mussolini counted himself an early convert to pragmatism; it is relevant to remark that it was Santayana, not John Dewey, who found it convenient to take up residence in Italy.

The cult of irrationality indulged in vicariously by Freud and Pareto, by Hitler and Mussolini, neither derived from nor needed the dubious support of the pragmatists or of any other philosophers.

It was, in fact, not an elaboration but a repudiation of philosophy. Its inspiration was science, and it raised the question whether any philosophy could be longer tolerated in a universe wholly without meaning and as indifferent to any meaning that the paltry mind of man might read into it as man himself was to the response that the ephemera might make to his own conduct.

5

Even as James was combating the determinism of Spencer, Royce seeking absolute good through inevitable evil, Santayana letting his imagination roam over the multicolored panorama of nature, a new physics, chemistry, and biology emerged which threatened to reduce the whole of human thought and art, all the stirrings of the body and the strivings of the mind and the soul, to insignificance. The universe unveiled by the new science was illimitable, impersonal, amoral, and incomprehensible. Not only was man's place in the earth evanescent, accidental, and meaningless; the earth itself was but a flyspeck in a universe equally without purpose or meaning. Matter, which had once seemed so unimpeachable, lost its solidity and became in the new physics but a complex of electrical reactions, indistinguishable from pulsating energy—a "wave of probability undulating into nothingness" in "a vibrating mechanism shot through with energy"; mind, which had once seemed to distinguish Man from all other creatures here below, was seen to be indistinguishable from matter. God, Providence, Design, first causes, and teleological ends all evaporated; such concepts as the soul, immortality, free will, were seen as whimsies with which men tried to console themselves; the line between life and death like the line between mind and matter was blurred, and life itself was explained as a convenient but not very accurate term for the chemical process of oxidation.

As the telescope and mathematics disclosed a universe so vast that it defied computation except in thousands of millions of light-years and reduced the earth to a grain of pollen floating in illimitable space; as the microscope discovered a universe surging about in each atom as the earth whirled about in its solar system; as biology found the source of life itself in a series of apparently fortuitous chemical reactions; as psychologists reduced the most profound reflections, the most dazzling flights of genius, to mechanical impulses and uncontrollable reactions—the cosmic system familiar to John Fiske in which man possessed a soul, even an immortal soul, cherished beliefs about conduct, read meaning into such terms as love, faith, loyalty, and fortitude, slipped quietly away. Man knew only that he was the creature of forces whose origins he did not know, whose functions—if they indeed had functions—he could not comprehend, whose operations he could not control. The only conclusion he could rely on with any confidence was that he and everything connected with him was reduced to such insignificance as mathematics could with difficulty express. The metaphor of man as a moth beating his wings with suicidal vanity against the flame took on grim reality as Jacques Loeb pointed out that man's response to his environment—such things as love and piety—was in no way different from the insects' purely mechanical response to light. It was a dusty answer that science gave to the hot certainties of the past.

The layman could follow the scientists but a short way in their audacious exploration of the universe, but a host of interpreters stood ready to explain the implications of their findings for mankind. Thus he could read Ernst Haeckel—that "Rocky Mountain tough," James called him:

The so-called history of the world . . . is an evanescently short episode in the long course of organic evolution, just as this, in turn, is merely a small portion of the history of our planetary system; and as our mother-earth is a mere speck in the sunbeam in the illimitable universe, so man himself is but a tiny grain of protoplasm in the perishable framework of organic nature.

Or the statesman-philosopher, Arthur Balfour:

Man, so far as natural science by itself is able to teach, is no longer the final cause of the universe, the Heaven-descended heir of all the ages. His very existence is an accident, his story a brief and transitory episode in the life of one of the meanest of the planets. Of the combination of causes which first converted a dead organic compound into the living progenitors of humanity, science, indeed, as yet knows nothing. It is enough that from such beginnings . . . have gradually evolved, after infinite travail, a race with conscience enough to feel that it is vile, and intelligence enough to know that it is insignificant. We survey the past, and see that its history is of blood and tears, of helpless blundering, of wild revolt, of stupid acquiescence, of empty aspirations. We sound the future, and learn that after a period, long compared with the individual life but short indeed compared with the divisions of time open to our investigation, the energies of our system will decay, the glory of the sun will be dimmed, and the earth, tideless and inert, will no longer tolerate the race which for a moment disturbed its solitude. Man will go down into the pit, and all his thoughts will perish. The uneasy consciousness, which in this obscure corner has for a brief space broken the contented silence of the universe, will be at rest. Matter will know itself no longer. . . . Nor will anything that *is* be better or worse for all that the labor, genius, devotion, and suffering of man have striven through countless ages to effect. (*Foundations of Belief,* pp. 29-31)

A little later the American physicist, Percy Bridgman, reinforced this melancholy conclusion:

The physicist finds himself in a world from which the bottom has dropped clean out; as he penetrates deeper and deeper it eludes him and fades away by the highly unsportsmanlike device of just becoming meaningless. No refinement of measurement will avail to carry him beyond the portals of this shadowy domain which he cannot even mention without logical inconsistency. A bound is thus forever set to the curiosity of the physicist. What is more, the mere existence of this bound means that he must give up his most cherished convictions and faith. The world is not a world of reason, understandable by the intellect of man, but as we penetrate ever deeper, the very law of cause and effect, which we had thought to be a formula to which we could force God himself to subscribe, ceases to have any meaning. ("The New Version of Science," *Harper's Magazine,* March, 1929)

That life is brief, fate harsh, nature ruthless, the past a tragedy, and the future a blank was scarcely an original observation. Every schoolboy knew that life was a tale told by an idiot, full of sound and fury, signifying nothing, and no other philosophical poem had enjoyed the continuous popularity of the *Rubaiyat,* the bible of a thousand village atheists. Most of the great Victorians, too, had taken up the refrain— though, interestingly enough, in England rather than in America. Yet in the past the challenge of a malignant fate or a vindictive nature had but inspired ardent spirits to their greatest triumphs. For they were not without resources. Although Matthew Arnold knew that the world which seemed to lie about him as a land of dreams had really neither joy nor love nor light nor certitude nor peace nor help for pain, he had, after all, one consolation. O love, he said, let us be true to one another. So, too, out of the night that covered him, black as the pit from pole to pole, William Henley thanked whatever gods might be for his unconquerable soul. No such consolations were available to those who had immersed themselves in the new science and the new psychology. They knew too well that such terms as love, fate, and soul were but poetical fancies and that the whole Victorian vocabulary had to be interpreted much as one interpreted the vocabulary of fairy tales. They knew that love was not a spiritual ecstasy but a biological phenomenon, a series of chemical reactions, and that the soul was either a poetic whimsy or a complex of purely mechanical responses. The universe which confronted them was neither benevolent nor malignant; it was impersonal and indifferent, and it made ridiculous all the hopes and ambitions, heroisms and gallantries, of the past. Logically it made philosophy itself irrelevant if not absurd.

"My generation," wrote Dewey's colleague, James H. Tufts, "has seen the passing of systems of thought which had reigned since Augustus. The conception of the world as a kingdom ruled by God, subject to his laws and their penalties, which had been undisturbed by the Protestant Reformation, has dissolved. . . . The sanctions of our inherited morality have gone. Principles and standards which had stood for nearly two thousand years are questioned." Certainly Americans might feel the foundations of all their beliefs slipping out from under them, might repeat with William Vaughn Moody: "This earth is not the steadfast place we landsmen build upon. From deep to deep she varies pace, and while she comes is gone."

American philosophy had been, on the whole, popular; democratic in vocabulary and ideas, it had appealed to and inspired the average man. Because it was teleological and optimistic, it was unprepared for the shock of the new science. The findings of the physicists and the biologists seemed to close all the familiar doors and barricade all the habitual roads to salvation. The familiar orthodoxy of the Scriptures, the Jeffersonian faith in happiness now and greater happiness hereafter, the Emersonian doctrine that divinity inheres in all men, the Spencerian principle of necessary progress which Fiske applied to the spiritual realm, the adventurous pragmatism of James and the cooperative instrumentalism of Dewey, Royce's vision of loyalty to the great community and to an ideal, Santayana's view of nature and science as poetry or mythology—all these came to seem outmoded and ineffectual.

Yet the impact of the new science on philosophy was by no

means catastrophic, and philosophy made no convulsive gesture either toward accommodation or suicide. From Plato to Kant, it had addressed itself to just such problems as those which now confronted it, for neither determinism, the insignificance of man, nor the ruthlessness of nature were new ideas, only the scientific formulas which now gave them such stout support. Nor did either Royce or Santayana find the new science any insuperable barrier to the formulation of their doctrines, for their philosophies accepted naturalism and pessimism as points of departure. It was rather the social sciences, art, and literature that reacted most violently to the implications of scientific determinism. Under the leadership of Sigmund Freud, psychology broke down the border between the normal and the abnormal, revealing the unconscious and uncontrollable origins of most impulses. Politicians, who had never lacked the instinct, now found a scientific basis for demagoguery, the abandonment of principles and logic, and the cultivation of the passions and emotions; and many old and famous peoples confessed the flight from reason in the politics they pursued. Henry Adams tried to interpret history as force and to formulate a law of history that would accommodate itself to the second law of thermodynamics: the universe, he said, was a clock that was running down, and all history should record its enervation. Under the prodding of Thorstein Veblen, economists began to consider the possibility that economic behavior was as irrational as public opinion had long suspected. Rebellious artists found impressionism too mild a revolt from the academic and resorted to mathematical symbols such as cubism, grotesque exaggerations of the human figure, or the use of colors designed to shock the beholder rather than to reproduce nature. "Nude Descending a Staircase" was thought fantastic when it was exhibited at the Armory Show in 1913, but thirty years later Salvador Dali, whose assault on sanity and morality was far more blasphemous, was welcomed by the popular magazines and the advertisers.

CHAPTER VI

Determinism in Literature

I

I
T WAS IMAGINATIVE literature that provided the most extensive sounding board to the fluctuating waves of science and philosophy which we have described. The adjective is important: imaginative literature was not concerned with the careful analyses and the nice distinctions of science, but with the dramatic and imaginative exploitation of its findings. Its purpose was not to explain scientific facts but to discover spiritual truths: a purpose which it did not, to be sure, invariably achieve. Where science might legitimately be interested in man only as he affected the cosmos, literature was interested in the cosmos only as it affected man. It was the privilege therefore of the novelists to be eclectic and of poets to be inspired. Some abused this privilege. They shamelessly mixed Darwinian biology with Freudian psychology and blended in contributions from Spencer, Haeckel, Loeb, Nietzsche, Einstein, Pavlov, and Jung to make what passed for a naturalistic brew. They were naturalists, they were determinists, they were behaviorists. They seldom paused to formulate their philosophy or even to defend their terms, and they rarely agreed in their use of these terms or these concepts. All was grist that came to their literary mill.

The impulse behind Jack London, Frank Norris, and Theodore Dreiser around the turn of the century, behind Sherwood Anderson, Edgar Lee Masters, James Branch Cabell, Joseph Hergesheimer, Waldo Frank, and Robinson Jeffers after 1910, was not primarily philosophical. Too often the philosophy, or the science, which glimmers on their pages seems at best a calculated rationalization, at worst a pretentious *décor*. The disillusion to which they yielded so eagerly found its primary justification, after all, not in science but in economy. It was because the air of the nineties and of the new century was already heavy with pessimism that artists found it so easy to take refuge in scientific doctrines which seemed to provide some ultimate justification for that pessimism. These doctrines did more. They not only explained away evil, otherwise so outrageous a phenomenon in America, but seemed to wash away guilt. For they shifted the responsibility for the sorry mess into which mankind had drifted from society itself to the cosmos. It was a new Calvinism, indulged in most recklessly by those who most vehemently repudiated all religion: denying free will to men, it placed responsibility for what seemed evil not on an omnipotent and inscrutable God but on an omnipotent and inexorable Nature. As Henry Adams observed:

He could not deny that the law of the new multiverse explained much that had been most obscure, especially the persistently fiendish treatment of man by man; the perpetual effort of society to establish law, and the perpetual revolt of society against the law it had established; the perpetual building up of authority by force, and the perpetual appeal to force to overthrow it; the perpetual symbolism of a higher law, and the perpetual relapse to a lower one; the perpetual victory of the principles of freedom, and their perpetual conversion into principles of power. . . . All that a historian won was a vehement wish to escape. (*Education of Henry Adams,* p. 458)

The protest against the economic and social evils of the time, together with a philosophy which neatly lifted responsibility for those evils from the conscience of men, is best presented in the chaotic pages of Jack London and Theodore Dreiser. For while Fiske and his rapt followers emphasized the spiritual implications of the evolutionary doctrine, evolution appeared to London and Dreiser as the struggle for existence and the survival of the fittest. It was not a subtle idea, made few demands upon the intellect or the imagination, but provided a powerful stimulus to the more violent emotions. And violence characterizes the writings of all those who succumbed to this version of Darwin. It is to be found in Mark Twain's extravaganza, *A Connecticut Yankee* and in the posthumous *Mysterious Stranger.* It stains the pages of Stephen Crane's *Maggie* which shocked readers in 1893, and of Frank Norris' *McTeague* and *Vandover and the Brute* which appeared shortly before 1900. It riots unrestrained through twenty volumes of Jack London. It infects alike Spoon River and Winesburg, Ohio. It hovers in the background of Dreiser's *Sister Carrie* and *Jennie Gerhardt,* of *The Titan* and *The*

Financier and *An American Tragedy.* It is what Hemingway celebrated later in *Death in the Afternoon,* and *The Green Hills of
Africa;* it haunted Thomas Wolfe, and it is the sum and substance
of most of the novels of William Faulkner. It speaks the lines in
Eugene O'Neill's *Anna Christie* and the *Hairy Ape,* in *Desire under
the Elms* and *Mourning Becomes Electra.* With Robinson Jeffers it
almost rises to the dignity of a philosophy.

2

Of all those who applied the doctrine of the survival of the fittest
to human society, Jack London was the most enthusiastic and the
most naïve: it is suggestive that he was, also, the most widely read,
at home and abroad. Within five years, at the beginning of the century, *The Sea Wolf, The Call of the Wild,* and *White Fang,* caught
the attention of the English-speaking world much as Kipling's stories
had done fifteen years earlier. London translated Darwinism into the
vernacular, presented it in a guise so romantic, boisterous, and extravagant that it proved irresistible; he wrote it up in dime novels and
purveyed it as literature and philosophy. The stuff of his endless adventure stories was dredged up from his own fabulous career as
newsboy, oyster pirate, tramp, sailor, prospector, and rancher; the
philosophy was laid on like ornamental scrollwork on Eastlake
buildings. London read Spencer and Haeckel and took the struggle
for existence to be but a prophecy of his own struggles with the thugs
of the San Francisco water front; he read Nietzsche and imagined
himself a Superman. Science and philosophy conspired to explain his
career and justify his fiction.

That fiction was a sustained celebration of physical power. Man
was nothing but an animal, life nothing but a brawl, nature as indifferent to man as to the wolf or the shark.

Civilization has spread a veneer over the surface of the soft shelled animal
known as man. It is a very thin veneer. . . . Starve him, let him miss six
meals, and see gape through the veneer the hungry maw of the animal beneath. Get between him and the female of his kind upon whom his mating
instinct is bent, and see his eyes blaze like any angry cat's, hear in his throat
the scream of wild stallions, and watch his fist clench like an orang-outang's.
. . . Touch his silly vanity, which he exalts into high-sounding pride, call
him a liar, and behold the red animal in him that makes a hand clutching

that is quick like the tensing of a tiger's claw, or an eagle's talon, incarnate with desire to rip and destroy.

This was the philosophy, too, of Wolf Larsen, one of the first sadists in American fiction:

I believe that life is a mess. It is like a yeast, a ferment, a thing that moves or may move for a minute, an hour, a year, or a hundred years, but that in the end it will cease to move. The big eat the little, that they may continue to move, the strong eat the weak that they may retain their strength. The lucky eat the most and move the longest, that is all.

It is with this philosophy that London justifies the tortures and beatings that Larsen inflicts upon his crew, and when the inept Humphrey Van Weyden protests that this is a misreading of Darwin, the Superman puts him in his place. Clearly London identifies himself with Wolf Larsen rather than with Humphrey. In a letter he confessed that:

I have always inclined towards Haeckel's position. In fact incline is too weak a word. I am a hopeless materialist. I see the soul as nothing else than the sum of activities of the organism plus personal habits, plus inherited habits, memories, experiences of the organism. I believe that when I am dead I am dead.

All this blood and thunder was designed to portray an elemental and amoral toughness. Yet along with it went an unconquerable romanticism, a romanticism that revealed itself at its worst in the insipid handling of love, and at its best in half-baked socialism that furnished the theme for so many London books. For London was at once a disciple of Marx and Nietzsche, a champion of the proletariat and of the superman. He proved that nature had nothing to do with justice and clamored for justice with a voice of brass. He subscribed to a philosophy which dictated the inexorable triumph of the strong over the weak and advocated a revolution by the weak against the strong. His own life advertised the same contradictions. He described *The People of the Abyss* but had no use for weaklings; he marched with Kelley's army of the unemployed and tried to build himself the most palatial ranch house in the West.

The confusion which permeated most of the naturalistic literature from the nineties well into the new century was similarly disclosed in the pages of Frank Norris. Most gifted and articulate of Zola's

American disciples, Norris was a more skillful and versatile artist than his fellow Californian, but his philosophy was scarcely more mature. He early set himself to combat "false views of life, false characters, false sentiment, false morality, false history, false philosophy, false emotions, false heroism," and his method was to substitute for sentimentalism a tortured toughness no less romantic. "The world of Zola," he had written, "is a world of big things. The enormous, the formidable, the terrible, is what counts," and he tried conscientiously to depict the formidable and the terrible. Like London he was fascinated by the animal in man and portrayed, by preference, the "great blond brute," creature of instincts and impulses. Everywhere in his early novels there is violence and bloodshed and lust, everywhere an almost naïve invocation of the doctrine of the survival of the fittest. The argument of *Vandover and the Brute* is more explicit than anything in London, for Vandover's degeneration into an animal is not spiritual but physical. Yet London himself might have written the words Norris ascribes to Charlie Geary:

Every man for himself—that was his maxim. It might be damned selfish, but it was human nature; the weakest to the wall, the strongest to the front. . . . All life was but a struggle to keep from under those myriad spinning wheels that dashed so close behind. Those were the happiest who were farthest to the front. To lag behind was peril; to fall was to perish; to be ridden down, to be beaten to the dust, to be inexorably crushed and blotted out beneath that myriad of spinning wheels.

Moran of the *Lady Letty,* in the book of that title, is filled with exultation at the discovery that he could kill. "The knowledge filled him with a sense of power that was veritably royal. . . . It was the joy of battle, the horrid exhilaration of killing, the animal of the race, the human brute suddenly aroused." When McTeague tasted blood, "the brute that lay so close to the surface leaped instantly to life, monstrous, not to be resisted." That was the point: the brute in man was not to be resisted. Like the Arctic explorer, Bennett, in *A Man's Woman,* Norris "ignored two thousand years of civilization."

In *The Octopus,* his most ambitious work and his best, the protagonist was a railroad. The book, appearing as Theodore Roosevelt became president, was designed to be the first part of an epic of wheat and to celebrate the vast impersonal forces that control human destinies.

Men were mere nothings, mere animalculae, mere ephemerides that fluttered and fell and were forgotten between dawn and dusk. . . . Force only existed—Force that brought men into the world—Force that crowded them out of it to make way for the succeeding generation—Force that made the wheat grow—Force that garnered it from the soil to give place to the succeeding crops.

Even the railroad was not a product of civilization but a symbol of brute force:

The map was white, and it seemed as if all the color which should have gone to vivify the various counties, towns, and cities marked upon it had been absorbed by that huge sprawling organism, with its ruddy arteries. . . . It was as though the State had been sucked white and colorless, and against this pallid background the red arteries of the monster stood out, swollen with life-blood, reaching out to infinity, gorged to bursting, an excrescence, a gigantic parasite fattening upon the life-blood of an entire commonwealth.

Yet *The Octopus* turned into an attack on the Southern Pacific Railway, a Populist tract, and an argument for Hiram Johnson, and concluded on a note of lyrical romanticism closer by far to Browning than to Haeckel. For it asserted that "the Truth will in the end prevail, and all things surely, inevitably, resistlessly work together for good." In his essay on "The Responsibilities of the Novelist," Norris adjured writers to work "with the pulpit and the universities for the good of the people, proving that power is abused, that the strong grind the faces of the weak." Spencer and Haeckel might have agreed with the description, but the injunction was as much at variance with their philosophy as it was with the logic of naturalism.

In Theodore Dreiser, determinism was less violent but scarcely less confused than in London and Norris. His emphasis was rather on the remorselessness of fate than on its malevolence, on the helplessness of man than on his brutality. His volumes assert more of a mechanical and less of an animalistic interpretation of life, more of Haeckel and Loeb and less of Nietzsche. To Dreiser, man was not a wild animal but a poor fool, and pity intruded itself perversely upon his pages. Like London, Dreiser was obsessed with power, but it was not so much sheer animal power as the more complicated and less amenable power of social and economic machinery. The city rather than the wilderness provided his background, and his characters did not pit their strength against the strength of the sea or the Arctic cold, the shark or the wolf, but against the cunning, greed, and ruthlessness of their fellow men. As the analysis of social forces requires more subtlety than the analysis of natural, there is some advance in maturity here: Frank Cowperwood is never a mere caricature of Mammon as Wolf Larsen is of the Superman, nor do social problems ever yield to the simple solution of the anarchist's bomb.

In his youth, Dreiser had come across Spencer and Haeckel, and he never got over them; *First Principles,* he recalled, blew him to bits, and in the heat of its pages "all that he deemed substantial—man's place in nature, his importance in the universe . . . man's very identity save as an infinitesimal speck of energy" dissolved. Later he was to read Carl Snyder's *World Machine* and Jacques Loeb's "Mechanistic Conception of Life," and these confirmed him in his wintry determinism. The lesson he learned was simple enough; it was that

Spiritually one got nowhere, that there was no hereafter, that one lived and had his being because one had to, and that it was of no importance. Of one's ideals, struggles, deprivations, sorrows and joys, it could only be said that they were chemic compulsions, something which for some inexplicable but unimportant reason responded to and resulted from the hope of pleasure and the fear of pain. Man was a mechanism . . . and a badly and carelessly driven one at that.

Years later Dreiser was to write that "life was too much a welter and play of inscrutable forces to permit . . . any significant comment," but comment he did in one behemoth book after another, energetically and monotonously. His novels furnished an extensive commentary on the social implications of determinism: his stories were all morality plays, his characters all but allegorical figures representing not virtue and vice but power and weaknesss. From *Sister Carrie* (1900) to *An American Tragedy* (1925) the moral is the same: men and women are poor creatures driven by chemical compulsions to act out their folly, fulfill their desires, satisfy their mental and physical appetites.

Neither Sister Carrie nor Jennie Gerhardt are responsible for the mess they make of their lives, nor are their seducers and betrayers responsible in any scientific sense, for they, like their victims, are but creatures of circumstance driven by violent desires which they did not create and cannot control. So Eugene Witla, of *The Genius,* exhausted art and sex and discovered, in the end, that "life was nothing save dark forces moving aimlessly." Cowperwood, of *The Titan,* one of the great figures of American fiction, is, for all his authenticity, but a symbol of force—force in business, politics, and love. As a boy he had watched in fascination a lobster devour a squid, had learned that in nature all things live on each other, and concluded that men were no exception to the universal rule. So he lived on the weakness of men, and of women, and congratulated himself that his life was consistent with the laws of nature. He was a Wolf Larsen in business, politics, and love; his weapons were cunning and corruption rather than fists but none the less natural for that, and his justification, like Wolf's, was that he needed no justification:

He had no consciousness of what is currently known as sin. He never gave a thought to the vast palaver concerning evil which is constantly going on. There were just two faces to the shield of life—strength and weakness. Right and wrong? He did not know about those. They were bound up in metaphysical abstrusities about which he did not care to bother. Good and evil? Those were the toys of clerics, by which they made money. Morality and immorality? He never considered them. But strength and weakness— oh yes! If you had strength you could protect yourself always and be something. If you were weak—pass quickly to the rear and get out of the range of the guns.

Clyde Griffiths, the protagonist of *An American Tragedy,* is a weakling rather than a titan, but the moral of his story is much the same. He, too, is the victim of "bio-chemic compulsions"—of the sexual urge and the no less natural passion for money and social position. It was not an American tragedy that Dreiser told but the tragedy of life itself, and he might better have given it the title which he gave to one of his plays—*The Hand of the Potter.* For he not only records how, in fashioning Clyde Griffiths, the hand of the Potter shook, but asks, like one "of the loquacious Lot"

> All this of Pot and Potter—tell me then,
> Who is the Potter, pray, and who the Pot?

An American Tragedy is Jacques Loeb crossed with Omar Khayyam. And notwithstanding all the palaver about chemic compulsions, it is perhaps Omar Khayyam that is dominant. For, as with London, Norris, and Crane, Dreiser's determination is confused and incoherent. For all his mechanistic determinism, he was never wholly objective, and his novels belong as much to the history of the Progressive movement as to philosophical naturalism. "This world, as we know it," he asked characteristically,

the human race and the accompanying welter of animals and insects, do they not, aside from momentary phases of delight and beauty, often strike you as dull, cruel, useless? Are not the processes by which they are produced or those by which they live stark, relentless, brutal, shameful even?

But what has chemistry to do with such purely subjective concepts as dullness or shame? It is not only Dreiser's vocabulary that betrays him but his themes, for his novels, like those of Zola, constitute as much an indictment of society as a transcript of nature. It is a measure of his despair with that society that he could explain its grossness and its inhumanity only on the theory that men could not, after all, help themselves; it was an indication of his own identification with that society that he tried, nevertheless, through his novels, to paint a picture so revolting that his fellow men might be moved to repudiate it and to imagine a better one.

3

It may seem curious to couple the name of James Branch Cabell with that of Theodore Dreiser, for in everything but philosophy they are profoundly unlike, and Cabell himself has underlined the inadequacies of Dreiser's realism. Where Dreiser was heavy handed and ponderous, Cabell is urbane and polished; where Dreiser's technique is that of the newspaper, cruelly descriptive, Cabell's is that of those Restoration dramatists whom he so inordinately admires, brilliant and impudent; where Dreiser was content with the tumultuous life of the modern city or the chaos of industrialism and finance, Cabell wanders blithely in his dream world of Poictesme or in the world of Litchfield, scarcely less shadowy.

Yet we must not be confused by differences of technique and of subject matter, wide as they are. The reactions of Dreiser and of Cabell to the world in which they were so helplessly lodged were much the same. "It was wonderful to discover America," wrote

Dreiser, "but it would have been more wonderful to lose it," and Cabell found his "country an inadequate place in which to live." It is not in philosophy that Cabell differs from such determinists as London, Norris, and Dreiser but in the impact of that philosophy upon his mind and his art. For he did not indulge in a Promethean protest against a world which he found intolerable but sought fastidiously to escape from it.

If Dreiser derived inspiration from Haeckel, Cabell seems to stem from Santayana. The author of the *Life of Reason,* we must remember, counted himself a thoroughgoing naturalist, and of American philosophers he was perhaps the only one who adjusted himself cheerfully to the new universe which science revealed to the contemplation of men. "My naturalism," Santayana wrote, "is not at all afraid of the latest theories of space, time, or matter: what I understand of them I like, and am ready to believe, for I am a follower of Plato in his doctrine that only knowledge of ideas can be literal and exact whilst practical knowledge is necessarily mythological in form, precisely because its object exists and is external to us." Where he differed most sharply from Royce and James—both of whom were familiar enough with the findings of the physicists—was in his genial acquiescence in the cosmos, in his readiness to take such delight as might come from a contemplation of its beauties, and to

remember that madness is human, that dreams have their springs in the depths of human nature; and that the illusion they cause may be kindly and even gloriously dispelled by showing what the solid truth was which they expressed allegorically. Why should one be angry with dreams, with myth, with allegory, with madness? We must not kill the mind, as some rationalists do, in trying to cure it. The life of reason, as I conceive it, is simply the dreaming mind becoming coherent, devising symbols and methods . . . by which it may fitly survive its own career.

Like Santayana, Cabell escapes from the world of material things, which seems repulsive, into a world of imagination and of dreams, and asserts jauntily that man's dreams are as real and as significant as his mundane life—and incomparably more agreeable. Like Santayana, he has found it possible to be happy "in human ignorance mitigated by pictures, for it yields practical security and poetic beauty." For life itself, Cabell submits, the life of even the best of men, is not tolerable. "No one on the preferable side of Bedlam." he wrote, "wishes to be reminded of what we are in actuality," for "one moment of clear vision as to man's plight in the universe would be quite sufficient to set the most philosophic gibbering." Man, with his puny strivings, his vanities and conceits, his incessant pursuit of the trivial, his vulgar concern for material things, his prosaic contentment with his shabby lot, his blindness to the cruelty, the vileness, and the dullness of life, is an object either of horror or of humor. He is "a parasite infesting the epidermis of a midge among planets"; he is "an ape, reft of his tail and grown rusty at climbing, who has reeled blunderingly from mystery to mystery with pathetic makeshifts, not understanding anything, greedy in all desires, and always honeycombed with poltroonery." Yet he is, too, a "maimed god," privileged to dream greatly, and ready "to give all and to die fighting" for the sake of his dream.

So Cabell is hot for romance—romance which may be just as near some unattainable truth as what we call reality. Who, after all, wants a transcript of daily life, scarcely of such excellence or nobility as to justify literary rehearsal? Who wants to meet in fiction, or in imagination, the dullards whom he of necessity meets every day? As Cabell expounds it to his alter ego, John Charteris:

Living is a drab transaction, a concatenation of unimportant events; man is impotent and aimless; beauty, and indeed all the fine things which you desiderate in literature—and in your personal existence . . . are nowhere attainable save in imagination. To the problem of living romance propounds the only possible answer, which is, not understanding, but escape. And the method of that escape is, . . . the creation of a pleasing dream, which will somehow engender a reality as lovely. So romance in literature invests its "dynamic illusions" . . . to the sole end that mankind may play Peter Ibbetson upon a cosmic scale. (*Beyond Life*, p. 327)

It is the dreams that count. In dreams alone can man attain to something approaching dignity and beauty, in dreams alone redress the balance of real life. With Santayana, Cabell might say:

> The crown of olive let another wear;
> It is my crown to mock the runner's heat
> With gentle wonder and with laughter sweet.

So in a score of novels, intricately contrived, subtle, allusive, and precious, Cabell has projected his characters into a gossamer world of dreams. They leave behind them their humdrum world of business or of housekeeping or of dull wives and disport themselves in the magic land of Poictesme, where they are permitted to drink deeply of the wisdom of the ages, to enjoy wonderful adventures, to display admirable gallantry. They are transformed, these Jurgens and Florians and Felix Kennastons—but not wholly transformed: they are still creatures of earth, still, even when they venture onto the High Places, honeycombed with poltroonery. For the beauty they find remains elusive, their gallantry turns too easily into unlovely passion, adventures peter out, and wisdom mocks them; even their dreams prove too much for them. It is the very cream of the jest not that dreams are unattainable but that once attained they are so disappointing. Jurgen, after all, gives up the beauty and the pleasures that are his for the taking and returns to his shrew and his pawnshop.

So it is vanity that makes men dream, and the dream is vanity. Romance, love, gallantry, beauty, all these notions have their origin in man's unconquerable vanity, and all are equally vain except, perhaps, to assuage a fleeting moment. The dream itself is an illusion and so, too, the hope of escape through dreams. "To submit is the great lesson . . . to submit, without dreaming any more . . . without either understanding or repining, and without demanding of life too much of beauty or of holiness."

All this is titillating rather than convincing, and there is no illusion more deceptive than the illusion that Cabell's urbanity conceals some profound philosophy. Cabell is caught in the dilemma that confounds most of the determinists, namely that his reaction from determinism is subjective and romantic. For it is not clear how the concepts of vanity or of sophistication differ from the concepts of romance or of beauty. To that cosmos in which man is insignificant, what man calls dreams and what man calls reality are equally legitimate or illegitimate, the cloak-and-dagger romance which Cabell scorns or the esoteric romance in which he indulges equally the product of some fortuitous concatenation of atoms. If there is no final escape in dreams, there is no final escape in submission, for the concept of submission is as subjective as the concept of dreaming.

CHAPTER VII

The Cult of the Irrational

I

"FINDING THEIR intelligence enslaved," wrote George Santayana in that remarkable essay on the "Intellectual Temper of the Age" which indicted alike evolution and pragmatism, determinism and irrationalism, "our contemporaries supposed that intelligence is essentially servile; instead of freeing it, they try to elude it. Not free enough themselves morally . . . they cannot think of rising to a detached contemplation of earthly things, and of life itself and evolution; they revert rather to sensibility, and seek some by-path of instinct or dramatic sympathy in which to wander. Having no stomach for the ultimate, they burrow themselves downwards towards the primitive." It was a just indictment of the irrationalists and the primitivists, of that whole school of thought and emotion represented variously by Sherwood Anderson and Ernest Hemingway, Gertrude Stein and Ezra Pound, Henry Adams and Robinson Jeffers.

In a broad way, this school subscribed to the philosophy which commanded the allegiance of London, Norris, Crane, and Dreiser and arrived at much the same conclusions, but the inspiration was somewhat different. Dreiser, whose *An American Tragedy* appeared in 1925, was probably the last of the naturalists whose determinism stemmed from Darwin and Haeckel, and the last, too, who ostentatiously confessed the influence of Nietzsche. Even as he was hammering out his iron novels, a new school of poets and novelists, who owed allegiance to Vienna rather than to Down, began to formulate a variation on Darwinian determinism. Man, as they dissected him, was still the creature of uncontrollable forces, but the forces which they recognized as sovereign were not outside but within man. Not the stars in their courses but the glands in their secretions fixed the destiny of men. Darwin and Haeckel had rejected the sovereignty of reason; Freud, Pavlov, and Jung, whose praises the new school sang, rejected its very existence and placed unreason upon the throne.

The attack upon reason, meaning, coherence, normality, grammar, and morality was the distinguishing characteristic of this new school of literature. Romanticism had challenged rationalism, and from that defiant gesture conservatives like W. C. Brownell, humanists like Irving Babbitt, and classicists like Paul Elmer More were to date the beginning of chaos while, with mounting pathos, they tried to recall a heedless generation to ethical and artistic standards that had stood the test of time. The Transcendentalists had exalted intuition over logic, insisting with Pascal that the heart has its reasons which reason does not know, and while practically the Transcendentalists observed ethical standards with utmost scrupulousness, philosophically they rejected them. Darwinian biology had confounded free will, and the new physics had unhinged the firmament itself. Yet reason had survived all these, and the rules of logic and of grammar had held fast. Poe had indulged in symbolism, but he had been, too, the creator of the scientific tale of mystery; Emerson had appealed to a higher law than that framed in the laboratory but only to enhance the dignity of man. Even those novelists who read in Haeckel or Jacques Loeb the doom of free will and of progressive evolution were able to report their surrender in coherent and logical terms.

Not so the novelists and poets of what may, for convenience, be called the psychological school—Sherwood Anderson and Waldo Frank, Evelyn Scott and Gertrude Stein, E. E. Cummings and William Faulkner, Hart Crane and Ezra Pound, Wallace Stevens and Conrad Aiken, and a host of others equally abandoned to irrationality. For the new attack upon reason was more insidious than any that had heretofore been launched. It confronted man not with the implacable forces of Nature but with the uncontrollable forces of human nature. It left him not the victim of circumstances or environment but of vagrant impulses, restless instincts, and haphazard desires, of neuroses, phobias, and conditioned reflexes that made a mockery of everything that he had formerly called mind and spirit.

The sources of the new irrationality were largely modern and exclusively European, and it is suggestive that where American literature was most derivative it was least articulate and where it was least mature it was most decadent. It owed something to the French—to the Symbolist poets, Mallarmé, Verlaine, Rimbaud, Valéry, Laforgue, and Paul Fort, to critics like Rémy de Gourmont and philosophers like Henri Bergson with his apotheosis of the *élan vital,* to novelists like André Gide and, above all, Marcel Proust. It owed more to Freud of Vienna and Jung of Zurich and the Russian Pavlov who made the western world not only conscious but self-conscious of the subconscious. It owed most of all—doubtless through the accident of language—to the philosophers, poets, and novelists from the British Isles: pioneers in the scientific study of the psychology of sex like Edward Carpenter and the magisterial Havelock Ellis; novelists like the indefatigable Dorothy Richardson and the brilliant Aldous Huxley and the brooding D. H. Lawrence and Virginia Woolf, not only practitioner but critic; the Irish experimentalists, William Butler Yeats and George Moore and Oscar Wilde and, above all, James Joyce, most successful of all those who floated their literary barks down the stream of consciousness.

What were the stigmata—for we can scarcely use the term principles for a persuasion that rejected the very concept of principle—of the new school? First, the rejection—on pseudoscientific grounds—of reason, meaning, normality, morality, continuity, and coherence, the rejection of civilization itself as eccentric and decadent. Second, a passionate interest in the subconscious and the unconscious and an enthusiasm for emotion rather than thought, instinct rather than reason, anarchy rather than discipline. Third, an obsession with sex, especially in its abnormal manifestations, as the most powerful and pervasive of all the instincts and the interpretation of all conduct in terms of sex. Fourth, a weakness for the primitive, for primitive people such as Africans, Indians, peasants, and children, for primitive emotions and activities—eating, drinking, sleeping, fighting, making love—and closely connected with this a predilection for violence in all forms. Fifth, the unqualified repudiation of all orthodox moral standards, all conformities and conventions, and acquiescence in a perverse amorality in which submission to instincts became the highest virtue. And, finally, the formulation of a new language and a new grammar to express more faithfully the fitful impulses emanating from the subconscious.

To Plato, the doctrine that there was "no knowing and no use in seeking to know what we do not know" was but "idle fancy," and to Henry Adams the "idea that he must give up, that he must meet his

Creator with the admission that creation had taught him nothing"
seemed "sheer senility." But the psychological school had nothing
but enthusiasm for idle fancy and held all that passed for learning as
but the product of inheritance and infant experience. Its characters
knew nothing but what their bodies told them. Consciousness was
merely the by-product of the unconscious, and the unconscious, as
Joad has put it, "a restless sea of instinct and impulse, a sea agitated
by gusts of libido, swept by waves of desires, threaded by currents of
urge and drive." Thought was but a phantasmagoria, the will but an
illusion, the values that men cherished but the sublimation of unconscious desires, and all the noble fabric of ethics and law but a compensation for instinctual renunciations.

Of all the impulses that animated men, the sexual was the most
powerful, and the new school of literature was drenched in sex.
Henry Adams had complained that "American art, like the American
language and American education, was as far as possible, sexless,"
and, in its obvious meaning, the generalization applied equally to
American literature from Cooper to Howells. With Crane and Norris
and Dreiser, the barriers were down, but it was not until after Freud's
first visit to America in 1909 that sex became a literary obsession. In
the fantasies of the novelists, gamekeepers ceased to keep game,
artists abandoned their paintpots, and businessmen fled their desks,
all to indulge an insatiable curiosity. Paris became a symbol and
Greenwich Village a synonym for nameless orgies; Americans unable
to admire André Gide from attics on the Left Bank imitated him
from attics in Bank Street. Reticence became prudery, modesty hypocrisy, and virginity a reproach.

Sex, Adams had added, speaking for his own Victorian generation,
"was sin. In any previous age, sex was strength." Freud, and perhaps
Margaret Sanger, wiped from sex the stain of sin, but none who read
the novels of Sherwood Anderson, Waldo Frank, or Ludwig Lewisohn, the poetry of Conrad Aiken, William Ellery Leonard, or Robinson Jeffers, or the plays of Eugene O'Neill could suppose that under
the new dispensation sex was strength. It was, on the contrary, a fury,
a madness, a misery; certainly the school that took over the term
"sublimation" knew nothing of the sublime. That sex is the well-
spring of all motives and impulses and dominates thought and conduct, was taken for granted, yet it was, curiously enough, in its physio-
logical rather than in its psychological character that sex was most

elaborately explored. Romance was repudiated, and love took on purely physical connotations. Expert in anatomy and biology, it was precisely in the realms of psychology—their private hunting ground —that the Freudian novelists proved weakest. Certainly they discovered little that Hawthorne had not guessed or that, in their own way, Henry James, Willa Cather, and Edwin Arlington Robinson did not know.

An essential part of the repudiation of reason was the rejection of the concept of normality, for what was called normal was merely what escaped the repressions and inhibitions imposed by Freud's "censors." To be sure, if normality was abandoned, abnormality became meaningless, but those who repudiated logic were untroubled by this elementary confusion. The abnormal was not only more important than the normal, it was, it appeared, more interesting, and a thousand novels and poems celebrated its eccentric manifestations. The line between sanity and insanity was blurred, and complexes, neuroses, and phobias took on dignity. Of all abnormalities, those caused by or related to sex were the most sensational, and Havelock Ellis and Krafft-Ebing were to the new school of novelists what Darwin and Spencer had been to their predecessors. Soon every novelist and playwright who hoped for a popular audience was salting his pages with complexes and perversions, until those who neglected the census reports might suppose that romantic love and marriage had ceased.

To the psychological novelists, perversion was untainted by immorality, for the concept of immorality was itself but one of the inhibitions which were best abandoned. The men and women who indulge their natural instincts so riotously in the pages of Faulkner, Caldwell, Farrell, and Hemingway, of Waldo Frank, Evelyn Scott, and Eugene O'Neill, are as amoral as animals. With them, the only unpardonable sin—if the word itself can be admitted—is repression, and the highest virtue self-expression. And by self-expression is meant the jaunty yielding to all impulses, especially the impulse to drink, to love, and to fight. Where these impulses take vagrant form, as in so much of Faulkner and Hergesheimer, or where they take violent form, as in Hemingway, Caldwell, and O'Neill, the experience is supposed to be purifying. Impulses are, after all, more to be trusted than reason, and those who yield to them more admirable than those who repress them. Not only private but social morality is repudiated:

the characters who people the lurid pages of these novelists and poets concern themselves not with consequences, nor has society, apparently, more than a casual interest in their misconduct.

Since those who indulged their impulses were more admirable than those who repressed them, the psychological school was enchanted with the primitive. "Our so-called civilization," Freud had written, "is itself to blame for a great part of our misery, and we should be happier if we were to give it up and go back to primitive conditions." Faulkner and Caldwell, Hemingway and O'Neill, and a dozen others were ready enough to give it up, though it cannot be said that they achieved happiness in the process. "I was not made for thinking," cried Frederic Henry of *Farewell to Arms,* "I was made to eat. My God, yes. Eat and drink and sleep with Catherine." Add fight, and it was pretty much the code of the primitivists. "For a long time," Sherwood Anderson asserted, "I have believed that crudity is an inevitable quality in the production of a really significant American literature." Inevitable or not, it was forthcoming, both in the delineation of what passed for character and the construction of what served as plot. As it was the reactions of the body rather than the workings of the mind that interested this school most, it confined itself as far as possible to characters with the mentality of the Jukes and the Kallikaks: the hunters, bullfighters, pugilists, and killers of Hemingway's stories, the subhuman louts who swarm through the pages of Faulkner's *Light in August* and *The Hamlet,* the Jecter Lesters of *Tobacco Road* and the Ty-Tys and Darling Jills and Plutos of *God's Little Acre,* O'Neill's Anna Christie and Emperor Jones, the frustrated John Webster of Anderson's *Many Marriages,* and the Negroes of *Dark Laughter* and of Gertrude Stein's *Three Lives.* As with Rimbaud and Gide, there was a lively appreciation of the Negro, but where an earlier romanticism had made him a symbol of happiness and loyalty, primitivism made him a symbol of unrepressed passion. Plots came to be as confused and as crude as the characters: a series of kaleidoscopic scenes, or a stream of consciousness, took the place of narrative.

It was the distinguishing characteristic of the stream of consciousness that it was unselective. The rejection of reason, indeed, imposed upon the psychological school the duty or the necessity of recording the incoherent and the trivial, and never did scholars perform duty more faithfully. To a philosophy which recognized no standard of values, the most casual gesture, the most vagrant thought, was as significant as the heroic deed or the noble word.

"Let us record the atoms as they fall upon the mind in the order in which they fall," wrote Virginia Woolf in *The Common Reader*. "Let us trace the pattern, however disconnected and incoherent in appearance, which each sight or incident scores upon the consciousness. Let us not take it for granted that life exists more fully in what is commonly thought big than in what is commonly thought small." If no American charted the stream of consciousness as skillfully as Marcel Proust or James Joyce or Virginia Woolf herself, there were a number who dove into it successfully enough: Faulkner in *As I Lay Dying* and *The Sound and the Fury*, E. E. Cummings in *The Enormous Room*, Evelyn Scott in *The Narrow House*, and Conrad Aiken in *Blue Voyage*.

It was Aiken who furnished a formula for the school that compares favorably with that furnished by T. S. Eliot in "Portrait of a Lady":

> Or as the cloud does on the northeast wind—
> Fluent and formless; or as the tree that withers,
> What are we made of, strumpet, but of these?
> Nothing. We are the sum of all these accidents—
> Compounded all our days of idiot trifles,—
> The this, the that, the other, and the next;
> What x or y said, or old uncle thought;
> Whether it rained or not, and at what hour;
> Whether the pudding had two eggs or three,
> And those we loved were ladies . . .
>
> (*Preludes for Memnon*)

And it was Aiken, too, who through William Demarest of *Blue Voyage* passed judgment on what he and his school were doing:

What if, in choosing this literary method, this deliberate indulgence in the prolix and the fragmentary, I merely show myself at the mercy of a personal weakness which is not universal, or ever likely to be. . . . I frequently suspect that I am nothing on earth but a case of dementia praecox, manqué or arrested. Isn't all this passion for aspects and qualifications and relativities a clear enough symptom of schizophrenia?

A new language and a new grammar were required to do justice to the impulses of the unconscious just as new combinations of light and color and of sound were necessary to express insurgent ideas in art and music. The formulation of this new language—which can be deciphered best in Joyce's *Ulysses* or *Finnegan's Wake*—was an attempt to make unintelligibility articulate, to make language itself a more supple instrument, to break through the molds of convention, and to achieve a highly intellectualized—and exclusive—obscurity: no one who studies the career of Ezra Pound can doubt that the search for obscurity was related to hatred of democracy. Words were used not to convey meaning but to suggest moods and impulses or were given entirely arbitrary meanings. "When I used a word," said Humpty Dumpty, "it means just what I choose it to mean," and everywhere in this school there was an unacknowledged debt to Lewis Carroll. What Aiken wrote of John Gould Fletcher's *Scepticisms* might be applied to this whole body of literature:

It is a sort of absolute poetry of detached waver and brilliance, a beautiful flowering of language alone, a parathenogenesis, as if language were fertilized by itself rather than by thought or feeling. Remove the magic of phrase and sound, and there is nothing left; no thread of continuity, no relation between one page and the next, no thought, no story, no emotion.

And Sherwood Anderson's reaction to Gertrude Stein's *Tender Buttons* was much the same. "How it excited me," he recalled, "here was something dealing with words separated from sense."

The Imagists had led the way with their polyphonic prose, but Imagism soon proved too conventional, and some of its earliest adherents, like Ezra Pound, revolted into more violent experimentation. Of all American disciples of the cult of unintelligibility, Pound was the most recondite, Pound to whom T. S. Eliot so appropriately dedicated *The Waste Land*. Open the famous *Cantos* at random (and why not?) and we find an infallible combination of obscurity and erudition, both calculated, both false.

Where Pound strove for intricacy, Gertrude Stein yearned for simplicity, yet she, too, was erudite and complex. She had studied psychology with William James, experimented with automatic writing, was familiar with the philosophy of Bergson and the painting of Picasso; she was a friend and patron to scores of American expatriates who swarmed across the Left Bank in the twenties, and to Hemingway and Anderson and Van Vechten and Wallace Stevens and others she was an inspiration. Oxford and Cambridge heard her gladly when she discoursed on "Composition as Explanation," and students at the University of Chicago could rejoice at her exposition of the *Geographical History of America*. She dabbled in primitivism, she experimented with the association of words and sound, she related literature to the art of the motion picture; she was original and creative and could be sincere.

The cult of irrationality was, from the beginning, doomed to self-destruction, for no literature built upon the quagmire of futility can survive. The attack upon reason, which flourished so furiously in the second and third decades of the century, was designed to pronounce the ultimate degradation of man—a degradation which reduced man, in the end, to gibbering. It carried to logical conclusion the findings of the naturalists and the determinists and revealed, more dramatically than any other inquiry, the bankruptcy of determinism. It was nihilism, but it was nihilism which proved its impotence by its very proclamation. It was the palpable insincerity of the revolt against reason which was, in the end, its most encouraging feature, for revolt is an act of will—even of free will—and those writers who engage in it confess their inconsistency. They confess faith in their own reason by the act of composition, social consciousness by their appeal for a hearing, and recognition of a moral order by the establishment of standards, however eccentric, and the insistence upon values, however esoteric.

2

Robinson Jeffers is peculiarly the victim of this paradox, though his statement of it is more eloquent and more dignified than that of most of the irrationalists, as his logic—or his illogic—is more thorough. The most uncompromisingly scientific of the literary spokesmen of determinism, Jeffers is, at the same time, the most romantic. Trained to medicine, familiar with psychiatry, biology, geology, and physics, living, by choice, close to nature and acknowledging no obligation but to nature, his affluent poetry is a scientific as well as a philosophical commentary on the life of man.

So completely does nature fill his poetic vision that man is scarcely admitted even as a part of nature. The men and women who infect his pages are so vile and perverse that they seem to contaminate nature herself. For aeons nature did not know man, and in a short time she will forget the stain he has put upon her:

I believe this hurt will be healed
Some age of time after mankind has died,
Then the sun will say, "What ailed me a moment" and resume
The old soulless triumph, and the iron and stone earth
With confident inorganic glory obliterate
Her ruins and fossils . . . After some million
Courses around the sun her sadness may pass.

(Margrave)

For man is born to pain, as are all living things, but man alone adds moral depravity to physical torture: human beings alone are inhuman. "Lord God," Jeffers prays,

Exterminate
The race of man. For man only in the world, except a few kinds of insect,
   is essentially cruel.
Therefore slay also these if you will: the driver ant,
And the slave-maker ant, and the slick wasp
That paralyzes living meat for her brood: but first
The human race.

("The Inhumanist," The Double Axe)

From *Tamar* to *The Double Axe* Jeffers spreads before us such a pageant of violence, cruelty, bloodshed, depravity, and perversion as we have not heretofore encountered in our literature—not even in Faulkner or Caldwell. He violates our innocence and confounds our philosophy with a picture of unmitigated evil, or of evil mitigated only by endurance. Life is one long agony of pain, interrupted by pleasure that is fleeting and ecstasy that turns upon us and wounds us:

. . . We know what life is:
That mercy's weakness, and honesty
The simple fear of detection; and beauty, pain,
And love, a furious longing to join the sewers of two bodies
That's how God made us. . . .

Only Nature is worthy of our contemplation, for only Nature has beauty and endurance:

A lion has dignity,
So has a hawk; even a barnyard bull or common whipped horse has a kind
   of grace; but these
Peeled apes teetering on their back legs,
Male and female,

Snickering with little shames, pleasures and wisecracks,
Or howling horror: and two million of them:
As for that, no. And take notice, their minds are as ludicrous
As their bodies and societies.

(The Double Axe)

The mountains, the sea, granite boulders, the redwood and the
cypress trees, the eagle and the hawk—give your heart to these, says
Jeffers, but not to men. It is the Lovely Rock he praises, or

> . . . the wild rock coast . . . and the reckless wind
> In the beaten trees and the gaunt booming crashes
> Of breakers under the rocks . . .

And from Hawk Tower, built by his own hands of granite boulders,
he looks out over "the great shed of the mountain shot in bronze
folds" and the "sea like a blue steel breakless to Asia."

What we have here, to be sure, is a scientific version of the Christian view where every prospect pleases and only man is vile. And
for all his desperate repudiation of orthodox religion, there is a strain
of religious mysticism in Jeffers. He, too, lifts up his eyes unto the
hills from whence cometh his help; he confesses, on behalf of ruined
man, that we have followed too much the devices and desires of our
own hearts and there is no health in us. The mortal flaw, the fatal
stain, is introversion—"man regarding man exclusively, founding
his values, desires, his picture of the universe, all on his own humanity." Thus he tells us that it is the purpose of the "Women at
Point Sur" to show that

there is no health for the individual whose attention is taken up with his
own mind and processes; equally there is no health for the society that is
always introverted on its own members, as ours becomes more and more,
the interest engaged inward in love and hatred, companionship and competition.

And it is as a symbol of this suicidal introversion that he uses incest
again and again.

Yet for all his scientific and psychiatric vocabulary, Jeffers lingers
in the romantic tradition, closer to Wordsworth and Arnold than
to Haeckel or even to Freud and Jung, whose books, we are assured,
adorn his shelves. What could be more romantic than this passion
for the mountains and the sea and for granite boulders? For to im-

partial nature the loftiest peak of the Sierras is no nobler than a ditch, or the heaving Pacific than a stagnant pool, and in the long catalogue of time Hawk Tower will have no more permanence than a soap bubble. So, too, with the habit of ascribing dignity and no-bility to birds and beasts; the concepts themselves are but tributes to man. Mankind, says Jeffers, has turned inward, and is corrupt. But what more shameless conceit than to ascribe human values to the works of nature, what more extreme introversion than to subject the universe to man's secular judgment?

Romantic though he is, Jeffers does not permit himself the recourse of earlier romantics, of Shelley whom he imitates or Arnold whom he recalls. There is no room in his cosmic philosophy either for Promethean defiance or for escape. Death alone can solace man, death and annihilation and the assurance that this is the fortunate destiny of all living things. Thus, musing at Shakespeare's Grave:

> . . . He wanted quietness.
> He had tasted enough life in his time
> To stuff a thousand; he wanted not to swim wide
> In waters, nor wander the enormous air,
> Nor grow into grass, enter through the mouths of cattle
> The bodies of lusty women and warriors,
> But all be finished. He knew it feelingly; the game
> Of the whirling circles had become tiresome.

Or Tamar, more bluntly, "Only that I want death. You lie if you think another thing."

This is nihilism, and it is a logical conclusion to scientific de-terminism, its consistency flawed only by the subjective view of na-ture that permeates every line and—it must be added—by the par-ticular inspiration for the outbursts of despair. Thus, apropos the American participation in the second World War—Nazi guilt gave him no concern—Jeffers tells us that

> . . . The whole human race ought to be scrapped and is on the way to it;
>   ground like fish-meal for soil-food.
> What does the vast and rushing drama of the universe, seas, rocks, condor-
>   winged storms, icy-fiery galaxies,
> The flaming and whirling universe like a handful of gems falling down a
>   dark well,
> Want clowns for?

("The Inhumanist," *The Double Axe*)

With Jeffers, the philosophical reaction to the world of science opened up first by Darwin came full circle. Man, the last born of nature's long travail, was seen not as her chiefest glory but as her most cruel blunder, because having endowed man with the critical faculty, she enabled him to realize the futility and horror of his existence.

3

That man was one of nature's blunders was, to many of the determinists, a literary conceit; sometimes, one suspects, the importance of the doctrine was not unrelated to its availability for literary exploitation. To Henry Adams it was an urgent scientific fact. Where London or Dreiser invoked the doctrine as an explanation of what theologians called evil, where Santayana and Cabell found in it justification for escape to a better world of the imagination, where Jeffers was seduced by it to embrace lovely and soothing death, where the Freudians and the Behaviorists found in it an invitation to self-indulgence, Adams wrestled courageously with its implications to society and to history.

Courage is not the word most commonly associated with the frail recluse of Lafayette Square, and some critics, exhausted by his paradoxes, have thought him pretentious and affected. Wendell Holmes, who had known him in Cambridge, used to take tea with him in the great house that Richardson had built for him on Lafayette Square, but after a time he stayed away. He was tired, he said, of death and ashes, he who had ceased asking the cosmos to explain itself to him. He was not without justification, for he felt the years closing in on him, and there were too many books unread, too many experiences untasted; yet the acerbity of the phrase was uncalled for. A desperate pessimism haunted Adams, but the pessimism which he revealed to his friends was something of a pose, and affection enabled most of them to penetrate beneath the pose. For while philosophically Adams' determinism went deeper than that of almost any of his contemporaries, it was at the same time more robust and less personal than with most of those who paraded it in print—and this notwithstanding the ostentatious withdrawal from public life and the concentration on that autobiography which has been the delight and despair of students for a generation.

For Adams was not content with a merely private reaction to the instruction of the scientists nor yet with escape, desperate though his need was. He was, for all his pose of aloofness, deeply concerned with his society and with the country to which his family had contributed so generously. For years he labored prodigiously to illuminate the history of that country and the character of its people, and only he was dissatisfied with the result. Science played him a scurvy trick in presenting its findings after he had formulated his answers. He might have ignored it or left it to others to make the necessary accommodations; instead he was prepared to scrap all that he had written and start over again. For

to the tired student the idea that he must give it up seemed sheer senility. As long as he could whisper he would go on as he had begun, bluntly refusing to meet his Creator with the admission that creation had taught him nothing. . . . Every man with self-respect enough to become effective, if only as a machine, has had to account to himself for himself somehow, and to invent a formula of his own for his own universe, if the standard formulas failed. (*Education*, p. 472)

It was no pose that persuaded this old man, weary and shattered, to tramp the corridors of expositions, to pore over the reports of the Smithsonian Institution, to wrestle with French and German treatises on geology, biology, mathematics, and atomic physics, in a search for a formula. Those who have been misled by the mocking note in his letters or the seeming cynicism of his autobiography, profoundly mistake his character. There was perverseness, to be sure, and some Yankee humor, but no American of his generation embarked more earnestly on the search for truth or labored more disinterestedly to rationalize history into a science. "A historical formula that should satisfy the conditions of the stellar universe," he confessed, "weighed heavily on his mind."

Certainly he had paid his debt to the other kind of history, arranging in volume after volume "such facts as seemed sure, in such order as seemed rigorously consequent," in order "to fix for a familiar moment a necessary sequence of human movement." *The History of the United States during the Administrations of Jefferson and Madison* was, by universal consent, a masterpiece. Everyone agreed that it was good history, but Adams found himself quite unable to say just what it was good for. It was good for facts, to be sure, but he confessed that "I never loved or taught facts, if I could help it, having that antipathy to facts which only idiots and philosophers attain." It was good for what it told of the American character and for what it predicted of the American future, but that character might change and the predictions be invalidated by science. It was good for the purposes of philosophy insofar as it "fixed a sequence of human movement"; but Adams came to doubt that it was a necessary sequence and concluded that "the sequence of men led to nothing, and that the sequence of their society could lead no further, while the mere sequence of time was artificial, and the sequence of thought was chaos."

At no time had Adams ever been an optimist—heredity could not be so easily renounced—yet his histories and biographies were drenched in the atmosphere of Victorian liberalism. "He had begun as the confident child of Darwin and Lyell" and had "entered gaily the door of the glacial epoch, and had surveyed a universe of unities and uniformities." It did not seem incongruous, then, to interpret history as politics and diplomacy or to ascribe to statesmen some influence on the course of events. And though Jefferson was but a dubious advance over John Adams, and Jackson a disorderly retreat from John Quincy Adams, there seemed no conclusive reason to suppose that American society might not, in the end, justify the hazardous experiment upon which it had embarked. That, at least, was the conclusion of the famous last chapter of the *History*. But the geology of Lyell and the biology of Darwin—together with the interpretations Herbert Spencer had read into them—were repudiated, and by the turn of the century Adams had put this earlier, more simple, and more innocent version of history behind him and had "entered a far vaster universe, where all the old roads ran about in every direction, overrunning, dividing, subdividing, stopping abruptly, vanishing slowly, with side-paths that led nowhere, and sequences that could not be proved." The new science made all orthodox history an anachronism and transformed his own stately volumes into a monument—he would have said a sepulcher—for it dictated a revolution not only in the character of the nation, but in the interpretation of that character. "My country in 1900," he wrote,

is something totally different from my own country in 1860. I am wholly a stranger in it. Neither I, nor anyone else, understands it. The turning of a nebula into a star may somewhat resemble the change. All I can see is that it is one of compression, concentration, and consequent development of terrific energy, represented not by souls, but by coal and iron and steam. (*Letters, 1892–1918*, p. 279)

The education to which Henry Adams had been subjected—and to which he had contributed at Harvard and through his books—was confounded by the spectacle which science revealed:

The child born in 1900 would . . . be born into a new world which would be not a unity but a multiple. Adams tried to imagine it, and an education that would fit it. He found himself in a land where no one had ever penetrated before; where order was an accidental relation obnoxious to nature; artificial compulsion imposed on motion; against which every free energy of the universe revolted; and which, being merely occasional, resolved itself back into anarchy at last. He could not deny that the law of the new multiverse explained much that had been most obscure . . . but the staggering problem was the outlook ahead into the despotism of artificial order which nature abhorred. The physicists had a phrase for it, unintelligible to the vulgar: "All that we win is a battle—lost in advance—with the irreversible phenomena in the background of nature." (*Education*, pp. 457–458)

It was, in short, force alone that counted. And it was the business of the historian to follow the track of energy wherever it led. Nothing more could be expected from the kind of history represented by the *Jefferson and Madison:* "the future of thought, and therefore of History, lies in the hands of the physicists, and . . . the historian must seek his education in the world of mathematical physics."

So, abandoning the sequence of time and of thought, Adams turned to the sequence of force and attempted to elaborate a formula which would bring human history within the scope of the organic law of the universe. And the law whose constitutionality he recognized was not that of progressive evolution, laid down by Darwin and Spencer, but that of the degradation of energy, formulated by Lord Kelvin, Herman von Helmholtz, and Louis Charles Saporta. "For human purposes," he wrote in his *Letter to American Teachers of History*, "whatever does work is a form of energy, and since historians exist only to recount and sum up the work that society has done . . . they will, if they obey the physical law, hold that society does work by degrading its energies."

The law of the degradation or dissipation of energy had many ramifications and was supported by what seemed to Adams an impressive array of scientific data; from those early years when he had hobnobbed with Sir Charles Lyell and with the *Pteraspis,* Adams had fancied himself a scientist. Those who will can read the evidence and ponder the conclusions as set forth with uncharacteristic grimness in the *Letter* and the *Rule of Phase Applied to History;* the argument, for all its curious mathematical formulas, is simple enough. The second law of thermodynamics announced that energy was constantly being expended without being replaced. The idea of progress, therefore, was a delusion, and the evidence customarily submitted to substantiate the idea sustained, instead, a very different conclusion. Civilization itself had been brought about by the operation of the law of entropy—the dissipation of energy by the constant degradation of its vital power. Society, as an organism, is subject to this law precisely like any other organism and faces therefore the certainty of running down until at last total stagnation is reached. The period of stagnation, Adams continued, is not in some infinite future but in the present. In the first quarter of the twentieth century, thought "would reach the limit of its possibilities," and the honest historian might logically "treat the history of modern Europe and America as a typical example of energies indicating degradation with headlong rapidity towards inevitable death." Already, Adams concluded, "History and Sociology gasp for breath."

Certainly History would gasp for breath if she were required to live in this rarefied scientific air. Perhaps the safest commentary that can be made on this thesis is that which Adams himself hazarded in his *Education:* "Historians," he had observed, "have got into far too much trouble by following schools of theology in their efforts to enlarge their synthesis, that they should willingly repeat the process in science. For human purposes a point must always be soon reached where larger synthesis is suicide."

Fortunately Adams had not completely subjugated history to physics nor followed his admonition that "silence is best." In those two books which must always be counted his peculiar triumph, *Mont-Saint-Michel and Chartres* and *The Education of Henry Adams,* he attempted to illustrate the theory of the drift from unity to multiplicity in more familiar terms:

Any schoolboy [he wrote] could see that man as a force must be measured by motion, from a fixed point. Psychology helped here by suggesting a unit —the point of history when man held the highest idea of himself as a unit in a unified universe. Eight or ten years of study had led Adams to think he might use the century 1150–1250, expressed in Amiens Cathedral and the Works of Thomas Aquinas, as the unit from which he might measure motion down to his own time. . . . From that point he proposed to fix a position for himself, which he could label "The Education of Henry Adams: a Study of Twentieth-Century Multiplicity." With the help of these two points of relation, he hoped to project his lines forward and backward indefinitely.

The *Mont-Saint-Michel* is in many ways a more moving book, perhaps a more profound one, than the *Education*. But its relevance to twentieth-century America was, designedly, by way of contrast, and medievalists have insisted that it throws more light on Henry Adams than on Thomas Aquinas. The *Education,* however, is clearly relevant to our inquiry, for it is not only the most successful but almost the only attempt to trace the impact of scientific ideas upon the course of modern American history. The method, to be sure, is allusive, discursive, and subtle, yet Adams was right in feeling that he himself furnished the most convenient "spool on which to wind the thread of history without breaking it."

For Adams was not only a historian; he was, himself, a historical fact. And though what he wrote surpasses in interest the writings of any other American historian except Francis Parkman, it can fairly be said that what he was is more significant than what he wrote. Whether we confine ourselves to the mere outward aspects of his career or embrace the history of the famous family which he so largely recapitulated or penetrate to his own intellectual and psychological reactions to his generation, we must conclude that he illuminates better than any of his contemporaries the nature and operations of the complex forces that were hurrying the older America across the threshold of the twentieth century.

He explains for us the shift in political power from New England to the West, from agriculture to industry and then to finance, from the individual to the mass, and the change in the nature of political power from intelligence to instinct and from reason to force. He reveals what his brother, Brooks, called the "degradation of the democratic dogma"—a phrase pointing to the decline in intellect and integrity from John Quincy Adams to Conkling, Platt, and Mark Hanna. Intellectually, he represents the transition from evolutionary optimism to mechanistic pessimism, from unity to multiplicity, and from order to chaos. He illustrates the rejection of the Victorian idea of progress for the idea of entropy, and of a theological for a mechanistic universe, and the substitution of science for philosophy, of the machine for man, of the dynamo for the Virgin.

That Adams was ill at ease in twentieth-century America is admitted; it is more significant that twentieth-century America for so long continued to be ill at ease with Adams, for he, after all, furnished the traditional standard. He had long recognized the inevitability of his defeat:

He had stood up for his eighteenth century, his Constitution of 1789, his George Washington, his Harvard College, his Quincy, and his Plymouth Pilgrims, as long as any one would stand up with him. He had said it was hopeless twenty years before, but he had kept on, in the same old attitude, by habit and taste, until he found himself altogether alone. He had hugged his antiquated dislike of bankers and capitalistic society until he had become little better than a crank. He had known for years that he must accept the regime, but he had known a great many other disagreeable certainties —like age, senility, and death—against which one made what little resistance one could.

The tragedy was indubitably personal—how could it be otherwise when the descendant of two presidents was offered a consulship in Guatemala?—but that it was more than personal no one familiar with the literature and politics of late nineteenth- and early twentieth-century America can doubt. For the old faiths were gone, the muscular Calvinism of the seventeenth century, the enlightened Deism of the eighteenth, the romantic Transcendentalism of the nineteenth. Spencerian determinism condemned the present for some indeterminate future, and Fiske's version of it satisfied only those whose orthodoxy needed easy reassurance, while pragmatism had not yet elbowed its way into philosophical respectability. Multiplicity, chaos, and stagnation were the answers that Adams read to the high hopes of the past.

Yet he was not wholly bereft. His revolt against the chaos of modern science threw him back on the unity of the church. It was not a matter of taste alone, though every page of the *Mont-Saint-Michel* is eloquent of the aesthetic appeal. Force for force, as Adams never tired of observing, the Virgin was as intelligible as the dynamo and as powerful. So, "happy in the thought that he had at last found a mistress who could see no difference in the age of her lovers," he turned to the adoration of the Virgin. It was, to be sure, an emotional response, yet emotion was no less a force than reason, and Adams was quick to point out that Faraday and Clerk-Maxwell would have joined Bernard in condemnation of Abelard's scholasticism. Saint Thomas Aquinas had formulated a philosophy which explained the universe as a unity, but Adams found unity not in the conclusion of a syllogism—though he was fascinated by the syllogism—but in the life, thought, and emotion of generations of men. He was persuaded not by the *Summa Theologiae* but by the Merveille of the cathedral of St. Michel, by the rose windows of Chartres, by the Chanson de Roland, and by the miracles of the Virgin.

Mary concentrated in herself the whole rebellion of man against fate; the whole protest against divine law; the whole contempt for human law as its outcome; the whole unutterable fury of human nature beating itself against the walls of its prison house, and suddenly seized by a hope that in the Virgin man had found a door of escape. She was above law; she took a feminine pleasure in turning hell into an ornament; she delighted in trampling on every social distinction in this world and the next. She knew that the universe was as unintelligible to her, on any theory of morals, as it was to her worshippers, and she felt, like them, no sure conviction that it was any more intelligible to the Creator of it. (*Mont-Saint-Michel and Chartres,* p. 213)

Uprooted and demoralized, tortured by a restlessness that found no repose in thought and no purpose in action, resigned to the bankruptcy of reason and the futility of knowledge, disillusioned of progress and of evolution, reconciled to the degradation of energy, the exhaustion of society, and the fall of man, lost in a universe that was mechanistic and chaotic, Adams turned in desperation to the one symbol of unity that seemed to have meaning and beauty, and found there such solace as he could. In spirit far removed from the modern Catholic church, he delighted in his picture of what the Virgin had meant to a simpler age. "Her pity," he knew, "had no limit." Not only Adams but his whole generation needed limitless pity, and the dynamo, symbol of the modern world, was not a reassuring comforter:

We know that prayer is thrown away,
For you are only force and light;
A shifting current; night and day;
We know this well, and yet we pray,
For prayer is infinite.

("Prayer to the Virgin")

CHAPTER VIII

The Traditionalists

I

THE NATURALISTS—London, Crane, Norris, Dreiser, even Cabell—did their most important work betweeen the nineties and the close of the first World War. The primitivists and irrationalists—Anderson, Hemingway, Faulkner, Caldwell, Pound, Jeffers—belong clearly to the troubled decades between the two world wars, as do those more substantial novelists whose significance is to be read largely in their reaction to the dislocations of the new era—Fitzgerald, Dos Passos, Steinbeck, and Wolfe. The first group reflects philosophically the mood of doubt that succeeded the earlier Victorian optimism and the impact of naturalism and of determinism. The second mirrors the disillusionment that came after the Wilsonian crusade and Republican normalcy, and the flight from reason that was inspired by the final collapse of Newtonian physics, the triumph of Freudian psychology, and the political disintegration of the Old World. Both were deeply affected by the economic malaise that furnished the background to so much of American history from the early nineties to the 1930's.

Paralleling and overlapping both was a group who may be called the traditionalists: Edith Wharton, Ellen Glasgow, Willa Cather, Rachel Field, Dorothy Canfield, Stark Young, Ole Rølvaag, among the novelists; E. A. Robinson, Santayana, Robert Frost, Stephen Vincent Benét among the poets. They were those who, in the great line of Wordsworth, had felt the weight of too much liberty. Philosophically, and artistically as well, they seemed more at home with the Victorians than with the modernists. They shared with the Victorians not so much particular philosophical doctrines as the conviction that there were such doctrines, not so much particular standards as acquiescence in the authority of standards, not so much an orthodox literary style as a respect for style. Where Norris, Crane, and

Dreiser represented change, they represented tradition; where the irrationalists rejoiced in revolution, they respected the conventions. What Edith Wharton wrote of Henry James might be said of the whole school: "For him every great novel must first of all be based on a profound sense of moral values," and it is their anxious concern for moral values that gives them their special distinction in twentieth-century America.

Because they reflected the traditional rather than the experimental, and the permanent rather than the ephemeral, they make few demands upon us. What they had to say—or more frequently to ask—is familiar, and so too the vocabulary and the accent with which they spoke. They can be understood better in terms of the nineteenth than of the twentieth century; it is a safe prophecy that they will speak to the twenty-first more directly than most of their more vociferous and sensational contemporaries.

Yet for all their artistic orthodoxy, their philosophical conservatism, and their respect for established values, the traditionalists subscribed nevertheless, with varying degrees of enthusiasm or reluctance, to the philosophy of determinism and reflected the swirling currents of social and economic change in the modern world. They were, willy-nilly, children of their age: they were naturalists, they were protestants, they were pessimists. They were closer to Arthur Clough and Francis Thompson and Thomas Hardy, among the Victorians, than to Tennyson or Arnold or Rossetti; in the American tradition, they were in the line of succession from Hawthorne to Melville rather than in the erratic line from Cooper to Mark Twain. They were not obsessed with sociological descriptions—Willa Cather specifically repudiated the overfurnished novel—but they could no more escape their own society than they could conceal their nostalgia for an earlier one. They were aloof from rather than immune to politics, fastidious rather than genuinely independent.

Insofar as they reacted to the contemporaneous scene their repudiation of it was scarcely less decisive, though far less vehement, than that of the economic rebels of the nineties or the satirists of the twenties. That repudiation can be read in Henry James, who reacted so disdainfully to the values of a pecuniary civilization; it can be read in Ellen Glasgow, who began with a challenge to the romantic tradition of the Old South and ended with a defense of those values still inherent in that tradition; it can be read in Willa Cather, who never acquiesced in the triumph of the speculators over the pioneers and builders of an earlier generation. It can be read, too, in the Robinson of "King Jasper" and the William Ellery Leonard of "Two Lives"; it is implicit in the poetry of Anna Hempstead Branch, Robert Frost, and Santayana; it can be found between the lines in purely lyrical poets like Edna Millay and Elinor Wylie. It inspired a group of unreconstructed Southerners to take their stand on a rickety platform of ante-bellum virtues; it united a group of critics in an uncertain school of humanism which had more professors than students and was, for all its arrogance, stronger in negation than in affirmation.

What distinguished the traditionalists from their journalistic contemporaries was not the conclusions at which they arrived but the premises from which they started and the roads they traveled. Like the late Victorians, in America as in Britain, they were troubled rather than shattered by the impact of science on faith and by the disintegration of values that had stood the test of centuries, and they yielded to pessimism rather than to despair, yielded gracefully rather than sullenly. Like the Victorians, too, they were more concerned about the spiritual well-being of the individual than about the material well-being of society. They were ready enough to agree with the rebels and reformers that life in America was inadequate, but the reasons for which they found America inadequate were not those which appealed to the Norris-Dreiser or the Lewis–Dos Passos schools, for where these were so often outraged that America did not change, they were dismayed by such changes as had occurred. They were prepared to agree with the naturalists and the irrationalists that life itself was a desperate business, but the reasons for which they found life desperate were not those which inspired the Faulkner-Jeffers school, for where those asserted that life was without meaning, they were all too sure that its meaning was tragic.

Both the old and the new schools—the distinction is not a chronological one—could have subscribed to Santayana's protest:

> My heart rebels against my generation
> That talks of freedom and is slave to riches,
> And, toiling 'neath each day's ignoble burden
> Boasts of the morrow

but only the traditionalists would have echoed his lament:

　　　　No space for noonday rest, or midnight watches,
　　　　No purest joy of breathing under heaven!

or his admonition that

　　　　　　Nature hath made us . . .
　　　　That we might, half knowing, worship
　　　　The deathless beauty of her guiding vision,
　　　　And learn to love, in all things mortal, only
　　　　　　What is eternal.

Neither the naturalists nor the irrationalists would willingly have conceded the existence of eternal values or logically have ascribed to nature such subjective notions as "deathless beauty." But it was the special distinction of the traditionalists that they were not only concerned but preoccupied with values, and that they found in the contemplation of nature that reassurance which had consoled the great romantics of the past.

2

It may have been more than fortuitous that, among the novelists, it was especially the women who addressed themselves so largely to the problem of preserving moral integrity and artistic values in a world which seemed increasingly indifferent to both. In the late nineteenth century, Howells, to be sure, had been vastly concerned with this problem—witness *A Modern Instance* and *A Hazard of New Fortunes*—and from *Daisy Miller* to *The Ivory Tower* it had been, for Henry James, an absorbing preoccupation. In the twentieth century, it was peculiarly James's disciples who clung to the belief that the problems of the novelist were predominantly ethical and who were persuaded that passion for social justice did not excuse a slovenly style, that there could be no final virtue in a society that did not cherish individual virtue, and that kindness, charity, loyalty, honesty, had more meaning than abstractions like equality or liberalism or reform.

The most articulate of Henry James's disciples was Edith Wharton, who for all the authenticity of her contributions to the social history of New York City was not primarily historian, or even sociologist, but artist. We need only compare her panels of New York society with those drawn by David Graham Phillips, Ernest Poole, or Abraham Cahan to appreciate how deep was her interest in ethical rather than merely social or material values. Her stories of Italy and France, too, suggest the extent of her debt to James, and again the debt was not merely one of literary technique but of philosophy. Like James, she was fascinated by the impact of the clash of cultures on traditional moral standards, and like her contemporary, Ellen Glasgow, she who began as a rebel against those traditional standards ended as something of an apologist for them. Even when, as in *Ethan Frome,* she turned from the complex pattern of New York society to a simple tragedy of rural New England, it was the moral implications of the violation of custom and code that concerned her, and *Ethan Frome* might have been a poem by Edwin Arlington Robinson.

Even more illuminating in its sharp reflection of shifting social mores was the work of Ellen Glasgow, the most ambitious historian of the Tidewater South and its most penetrating. She had begun, at the turn of the century, as a simple chronicler of the decline of the Old South and the rise of the New, performing for Virginia much the same task that Mary Wilkins Freeman and Sarah Orne Jewett had performed for New England, though not in a mood quite so autumnal. The patrician South which she portrayed was already decadent, its interests artificial, its standards meretricious, its defenses palpably vulnerable: she did not need to attack it but could regard its lingering pretensions and its inevitable collapse with ironic detachment, as she could regard the triumph of the New South with equanimity. But by the twenties, the threat to those moral values Miss Glasgow held precious came not from the persistence of the sentimental traditions of the Old South but from the absence of any tradition in the New, not from the dead hand of the past—a past which proved, indeed, surprisingly vital—but from the heavy hand of the present. Beginning with *Barren Ground* came a growing distaste for the vulgarity and emptiness of the new day and a grudging appreciation of the virtues still to be found in the old. With *The Sheltered Life,* best of all her novels, the appreciation was no longer grudging, and with *Vein of Iron* and *In This Our Life,* it became eloquent. For, as Miss Glasgow tells us in her later preface to *Virginia:*

Although in the beginning I had intended to deal ironically with both the Southern Lady and the Victorian tradition, I discovered, as I went on, that my irony grew fainter, while it yielded at last to sympathetic compassion.

After *The Romantic Comedians* and *They Stooped to Folly* the irony grew faint indeed, and sympathetic compassion permeates *The Sheltered Life*—compassion for the lovely Eva Birdsong who, in response to tradition, "gave up too much for happiness," compassion for the gallant old General Archbold who had been, all his life, a victim of that tradition but who, in the end, found nothing better to take its place and became reconciled to it as one becomes reconciled to an infirmity. For, "a world made, or even made over, by science was only a stark and colorless spectacle. . . . A thin-lipped world of facts without faith, of bones without flesh. Better the red waist-coats and the soulful vaporing of early Romanticism. Better even the excessive sensibility of mid-Victorian aesthetics." So thought General Archbold, and, musing on the "deep past," he asked himself:

were material ends all the world needed to build on? Was passion, even in the old, a simple problem of lowering your blood pressure and abandoning salt? Could a man discard his thinking self as lightly as he discarded the doctrine of an ultimate truth?

Certainly Miss Glasgow was unprepared to discard the doctrine of ultimate truth, unpopular as that doctrine was in the skeptical twenties. With *Vein of Iron* her revolt against the new generation became explicit and calculated. Now it was the vein of iron one remembered in the old generation, not the foundation of clay; now it was in that generation, which had once seemed so artificial and insincere, that one found integrity and dignity. "Having held fast through the generations, would this breed yield nowadays to the disintegrating forces in the modern world?" she asked.

Would that instinct for survival we used to call "the soul of man" be content to wear, for the future, the tarnished label of psychology? Would those intrepid Scottish metaphysicians who had placed freedom to believe above freedom to doubt, and had valued immaterial safety more than material comfort, would they sink in the end, under the dead weight of an age that believed only in the machine?

In the last of her novels, *In This Our Life,* Miss Glasgow turned from a defense of the old moralities to an attack upon the new immoralities. "The problem I had set myself," she wrote, "was an analysis in fiction of the modern temper; and the modern temper, as it pressed round me, appeared confused, vacillating, uncertain and distracted from permanent values. . . . I was dealing less with a declining social order than with a dissolving moment in time, with one of those perpetually returning epochs which fall between an age that is slipping out and an age that is hastening in."

In the end, then, Miss Glasgow found strength where before she had seen only weakness, inspiration where before she had detected insincerity. She had come out of the deep past, and it was to the deep past that she returned in the end, for she learned that the past had not only adorned a tale but pointed a moral. She who had been the historian of change became its elegist, her novels exercises not in irony but in nostalgia.

Ellen Glasgow succumbed to nostalgia; a younger school of southern writers—most of whom eventually found refuge in the North—embraced it with self-conscious enthusiasm. Alarmed by the ravages of industrialism, they turned wistfully back to agrarianism; repelled by a commercial civilization they rejoiced in the recollection of one whose purposes were not pecuniary and whose destiny was not success; dismayed by a society which seemed rootless, which forgot the past and ignored the future, they recreated one whose roots were deep-struck, one which found comfort in the past. At the height of the great boom of the twenties, a group of them issued a public declaration of faith, a series of essays in praise of the Southern way of life appropriately called *I'll Take My Stand*. It was a plea for provincialism, a celebration of tradition, a re-creation of the Golden Age; nothing more sentimental had appeared since the days of James Lane Allen and Thomas Nelson Page.

The most eloquent of the Southern romantics, and the most persuasive, was Stark Young, who more felicitously than any of his compatriots—the term is not without justification—presented the case for traditionalism in modern America. "Not in Memoriam but in Defense," he called his contribution to the statement of agrarian principles, and the phrase might serve for the whole school which he represented. What was it that he defended in this essay, in novels like *River House* and *Heaven Trees* and *So Red the Rose,* in those exquisite stories and sketches so appropriately called *Feliciana*? It was provincialism which "is a fine trait . . . akin to man's interest in his own center, which is the most deeply-rooted consideration that he has, the source of his direction, soul, and health." It was tradition, which was its own justification, for "everything worth anything, in the end, is an echo." It was the sense of belonging to something bigger than one's self—the only protection against the isolation, the anonymity, the rootlessness of modern life. "These days," says the philosophical priest in *Echoes at Livorno,* "everybody is himself without reference to an idea—God for example. . . . Everybody is himself without reference to anything larger than himself; and so nobody is anybody." It was the life of the affections—the only trait the McGehees couldn't abide was to be thin lipped and cold—affection for family and land and for the memories of the past.

His characters everywhere—in *So Red the Rose,* in *Heaven Trees,* in *River House* with its sense of currents running deeper by far than those of the placid river, in the sketches of *Feliciana*—confess this ever-present sense of the past. That sense of the past comes out in the feeling for tradition and usage, in affection for family and place and for material things even, when sanctified by time and familiarity: the old plantation houses, lovely in themselves and dearer because built by ancestors; the rosewood and mahogany furniture, brought over from France or England, perhaps, or carted across the mountains to what was a remote frontier; the family portraits, be they ever so bad, and the bright silverware and gleaming crystal glasses, polished by devoted hands; the magnolias and oak and crepe myrtle, the roses and camellias and yellow jasmine, whose shade and fragrance recalled daily the faith and affection of those remote ancestors who had planted them. For the world which Stark Young re-created was, like that which Henry James re-created, filled with furniture, but it was not in any sense that furniture which Willa Cather repudiated nor yet the mere stage furniture so carefully installed by historical novelists. It was rather a set of properties which united the present with the past and acknowledged its indebtedness, as the carvings and stained glass windows of medieval churches unite present with past in acknowledgement of the eternal truths of religion. It all gave a sense of continuity and thus of security, reminded men that they belonged in the stream of history and that their lives had meaning only as they touched other lives. Thus, Hugh McGehee to his son, about to go off to war:

The way I've been obliged to see it is this: our ideas and instincts work upon our memory of these people who have lived before us, and so they take on some clarity of outline. It's not to our credit to think we began today, and it's not to our glory to think we end today. All through time we keep coming into the shore like waves—like waves. You stick to your blood, son; there's a certain fierceness in blood that can bind you up with a long community of life.

The long community of life—that was what Stark Young and the southern traditionalists were concerned about. It existed in material things; it existed in ideas and the records of ideas—the carefully kept diaries and the packets of letters; it existed, most surely, in the affections. "You know how 'tis in our family," says Hugh McGehee. "It's something to know that you were loved before you were born." Stark Young never wrote a formal love story, but all his stories are suffused with tenderness, and the tenderness is for a way of life and for all those who were ennobled by it.

The merits of the traditionalist argument are irrelevant to our inquiry but not its indissoluble connection with the Old South. The fact that, in the twentieth century, the case for traditionalism should come to rest upon the aristocratic and self-indulgent South rather than upon the democratic and austere New England, upon that region which used tradition as a refuge rather than as an instrument, is illuminating. The American tradition was not, after all, either feudal or self-indulgent, and the authors who so studiously took their stand in Dixie Land were right in recognizing that the tradition which the South perpetuated was European rather than American. That other regions had their own traditions was not to be denied, and these had their own memorialists, but in literature and the popular arts it was the South that came increasingly to symbolize tradition and to represent such qualities as courtesy, generosity, hospitality, gallantry, and even beauty. Whether the association was more than fortuitous, whether it was not, indeed, fictitious, belongs to the domain of historical rather than literary investigation; what is important is that it was pervasive and conclusive. Its pervasiveness suggests that the American nostalgia for the past was romantic rather than moral. That Ellen Glasgow and Stark Young and their compatriots were deeply concerned with the moral problems is clear, but we have only to note what happened to the southern tradition when it was taken over by film producers and song writers and advertisers to realize that it was the romantic rather than the moral qualities which explained its popular appeal.

3

To Willa Cather the past was significant for its moral qualities, and only gradually did romanticism triumph over morality. Throughout her long literary life she was engaged in an elaborate remembrance of things past—the past of the pioneers who had built the West, of the immigrants who had carried with them into the New World their sense of beauty and art, of those earlier spiritual pathfinders, the Franciscans and Jesuits, who had served their fellow-men and their God so selflessly. And all her novels and stories—those of the Arcadian Virginia of her childhood, of the golden Nebraska of her youth, of the New York she had known as a young journalist, of the shimmering Southwest that belonged to the past even in the present, and the Quebec that seemed to have only a past—were animated by a single great theme as they were graced by a single felicitous style. The theme was that of the supremacy of moral and spiritual over material values, the ever recurrent but inexhaustible theme of gaining the whole world and losing one's soul.

Willa Cather was a traditionalist and a conformer; the tradition that she so triumphantly maintained was peculiarly American, the standards to which she so instinctively conformed those that had sufficed her mentors, Sarah Orne Jewett and Henry James and, in an earlier day, Hawthorne. Her roots were deep in the American and the Christian past; she had inherited the best of Virginia—not the Tidewater, but that Valley where Ellen Glasgow finally found her vein of iron; she had known the Middle Border in the days of its primitive beauty and all her life drew strength from it; she had lived and worked in eastern cities and abroad and could re-create the artistic world of New York with flawless deftness, but she never came to terms with that world. "It's a queer thing about the flat country," she once wrote, "it takes hold of you, or it leaves you perfectly cold. A great many people find it dull and monotonous; they like a church steeple, an old mill, a waterfall, country all touched up and furnished, like a German Christmas card. I go everywhere—I admire all kinds of country. I tried to live in France. But when I strike the open plains, something happens. I'm home. I breathe differently."

Miss Cather rejected the "overfurnished" novel as she rejected the overfurnished countryside—rejected alike the furniture of sociology, of psychology, and of physiology, for "a novel crowded with physical sensations is no less a catalogue than one crowded with furniture." She thought the traditional themes of love and despair, truth and beauty, the struggle with the soil and the struggle for artistic honesty, far from exhausted; indeed she held, with Henry James and Ellen Glasgow, that these were the only themes capable of inspiring great art. "Ideals," she wrote, "were not archaic things, beautiful and impotent; they were the real sources of power among men," and unlike so many of her contemporaries—Hemingway, for example—she was not embarrassed by this vocabulary. Sarah Orne Jewett had admonished her, when she was scarcely more than a girl, that "you must write to the human heart, the great consciousness that all humanity goes to make up. Otherwise what might be strength . . . is only crudeness, and what might be insight is only observation, sentiment falls to sentimentality—you can write about life but never write life itself." From *Alexander's Bridge* to *The Old Beauty* she wrote life itself, wrote it so passionately that the characters she created seem to us more authentic than the characters of history.

The best of Miss Cather's novels all deal with the frontier, in one sense or another, but the frontier is never the object but rather the setting, and her stories are never, as with Bret Harte or Hamlin Garland, frontier stories. For just as Turner, when he placed himself on the vantage point of the frontier, was able to see the significance of the whole of American history, so Willa Cather, when she looked out upon life from the prairie or mesa or from one of those Rocks which figure so largely in her books, was able to see, from those vantage points, the real meaning of life in America. It was because the frontier simplified, clarified, and dramatized universal moral problems that she returned to it again and again for inspiration, and rarely in vain.

What was it about the pioneer West that inspired Miss Cather's elegiac mood, commanded her affection and respect, and, by contrast, made the busy world of the East seem so brash and pushing? It was, first of all, the land itself, and Miss Cather indulged in that pathetic fallacy which ascribed to the land not only spaciousness and beauty but endurance and serenity and strength. "It fortified her," she wrote of Alexandra Bergson, "to reflect upon the great operations of nature, and when she thought of the law that lay behind them she felt a sense of personal security." She subscribed to that romantic tradition, so

strong in American literature and art, that saw nature splendid in
all its manifestations and man virtuous only when he accommodated
himself to nature—the tradition that stretched, politically, from Jefferson to Bryan, that found literary expression in so many writers
from Cooper to Rølvaag, that was reflected in the work of naturalists like Burroughs and Muir and in landscape painters from the
Hudson River school to Winslow Homer and Grant Wood. Thus
when Thea Kronberg heard the "New World Symphony" she recalled

The sandhills, the grasshoppers and locusts, all the things that wakened
and chirped in the early morning; the reaching and reaching of the high
plains, the immeasurable yearning of all flat lands. There was home in it,
too; first memories, first mornings long ago; the amazement of a new soul
in a new world, that had dreamed something despairing, something glorious, in the dark before it was born.

And thus, in a somewhat different vein, of the Rock of Acoma:

the rock, when one came to think of it, was the utmost expression of human
need; even mere feeling yearned for it; it was the highest comparison of
loyalty in love and friendship. . . . The Acomas, who must share the
universal human yearning for something permanent, enduring, without
shadow of change, had their idea in substance.

Nature, however, was usually something that seemed to belong
to the past; modern man had ignored it or exploited it, and therein
lay its weakness. But those pioneers who had first gone out to the
high plains, Miss Cather asserted, had been concerned with more
than material conquest or exploitation: it was a romantic assertion,
to be sure, and not wholly supported by the facts, but it was a mark
of Miss Cather's triumph that she made nature and history conform
to her art. The pioneers had a special relationship to the soil and
drew from the soil strength and courage; they came not merely to
make money but to live, and they built not merely an economy but
a civilization, and there was integrity and dignity and piety in their
work and their lives.

When an adventurer carries his gods with him into a remote and savage
country [she wrote in Shadows on the Rock—and the words apply as well
to the Nebraska pioneers], the colony he founds will, from the beginning,
have grace, traditions, riches of the mind and spirit. Its history will shine
with bright incidents, slight perhaps, but precious, as in life itself, where the

great matters are often as worthless as astronomical distances, and the trifles dear as the heart's blood.

But after the pioneer and the builder, after the Ántonias and the Alexandras, the Captain Forresters and the Tom Outlands, came the exploiters and the spoilers. Thus Niel Herbert, who loved the Lost Lady,

had seen the end of an era, the sunset of the pioneer. He had come upon it when already its glory was nearly spent. So in the buffalo days a traveler used to come upon the embers of a hunter's fire on the prairie, after the hunter was up and gone. . . . This was the very end of the road-making West; the men who had put plains and mountains under the iron harness were old; some were poor; and even the successful ones were hunting for rest and a brief reprieve, death. It was already gone, that age; nothing could ever bring it back.

Nothing could ever bring it back, but Miss Cather found a sort of mournful consolation in recalling its heroic virtues.

This moral is implicit in all the early novels—notably in *O Pioneers* and *My Ántonia*. With *A Lost Lady* and *The Professor's House*—both dating from the early twenties—it becomes explicit. "The whole world broke in two in 1922 or thereabouts," Miss Cather later wrote, and it was perhaps a consciousness of the passing of that old world that gave such poignancy to her recollection of the past. *A Lost Lady* is almost an allegory. The lovely Marian Forrester draws her strength, even her beauty and her charm, from that husband who represented all the old integrities. "It was as Captain Forrester's wife that she most interested Niel," says Miss Cather,

and it was in her relation to her husband that he most admired her. Given her other charming attributes, her comprehension of a man like the railroad-builder, her loyalty to him, stamped her more than anything else. That, he felt, was quality. . . . His admiration for Mrs. Forrester went back to that, just as, he felt, she herself went back to it. (*A Lost Lady*, p. 78)

When the Captain fails and then dies, Mrs. Forrester is indeed lost; her beauty remains and something of her charm, but they are tarnished, as the Old West was tarnished, because put to shabby use. That the gross and greedy Ivy Peters should supplant Captain Forrester is symbolic of the triumph of the speculator over the builder:

The Old West had been settled by dreamers, great-hearted adventurers who were unpractical to the point of magnificence; a courteous brotherhood strong in attack but weak in defense, who could conquer but could not hold. Now all the vast territory they had won was to be at the mercy of men like Ivy Peters who had never dared anything, never risked anything. They would drink up the mirage, dispel the morning freshness, root out the great brooding spirit of freedom, the generous, easy life of the great land-holders. The space, the colour, the princely carelessness of the pioneer they would destroy and cut up into profitable bits, as the match factory splinters up the primeval forest. All the way from the Missouri to the mountains this generation of shrewd young men, trained to petty economies by hard times, would do exactly what Ivy Peters had done when he drained the Forrester marsh. (*A Lost Lady,* pp. 106–107)

The passing of this pioneer generation meant, to Miss Cather, the passing of all the old virtues, and she was incapable of believing that there could be different virtues in a civilization whose standards were those of the countinghouse, whose habits were predatory, and whose rewards were social and ostentatious rather than spiritual and private. "We must face the fact," she said in a tribute to Nebraska penned just as she finished *A Lost Lady,*

that the splendid story of the pioneers is finished, and that no new story worthy to take its place has yet begun. . . . The generation now in the drivers' seat hates to make anything, wants to live and die in an automobile, scudding past those acres where the old men used to follow the corn-rows up and down. They want to buy everything ready-made: clothes, food, education, music, pleasure. Will the third generation—the full-blooded joyous ones just coming over the hill—be fooled? Will it believe that to live easily is to live happily?

Miss Cather's next novel—in many ways her most interesting—answered this rhetorical question with a clear negative. If *A Lost Lady* was an allegory, *The Professor's House* was a morality play, its characters authentic enough but symbols, each of them, of virtues and vices. It presented the contrast between spiritual integrity and worldly success even more dramatically than had *A Lost Lady.* For here, as if to underline the moral, were two complementary themes: Professor St. Peter's devotion to scholarship, threatened by the social ambitions of his family, and Tom Outland's passion for his miraculous mesa, thwarted by commercialism. The professor's house is a symbol of all the artistic and moral values he cherishes, the shabby house with the attic room which he shared with Augusta's "form," where he had written the eight volumes of his Spanish Adventurers, where he had known the happiest hours of his life, just as the new house he had built for his ambitious wife and spoiled daughters is a symbol of the pretentiousness of the new day. As for Tom Outland —the elusive Tom who had come out of nowhere and slipped away as quietly—the symbol is the mesa where he had discovered the remains of an extinct civilization, the mesa so remote, so private, so far above mere exploitation, a work of art, a projection, almost, of his own spirit. But the professor's house was doomed to abandonment; Tom Outland was killed, leaving a formula which made others rich, and greedy hands put the lovely pots and jars and tools he had found to commercial use. In the end, St. Peter found solace only in a crumbling diary which recalled for him the one stirring experience of his life.

The Professor's House was an acknowledgement of defeat, and after that Miss Cather seemed to give up even the pretense of finding something worth while in contemporary life. "The United States," she wrote, "had got ahead wonderfully, but somehow ahead on the wrong road." She turned back, instead, to Spanish New Mexico, to French Quebec, to ante-bellum Virginia. It was entirely natural that her search for the permanent should have led her, as it led Henry Adams, to the Catholic church, with "its safe, lovingly arranged and ordered universe, not too vast, though nobly spacious."

"It takes a great deal of history to produce a little literature," Henry James had written, and the sense of history was strong in Willa Cather, stronger by far than in most of those "historical" novelists whose recreation of the past was so calculated and so artificial. Better than any of her literary contemporaries, she represented the force of tradition in twentieth-century America—the tradition of the artist, the tradition of the pioneer, the tradition, eventually, of the universal church.

4

The most distinguished of American men of letters of his generation, Edwin Arlington Robinson, was an altogether more complex artist than either Willa Cather or Ellen Glasgow, while by comparison with him the muckrakers and reformers like Norris and Phillips, the sociologists and journalists like Dreiser and Farrell, the satirists like Edgar Lee Masters, and the irrationalists like Robinson Jeffers, all seem simple and immature. Aloof, almost isolated, from the surface manifestations of American life, he responded sensitively to its deeper undercurrents. Rooted in New England, provincial, almost parochial, he transcended his section and his country as he transcended his time: the creator of Tilbury Town—so much more authentic than Spoon River—was also the re-creator of Camelot and Joyous Gard, the poet who wrote the most felicitous tributes to Shakespeare and to Rembrandt in our literature. Content himself with a monastic life, he probed more deeply into the heart of lovers, and especially of women, than any other poet of his time, and the Arthurian triology —"Merlin," "Lancelot," and "Tristram"—is surely the greatest love poetry in modern literature. Heir to Calvinism and to Transcendentalism, he was at the same time indubitably a modern: compare his use of the Arthurian legends with that by Tennyson! Confessing that life was a desperate business, he found its very desperation a source of strength; acknowledging the impossibility of finding the ultimate meaning of life, he insisted that its only significance was to be found in the search for that meaning:

> Say the gleam was not for us, but never say we doubted it,
> Say the wrong road was right before we followed it.

Philosophically and stylistically, Robinson belongs with the late Victorians rather than with the modernists—with Browning, above all, whom he resembled in so many and such interesting ways—with Gerard Manley Hopkins and Thomas Hardy. He came to maturity, indeed at the end of the Victorian era, and the pattern of his thought and of his verse form was fixed then and never thereafter more than modified. He himself matured early, and there is no perceptible advance, either in philosophy or in style, from *Children of the Night* and *Captain Craig* to *Amaranth* and *King Jasper*. Except for the ill-considered *Dionysus in Doubt* and the ambitious but confusing *King Jasper,* he deliberately ignored the social and economic problems of his own day, and it is suggestive that these, with perhaps *The Glory of the Nightingales,* are the only long poems where his talent clearly flagged.

Robinson's traditionalism was not merely a negative matter of aloofness from the contemporary scene, an aloofness which was personal as well as literary, it was positive, both in syle and in content.

In the first of his volumes of poetry, *Children of the Night,* he confessed that

> We lack the courage to be where we are:—
> We love too much to travel on old roads,
> To triumph on old fields,

and he himself preferred to travel on old roads and—witness the use he made of the Arthurian legends—to triumph on old fields. He addressed himself consistently to those great philosophical and religious themes that had engaged poets and dramatists from the days of Periclean Greece to those of Victorian England: the persistent themes of love and renunciation, exaltation and despair, ambition and frustration, vanity and humility, the search for artistic integrity, for spiritual peace, and for the meaning of life. Nor did he find it necessary, in dealing with these familiar themes, to cast around for new verse forms. "Nowadays," he wrote,

> Sinners in art believe there are short roads
> To glory without form

and those roads he shunned, preferring rather the well-worn paths that generation of poets had traveled and made serviceable.

Yet for all his acceptance of conventional forms and his absorption in traditional problems, Robinson was as indubitably a child of his age as was Henry Adams, whom he resembled in so many ways, of the age of confusion and disintegration that came in with Haeckel and Freud. Almost alone among the major American poets of his time, he was immersed in what Joseph Wood Krutch has called the modern temper, and his significance emerges more sharply when we place him in his American setting, see him in relation to the poetry of his day. Robert Frost was all but innocent of philosophy; Elinor Wylie's great sonnets celebrated love; Stephen Vincent Benét was content to dramatize the American past and inspire the present; Sandburg, Masters, and Vachel Lindsay, for all their talents, reflected only the surface manifestations of contemporary life; Jeffers sounded, with wearying monotony, a single strident note of violent despair; while the three poets who were closest to Robinson—William Vaughn Moody, Anna Hempstead Branch, and George Santayana—wrote too little to enable us to piece out a consistent philosophy from their poetry alone. Robinson's poetic production was as large as that of any other

major American poet—larger by far than that of Emerson or Poe or
Whitman or Lanier, for example—and the range of his philosophy
was broader, his emotions deeper, his imagination richer, than that of
any other poet of his age.

His was, above all, the tragic muse; sadness and compassion permeate all his lines. He was a Calvinist who yielded occasionally and
reluctantly to the lure of Transcendentalism and then returned peni-
tently to brood on the depravity of man, the inscrutability of God or
of fate, the necessity of suffering and defeat. Man's fate, as Robinson
read it, is forever tragic; he cannot avoid that fate but he can, if he
will, ennoble it by acquiescence, by fortitude, and by loyalty to some
ultimate truth, some gleam, some vision, some light—the terms appear again and again and are interchangeable. So Merlin, musing on
the destiny of man:

> . . . there may still be charted for his feet
> A dimmer faring, where the touch of time
> Were like the passing of a twilight moth
> From flower to flower, into oblivion,
> If there were not somewhere a barren end
> Of moths and flowers, and glimmering far away
> Beyond a desert where the flowering days
> Are told in slow defeats and agonies,
> The guiding of a nameless light . . .
> ("Merlin," *Collected Poems,* p. 294)

And so, too, Robinson himself, in that baffling *Credo* written at the
beginning of his long poetic career,

> No, there is not a glimmer, nor a call,
> For one that welcomes, welcomes when he fears,
> The black and awful chaos of the night;
> For through it all—above, beyond it all—
> I know the far-sent message of the years,
> I feel the coming glory of the Light
> (*Collected Poems,* p. 94)

He is obsessed by the sense of sin, the necessity of humility, the no-
bility of renunciation. It is suggestive that where Tennyson, in *The
Idylls of the King,* makes his King Arthur stainless and ascribes his
downfall purely to external forces, Robinson makes the hapless king
a sinner, like other men, and traces the catastrophe that overtook him

and his kingdom to his own weakness, as well as to fate. It is suggestive, too, that both Merlin and Arthur, conscious of their sins and their weaknesses, renounce the Holy Grail. "I have enough," says Arthur,

> Until my new knight comes to prove and find
> The promise and the glory of the Grail,
> Though I shall see no Grail. For I have built
> On sand and mud, and I shall see no Grail."
> "Nor I," said Merlin. "Once I dreamed of it,
> But I was buried. I shall see no Grail,
> Nor would I have it otherwise. I saw
> Too much, and that was never good for man."
> ("Merlin," *Collected Poems,* p. 254)

It is never good for man to see too much—when that happened to Elaine Amelia Watchman, in the wryly humorous *Amaranth,* she turned to dust. But there is little danger here, as Robinson saw it: the Light, if it exists at all, is dim and flickering, the Vision something faintly remembered, as in a dream, though no less dear for that.

> "I see no answer shining in the dark"
> Said Fargo, "All I know is, I am here.
> I have no other knowledge than a dimness
> That is not quite remembrance, yet remembers.
> And I am not here because I would be here;
> And God knows why I must."
> ("Amaranth," *Collected Poems,* p. 1332)

It is a note that recurs again and again in Robinson. God alone knows the why, the whence, and the whither of life, and He has not chosen to let man in on the secret.

> Was ever an insect flying between two flowers
> Told less than we are told of what we are?

says Cavender's wife—the wife who returns to haunt him with the question of her faithfulness. And again—it is Captain Craig speaking this time—

> What men lose,
> Man gains; and what man gains reports itself
> In losses we but vaguely deprecate,

So they be not for us;—and this is right,
Except that when the devil in the sun
Misguides us, we go darkly where the shine
Misleads us, and we know not what we see;
We know not if we climb or if we fall;
And if we fly, we know not where we fly.

("Captain Craig," *Collected Poems*, p. 150)

Yet, though an inexorable fate has predestined man to sorrow and suffering, men must go on as best they can, groping their way toward the truth. "The world," Robinson wrote, "is a kind of spiritual kindergarten where bewildered infants are trying to spell God with the wrong blocks," but the important thing was, after all, the valiant effort to spell God. "It is the flesh that ails us," says Captain Craig, who is so clearly the spokesman for Robinson himself,

. . . for the spirit knows no qualm,
No failure, no down-falling; so climb high,
And having set your steps regard not much
The downward laughter clinging at your feet,
Nor overmuch the warning; only know
As well as you know dawn from lantern-light
That far above you, for you, and within you,
There burns and shines and lives, unwavering
And always yours, the truth. Take on yourself
But your sincerity, and you take on
Good promise for all climbing; fly for truth,
And hell shall have no storm to crush your flight.

("Captain Craig,"*Collected Poems,* p. 151)

For Robinson was the poet of doubt, but doubt requires the existence of belief. He was the poet of failure, but failure implied some standard of success. He was the poet of defeat, but the defeat was never final—as with Masters or Jeffers, for example—and if it involved misery, it involved, too, grandeur. He was the poet of remorse and of the tortured conscience, but conscience necessitated faith in some ultimate right, or some God.

It is significant that the most profound of American poets of the twentieth century should have been so preoccupied, obsessed even, with failure, frustration, desolation, and death. Not for him the easy paths, the glib answers, the simple solutions, of a material civilization. Dedicated to his art, he pursued it with lonely devotion, content to ask questions to which there were no final answers, content to hold dear such virtues as love and loyalty and duty and humility, content with a mournful faith in some glimmering ideal of truth whose very nature must mock and elude us forever. For he knew that

> We, with all our wounds and all our powers,
> Must each wait alone at his own height
> Another darkness or another light.

CHAPTER IX

Religious Thought and Practice

I

IT WOULD BE naïve to suppose that any substantial number of Americans acquiesced in scientific determinism or in those implications and consequences which a Dreiser, a Cabell, a Jeffers logically drew from it. A kindly and amiable people, Americans were not to be impelled by dubious logic to a violence that was foreign to their character, nor did they seek escape from a world which most of them considered unquestionably the best of all possible worlds. For three hundred years Calvinism had taught the depravity of man without any perceptible effect on the cheerfulness, kindliness, or optimism of Americans, and it was scarcely to be expected that a handful of scientists, novelists, and poets would succeed where generations of stout clergymen had failed. American optimism was, in fact, impenetrable and unconquerable.

Few things were more remarkable than the unanimity with which Americans professed a religious faith, for the most part Calvinistic, and the indifference which they displayed to its doctrines. What was remarkable was not the indifference but the persistent profession. Those doctrines had been formulated to explain and, if possible, alleviate the misery of man, to enable him to bear burdens and sorrows otherwise more than he could bear, to sustain him with the assurance that everlasting bliss would be the reward for faith and patience in this vale of wrath and tears. But from the beginning most Americans, except Negro slaves, found this world a paradise rather than a purgatory. Whatever they may have said, or sung, they preferred this life to the next, and when they imagined heaven, they thought of it as operating under an American constitution.

Logically, perhaps, they should have abandoned a religion which, in flagrant contradiction to all experience, taught the depravity of man and the corruption of society and subordinated this life to the next, but Americans were not a logical people. Santayana has observed that in America ideas are abandoned by virtue of a mere change of feeling, without the pressure of new evidence or new arguments: "We do not nowadays refute our predecessors, we pleasantly bid them good-bye." This was what Americans did, almost from the beginning, with those inherited religious doctrines which seemed so inconsistent with observation: it is interesting to recall that the Northampton congregation which, in the mid-eighteenth century, dismissed Jonathan Edwards, did not find it convenient to refute his doctrines but merely to avoid them. The revolt, in short, was moral and social, not intellectual. Americans rejected the application of Calvinism rather than the philosophy, the conclusions rather than the premises or the logic. There were, to be sure, scattered revolts against the logic. Deism had its day, and Unitarianism and Universalism commanded, for a time, the allegiance of a distinguished if not a numerous body. Yet the only well-established churches whose membership declined, absolutely, during the twentieth century were the Unitarian, Universalist, and Quaker. And though deism and agnosticism undoubtedly persisted and flourished, atheism (or free thought, as it was quaintly called) became a curiosity, repudiated even by the physicists, who all turned mystics. It was the Calvinistic, the Evangelical, and the Catholic churches that increased steadily in membership and in authority.

Indeed, in everything but law, America, at the opening of the twentieth century, was a Christian nation. Some states recognized Christianity as the official—though not the established—religion. Jurors were required to believe in God, teachers to read from the Bible, and in some states a religious observance of the "Lord's Day" was a legal obligation. Almost a century earlier, the perspicacious Tocqueville had remarked this unofficial establishment and rejoiced in it:

There is no country in the whole world in which the Christian religion retains a greater influence over the souls of men than in America, and there can be no greater proof of its utility, and of its conformity to human nature, than that its influence is most powerfully felt over the most enlightened and free nation on earth. . . . In the United States religion exercises but little influence upon the laws and upon the details of public opinion, but it directs the manners of the community, and by regulating domestic life, it regulates the state.

Fifty years later, Bryce confirmed this interpretation:

Christianity is in fact understood to be, though not the legally established religion, yet the national religion. So far from thinking their common-wealth Godless, the Americans conceive that the religious character of a government consists in nothing but the religious beliefs of the individual citizens, and the conformity of their conduct to that belief. They deem the general acceptance of Christianity to be one of the main sources of their national prosperity, and their nation as a special object of the Divine favor.

There was no Scriptural authority for this notion, yet none was more deeply implanted or more widely held. That God had sifted a whole nation that He might send over choice grain into this wilder-ness was accepted as an elementary fact of divine husbandry, and the theory of special favor was restated, generation after generation, with what must have seemed to non-Americans monotonous conceit. Every people makes God in its own image, and the Americans were no exception, nor did the variety of sects that flourished here blur the image beyond recognition. The God of Puritanism and of camp meetings was an angry God, and as late as 1911 the Southern Pres-byterian church clung stubbornly to the doctrine of infant damna-tion, yet no American could believe that he was damned, and Jeffer-son spoke for most of them when he acknowledged "an overruling Providence which by all its dispensations proves that it delights in the happiness of man here and his greater happiness hereafter."

Americans naturalized God, as they naturalized so many other concepts. Because they were optimistic, they insisted upon His be-nevolence and found everywhere manifestations of His favor. Because they distrusted arbitrary authority, they qualified His omnipo-tence by reading into it respect for law. Because they were easy-going and careless, they did not permit Him to lay upon them bur-dens heavier than they could bear and persuaded Him to be satisfied with formal and occasional worship. Because they enjoyed greater natural bounty than any other people had known, they invoked His approval of material success as a reward for virtue, industry, and thrift. Confident that God was vitally concerned with their affairs, they solicited His participation in their most trivial activities, inviting Him, as it were, to give a weekly editorial commentary on the va-garies of their society. In defiance of all history they explained away the Devil and ignored Sin and, in the words of Dean Sperry, "struck straight for the ultimate optimism in neglect of that preliminary pessimism which the great religions of the world have all presupposed as their premise." They read Hawthorne as a historical novelist, and they neglected Melville; a generation later it was William James who captured their imagination, not poor Josiah Royce, wrestling heroically with the problem of evil; and even after the agony of the second World War, Reinhold Niebuhr was more widely appreciated in Britain and on the European continent than in his own country.

Although the theological implications of Puritanism wore off in the course of the eighteenth and nineteenth centuries, many of its moral and political implications persisted. Two centuries of reaction could not dissolve the Puritan inheritance of respect for the individual and for the dignity of man, of recognition of the ultimate authority of reason, of allegiance to principles rather than to persons, to the doctrine of government by compact and by consent, and to spiritual and moral democracy. These things, along with Puritanism's deep-seated moral purpose, its ceaseless search for salvation, its passion for righteousness and for justice, and its subordination of material to spiritual ends, entered into the current of secular thought and retained their vitality long after the theological and metaphysical arguments which sustained them had been forgotten.

2

It is scarcely an exaggeration to say that during the nineteenth century and well into the twentieth, religion prospered while theology went slowly bankrupt. From Edwards to Royce, America did not produce a first-rate religious philosopher: the achievement of a seer like Emerson or a scholar like Parker or an evangelist like Beecher was rather to escape from the coils of theology than to wrestle with them and reduce them to some harmonious design. Even the fabulous sectarianism of American religion did not stimulate philosophical inquiry, for the differences that seemed to justify denominational splits were rarely dogmatic, and most of the new sects which clustered along the fringes of Protestantism represented a flight from reason rather than an exercise of it. Except in the Unitarian and Universalist churches there was little effort to accommodate inherited theology to the realities of American experience: as a result, the gap between the authoritative dogma of Protestant churches and the actual beliefs of their communicants widened steadily—and heedlessly.

The Higher Criticism and comparative religion, to be sure, both made inroads upon orthodoxy, and both produced some defections and some readjustments. The impact of science, and especially of the Darwinian theory, was violent but not shattering. The cosmic philosophy which John Fiske elaborated, and to which liberal church-men everywhere rallied, represented in fact but little advance over the liberal theology of Theodore Parker, but it did enable devout Christians to conclude that there was no necessary conflict between science and religion and that evolution was but God's way of doing things. It was a tribute either to the skill of Fiske, Beecher, Lyman Abbott, and their allies, or to the ability of Americans to divorce their Sunday from their weekday world, that the most scientific-minded people in the western world were, on the whole, those whose faith was least impaired by science.

Certainly by every test but that of influence the church had never been stronger than it was at the opening of the twentieth century, and its strength increased steadily. Everyone was a Christian, and almost everyone joined some church, though few for reasons that would have earned them admission to Jonathan Edwards' Northampton congregation. The typical Protestant of the twentieth century in-herited his religion as he did his politics, though rather more casually, and was quite unable to explain the differences between denomina-tions. He found himself a church member by accident and persisted in his affiliation by habit; he greeted each recurring Sunday service with a sense of surprise and was persuaded that he conferred a benefit upon his rector and his community by participating in church services. The church was something to be "supported," like some aged rela-tive whose claim was vague but inescapable.

That it was supported is clear, and whatever the spiritual quality of American Christianity, the material and quantitative standards were high. There were forty-two million church members in 1916, fifty-five million in 1926, and seventy-two million in 1942; though church statistics attain an unreliability that would be a penal offense in a corporation, it was apparent that church membership was growing more rapidly than population. The increase in wealth and in social activities was even more impressive; the churches, of necessity, borrowed the techniques of big business, and bishops were often chosen for their administrative talents rather than for their spiritual qualities.

Never before had the church been materially more powerful or spiritually less effective. After Phillips Brooks, no Protestant churchman spoke with authority: certainly Channing and Parker had no successors, and for all the vast growth in population and literacy, it is difficult to imagine any preacher selling fifty thousand copies of his sermons as Parker so commonly did. The clergy had been leaders in the great reform movements of the early nineteenth century, but they played only a timid role in the reforms of the nineties and the Roosevelt era. The great moral crises of two world wars failed to elicit any authoritative religious leadership or even to inspire any spiritual interpretation, and not the clergy but the scientists instructed the American people in the moral consequences of the use of the atomic bomb.

The church itself confessed to a steady secularization: as it invaded the social and economic fields, it retreated from the intellectual. Philosophy, which for over two centuries had been almost the exclusive property of the clergy, slipped quietly from their hands. With the exception of James Mark Baldwin and George T. Ladd, both of them transitional figures, all the leading philosophers of the new day were laymen: Wright, Peirce, James, Royce, Santayana, Münsterberg, Lovejoy, Montague, Dewey, Tufts. No longer did the Protestant churches control higher education. Denominational colleges, to be sure, still flourished, particularly in the South, but it was beyond the competence of the most subtle students to discover the religious implications of those affiliations for such institutions as Harvard, Yale, Columbia, or Chicago Universities. In 1840 the president of every important college in the country was a clergyman or trained to the church; a century later no clergyman adorned the presidential chair of any of the leading institutions of learning.

Notwithstanding its Calvinistic antecedents and numerous revivals which sought to lead sinners back to the straight Gospel, religion became increasingly a social activity rather than a spiritual experience. William Dean Howells, the most acute observer of the social habits of the plain people, noted the ravages of secularization even in Puritan New England. "Religion there," he wrote of Equity, New Hampshire, had largely ceased to be a fact of spiritual experience, and the visible church flourished on condition of providing for the social needs of the community. It was practically held that the salvation of one's soul must not be made too depressing, or the young people would have nothing to do with it. Professors of the sternest creeds temporized with the sinners, and did what might be done to win them to heaven by helping them to have a good time here. The church embraced and included the world. (*A Modern Instance,* p. 27)

Yet everyone in Equity went to church, everyone but Squire Gaylord who confounded the godly with his austere Puritanism.

When William James came to analyze *Varieties of Religious Experience,* he had to depend chiefly on the obscure little sects or on individuals whose religious attitudes would ordinarily be called psychopathic. The American notion, as Santayana put it, was that religion "should be disentangled as much as possible from history and authority and metaphysics, and made to rest honestly upon one's own feelings, on one's indomitable optimism and trust in life." Religion came to be largely a matter of observing certain formalities and of doing good. The formalities were a concession to tradition and convention; the practical humanitarianism an authentic expression of the national character. The church was, on the whole, the most convenient and probably the most effective organization for giving expression to the American passion for humanitarianism, and it rarely interposed any awkward dogmatic prerequisites. Doing good was interpreted broadly: it might mean saving men from drunkenness, rescuing fallen women, sending flowers to the local hospital, organizing a basketball team for the young folks, maintaining a settlement house in the slums, supporting a missionary in darkest Africa, or holding forums for the discussion of current affairs.

This recognition of the obligation of the church to society came to be called the socialization of Christianity. Although the phrase was new, the attitude was old. The Catholic church had never failed to recognize its obligation to society and, since the seventies, had consistently allied itself with economic, though not with intellectual, liberalism. Among Protestants, however, that sense of responsibility for community welfare which distinguished the Puritan church in the seventeenth century had declined, and during the nineteenth century the evangelical churches concentrated on preparing the individual for the next world rather than for this. They took to heart the assurance that there would be more joy in heaven over one sinner that repenteth than over ninety and nine just persons which need no repentance, and regarded as sinners all who had not experienced conversion. Washington Gladden remembered that, in his youth, in the mid-century,

the conversion of sinners was supposed to be the preacher's main business. . . . The immense importance of saving men . . . overshadowed all other interests. The appeal was, therefore, almost wholly individualistic. It constantly directed the thoughts of men to the consideration of their own personal welfare. (*Recollections*, p. 58)

And Mary Ellen Chase, writing of Maine in the nineties, recalled that

Conversion . . . was not considered, as it is today, one of those varieties of religious experience interesting alike to the philosopher and to the psychologist. Instead, in communities like ours . . . it was regarded as a necessary and fearfully important occurence in one's life, usually undergone in adolescence but sometimes sadly, yea, *dangerously,* deferred until maturer years. The conversion of the young in their parishes was the deepest concern of both our ministers; and machinery was each year set in operation by means of which it might be facilitated. This machinery consisted always of the January Week of Prayer and not infrequently also of revival meetings, held whenever the fields seemed especially ripe for harvest. (*A Goodly Heritage,* p. 136)

The Middle Border, with its missionary background, was if anything even more abandoned to revivals than Pennsylvania or New England. Ed Howe recalled the religion of Fairview:

As soon as a sufficient number of children reached a suitable age to make their conversion a harvest, a revival was commenced for their benefit, and they were called upon to make a full confession with such energy, and warned to cling to the cross for safety with such earnestness, that they generally did it, and but few escaped. If there was one so stubborn that he would not yield from worldly pride, the meetings were continued from Sunday until Monday, and kept up every night of the week at the house where the owner of the obdurant heart lived, so that he finally gave in. . . . If two or three, or four or five, would not relent within a reasonable time, the people gave up every other work, and gathered at the church in great alarm, in response to the ringing of the bell, and there they prayed and shouted the livelong day for the Lord to come down among them. (*Story of a Country Town,* pp. 31–32)

Yet even among the Protestants there had been notable exceptions to this absorption in individual soul-saving, and none of the twentieth-

century champions of the "religion of humanity" went further than
Theodore Parker in pleading the cause of the "dangerous and perishing classes" of society, or recognized more fully the duty of the church
toward such problems as labor, woman's rights, business malpractices, and war. Logically the Transcendentalists, like the Calvinists,
should have concentrated on individual salvation, but in fact they
devoted themselves and their churches to social reform, and in such
men as George Ripley, James Freeman Clarke, Edward Everett Hale,
and Octavius Brooks Frothingham, the tradition persisted even after
the sun of Transcendentalism had set.

The challenge which the new urban, industrial, and corporate order presented to the church was less dramatic, but more immediate
and complex, than that with which either Darwinism or the Higher
Criticism confronted it. The accommodation to these concepts was
intellectual merely: either a church, or a denomination, could refuse
to recognize them—in which case it went on as before, clinging to
what it called fundamentals—or it could recognize them and assimilate them, interpreting their findings as but new evidence of the
power and the glory of God and invoking poetry, imagination, and
symbolism to explain away what seemed inconsistencies in the Scriptures. In either case religious practices and conduct remained substantially unaffected, and it was, in fact, as difficult to distinguish by
their conduct or their character between fundamentalists and modernists as between Shriners and Elks.

The recognition by the church of social duties and ·obligations,
however, involved more practical, and perhaps more far-reaching,
readjustments. Darwinism, once either dismissed as impious or accepted as poetic, could be put aside and forgotten, but social responsibilities were clamorous and persistent. The easy course—and the
one which the fundamentalist churches were inclined to follow—
was to concentrate on such obvious social problems as intemperance
and vice, and these churches won their most spectacular, and elusive,
victory when the Volstead Act was passed and the Eighteenth Amendment ratified. Some of the more liberal churches—the Unitarian,
the Congregational, and the Episcopal, for example—were not content with attacking the saloon and the brothel but raised awkward
questions about ultimate responsibility for the maintenance of these
and other immoral institutions. So the champions of socialized Christianity examined the labor question, slums, predatory wealth, ab-

sentee ownership and the corporation, political corruption, and a host of related issues that brought it inevitably in conflict with the rich who built the churches, endowed the denominational colleges, and subsidized missionary activities overseas.

These apostles of the religion of humanity borrowed from Toynbee Hall the idea of settlement houses and enlisted the colleges in the effort to bring practical Christianity to the underprivileged of the great cities. They championed the cause of labor and were active in the crusade to abolish the sweatshop and child labor. They sought to break down denominational barriers and helped form a Federal Council of Churches which injected itself into all kinds of social and economic reform movements. They recognized that the admonition to render unto Caesar that which is Caesar's had been misinterpreted and participated in campaigns against bosses and rings. With the Reverend C. M. Sheldon, they asked what would happen if a congregation should follow literally In His Steps for a year. With George D. Herron, they called for a New Redemption through populism and the single tax; with W. D. P. Bliss, they ventured into socialism, then almost as disreputable as communism was to become; with Walter Rauschenbusch, they denounced capitalism and espoused industrial democracy. They challenged the evangelical churches with the assertion that individual salvation could not be divorced from social reconstruction. They sought to establish the Kingdom of God on earth and were unwilling to wait for the millennium.

3

There was no more representative spokesman for socialized Christianity than Washington Gladden of Springfield, Massachusetts, and Columbus, Ohio. He had been brought up in strictest orthodoxy, and what impressed him most about the church of the mid-century was not its insistence upon conformity or even its hostility to the most innocent diversions, but its emphasis on individual salvation. He came early under the influence of the gentle Horace Bushnell and never lost sight of the vision which Bushnell imparted to him of Christianity as a fellowship of love and of the church as a social agency. Four years on the *Independent* gave him a taste for social and economic reform and some training in the technique of advancing it, and association with the great Samuel Bowles of the *Springfield Republican* confirmed him in his liberalism and his independence. Neither Darwinism nor the Higher Criticism embarrassed him; he welcomed them rather as allies which freed Christianity from literalism and enabled the church to reclaim those who had been affronted by its irrationality.

Gladden had already written widely on the application of Christian principles to public affairs when, in 1882, his move to the capital of Ohio gave him an opportunity to translate his principles into policies. At a time when Spencerian laissez faire was accepted by respectable folk everywhere, he announced that

What men call "natural law," by which they mean the law of greed and strife . . . is not a natural law: it is unnatural; it is a crime against nature; the law of brotherhood is the only natural law. The law of nature is the law of sympathy, of fellowship, of mutual help and service.

At a time when Ohio was dominated by ruthless industrial overlords, he championed the right of labor to organize and to strike, even against members of his own wealthy congregation.

The Christian moralist [he said] is bound to admonish the Christian employer that the wage-system, when it rests on competition as its sole basis, is anti-social and anti-Christian. "Thou shalt love thy neighbor as thyself" is the Christian law, and he must find some way of incorporating that law into the organization of labor. . . . It must be possible to shape the organization of our industries in such a way that it shall be the daily habit of the workman to think of the interest of the employer, and of the employer to think of the interest of the workman.

He led the fight against accepting "tainted money" for religious purposes, finding himself in unexpected alliance with William Jennings Bryan, whose theology he thought pernicious. He served on the Columbus city council and learned at first hand how public utility corporations got valuable franchises for a pittance. He fought the American Protective Association and exposed himself to the charge that he was in the pay of Rome; he espoused the right of the Negro to equal educational and economic opportunities with whites. He combined James's faith in the pragmatic test of the consequences of conduct with Royce's loyalty to the community.

Gladden had been born early in Victoria's reign, and throughout his long life he shared something of that optimism which sustained the American even more than the English Victorians. His criticisms of the economic system were harsh but not radical, and he advocated reform rather than revolution. Temperamentally he was closer to Bryan and Roosevelt than to Altgeld or Debs: aware that American economy and society were afflicted by grave ills, he was confident of the curative power of common sense and moral persuasion.

Walter Rauschenbusch confessed to no such confidence, nor could he delude himself that either the old parties or the old shibboleths had anything to offer a people afflicted by evils that were fundamental. He came to maturity in that decade when, in Parrington's phrase, "a film of haze slowly gathered upon the face of the brilliant sun and the light of men's hopes grew dimmer." Where Gladden's natural optimism had been qualified by experience, Rauschenbusch's pessimism was qualified by faith. Better read than Gladden in theology and philosophy, he was likewise better trained in economics and sociology: New York's Hell's Kitchen rather than a Pennsylvania farm taught him the facts of social life. His background and education, too, set him apart from most of the leaders of Christian socialism—men like Edward Everett Hale, Lyman Abbott, Octavius Frothingham, Josiah Strong, W. D. P. Bliss, and others—New Englanders, most of them, and god-children of the Transcendentalists. What distinguished Rauschenbusch from these was not only his Baptist faith and his German origins but a combination of piety and tough-mindedness, religious orthodoxy and economic heterodoxy. The first American in seven generations of Lutheran and Baptist clergymen in his family, Rauschenbusch was a disciple of Schleiermacher, Troeltsch, Albrecht, and Otto Ritschl, and it was probably from the latter that he got his idea for that Brotherhood of the Kingdom which was for so many years the clearinghouse for religious thought. He was imbued with pietism rather than Transcendentalism; no more than his spiritual successor, Reinhold Niebuhr, was he prepared to dispense with the Old Testament for the New or to blink Sin, and at the Rochester Theological Seminary, where he taught for twenty years, he gave a course on The Devil.

Significant as were the Germanic contributions to his theology, Rauschenbusch's Christian socialism was an indigenous product. It was in 1886 that he came to New York to serve a poor struggling church at the edge of Hell's Kitchen. That was the year of the Haymarket riot and the abortive national strike; that was the year Henry

George made his spectacular bid for the mayoralty of New York. Soon the young German pastor found himself reading Henry George and Edward Bellamy and Jacob Riis; soon, like Howells—then enjoying a similar education in New York—he acknowledged himself a disciple of Tolstoy. These teachers, along with others—Richard Ely, Robert Hunter, John R. Commons—opened his eyes to a world he had not known in pastoral Rochester or in Old World Bonn. As early as 1887 he wrote an essay in praise of Henry George, and two years later he launched his own paper, *For the Right*. It was edited, he said, "from the standpoint of Christian Socialism," and with it and the organization of the Brotherhood of the Kingdom, he was embarked on that career which was to make him the leader for his generation of the radical religious movement.

He matured slowly, but he never deviated from the path he had marked out in those early years. In 1892 he supported the Homestead strikers and wrote a series of articles designed to prove that populism was the Christian approach to politics. With the collapse of populism, he veered to the left rather than to the right; by 1900 his reaction to the industrial scene led him to support Debs, and thereafter he was a Socialist by conviction, if not by party membership. His shift from New York to Rochester, from preaching to teaching, did not lead him to abate his anxious concern for the morality of the economic order, and in 1907 he brought out *Christianity and the Social Crisis*—with Ross's *Sin and Society* the best diagnosis of the moral confusion underlying the economic malaise that had yet appeared.

The argument of *Christianity and the Social Crisis,* as of Rauschenbusch's later books, was primarily religious. The criticism of capitalism, the competitive system, the industrial revolution, was all familiar enough; the point of departure, and the conclusions, less familiar. For Rauschenbusch's indictment of capitalism was not merely that it was antisocial but that it was anti-Christian, not that it stunted men and women in their physical growth and corrupted social and political life but that it stunted moral growth and corrupted the spirit of men.

Capitalism, Rauschenbusch asserted, was the most formidable of all enemies to the Kingdom of God. For twenty years he had studied the Bible, working his way back through the Higher Criticism to primitive Christianity, finding new truths in the sacraments and in such doctrines of orthodox theology as original sin, atonement, and redemption. What he found—it seemed simple as he stated it—was that primitive Christianity had been not just a church or a theology but a way of life, embracing church, state, family, economy, education, and all other social institutions, and that it had originally been committed to the complete moral reconstruction of society.

That it had failed in this task of moral regeneration was of interest to the historian; its present failure commanded the interest of the moralist and the reformer. Responsibility for the present failure of society to live up to Christian principles Rauschenbusch ascribed chiefly to the industrial revolution and capitalism. The industrial revolution, tapping boundless sources of energy, had promised to free men from many of the evils which had afflicted them for centuries; instead it compounded those evils.

Now at last the weary hum of the hand-spindle and the pounding of the hand-loom would cease. Nature bent her willing neck to the yoke, and the economic production of our race took a leap forward. . . . If some angel with prophetic foresight had witnessed that epoch, would he not have winged his way back to heaven to tell God that human suffering was drawing to its end? Instead of that a long-drawn wail of misery followed wherever the power-machine came. It swept the bread from men's tables and the pride from their hearts.

And capitalism, which triumphed with the industrial revolution, encouraged fear, intolerance, inequality, covetousness, pride, and other sins.

If it were proposed to invent some social system in which covetousness would be deliberately fostered and intensified in human nature, what system could be devised which would excel our own for this purpose? Competitive commerce exalts selfishness to the dignity of a moral principle. It pits men against one another in a gladiatorial game in which there is no mercy and in which ninety per cent of the combatants finally strew the arena. It makes Ishmaels of our best men and teaches them that their hand must be against every man, since every man's hand is against them. It makes men who are the gentlest and kindliest friends and neighbors, relentless taskmasters in their shops and stores, who will drain the strength of their men and pay their female employees wages on which no girl can live without supplementing them in some way. (*Christianity and the Social Crisis,* p. 265)

A Theology for the Social Gospel, written in 1917, gave a theological gloss to E. A. Ross's argument that sin was social rather than personal and that no more for religion than for law or politics did the old litanies suffice. War, oppression, intolerance, injustice, prostitution, intemperance, all were social sins, all inherent in a social system that exalted profit and position above virtue and an economy that "taught us to approach economic questions from the point of view of goods and not of men."

Rauschenbusch called boldly for a revolution in economy as well as in morals. "It is hardly likely," he wrote, "that any social revolution by which hereafter capitalism may be overthrown will cause more injustice, more physical suffering, and more heartache than the industrial revolution by which capitalism rose to power." He did not hesitate to advocate communism, though he had in mind the communism of early Christianity rather than that of Karl Marx, and his program was actually drawn largely from Henry George and Eugene Debs. "Down to modern times," he wrote,

the universal judgment of Christian thought was in favor of communism as more in harmony with the genius of Christianity and with the classical precedents of its early social life. . . . One of the greatest services which Christianity could render humanity in the throes of the present transition would be to aid those social forces which are making for the increase of communism. The Church should help public opinion to understand clearly the difference between the moral qualities of the competitive and the communistic principle, and enlist religious enthusiasm on behalf of that which is essentially Christian.

Even as he spoke, his father's country and his own were locked in a war that made a mockery of his faith in moral regeneration and left among its ruins the hopes that had sustained his generation.

We need not inquire into the effectiveness of the socialization of Christianity or ask whether, after half a century, industrial relations were more humane, race prejudice less rancorous, capital less predatory, or war less brutal than before the church undertook to ameliorate social evils, nor need we try to balance probable gains in social welfare against possible losses in individual spiritual enrichment. It is sufficient to note that the phenomenon of socialization was a logical expression of the American temperament in the new century. It reflected that decline of the importance of individualism and that growing awareness of social responsibility that could be noted, similarly, in law, education, business, and legislation, and it paralleled a similar shift in philosophy from Spencer and Sumner to Ward and Dewey. It was perhaps inevitable that an optimistic and easygoing people should develop a religion whose tests were ethical rather than intellectual, a practical people a religion whose demands could be satisfied by material concessions, an efficient people a religion that justified itself by calculable results, a democratic people a religion which embraced humanity indiscriminately rather than merely a chosen few. And it was, perhaps, equally inevitable that a people who were complacent about their own achievements should not take too seriously the jeremiads of their preachers, a people whose standards were material should reject clerical warnings against the sins of avarice, covetousness, and pride, and a people who were careless should be content with gestures toward reform.

4

It was no accident that the Unitarian and Congregational churches were the first to accept the findings of the Higher Criticism, to absorb Darwinian evolution, and to attempt to socialize the Christian doctrine. Both New England in origin, innocent of dogma or creed or of central governing authority, they drew their membership largely from the educated, native-born middle classes. But the difficulty with such liberalism as they represented was that it tended to become increasingly secular. Just as liberals in politics abandoned party affiliations and drifted into independence, so liberals in religion found it more convenient to practice their ethics or their philanthropies without benefit of church affiliation. As a result, these churches, notwithstanding their intellectual distinction, came to occupy but a marginal place in the American religious scene.

The central place in the American religious picture was filled by the Baptist, Methodist, Lutheran, Presbyterian, and Episcopal among the Protestant churches and by the vast and powerful Roman Catholic church. On the eve of the first World War these Protestant churches counted some twenty-two million communicants; by the time of the second World War their membership had increased to about thirty million, while the Roman Catholic church grew, in the same years, from sixteen to twenty-three million and Jewish congregations increased to almost five million. With the occasional exception of the Protestant Episcopal, which drew a disproportionate number of its communicants from the rich and the educated, and of some Baptist congregations which took advantage of a congregational church policy to indulge in theological liberalism, these churches were conservative in their social program and fundamentalist in their theology.

The strength and persistence of fundamentalism well into the twentieth century is one of the curiosities of the history of American thought. That a people so optimistic and self-confident should accept a theology which insisted on the depravity of man, that a people so distrustful of all authority should yield so readily to the authority of the Scriptures as interpreted by men like themselves, that a people so inclined to independence should take their religious ideas at second hand, that a people so scientific minded should resolutely ignore the impact of science in the realm of religion—all this is difficult to explain, except on fundamentalist grounds.

Other explanations suggest a divorce between religious and secular thought, a dichotomy in the American mind which the student is reluctant to accept. That, in a world which trembled and reeled beneath them, where life seemed a matter of endless adjustments and readjustments to the obscure and shifting facts of science, men should cling to something that seemed stable and familiar was not wonderful; that they should find it exclusively in the fundamentalist version of the Scriptures was. They sang Henry Lyte's great hymn as a prayer:

> Swift to its close ebbs out life's little day;
> Earth's joys grow dim, its glories pass away;
> Change and decay in all around I see;
> O Thou who changest not, abide with me.

With Henry Adams, whom they did not read, they were ready to believe that, force for force, the Virgin was as intelligible as the dynamo. With T. S. Eliot, whom they did not know, they cried:

> God is leaving us, God is leaving us, more pang,
>   more pain, than birth or death.
> Sweet and cloying through the dark air
> Falls the stifling sense of despair.

(The Cathedral)

As science revealed a mysterious universe, they clung all the more devoutly to their familiar God. They did not wish to inquire into the truth of revealed religion, for that old-time religion gave them assurance of salvation, just as it was. They resented the invasion of religion by science just as many Southerners resented the invasion of race relations by science; they preferred to cling to the doctrine of the inspiration and the inerrancy of the Scriptures, as many Southerners preferred to cling to the notion of white supremacy—as an article of faith. They felt instinctively that to subject the Bible to the test of textual criticism or of the laboratory was both shabby and dangerous.

Yet other beliefs as deeply imbedded in tradition and custom, and almost as sacrosanct, had yielded to the findings of scholarship and science, and even Southerners were forced, in time, to modify some of their notions about the Negro. That religion could be brought into conformity with new currents of thought and fitted to the practical needs of society without consequences fatal to its spiritual content had been asserted by their greatest religious leaders—men like Henry Ward Beecher and Lyman Abbott and Phillips Brooks—and abundantly demonstrated by the modernists. Why were the assertions so widely ignored, the demonstrations so commonly rejected?

Perhaps it was because religion meant, on the whole, so little; because, divorced as it was from the intimate realities of daily life and excused from active participation in the affairs of business, politics, or society, it could be regarded as a thing apart, not subject to the normal tests prescribed for secular faiths and doctrines. Fundamentalists resented a critical attitude toward their religion as they resented a critical attitude toward their mothers. They improvidently ignored religious precepts, just as they ignored the moral axioms inculcated by their mothers, but they did this, as it were, on weekdays and honored religion on Sundays—as they honored their mothers on Mother's Day, that curious American institution. Because they rarely subjected their religion to the test of experience and application, they could cherish it as they might cherish some museum piece which was never subject to such wear and tear as might expose its fragility.

For what is striking about fundamentalism is not alone the zeal with which it was maintained or the general acceptance it commanded but the superficiality with which it was observed. These terms may seem contradictory, just as it may seem contradictory to remark that the superpatriotism of the D.A.R. sometimes constituted disloyalty, but the contradiction is resolved if we keep in mind that fundamentalism came to be, increasingly, a ceremonial attitude, divorced from conduct. The fundamentalists themselves were rarely fundamentalist; they asserted the inerrancy of the Scriptures, but that literal interpretation of the New Testament upon which they insisted would have convulsed their society and economy. It is recorded that the Reverend C. M. Sheldon sold eight million copies of *In His Steps,* but the number who followed its precepts was probably somewhat smaller. Certainly some of the southern fundamentalists did not act as if they believed in the authority of the Biblical injunction to love thy neighbor as thyself; geographically, fundamentalism and lynching seemed to go together. It was typical of the fundamentalist position that the organized Fundamentalist movement, launched in 1909, was financed by two California oil millionaires who had somehow overlooked both Matthew 19:24 and Mark 10:25. Dwight Moody, most attractive of postwar revivalists, gave away all of his fabulous earnings, but his successors in spreading the straight Gospel—men like Bryan and Billy Sunday and John Alexander Dowie—did not display a comparable contempt for money.

After the first World War, fundamentalism lost much of its driving force, its authority, and its dignity, and became increasingly querulous, negative, and histrionic. The fundamentalists were eased out of the colleges and lost control of most theological schools; those which they retained, or founded, lacked prestige and good students. Heresy trials, painfully frequent even in the nineties and the early years of the century, were abandoned, and heretics went their way unmolested if not unrebuked. The contrast between the treatment accorded poor Tom Paine and Col. "Bob" Ingersoll is illuminating; even more illuminating is the fact that the next generation had no need for any devil's advocate and that organized Free Thought, which flourished on opposition and martyrdom, flickered and died out. Except in certain backward areas like southern California and the rural South, revivals petered out, and even Chautauqua, never aggressively fundamentalist or without dignity and beauty, declined sharply in popularity. The champions of fundamentalism in the twentieth century were men and women like Sam Jones, Gypsy Smith, Billy Sunday, John Roach Stratton, and Aimee Semple McPherson, who compared somewhat unfavorably with their predecessors in orthodoxy like Jonathan Edwards, Bishop Asbury, Charles Finney, or even Dwight L. Moody. Under such leadership, fundamentalism appealed, increasingly, to the uneducated and the half-educated; it exploited fear not only of hell-fire and damnation but of Catholics and Jews, and in the South and Middle West it formed an unofficial alliance with the Ku Klux Klan.

Two episodes which came at the conclusion of the first quarter of the new century dramatized at once the tenacious strength of fundamentalism and its intellectual decadence: the fight over the Ku Klux Klan plank in the Democratic national convention of 1924 and the Scopes trial at Dayton, Tennessee, the following year. Fundamentalism was not officially represented at the Democratic convention, but William Jennings Bryan was its unofficial spokesman, and it largely inspired the opposition both to the nomination of the Catholic Alfred E. Smith and to the plank denouncing the notorious Ku Klux Klan. For reasons not entirely connected with religion it was victorious on both issues: it is proper to recall, however, that Governor Smith was nominated in 1928 and that the Ku Klux Klan disintegrated. That fundamentalists should have opposed Governor Smith on religious grounds in 1924 and again in 1928 is a reflection either on their sincerity or their intelligence, for Catholics were extreme fundamentalists, and whatever else Romanism may have threatened, it scarcely threatened either religion or morality.

The issue at Dayton was more clear cut: here was one of the decisive battles in that warfare between science and theology which Andrew Dickson White had deplored more than a generation earlier. The religious question—the wisdom of the state law forbidding the teaching of evolution in public schools—was, to be sure, confused by the legal one—the right of the state to enact such a law. Both public opinion and counsel largely ignored the legal and concentrated on the religious issue. It was appropriate that Bryan should have appeared as counsel for the prosecution, for he was not only the most distinguished and eloquent of American fundamentalists but largely responsible for the enactment of antievolution laws in several southern states. It was less appropriate, perhaps, that Clarence Darrow should have been chief counsel for the defense, for in the eyes of most Americans he represented not modernist religion but irreligion, and his advocacy of evolution and assault upon Fundamentalism enabled the prosecution to identify science with atheism.

Bryan at Dayton is a spectacle that cannot fail to command the anxious interest of every student of the American mind, for it marked the end not only of a career but of an era. No one had more faithfully represented the American mind and character than the Great Commoner who had thrice led the democracy, the Peerless Leader who had championed righteousness and morality with a consistency without parallel in modern politics; but it was the mind and character of the mid-nineteenth, not the twentieth, century that he represented; it was for the America of the Middle Border, of the farm and the village, of the little red schoolhouse and the little brown church, of the Chautauqua tent and the Redpath circuit, of Puritanism and evangelism, of agrarian democracy and homespun equality that he spoke. He had spent his boyhood and youth in an atmosphere of piety and was never thereafter able to breathe any other without discomfort. His father had been a Baptist, his mother a Methodist, he himself was converted to Presbyterianism when still a boy; it was characteristic that he should have been attached to the three most numerous and conservative of Protestant denominations. From these fundamentalist churches he derived his religious ideas and habits and he never saw reason to modify them: the old-time religion was good enough for him and for everyone else. His sincere devotion to Jefferson did not embrace that statesman's religious views or concepts of toleration, and the evolution of democracy from Jefferson to Bryan went far to confirm Henry Adams' theory of entropy. History remembers the Cross of Gold, but his contemporaries knew Bryan rather for the oft-repeated eulogy of the Prince of Peace; to them he was the Peerless Leader not only of democracy but of morality, his very vocabulary freighted with the Scriptures, his political campaigns moral crusades. As he had founded his political morality on the Bible, there was no inconsistency in his advocacy of fundamentalism; as he had always been opposed by the rich, the privileged, and the learned, there was some consistency, too, in his hostility to a modernism which found its support in the eastern cities and seats of learning.

Constitutionally Bryan's case was unimpeachable, for in a democracy, as Justice Holmes never tired of pointing out, the people have a right to make fools of themselves. Bryan, however, did no adopt this logical but embarrassing position. Neither he nor Darrow argued the constitutional issue, and their evasion was encouraged by the Court, the press, and public opinion. It was not young John T. Scopes, after all, who was on trial but fundamentalism itself. To the delight of the newspapermen and the chagrin of the devout, the trial degenerated into a circus and a brawl. That was both unfortunate and misleading, but it was perhaps inevitable. It was unfortunate because it made a mockery of the faith of millions of men and women; it was misleading because fundamentalism, for all its glaring intellectual inadequacies, was not to be confounded by arguments which Colonel Ingersoll had already exhausted. If Bryan failed to meet the challenge of science, Darrow failed equally to meet the challenge which traditional religion presented to modern philosophy, and the failure of both illuminated the confusion that permeated the American mind in the twentieth century.

Technically Bryan won his case, for Scopes was convicted and the conviction sustained in the state Supreme Court; actually he lost it, and even his dramatic death could not reverse the decision which public opinion had rendered. It was not that Darrow and his colleagues made fundamentalism ridiculous; actually, by falling back on the arguments of Ingersoll and Brann "the Iconoclast," they made anti-fundamentalism almost equally ridiculous. It was rather that Bryan, for all his eloquence, was unable to demonstrate the connection between fundamentalism and morality or explain the relevance of fundamentalism to the complex problems of the twentieth century or infuse the fundamentalist cause with vitality or dignity.

Although fundamentalism persisted and the numbers of those who theoretically subscribed to its dogmas remained high, it never quite recovered from its connection with the Ku Klux Klan and the Dayton trial. By the mid-century it had lost power and prestige: the legal crusade against evolution was quietly dropped; the war on Higher Criticism became an anachronism and Fundamentalist churches found no religious obstacles to an interest in social welfare. Fundamentalism declined not so much because it was refuted—for its adherents were indifferent to secular refutation—as because it had lost whatever intellectual vitality and moral justification it had possessed.

5

It was not fundamentalism, however, but denominationalism that made the strongest impression on foreign observers of the American scene. Accustomed as most of them were to an established church and to the domination of the religious field—and of the social and intellectual as well—by one great church, they commonly found American religion a thing of shreds and tatters. As they traveled through the country, they found three or four major denominations represented in each village, a score in each city. If they turned for confirmation of their impressions to the official census of religious bodies, they would find some two hundred denominations claiming recognition. Nowhere else in the western world did religion display a comparable fecundity, nowhere else did individualism express itself so emphatically in the spiritual field.

Yet the observer who ventured beyond statistics shortly found himself involved in confusion and contradiction. If he went within the churches, he would find that though there were differences in ritual there was no perceptible difference in the Gospel which was preached, in the clergymen who preached it, or in the congregations who heard it. If he turned to the religious books which poured from the presses in undismayed numbers, he would discover the same essential harmony of philosophy if not of doctrine. If he visited the denominational colleges and the theological seminaries, he would be impressed not so much by their formal variety as by their basic uniformity of student body, faculty, and curriculum. Even church architecture, which had long had its own denominational pattern, was becoming increasingly uniform as Congregational and Unitarian churches abandoned their lovely and austere white-steepled meetinghouses, and Baptist, Methodist, and Presbyterian their dusty brown or hideous yellow brick auditoriums for imitation Gothic or Romanesque. The perspicacious observer, balancing the statistical multiformity against the cultural uniformity, would find it difficult to resist the conclusion that American Protestantism was miscellaneous rather than diverse, heterogeneous rather than inharmonious.

American denominationalism had its roots both in philosophy and in history. Philosophically it grew out of the inheritance of Protestantism, English and Continental, which was by its very nature disintegrating: only where the State was strong was fragmentation arrested, and the State was not strong in America. Historically it was a response to the environment of individualism and independence which the New World provided and to those religious and national divisions which were continually being transplanted from the Old World to the New.

Inheritance and environment were equally important. Nonconformity flourished most luxuriantly on the frontier, and all America was frontier to the Old World. Yet it was the English, not the French or Spanish, frontiers that nourished it. The principle that men could come together and make a church had been asserted in England by Puritans, Separatists, Brownists, and Quakers, but it was the American environment that so prodigiously stimulated the practice of religious independency and gave it such far-reaching significance: English religious fertility was not to be compared with American after the seventeenth century. The vast distances that separated the American colonials from Europe encouraged them to set up their own churches, and the lack of adequate machinery for supervision and—outside New England—of an educated ministry encouraged experiment and heterodoxy.

The effect of Old World religious and national divisions on American denominationalism was both more obvious and more persistent. From the very beginning each national and language group brought its own church with it, and with religious freedom guaranteed in federal and state constitutions there was official sanction for religious diversification. With the vast flood of immigration in the nineteenth century, denominations multiplied with bewildering rapidity: every racial and language division in the Old World was reproduced in the New, every schism took new root in favorable soil. Most of the two hundred-odd denominations recorded in the Census of Religious Bodies reflected not theological but racial, linguistic, historical, or even geographical differences. Thus the twenty-some separate Lutheran churches in America were divided not so much by dogma as by language. As the foreign-language church was the most effective of all agencies for the maintenance of transplanted languages and cultures, its leaders stubbornly resisted Americanization or even too close an affiliation with native denominational bodies. The emancipation of the Negro, too, aggravated the denominational divisions, for Negroes not only preferred their own organizations within the traditional denominational framework but displayed an astonishing originality in the establishment of new cults. Geography and sectionalism, too, played a role which should not surprise those familiar with the sharply differentiated churches of England, Scotland, and Wales. Some churches which had split on the slavery issue found it inconvenient to reunite; others, on successive frontiers, found that they had departed so far from the creed or ritual of their mother churches that independence was easier than a return to conformity.

Yet denominationalism was not to be accounted for entirely by these fortuitous historical circumstances. There was a continuous flowering of new religions, sects, and cults, which, however bizarre some of them may have appeared, testified to the strength of the creative instinct in the spiritual realm and to the characteristically American confidence that all religious truth was not exhausted by the Reformation.

The most notable of these native American religions were Mormonism and Christian Science. Mormonism is interesting chiefly because, although a product of the frontier, it departed so sharply from the customary pattern of frontier religions. Where these were individualistic, particularistic, and emotional, Mormonism was authoritative, centralized, regimented, and efficient. Its appeal was, in fact, more effective with the foreign than with the native-born, and its chief conquests were overseas; it was the most imperialistic of American religions and the only one with a territorial foundation. Its social and economic achievement was spectacular, its contribution to religious thought negligible. From the beginning it not only invaded but controlled the daily life of its constituents; it is perhaps the best illustration which American religion affords of the magnetic power of a secular appeal.

Christian Science, another religion which owes its origin to the inspiration of a single founder, appeared half a century after Mormonism. In the centralization of its authority, the rigidity of its discipline, its reliance on old truths in new forms—and, it might be added, its prosperity and success—it resembled Mormonism, but there the similarity ends. For Christian Science was urban where Mormonism was rural; its appeal was to the upper rather than to the lower middle classes, to women rather than to men, to the sophisticated rather than to the primitive. It derived from the New Testament rather than the Old, and its concern was with spiritual rather than material welfare. Although purporting to be a new dispensation, Christian Science taught what philosophers and theologians had asserted for two thousand years: that sin, pain, disease, and death have no reality, and that, through grace and faith, the mind can triumph over these and find its way to health, happiness, and salvation. Where philosophers from St. Augustine to Josiah Royce had propounded this doctrine as a metaphysical theory, Mrs. Eddy advanced it as a scientific fact and she called her bible *Science and Health.* Christian Science, though it remained comparatively small and uninfluential, attracted a vast amount of attention. It was the only major modern religion to be founded by a woman; its doctrine of faith healing brought it in conflict with the law; its proselytizing activities advertised it abroad; its classical architecture, its use of reading rooms, its substitution of readers and practitioners for clergy, differentiated it from Protestant denominations, and its remarkable newspaper, the *Christian Science Monitor,* gave it an intellectual standing which it might not otherwise have enjoyed.

Mormonism, Christian Science, and a host of other religions, such as the International Four Square Gospel, the Jehovah's Witnesses, the House of David, and the Holiness churches, gave variety and color to the American religious picture. Actually, however, the religious scene was by no means so diversified as the official record or the superficial view would suggest, and the American character, otherwise harmonious, was not inharmonious in its spiritual expression. For if we look more critically into the statistics of church membership, we find that in the middle of the twentieth century two thirds of all church members belonged to three denominations— the Roman Catholic, Baptist, and Methodist; and that over nine tenths adhered to the ten leading denominations—some of them, to be sure, like the Baptist and the Lutheran, divided into a dozen fragments. Nor does a statistical analysis reveal fully the deceptive character of mere denominational distinctions. While most Americans were vaguely conscious of the dogmatic differences which distinguished Protestants, Catholics, and Jews, few were able to explain or justify those which divided the various Protestant denominations, and there were no intellectual or social differences between Baptists, Methodists, Presbyterians, Lutherans, Disciples, and others, save those of the local mores. Church membership, indeed, rarely had anything to do with dogma: the vast majority of those who were not born to a particular church attached themselves to one for reasons that could not be called other than secular: accessibility, convenience, an engaging minister, or an attractive social program.

It might indeed be plausibly maintained that uniformity rather than multiformity characterized the American religious scene. The distinction between the churched and the unchurched was less sharp than in most other countries, the distinction between Protestants and Catholics less acute, and the practice of shifting from denomination to denomination far more common. With most Americans, religious allegiance was not unlike political allegiance: inherited rather than assumed, dictated, often, by geography or by interest rather than by intellectual conviction, it was embraced without solemnity, changed without spiritual travail, abandoned without pain.

With a few exceptions, denominational differences did not carry with them the social and even economic and political connotations that Church and Chapel, for example, possessed in England, and it was inconceivable that any churches should seek political power or privilege as they did, so commonly, on the Continent. In some of the older parts of the country, to be sure, denominational associations still retained some faint social significance. In Charleston it was still true that the gentry would rather be buried in St. Michael's or St. Philip's than alive anywhere else: perhaps the beauty of those churches and the haunting loveliness of their churchyards accounted for what might otherwise be thought a conceit. In Boston the Unitarian and in New York the Dutch Reformed shared social and intellectual leadership only with the Episcopal church, while around Philadelphia an aura of aristocracy still hovered, paradoxically and uncertainly, around the humble Friends. In some sections of the South the Presbyterian, in some parts of the North the Congregational, church retained a dubious primacy, and in Maryland and Louisiana, Catholicism enjoyed an incontestable social position. It is suggestive that although the Episcopal and Unitarian were among the smallest of denominations, they boasted, respectively, nine and four American presidents, while only four presidents confessed to the Methodist and two to the Baptist faith. If we look, however, at the record from 1890 to the mid-twentieth century, we find, among eleven presidents, two Methodists, two Presbyterians, two Baptists, and one each of the Unitarian, Dutch Reformed, Congregational, Quaker, and Episcopal faiths: it is perhaps a fairer index to the contemporary religious scene.

By and large it remained true that religious distinctions did not carry over to the social realm: American society, exposed to so many and dangerous divisions, escaped this most pernicious of all. The exceptions are significant, but their significance belongs to the nineteenth rather than the twentieth century. The most striking was, of course, that supplied by the Roman Catholic church. Historically Catholicism was associated with immigration: its communicants belonged, almost inevitably, to the poorer and less privileged elements of American society, and from the days of the Know-Nothing movement to the modern Ku Klux Klan much of the hostility to it was racial and economic rather than religious. Increasingly after 1900, as it became less dependent on immigrant contributions, achieved a broader native base, and grew in wealth and power, Catholicism attained a social position equal to that of most Protestant denominations and an intellectual position at least as high as the average. No Catholic had reached the White House, but two had presided over the Supreme Court, and from the days of Bishop Cheverus of Boston to those of Cardinal Gibbons of Baltimore the Catholic hierarchy has been able to command such social prestige as it cared to accept.

6

The growth of Catholicism was the most spectacular development in American religious history after the decade of the eighties. In 1890 the Roman Catholic church counted some nine million communicants; thirty years later the number had doubled, and every sixth person, every third church member, was Catholic. It was no accident that this giant growth coincided with that great flood of immigration which brought over sixteen million people from Europe to the New World, for well over half of these came from the Catholic countries of central and southern Europe. No church which had been in America a century before the Pilgrims landed at Cape Cod could be called an immigrant church, but probably the majority not only of Catholic communicants but of the hierarchy were first and second generation Americans. "Has the immigrant kept the faith?" was a question anxiously canvassed by Catholic writers in these years: a correlation of the figures of Catholic growth with immigration and birth-rate records indicated pretty clearly that he had.

The flood of immigration was dammed up, after 1920, by restrictive legislation, and in the next quarter-century the Catholic population increased by a mere twenty per cent—from twenty to twenty-four millions. For the first time the ratio of Catholic increase not only failed to exceed the ratio of population increase but was substantially smaller than the increases recorded for the Protestant Episcopal, the Lutheran, or the Eastern Orthodox churches. While a growth of four million was sufficiently impressive to give pause to those who believed that Catholicism was wholly dependent upon immigration, it by no means confirmed the hopes or fears of those who had confidently predicted that the United States was destined to become a Catholic country.

Yet a quarter-century was nothing in the life of a church which traced its history back to St. Peter, nor would a position temporarily second to the Protestant disquiet churchmen whose church could claim undisputed primacy among Christians on five continents. Other considerations than those of present numbers were relevant to the question of the future strength and influence of Catholicism in America. Of these the most significant were its racial and geographical distribution, its attitude toward the family and education, its organization, discipline, and history. Catholicism was strongest among the most prolific elements of the American population—the Irish, Poles, Italians, French-Canadians, and Mexicans—and while infant mortality was relatively high among these groups, increased prosperity and improved medical facilities promised to reduce it to the national average. The implacable hostility of the Catholic church to birth control and divorce suggested that the Catholic population would, in the future, increase more rapidly than the Protestant, while the success of the Catholic church in bringing the children of mixed marriages into the fold contrasted sharply with the failure of Judaism in this policy or with the casualness of most Protestant denominations. While comparisons are necessarily difficult, it would seem that the average Catholic took his religion somewhat more seriously than the average Protestant or Jew; if church attendance was an accurate index, the generalization could scarcely be challenged. The unassailable unity of the Catholic church, its centralized control and discipline, its far-flung and elaborate organization, its refusal to compromise with modernism or nationalism, its rejection or affiliation or ecclesiastical cooperation with non-Catholic bodies, its clear-cut program and purpose, its comprehensive and rigid control of education from the parochial school through the seminary and the university, all contrasted sharply with the secularism, individualism, liberalism, provincialism, and fragmentation of Protestantism. Finally, the geographical concentration of Catholicism in the North-east and in the larger cities gave it a potential power, political and cultural, enjoyed by no other denomination except the Baptist and Methodist in the South and the Mormon in Utah.

Was that power more than potential? Was it actually exercised, and was its exercise dangerous? Certainly many Americans thought so, and the fear that had inspired the Charlestown, Philadelphia, and St. Louis riots earlier in the nineteenth century inspired the blundering antics of the American Protective Association in the nineties and the hysteria of the Ku Klux Klan a quarter-century later, while in 1928 it was still powerful enough to swing Virginia, North Carolina, Florida, and Texas into the Republican column. Yet the *Menace* petered out, the *Maria Monk* type of shocker could not compete with Faulkner or Caldwell, and the conviction that every village priest was bent on undermining the foundations of the Republic and that every nunnery and monastery housed strange and fascinating iniquities lingered on only in backward parts of such states as Indiana and Arkansas.

It was easy to dismiss this type of anti-Catholicism as vulgar but insignificant. More serious were the apprehensions voiced by judicious and scholarly students such as Charles Marshall and W. E. Garrison that Catholic doctrine was inconsistent with the American principles of liberty and democracy, complete freedom of expression, separation of church and state, and secular control over public education. It was not mere prejudice that animated the Reverend Mr. Garrison's *Catholicism and the American Mind* or Mr. Marshall's famous open letter to Governor Smith.

The question of the harmony of Catholicism with American institutions can be approached logically and theologically or historically and pragmatically. Logically Catholicism would seem to be in conflict with many principles of the American political system, an observation which some may regard as a criticism of that political system rather than of Catholic doctrine. Thus the *Papal Syllabus of Errors* of 1864 pronounced it an error to assert that "it is no longer expedient that the Catholic religion shall be held as the only religion of the State, to the exclusion of all other modes of worship" or "that the church ought to be separated from the state and the state from the church." Thus the encyclical of November 1, 1885, pronounced at variance with Christian and natural law the principle that,

As all men are alike equal by race and nature, so in like manner all are equal in the control of their life; that each one is so far his own master as to be in no sense under the rule of any other individual; that each is free to think on every subject just as he may choose and to do whatever he may like to do; that no man has any right to rule over other men. In a society grounded upon such maxims, all government is nothing more or less than the will of the people, and the people, being under the power of itself alone, is alone its own ruler.

Thus so distinguished a Catholic as Monsignor John A. Ryan insisted that, "According to the Catholic position, the State has no right to make laws affecting the validity of the marriages of baptized persons. . . . She [the church] does not consider that human welfare, or social welfare, is promoted by State recognition of any marriage which she pronounces invalid or by State prohibition of any marriage that she declares valid."

In principle, too, the Catholic church presented a sharp challenge to the American philosophy of the relation of the state to education. Thus the encyclical of Pius XI, *Christian Education of Youth,* stated categorically that "all education belongs pre-eminently to the Church." Thus Archbishop John T. McNicholas of the National Catholic Educational Association called government monopoly of education "in reality Fascistic control of schools." Thus so judicious a Catholic layman as George N. Shuster blamed the rejection of a system of denominational and parochial schools for public schools on "the grotesque stupidity of Protestants."

Logically these doctrines and expressions spelled hostility to some of the principles and institutions which Americans cherished. The debate between Mr. Marshall and Governor Smith suggested, however, that there was no basis for any immediate fear that these doctrines would be urged in a doctrinaire manner. The Catholic church was one of the most logical of human institutions, but its logic, unlike that of communism, rejected the doctrinaire approach and adapted itself to realities. These doctrines, Catholic apologists explained, applied only to some ideal situation or to some country completely Catholic and had no present relevance to the United States. However, twenty years after Governor Smith had dissipated fears of Catholic intervention in political affairs, Cardinal Spellman showed himself ready to apply doctrine to a current situation by aggressive advocacy of federal aid to parochial schools and by intemperate denunciation of Eleanor Roosevelt for her temperate criticism of such use of public funds.

Yet, though Catholicism made itself heard on many matters of domestic and foreign policy, there was seldom convincing evidence that it concerned itself improperly with matters outside the legitimate interest of the church in the spiritual and moral welfare of its communicants, especially as the church itself decided what were its legitimate interests. Thus Catholics—rather than the Catholic church —opposed the federal child labor amendment, sponsored censorship of the stage, moving pictures, and books, and advocated legislation looking to the discouragement of birth control and of loose divorce laws. While to many Protestants all these matters seemed to belong to the civil realm, Catholics were not without justification in holding that they affected the moral welfare of their people. They could argue that Catholic interest in birth control or divorce was as legitimate as Methodist interest in prohibition or Presbyterian interest in evolution. In foreign affairs Catholics exercised some influence on the settlement of the Friars' lands dispute in the Philippines and on State Department attitudes toward Mexico in the twenties, Spain in the thirties, and Soviet Russia in the forties. No method has as yet been found, however, to distinguish the religious from the secular motives that inspire the expression of opinion or to sterilize political opinions of religious origin, nor could any democrat consistently deny voters their right to agitate for policies consistent with their moral convictions even though these happened to coincide with the convictions of their church.

Whatever conclusions might be drawn from a scrutiny of Catholic doctrine, the fact was that Catholicism had flourished as a major religion for three quarters of a century without raising serious difficulties except in the imaginations of men and that democratic institutions seemed as sound when the church numbered twenty-four million members as they had been when it counted its communicants by the hundred thousand. It might, indeed, be maintained that the Catholic church was, during this period, one of the most effective of all agencies for democracy and Americanization. Representing as it did a vast cross section of the American people, it could ignore class, section, and race; peculiarly the church of the newcomers, of those who all too often were regarded as aliens, it could give them not only spiritual refuge but social security. As late as 1891 Father Cahensly had advocated the organization of the Catholic church in America on racial and language lines, but Cardinal Gibbons set himself resolutely against this dangerous fragmentation of the Universal Church, and the Cahensly Memorial was rejected. "He was determined," wrote the Cardinal's biographer, "that the Church in this country should continue homogeneous, like the nation. If the discord of rival nationalist aims were definitely introduced, his work would go down a wreck." And Archbishop Ireland, who shared with the great Cardinal leadership of American Catholicism, insisted that "the Church of America must be, of course, as Catholic as even in Jerusalem or Rome, but as far as her garments assume color from local atmosphere, she must be American. Let no one dare paint on her brow with a foreign tint, or pin to her mantle foreign linings."

Not only did Catholicism accept America but more and more America accepted the Catholic church. This was in part a recognition of its strength, in part the tribute to its historical appeal by a people ever more conscious of their past. Montcalm had always been as heroic a figure as Wolfe, but he belonged to France; now Junipero Serra, Father De Smet, and Father Lamy were admitted to the American Valhalla. Skillful biographers like Agnes Repplier, novelists like Mary Austin, Thornton Wilder, and Willa Cather, threw an aura of romance over the beginnings of Catholicism in America, and it is suggestive that it was a Catholic priest who was the most admirable figure in Grace Zaring Stone's remarkable re-creation of Puritan New England, *The Cold Journey*. It is significant, too, that Catholicism was treated with unvarying respect in the newspapers, magazines, and radio and that Hollywood seemed to prefer Catholic priests to Protestant parsons for its more sentimental religious roles: whether Hollywood's gesture was a tribute to the spiritual authority or to the temporal strength of Catholicism it is unnecessary to determine.

Although Catholicism adapted itself to American democracy, it would be an error to suppose that it was, in any doctrinal sense, Americanized, for a Universal Church, dominated by Italian and French churchmen, could not be expected to accommodate its doctrines to the idiosyncrasies of a people whose contributions to theological thought were so negligible. Indeed it was "those views which . . . are called by some Americanism" that were condemned by the Apostolic Letter, *Testem Benevolentiae,* which Leo XIII addressed to Cardinal Gibbons in 1899. Precisely what those views were is a problem impenetrable to the layman for, when examined, they evaporate into thin air, like the Cheshire cat, leaving nothing but a sardonic—and we may assume a Gallic—grin behind. "Rome had caught something in the air," writes Theodore Maynard, the most recent historian of American Catholicism, "a readiness to yield to the *Zeitgeist* to win souls by accommodation. It was no more than a vague incipience. But it would quite possibly have developed and hardened had not Leo spoke." Just how something which the American Catholic hierarchy declared nonexistent could have hardened is a question best left to theologians, but in any event Leo spoke and "Americanism," if it had ever lived, was dead.

Nor was there any difficulty about modernism in American Catholicism. That heresy, which ravaged the Protestant denominations, was disposed of by a series of encyclicals of 1906–7, notably the great encyclical, *Pascendi Dominici Gregis*. In England the saintly George Tyrrell and in France the learned Alfred Loisy were forced out of the church by these encyclicals, but, as Theodore Maynard observes, "in America the anti-modernist oath was taken with no recalcitrance." "It has sometimes been suggested," he adds, "that what saved the American Church from these ravages was the fact that American Catholics were not much addicted to speculation." In this, in any event, they were thoroughly American.

PART II

CHAPTER X

Lester Ward and the Science of Society

I

THAT THE PROPER study of mankind is man was recognized long before Pope coined the aphorism, but the study was assumed to belong to philosophy or art rather than to science. When, in the eighteenth century, men began to indulge the hope that human institutions might be brought within the scope of science, the consequences were revolutionary. For if, indeed, all were

> but parts of one stupendous whole,
> Whose body Nature is, and God the soul,

then man and his institutions were subject to the same inexorable laws that governed the movements of heavenly bodies or the circulation of the blood. It remained merely to find those laws, and the science of society could take its place alongside the science of chemistry or of physics.

This notion, that there were fixed laws that ruled human destinies and molded human institutions, inspired generations of philosophers to formulate them and generations of bemused sovereigns to require their subjects to conform to them. It animated visionaries like Condorcet and Godwin and Jefferson and enlightened statesmen like Struensee and Joseph II and Benjamin Thompson, Count Rumford, and even seduced tyrants like Frederick and Catherine the Great temporarily from military to civil adventures. For a century the greatest minds dedicated themselves to the search for Law—in the realms of government, jurisprudence, political economy, history, and of what came with Comte to be known as sociology. Gradually the term "social sciences" came to be accepted for the study of mankind, and those who forgot that *scientia* meant merely knowledge were persuaded to expect from this study results comparable to those achieved in the natural sciences. It is suggestive that philosophers were permitted to play a larger role in government and public affairs in the eighteenth than in the nineteenth century.

It was not wonderful that the search for a science of society should be transferred to America or that American contributions should be impressive. On the contrary, the new land seemed to offer the fairest opportunity for the formulation of those laws which should guide society to Utopia, for here Nature was bountiful, man virtuous and intelligent, the past not too burdensome, and the future malleable. The great Declaration was grounded on principles drawn from the Laws of Nature and Nature's God, and the Constitution was designed to embody eternal truths about the nature of man and government and their mutual relations. Certainly the doctrines of constitutional law, as expounded by John Marshall and Joseph Story, were presumed to be rooted in the very nature of the universe. In the economic realm, Federalists like Hamilton, who tried to fasten mercantilism on America, and agrarians like George Logan, who elaborated the theories of the physiocrats, alike acknowledged the authority of scientific laws. Historians admitted that the American experience was a fulfillment of a Providential design, and destiny was made manifest by a priori reasoning.

Evolution—particularly in that Spencerian form which was accepted by social and economic fundamentalists, as the King James version of the Bible by religious fundamentalists—brought the social into the stream of the physical sciences. Although it hopelessly disrupted what we may call the Newtonian principle of social mechanics, it substituted not chaos but a different order and a different law. Nor was the law of evolution less impersonal than those Laws of Nature to which the eighteenth century had so hopefully subscribed. Indeed, the Spencerian version of law dispensed with man far more cavalierly than the Newtonian, for it conjectured a mechanism that, like some sealed engine, worked best without tinkering. That mechanism was self-starting and self-regulating; it was subject only to physical forces and immune from what Lester Ward called the psychic factors in civilization. Thus, where enlightened despots had hoped to relate social institutions to such laws of nature as philosophers might discover, Spencer and his disciples insisted that man's most signal virtue was acquiescence in the impersonal processes of evolution.

To such disciples as John Fiske, to be sure, who imported divine design into science, man was the object and the purpose of evolution. But William Graham Sumner's more scrupulous reading of the Spencerian text held that man was the subject, not the object, of the evolutionary process and that the success of that process was strictly correlated with his passivity. No one applied more rigorously to the social realm the Darwinian doctrine of the survival of the fittest than this Episcopal rector turned sociologist, who conceded to the commandments from Manchester an authority he could not concede to those from Mt. Sinai. He elevated laissez faire into a social and economic law and assigned to it the same standing as the law of gravity. His study of Folkways had diverted him from the standards of conventional morality, but he constructed a new moral system in which competition became a virtue and regulation a vice. "All experience," he wrote, "is against state regulation and in favor of liberty. The freer the civil institutions are, the more weak or mischievous state regulation is." Yet the liberty he extolled did not derive from Heaven or from some social contract but from the necessities of Nature itself. Where Nature was concerned he was a fundamentalist, and his fundamentalism was not unlike that of that Bryan whom he detested, for he insisted upon the infallibility of Nature's scripture and would not permit the hand of man to profane the sacred text.

Sumner was at once economist and sociologist, and from his study of each of these disciplines he drew the lesson of laissez faire with such consistency that he deprived them of their legitimate function, reducing them to a merely historical role. His contemplation of the long evolution of human society led to but one grand conclusion—that Nature required man to mind his own business—and wherever he turned, whether to the administration of Andrew Jackson or the growth of Folkways, the history of Protection or the lamentable lot of the Forgotten Man, he found evidence to support this conclusion:

If we can acquire a science of society [he wrote] based on observation of phenomena and study of forces, we may hope to gain some ground slowly toward the elimination of old errors and the re-establishment of a sound and natural social order. Whatever we gain that way will be by growth, never in the world by any reconstruction of society on the plan of some enthusiastic social architect. The latter is only repeating the old error over again, and postponing all our chances of real improvement. Society needs first of all to be free from these meddlers—that is, to be let alone. Here we

are, then, once more back at the old doctrine—laissez-faire. Let us translate it into blunt English, and it will read Mind your own business. It
is nothing but the doctrine of liberty. Let every man be happy in his own
way. (*What Social Classes Owe to Each Other*, pp. 119–120)

If Sumner's logic was dubious and his history tendentious, his consistency was beyond reproach, for he ruthlessly eliminated from the
arena of state authority even such matters as public education, sani-
tation, and child labor. He was not unaware of the price which society would have to pay for the removal of all restraints on individual
power and greed, but he was persuaded that it was, in the long run,
less exorbitant than the price which society paid for coddling the
weak and perpetuating the unfit. "If we do not like the survival of
the fittest," he wrote, "we have only one possible alternative, and
that is the survival of the unfittest. The former is the law of civilization; the latter is the law of anti-civilization."

In time, he was sure, competition, or the survival of the fit, would
justify itself in human nature as in nature. Progress was sure—but
slow; it was to be achieved through "growth, not reconstruction"
—and what happened to man in the process was nature's affair. His
position was neatly put by Edward L. Youmans in a conversation
with Henry George about the corruption of New York politics.
"What do you propose to do about it?" asked George. "Nothing,"
said Youmans. "You and I can do nothing at all. It's all a matter of
evolution. Perhaps in four or five thousand years evolution may have
carried men beyond this state of things." The willingness of the
Spencerians to wait that long gave their arguments an appearance of
objectivity, but Tammany bosses were content to take a shorter view
and were well aware of the usefulness of nonintervention in maintaining the status quo.

All this left no room for social reform and was useful chiefly as
an indictment of the Progressive movement, then threatening to
substitute political regulation for natural law. Sumner himself had
no patience with the vagaries of the reformers. "Projects to abolish
poverty," he wrote,

are worthy of an age which has undertaken to discuss the abolition of
disease. Why not abolish death and be as gods once and for all—why trifle
with details. If these agencies can get us anything they can just as well get us
everything.

What Sumner did not see was that his logic left no room for social science, either, for sociology and economy had literally nothing to do but teach object lessons warning men against interference with natural processes. Sumner had found theology arid; he left social science even more arid. For theology cherished at least the notion that it could save men's souls, but social science, as taught by Sumner, was doomed to negativism and impotence.

Thus the century-long search for law had ended with the law of evolution, but, as interpreted by Spencer and Sumner, it was, for all human purposes, a dead end. The authors of *Social Statics* and "The Absurd Attempt to Make the World Over" recognized readily enough that reason and will distinguished man from other animals but taught that for man the highest wisdom lay in treading the path which nature had marked out and the most solemn exercise of will in refraining from any effort to alter her laws. The generation of Jefferson had been enraptured by a vision of Reason guiding man along the paths of natural law; that of John Dewey was to be sustained by the conviction that men could participate in and direct the evolutionary process. But to Sumner and his disciples the contemplation of man's place in the evolutionary pattern could give only intellectual or artistic satisfaction. Thus while natural science felt an immediate stimulus from the doctrine of evolution, the generation after 1860 was one of singular aridity in the social sciences, and it is a striking fact that until the emergence, in the eighties and nineties, of such men as Ward, Holmes, Veblen, and Turner, no important advances in the study of social institutions were associated with the doctrine of evolution. Yet it was not the fault of that doctrine that its promises went unfulfilled. It was the fault of those who interpreted it as a mechanical law rather than as an instrument. Until man was emancipated from the subjection to which Spencer and Sumner had consigned him and accorded some share in the control of the evolutionary process, evolution could have no consequential effects on the social sciences. It could describe but it could not prescribe; it could explain but it could not create.

2

It was in 1882 that Herbert Spencer made his triumphal visit to the United States, warning Americans that their freedom was in danger. On his departure for England, the great and wise of the country gathered at Delmonico's to do him honor. Inevitably Sumner was there, and inevitably he spoke on the science of sociology. "As for the philosophy of the subject," he said, "we still need the master to show us how to handle and apply its most fundamental doctrines . . . Mr. Spencer is breaking a path for us into this domain. We stand eager to follow him into it." The next year he followed, with two of the most famous of all his essays—"The Forgotten Man" and "What Social Classes Owe to Each Other." That same year Lester Ward published *Dynamic Sociology,* and "the master" who was to show "how to handle and apply the most fundamental doctrines" presented his credentials. They were, however, unrecognized. While Sumner's fame grew into a legend and "The Forgotten Man" achieved the sacrosanctity of a gospel, *Dynamic Sociology* gathered dust on the booksellers' shelves. "Everything considered," wrote the dean of American sociologists, Albion Small, "I would rather have written *Dynamic Sociology* than any other book that has ever appeared in America." The tribute, though a bit extreme, was not unjustified, yet fifty years later Sumner was still the patron saint of American individualists and Ward still almost unknown.

The contrast between the mighty Sumner and the lonely, obscure Ward is fascinating and instructive. Both were born to respectable poverty, both learned early the necessity of hard work and elevated it to a virtue, both were deeply learned. Thereafter the parallel ceases. While Ward was desperately teaching himself Greek and Latin, French and German, and pouring out his soul in the only one of his voluminous diaries which has survived—diaries heroically written in French—Sumner entered Yale College to study under the authoritarian Theodore Dwight Woolsey and the devout Noah Porter. Three years later, with a substitute filling his place in the army, Sumner sailed for Europe to complete his studies at Geneva, Göttingen, and Oxford; Ward enlisted and was thrice wounded at Chancellorsville. Sumner returned and in 1872 took up his long association with Yale and embarked upon those studies and public pronouncements which were to assure him such popularity as no other American sociologist could command. Ward, poor and depressed, petitioned for a clerkship in the Treasury Department, and managed somehow to go to night school, take dubious degrees in law and science, and edit a curious free-thought magazine prophetically named *The Iconoclast*. While Sumner was hammering out his iron system of sociology and economics in the pleasant academic groves of New Haven, Ward was shifting from one government department to another—the Division of Immigration, the Bureau of Statistics, the Geological Survey—and finding neither servitude nor intellectual stultification in civil service. Notwithstanding the exacting demands of his official work—the painstaking compilation of statistics, the far-flung inquiries into botany and geology and paleontology which took him jogging over country roads in Alabama or into the rugged Black Hills of Dakota or floating down the Missouri in a flatboat— notwithstanding, too, the poverty which drove him into potboiling revision of the Century Dictionary at two dollars an hour and poorly-paid lecturing at various universities, Ward found time to amass that prodigious store of scientific and sociological information which made him, in the end, one of the most variously learned scholars of his generation. In the last years of his life he was attached to Brown University, where he gave a course entitled "A Survey of All Knowledge": perhaps he alone in the academic world of that time could give such a course meaning and dignity.

Dynamic Sociology, Ward wrote, was inspired by "a sense of the essential sterility of all that has thus far been done in the domain of social science." This was a sweeping indictment but not a reckless one. For since the days of Bentham and Comte the social sciences had been monopolized by those more interested in the discovery of laws than in the welfare of society. Certainly in America, where Theodore Dwight Woolsey and John W. Burgess dominated the political scene, Judge Cooley and Justice Field the legal, Francis A. Walker and David A. Wells the economic, and Sumner the sociological, the situation appeared desperate. Perhaps the most familiar comment made on the social sciences was that they had failed to keep pace with the natural, and the comment was a tribute to the efficacy of the Spencerian dogma which required that man refrain from meddling with nature's laws.

Ward was the first major scholar to attack this whole system of negativist and absolutist sociology, and he remains the ablest. "Is it true," he asked, "that man shall ultimately obtain dominion of the whole world except himself?" Those who subscribed rigorously to the doctrine of social statics were forced to confess that it was— at least for some thousands of years. But Ward insisted that sociology was a positive and dynamic science and that, properly applied, it would enable man to control the evolutionary process. The psychic factors, he submitted, count more than the natural in building civilization for they condition and control the natural. "The advent with man of the thinking, knowing, foreseeing, calculating, designing, inventing and constructing faculty, which is wanting in lower creatures, repealed . . . the law of nature, and enacted in its stead the psychologic law, or law of mind," Ward wrote. The capital error of the Spencerian system was its failure to appreciate the role of mind in creative evolution, and this error Ward set about to repair. "Thus far," he wrote, "social progress has in a certain awkward manner taken care of itself, but in the near future it will have to be cared for. To do this, and maintain the dynamic condition against all the hostile forces which thicken with every new advance, is the real problem of sociology considered as an applied science."

The first American who brought to the study of sociology an adequate scientific and philosophical equipment, Ward was likewise the first truly evolutionary sociologist. He saw that though environment transforms animals, man transforms environment, and he insisted that the transformation be not haphazard but planned—and so planned as to produce not only material abundance but intellectual and spiritual well-being. He set himself, almost singlehanded, to rescue evolution from the creeping paralysis with which Spencer had infected it, release its energies for the use of society, and make it the servant rather than the master of man. Throughout all his writings, as Franklin Giddings—himself a Spencerian—admitted, "there runs one dominating and organizing thought. Human society as we who live now know it, is not the passive product of unconscious forces. It lies within the domain of cosmic law, but so does the mind of man; and this mind of man has knowingly, artfully, adapted and readapted its social environment, and with reflective intelligence has begun to shape it into an instrument wherewith to fulfill man's will."

Before Ward could begin to formulate that science of society which he hoped would inaugurate an era of such progress as the world had not yet seen, he had to destroy the superstitions that still held domain over the mind of his generation. Of these, laissez faire was the most stupefying, and it was on the doctrine of laissez faire that he trained his heaviest guns. The work of demolition performed by *Dynamic*

Sociology, Psychic Factors of Civilization, and *Applied Sociology* was thorough. Yet the doctrine, demolished as a scientific law, persisted as a shibboleth, and the battle won in the arena of scholarship had to be refought in the arena of politics.

Laissez faire, Ward argued, was incoherent, fragmentary, insincere, and futile, scarcely consistent with the law of nature and wholly inconsistent with the law of man. It repudiated the past and condemned the future, denied scope to the creative faculty of man and barred the road to calculated progress. For civilization, as we know it, is the triumph of man over the blind forces of nature and the deliberate application of human genius to the task of emancipating man from the tyranny of those forces. "We are told," Ward wrote, "to let things alone, and allow nature to take its course. But has intelligent man ever done this? Is not civilization, with all it has accomplished, the result of man's not letting things alone, and of his not letting nature take its course?" Nature is prodigal and ruthless, indifferent to man's fate and to time; it is only when man breaks in upon nature's course that he can free himself from the fate to which all other forms of life are condemned:

This iron law of nature, as it may appropriately be called, was everywhere found to lie athwart the path of human progress, and the whole upward struggle of rational man . . . has been with this tyrant of nature—the law of competition. And in so far as he has progressed at all beyond the purely animal stage he has done so through triumphing little by little over this law and gaining somewhat the mastery of the struggle. In the physical world he has accomplished this through invention, from which have resulted the arts and material civilization. Every implement or utensil, every mechanical device . . . is a triumph of mind over the physical forces of nature in ceaseless and aimless competition. All human institutions—religion, government, law, marriage, custom—together with innumerable other modes of regulating social, industrial and commercial life are, broadly viewed, only so many ways of meeting and checkmating the principle of competition as it manifests itself in society. (*Psychic Factors of Civilization,* pp. 261–262)

The notion of the "survival of the fittest," which dazzled a whole generation, Ward repudiated as either meaningless or pernicious. For "fit" is not an absolute but a conditional term: fit for what? Assuredly, said Ward, mere fitness to survive is no criterion that civilization can accept, and here he echoed Huxley's statement that "social progress means a checking of the cosmic process at every step. The more advanced a society becomes the more it eliminates the struggle for existence." It was only when man intervened that nature's products became fit for man, and it is only when society or government intervenes, Ward asserted, that man's products become fit for society. Competition is, in fact, not the law of life, as so many of Ward's contemporaries believed, but the law of death: the whole of medicine and surgery is a violent interference with biological competition. Nature will undoubtedly evolve in its own way, but that way is not man's way. Man, thanks to the possession of mind, repudiates nature and applies art—or that which is *art*ificial. "The constant tendency," Ward pointed out,

is to render everything more artificial, which means more and more perfect. Human institutions are not exempt from this all-pervading spirit of improvement. They, too, are artificial, conceived in the ingenious brain and wrought with mental skill born of inventive genius. The passion for their improvement is of a piece with the impulse to improve the plow or the steam engine. Government is one of these artificial products of man's devising, and his right to change it is the same as his right to create it. (*Psychic Factors,* pp. 287–288)

Nor was collective action inconsistent with evolution, properly interpreted. Collectivism and individualism, Ward told an enthusiastic audience at the International Congress of Sociology, "are not opposites but concomitants. Spencer lost sight of the first law of evolution which is that it must take place in the direction of the advantage of the organism, and in the social organism this is the opposite of what it is in animals, and consists in securing the interests of the parts—i.e., individuals—instead of the whole. Every step in the direction of a true collectivism has been and must be a step in the direction of true individualism."

Ward protested equally the inconsistency and the insincerity of the doctrine of laissez faire as applied in America. It was applied to public associations but not to private, and Ward had been too long a civil servant to accept the curious theory that a peculiar iniquity attached to governmental activities from which the comparable activities of corporations were miraculously free. He knew that laissez faire was a rationalization rather than a first principle: business did not embrace competition in response to philosophical precepts; those precepts, rather, flowed from the felt needs of business. Laissez faire was rather the validation than the inspiration of the economic conduct of the age of big business.

Yet even here there was glaring inconsistency, for business did not practice its own precepts. Genuine competition was the last thing that business wanted, and even as Sumner celebrated its virtues and rewards, shrewd captains of industry like Rockefeller and imperial masters of capital like J. P. Morgan were moving to eliminate it and establish monopoly in its place. Certainly the power of the Standard Oil Company, then at its height, was a tribute to the virtues not of competition but of monopoly, and John D. Rockefeller used the very analogy which Ward himself had suggested when he observed that "the American Beauty rose can be produced in all the splendor and fragrance which bring cheer to its beholder only by sacrificing the early buds which grow up around it." Survival, as it revealed itself to Americans of the nineties, was in part evidence of fitness but in part, also, of privilege, capital, legal acumen, and ruthlessness.

Real competition, indeed, no longer existed, said Ward; only artificial competition remained, and it operated best in a framework of law so interpreted as to give the maximum protection with the minimum of interference. Ward had legal as well as scientific training, and his insights into the relations between jurisprudence and property anticipated the scholarly findings of economists like Ely, Commons, and Veblen and the judicial opinions of judges like Harlan, Holmes, and Brandeis. He saw how archaic notions of property, contract, and due process of law had taken on the character of Laws of Nature, and how the term "liberty" had been perverted to assure immunity from governmental interference to the practices of corporations. He insisted that the natural law which Marshall and Story had written into our constitutional system and which their successors had used to give sacrosanctity to property was in fact no more natural than was the law which Spencer and Sumner applied to society at large.

Finally Ward saw what even Sumner, for all his hostility to the protective tariff, had failed to see—that business had already made a travesty of the doctrine of laissez faire. In an article written in the year of the great Pullman strike he advertised the patent insincerity of the attack upon "paternalism" and of the plea for unfettered competition:

The charge of paternalism is chiefly made by the class that enjoys the largest share of government protection. Those who denounce state interference are the ones who most frequently and successfully invoke it. The cry of laissez-faire mainly goes up from the ones who, if really "let alone" would instantly lose their wealth absorbing power. . . . Nothing is more obvious today than the signal inability of capital and private enterprise to take care of themselves unaided by the state; and while they are incessantly denouncing paternalism—by which they mean the claim of the defenceless laborer and artisan to a share in this lavish state protection—they are all the while besieging legislatures for relief from their own incompetency, and "pleading the baby act" through a trained body of lawyers and lobbyists. (*The Forum*, XX, 1895)

3

It was a misfortune that Ward had to devote so much of his energy to clearing away the thickets and underbrush that blocked the path to social progress. In critical acumen he was matched only by Veblen, in his generation, but his mind was not primarily critical but creative. It is suggestive that *Dynamic Sociology* was originally named *The Great Panacea*. "I was an apostle of human progress," he confessed, and it was to positive sociology—sociocracy, he called it —that he made his most important and original contributions. He was no theorist but a practical man, no Utopian reformer but tough minded and hard bitten. Yet somehow he had caught a vision of a better life for the toiling and oppressed millions of mankind, and his spirit was quickened and his imagination fired by the belief that by taking thought man could rid himself of the evils that afflicted him and win his way to virtue and happiness. "I have a feeling, perhaps wholly unfounded," he wrote, "that the inculcation and spread of scientific principles, even such as I am able to work out, is essentially moral, and is almost the only real moral influence in the world." This dour, irascible scholar, who wore out his life in government offices and poured out the riches of his mind in a harsh and crabbed style, was withal a music-maker and dreamer of dreams.

"Man's destiny," he asserted, "is in his own hands. Any law that he can comprehend he can control. He cannot increase or diminish the powers of nature, but he can direct them . . . His power over nature is unlimited. He can make it his servant and appropriate to his own use all the mighty forces of the universe." Yet man cannot achieve this mastery over nature individually but only collectively, only through planning and organization. And what organization can be trusted with so solemn a responsibility? What, indeed, but government—a democratic government awake to the possibilities of social science and responsive to the needs of men?

"Modern society," wrote Ward, "is suffering from the very opposite of paternalism—from under-government. . . . The true function of government is not to fetter but to liberate the forces of society; not to diminish but to increase their effectiveness." It was a bold thing for a scholar to say in the nineties, when even the Interstate Commerce Act seemed vaguely socialistic and when Henry Wood, whose *Political Economy of Natural Law* purveyed Spencer in capsule form, was insisting that "freedom of the individual contract is the chief cornerstone in the structure of any system of liberal government. . . . Any legislation or even prevailing custom, which tends to its impairment, is tyrannous."

Ward cherished liberty as sincerely as did Henry Wood or William Graham Sumner, but he saw no cleavage between liberty and government. For what was government, after all, but "a collection of cases in which society in its corporate capacity has assumed certain operations and interfered with the unrestrained liberty of private enterprise"—a system of controls already extensive and efficacious. "Individual freedom," Ward insisted, "can come only through social regulation," and like so many of the reformers of his generation he believed that true liberty could flourish only where the state interposed itself between the strong and the weak, the privileged and the unprivileged, the cunning and the simple, and where it undertook to establish equality of opportunity and of bargaining power, insure economic security, and lift up the general level of intelligence. All this could be achieved through wise legislation. And legislation, after all—it was an obvious consideration the Spencerians had overlooked—was but an invention, like any of the other innumerable inventions with which man has circumvented nature, a mechanism for "the scientific control of the social forces by the collective mind of society for its own advantage."

All experience, Sumner had argued, "is against state regulation." But Sumner's experience was secondhand; Ward's was firsthand. He had worked in the Census Bureau, the Bureau of Navigation, and the Geological Survey: did even Yale University boast more distinguished geologists than Major Powell and Clarence King and Raphael Pumpelly and, yes, Ward himself? He was not inclined to apologize for the State. Government had already extended its jurisdiction over broad areas of life—over justice, national defense, agriculture and the public domain, science and education—and no one could say that it had done badly. "In all those affairs which the state can manage more advantageously than the individual," Ward concluded, "it has in fact managed well, and such as have passed from private to public control are better administered by the state than they were by the individual."

The question of government intervention, as Ward saw, was one not of theory but of fact, and the wisdom of particular legislation was to be determined by experience rather than by a priori reasoning. The realization of this made him impatient with discussions of abstractions like centralization, paternalism, bureaucracy, socialism, and similar terms that lost all their meaning when they were treated as absolutes rather than as techniques. Ward had the same test for legislation that James had for truth: good legislation was what worked. Nor was his political pragmatism less idealistic than James's philosophical. What worked was what contributed most, in the long run, to the spiritual and intellectual as well as the material welfare of mankind.

The trouble with legislation, as Ward saw it during the last quarter of the nineteenth century, was threefold: it was limited in scope and in imagination; it reflected the will of special pressure groups rather than the needs of society as a whole; it was haphazard and unscientific. Most legislation, Ward observed, was negative rather than "attractive," more concerned with preventing crime than with releasing the energies of men for constructive work. Government should adopt a positive program, should stimulate rather than suppress, should concern itself more with crimes against society than with crimes against persons. It was a notion which young E. A. Ross was to pick up and dramatize, years later, in his *Sin and Society*.

What was needed was a positive program—a program not hamstrung by those predatory interests that were so ready to use government for their own advantage and so reluctant to permit society to use it for social advantage. Ward himself was not tempted to shift from his scholar's study—or his office desk—to the political hustings. "I would probably go further toward populism than you," he wrote his nephew, E. A. Ross. "No one is more anxious to throttle the money power." But he was more concerned for the establishment of right principles than for the agitation of current issues. "It is not indifference now that resigns me to events," he confessed, "but a sense of the infinitesimal effect of anything I could do, especially of the utter powerlessness of the hortatory method." He had little faith in any mere tinkering with the political or economic machinery of society; he was after bigger game—the "manufacture of intelligence" and its application, through scientific planning, to the whole life of society.

Faith in education was nothing new in America, nor was the idea of planning original in sociology. Since Jefferson, education had been an American religion, and since the reform movement of the forties, visionaries had dreamed of a planned society. Ward's faith in the efficacy of education was, if not deeper than Jefferson's, better grounded scientifically and more catholic. He rejected the implications of eugenics as to the inheritance of ability or of genius (he had long warred on Weismann) and emphasized instead the role of environment and of training. There is, he asserted, no aristocracy of brains: intellectual supremacy is the product of opportunity and privilege, not of native capacity. The "denizens of the slums" he considered not inferior in potential capacity to the graduates of Harvard College, and as for criminals—"they are the geniuses of the slums. Society has forced them into this field, and they are making the best use they can of their native abilities." Ward rejected the theory of inherent intellectual superiority, as he rejected the theory of race, class, or sex superiority.

"The great demand of the world," Ward submitted, "is knowledge. The great problem is the equalization of intelligence, to put all knowledge in possession of every human being." It was an ambitious order, but the emphasis was doubtless on equalization rather than on omniscience, and Ward announced as a fundamental principle the axiom that "no matter what class of society you may select from—taking a corresponding number from each—the individuals from all classes will be equal in their native capacity for knowledge." The application of this principle required the elimination of all those artificial barriers, economic and social, that fostered intellectual inequalities and the creation of conditions that would make possible effective social planning. "Intelligence, heretofore a growth, is destined to become a manufacture. . . . The origination and distribution of knowledge can no longer be left to chance and to nature. They are to be systematized and erected into true arts."

This, as Ward saw it, was the primary problem of sociology—the problem without whose solution no other problems could be finally solved. "It is a frequent delusion," Spencer had said, in reply to an inquiry about the future of America, "that education is a universal remedy for political evils." But to Ward education was the "great panacea"—for political as for all other evils. And education—like civilization itself—was a purely artificial thing, a calculated interference with nature, a violent departure from laissez faire. Ward was confident that once a firm foundation of education had been laid, there could be no limit to social progress.

Education, however, should not be haphazard: it should be consciously directed to definite ends. It should be planned, as social progress should be planned.

Ward was no Utopian, and there is no evidence that he was ever excited by *Erewhon,* or by those pseudo novels so popular in the nineties—*News from Nowhere, Looking Backward,* or *A Traveler from Altruria.* Profound as was his distaste for the acquisitive society and the predatory economy of his own time, he did not indulge in any gesture of repudiation or take refuge in some imaginary commonwealth but addressed himself to improving the one he knew. Nor did he think that, given time, this was too difficult a task. "There are those who believe," he said, writing of the "ignorance, poverty, drudgery, and nameless misery" that he saw about him, "that the organization of society on such a basis as shall put these evils in the way of immediate mitigation and ultimate removal is not a chimera." The first step was the establishment of a genuine people's government. The second was the creation of a real science of politics and the training of legislators to be social scientists:

Before science taught man the nature of physical laws, all attempts at invention except of the simplest kind, were just such wretched miscarriages as attempts at progressive legislation are today, and for the same reason, viz., that the inventors possessed no science of the field of natural forces over which they sought to exert an influence. Before progressive legislation can become a success, every legislature must become, as it were, a polytechnic school, a laboratory of philosophical research, into the laws of society and of human nature. No legislator is qualified to vote on or propose measures designed to affect the destinies of millions of social units until he masters all that is known of the science of society. Every true legislator must be a sociologist.

The legislation of the future, he wrote elsewhere, "will consist of a series of exhaustive experiments on the part of true scientific sociologists and sociological inventors working on the problems of social physics from the practical point of view." And as a contribution to this end, Ward proposed the establishment of a national academy of the social sciences, staffed by the ablest scholars in the country and devoted to the training of public administrators and the illumination of social and economic problems.

The academies were to come, in the course of time, the bureaus for municipal research, the legislative reference bureaus, and the schools for public affairs; eventually the most distinguished champion of rugged individualism was to appoint committees of social scientists to investigate and advise on public policy, and then Ward was vindicated. More illuminating, however, was President Hoover's disregard of the findings of the committees he appointed and his acquiescence in the Smoot-Hawley tariff against the advice of almost every economist in the country. Far better than most of his contemporaries, Ward understood the problems which confronted society and the policies which would contribute to their solution, but he never fully understood the pressures which in the last analysis control policy. The most penetrating of men, he penetrated to possibilities rather than to actualities; the most rational of men, he made too little allowance for irrationality. Like Sumner he was a product of the age of reason, confident that in the end the reason of man would assure his felicity.

Yet for all his limitations—perhaps in part because of them—Ward was both a pathfinder and a prophet. The first major scholar to challenge the doctrine of laissez faire on scientific grounds and to articulate social with natural evolution, he was the first, too, to accept the full implications of pragmatism and to give sociology a philosophical foundation. He ranged himself unreservedly on the side of the plain people, fighting their battles with weapons more formidable even than those which Sumner and his disciples could muster. He inspired a whole generation of scholars and reformers to believe that it was possible to remake society along happier lines, and a new generation that did not know him worked with his tools and fought with his weapons. He was the prophet of the New Freedom and the New Deal, of all those movements looking to that reconstruction of society and economy through government intervention which is the most striking development in the political history of the last half-century in America. In perspicacity, intellectual acumen, and imagination, he was the equal of Henry Adams or Thorstein Veblen or Louis Sullivan, but he was better rounded and more constructive than these major critics. In the rugged vigor of his mind, the richness of his learning, the originality of his insights, the breadth of his conceptions, he takes place alongside William James, John Dewey, and Oliver Wendell Holmes as one of the creative spirits of twentieth-century America.

4

The issues raised by William Graham Sumner and Lester Ward, shorn of their scholarly trimmings and simplified into such rallying cries as free silver or sound money, private enterprise or socialism, regimentation or planned economy, rugged individualism or social security, filled half a century of history with an increasing clamor. They were hotly debated in remote schoolhouses on the prairies or in cotton fields, in Grange halls and labor temples, on Chautauqua platforms, in gaudy party conventions, in turbulent legislatice chambers, and in dignified courtrooms. They were fought out under strange banners and often with murderous weapons in the battles between the Pullman Company and the railway workers, the packers and the cattlemen, the railroads and the farmers, the coal operators and the United Mine Workers, the insurance companies and the state governments, the timber thieves and the Department of the Interior. They were the basic issues of the Populist crusade, the Progressive movement, the New Freedom, and most heatedly of all, the New Deal and the Fair Deal. Their champions were, in the end, not so much the scholars who had formulated them as the businessmen and labor leaders, farmers and bankers, muckrakers and editors, statesmen and judges, who came to see that ideas were weapons. Bryan and Mark Hanna, Theodore Roosevelt and Nelson Aldrich, Wilson and Lodge, Franklin D. Roosevelt and Hoover, translated the arguments of the social scientists into the vernacular and, when given the opportunity, into public policy.

Except to the view of purblind fanatics, none of these was an extremist as Sumner and Ward were, each in his own way, extremists: it was perhaps to be expected that politicians who practiced in the public arena should be more cautious and less doctrinaire than scholars who pursued logic in libraries. Clearly, in this matter the politicians represented more faithfully than the scholars the American character. That character was not given to extremes, certainly not in its political manifestations. Americans had, rather, much of the English genius for the middle way, for compromise and concession, for the logic of experience rather than of theory.

It was the logic of experience that politicians followed, in practice, at least, if not always in dogma. If that logic revealed the extravagance of Ward, it proclaimed the bankruptcy of Sumner. For though Ward was forgotten and Sumner extolled, government and economy were moving along the lines charted by the former rather than by the latter. As early as 1881 Ward had called the tendency to government regulation of social phenomena "an impulse without a philosophy, an instinct rather than a conviction." By the turn of the century, the philosophy had been formulated, the instinct had crystallized into popular conviction, and statesmen were preparing to translate that conviction into legislation.

Circumstances, indeed, were making almost irresistibly for the growth of governmental intervention throughout the economic and social life of the nation. An increasingly centralized economy required an increasingly centralized political control; a let-alone economy necessitated public assumption of responsibilities heretofore private; a pecuniary economy dictated the affirmation by government of social considerations. The old distrust of the State, deeply rooted in American experience, gave way before the inescapable realization that only the State was prepared to act effectively in many of the crises of national affairs—crises related to such basic matters as the conservation of natural and human resources or cycles of prosperity and depression. In a thousand ways government moved in to preserve the commonwealth which, being common, no longer seemed the concern of private agencies or individuals. The State as policeman gave way to the State as producer.

However much they might differ on other matters, the major political leaders of these transition years—Bryan, Roosevelt, LaFollette, and Wilson—agreed on this. All regarded themselves as liberals, all supported the expansion of government controls. If none of them entertained notions of a planned economy, all repudiated one whose planning was exclusively private. What was true of national was no less true of state leaders, "conservative" and "liberal" alike; from

Hughes in New York to Johnson in California, from Lind in Minnesota to Tillman in South Carolina, state governors took for granted the advent of the welfare state. It was this general agreement upon the enlarged functions of government that gives unity to the political history of the period.

The laissez-faire argument persisted, to be sure, but it became increasingly querulous and irrelevant, and Sumner did not find a respectable successor. Those who still rejoiced in Sumner's injunction, "mind your own business," were confronted with two insuperable difficulties. In the first place, it was no longer practicable to distinguish between public and private business, and the doctrine of "affectation with a public interest" was accepted even by the conservatives on the Supreme Court. In the second place, as both Ward and Sumner had seen, those who voiced this doctrine no longer believed in it, or believed in it only for others. For themselves they preferred the maintenance of the status quo with themselves as beneficiaries. They were not really prepared to urge the repeal of tariffs, corporation franchises, or patents, or to abandon the scores of other devices whereby, over the years, government had set the molds for the economy which had assured them their privileged position.

The story of the formal repudiation of laissez faire and the triumph of the principle of government regulation is too familiar to rehearse. With Wilson, it reached a climax and, with Wilson, shifted somewhat uncertainly from negative interposition to positive action. Wilson, himself an old-fashioned liberal who admired the English liberals, Mill and Bagehot, and distrusted alike special privilege and socialism, struck a compromise between the extremes of anarchy and paternalism: "There has been something crude and heartless and unfeeling in our haste to succeed and be great," he said in that First Inaugural Address which provides the key to much of American history in the first third of the new century.

Our thought has been, "Let every man look out for himself, let every generation look out for itself," while we reared giant machinery which made it impossible that any but those who stood at the levers of control should have a chance to look out for themselves. . . . We have not . . . studied and perfected the means by which government may be put at the service of humanity, in safeguarding the health of the Nation, the health of its men and its women and its children, as well as their rights in the struggle for existence. . . . Society must see to it that it does not itself crush or weaken or damage its own constituent parts. The first duty of law is to keep sound the society it serves.

To put government at the service of humanity—that was the ideal and the program of those liberals who who still regarded themselves as disciples of the philosopher who had insisted that that government was best that governed least. But how was it to be done without such an increase in governmental authority as would endanger the liberties of men? How was it to be done without such a centralization of governmental power as would hopelessly weaken community life? How was it to be done without such over-all planning as would confound intelligence and such bureaucratic supervision as would paralyze enterprise and initiative?

The Wilson administration provided a formula which satisfied the moderates in both camps. Where—outside the familiar field of conservation—Roosevelt's use of government had been chiefly negative, symbolized by the Big Stick, Wilson's was positive. Yet the shift from prevention to cure, recorded in such measures as the Federal Reserve Act and the Federal Farm Loan Act, was achieved without either frustration of private enterprise or impairment of personal liberties. War accelerated what reform had inaugurated: confronted by an emergency, government came closer to a planned economy than even Ward had anticipated.

The return to "normalcy" meant, in the public mind at least, an abandonment of government controls and a celebration of the virtues of private enterprise, and three successive Republican presidents insisted that the American system was irreconcilable with planning. Yet the dilemma of the American mind, tempted by the material rewards of private enterprise and frightened by its social costs, tempted by the security of government control and frightened by its dangers, was illuminated by the policies of Herbert Hoover. "We are passing," he said, "from a period of extreme individualistic action into a period of associated activities." As Secretary of Commerce he had not hesitated to invoke government aid to an extensive program of business expansion, and as president he enlisted distinguished social scientists in the work of social and economic planning. Yet the exigencies of politics, the bright temptations of a "new era" of prosperity, and the distant threat of communism led him, in the end, to an espousal of doctrines of laissez faire archaic even in the days of McKinley.

A sensible compromise between the extremes of individualism and paternalism—extremes which Hoover himself deplored—would doubtless have emerged had it not been for two unforeseen developments, each pulling in a different direction, each artificializing and exacerbating issues that called for realism and objectivity. The first of these was the rise, in Europe, of regimes which appeared to prove that a planned economy was ineradicably linked with totalitarian politics and that effective planning meant the destruction of life, liberty, and property. The second was the great depression which appeared to reveal the bankruptcy of a privately managed economy and imposed upon government the inescapable responsibility to save the commonwealth.

Franklin D. Roosevelt accepted that responsibility, and under the New Deal, government resumed the road toward "sociocracy" which Lester Ward had charted half a century earlier. As one measure after another came from Congress, organizing industry, agriculture, labor, banking, transportation, hydroelectric power, and centralizing, directing, and controlling the national economy, the air was filled with the laments of rugged individualists. Unreconstructed disciples of Sumner raised again the old battle cries of regimentation, bureaucracy, paternalism, and dictatorship, and identified all these indiscriminately with communism or fascism. Poor Thomas Jefferson was revived and conscripted into alien ranks; echoes of Calhoun resounded curiously in the halls of Congress, and the ghosts of Justices Taney and Field brooded over the confabulations of the Supreme Court. *The Man versus the State* was resurrected from the oblivion into which it had fallen, the didactic volumes of Sumner were dusted off, and battle-scarred veterans of Austrian and German campaigns were enlisted in the armies of the new liberalism. Planning was identified with totalitarianism, legislation with paternalism, and the executive power with tyranny; competition was equated with liberty, states' rights with constitutionalism, and individualism with the American system. There was thunder, too, from the left. Embittered victims of the business cycle, outraged critics of capitalism, deluded disciples of Moscow, undisillusioned technocrats, and visionary planners, all charged the New Deal with betraying the faith by feeble and insincere compromises and envisioned a shining goal of a planned economy certain to usher in a new Utopia.

5

At this juncture, when the American mind was distraught with charges and countercharges, the most sagacious of American publicists sought to distinguish between the real and the artificial issues which beclouded the public understanding and paralyzed the public will and to make clear the relation of the present crisis to the great tradition of American politics. *The Good Society* summed up a generation of controversy over laissez faire and planning and restated the issues of that controversy in terms valid for the generation to come.

Walter Lippmann was not only the most brilliant of the younger liberals associated with Herbert Croly and the *New Republic* at the beginning of the Wilson era, he was perhaps the most tough minded, the most realistic, the most pragmatic. He was a reformer who saw with disconcerting clarity the shortcomings of reform which came from the heart rather than the head; a visionary who knew well the inescapable limitations on all human vision. A quarter-century of study and comment on public affairs made him not only one of the best-informed students of the contemporary scene but perhaps the most perspicacious. To a familiarity with philosophy he added an understanding of modern psychology, to a knowledge of history some experience with practical politics and diplomacy. He knew that society was composed of men who were creatures of emotion and habit rather than of reason, but he did not despair of reason. He knew that stereotypes were, more often than not, acceptable counterfeit for the coin of thought and that history included not only the facts of the past but the shibboleths and myths that clustered about them; but he was confident that in the end Gresham's law would operate in the intellectual realm and that history could be instructive as well as entertaining. His was a mind that delighted in recognizing how complex were the factors that entered into any situation and in rearranging these factors into a symmetrical pattern; he early revealed that instinct for the jugular vein of any social or political problem which was later to distinguish his commentary on public affairs. The most pragmatic of thinkers, he did not fall into the error of disdaining principle or ignoring theory, nor did the obligation to comment on the transient in politics distract him from the study of the permanent. His judgment was objective, his mind austere, his logic persuasive.

In his youth, Mr. Lippmann confessed, he had cherished the belief that "in a regime of personal liberty each nation could, by the increasing exercise of popular sovereignty, create for itself gradually a spaciously planned and intelligently directed social order." The two decades after the war disillusioned him of that belief. In Italy and Germany, popular sovereignty had created tyranny, and there, as well as in Russia, planning had been directed not to a spacious but to a constricted social order. Not even in America had the bright promises of the prewar days been fulfilled. Mastery had indeed succeeded drift, but the tyranny of planning was no more palatable to Lippmann than the chaos of freedom against which he had once so vigorously protested. Now the very ground under his feet was heaving and shifting, the old freedoms inadequate to the crises of the new day, the brave new world of planning metamorphosed into totalitarian despotism. The past was unrecoverable, the future ominous, the alternatives that seemed to present themselves—freedom at the price of security, security at the cost of freedom—intolerable. "Everywhere," he wrote,

the movements which bid for men's allegiance are hostile to the movements in which men struggle to be free. The programmes of reform are everywhere at odds with the liberal tradition. Men are asked to choose between security and liberty. To improve their fortunes they are told that they must renounce their rights. To escape from want they must enter a prison. To regularize their work they must be regimented. To obtain greater equality they must have less freedom. To have national solidarity they must oppress the dissenters. To enhance their dignity they must lick the boots of tyrants. To realize the promise of science they must destroy free inquiry. To promote the truth they must not let it be examined. (*The Good Society*, Little Brown and Co.)

The Good Society attempted to resolve the dilemma of the American mind confronted with these unpalatable choices. It was an effort to find not so much a compromise as an escape, and the escape was into that eighteenth-century past which had laid so firmly, as Lippmann felt, the foundations of true liberalism.

What placed *The Good Society* unmistakably in the American tradition was its ringing reassertion of faith in a government of laws and not of men and its confidence in the efficacy of law as regulator and director of the social and economic system. What more obvious than a resort to this hoary aphorism—once indeed so meaningful— and what more antiquarian? And a flavor of the eighteenth century clings to the whole of the book, suffusing even the style. For not content with reliance upon the machinery of impersonal laws, Mr. Lippmann revived the Higher Law, defining it simply as "the denial that men may be arbitrary in human transactions." That was indeed bold, for the Higher Law had long been discredited, those who celebrated it regarded as either innocents or knaves. And as if to make clearer either his innocence or his guile, Mr. Lippmann added, for good measure, an ultimate test of all government which was nothing but Kant's categorical imperative: "whether men shall be treated as inviolable persons or as things to be disposed of."

All this was reminiscent of *The Man versus the State* and suggested comparison even with Herbert Hoover's popgun *Challenge to Liberty,* and there was great rejoicing among those who read into Mr. Lippmann's attack upon arbitrary government an advocacy of rugged individualism. Yet Lippmann was in fact closer to Huxley than to Spencer, to Ward than to Sumner. *The Good Society* repudiated alike the doctrines of the extreme right and the extreme left—if those terms still had meaning—but its most deadly attack was leveled not against government but against that perversion of classical economics which masqueraded as liberalism.

For what was freedom in society? Freedom was not the absence of planning or of government controls; it was not synonomous with anarchy, not even with anarchy plus the policeman. It was, in the great words of John Locke, to have a standing law to live by, and the crucial word was *law*. True liberalism, as Lippmann insisted, was not the repudiation but the elaboration of law. It was not

quietism and weak government. That is the corruption of liberalism. The effective liberals have always been concerned with the development of the law, with the definition of rights and duties, with the organizing of constitutions, with the absorption of all power to coerce in the hands of duly constituted authorities, with the liquidation or regulation of all kinds of private and petty powers within the community.

And what was it that threatened freedom of men in society? Abroad it was indeed government, but in America governmental restrictions were potential rather than actual. Here it was rather a bankrupt

laissez faire, a perverted liberalism, precisely that liberalism celebrated by William Graham Sumner and his political disciples from
Cleveland to Hoover. For by the 1880's, Mr. Lippmann pointed out
—it was the decade of Sumner's greatest activity—"liberalism had
ceased to guide the progressives who sought to improve the social
order. It had become a collection of querulous shibboleths invoked
by property owners when they resisted encroachments on their
vested interests." And the classical economics so clamorously invoked
to justify the exemption of the status quo from governmental interference was, in fact, a damning criticism of that status quo and an insistent claim for governmental action. For it revealed "how far short
of the promise . . . is the actual society in which we live." Had
liberals but realized this, they might have proceeded with the task
before them—the reformation of the economic order through the reconstruction of the legal. Instead they were obsessed with the notion
that their imaginary world was one to which the real world must conform, and this obsession "sterilized the scientific advance of liberal
thought, paralyzed the practical energies of liberal statesmen, and
destroyed the prestige of liberalism."

The words, addressed to Ricardo and his successors, were equally
applicable to the champions of rugged individualism in the generation
in which Mr. Lippmann wrote. Nor was the agenda of true liberalism,
as set forth in *The Good Society,* one to give comfort to the followers
of Herbert Hoover or, for that matter, of Friedrich von Hayek. Mr.
Lippmann's program rejected, to be sure, collectivism and economic
planning, but in its insistence upon the application of artificial controls to social and economic institutions, in its assertion of the responsibility of the State, through "invention," to preserve the commonwealth, develop the intelligence, and exalt the dignity of men,
equalize opportunities, level artificial barriers, and destroy all special
privileges, it went back to the dynamic sociology of Lester Ward.

Mr. Lippmann's agenda of liberalism was, it turned out, surprisingly like Mr. Roosevelt's agenda for the New Deal. It included,
among other things, large expenditures on eugenics and on education; the conservation of land and other natural resources; the development of the public estate through public works, reclamation,
and hydroelectric power; the supply of necessary facilities for the
transport and exchange of goods and services; the organization, in-
spection, and regulation of markets; insurance and indemnification

against such risks of technological change as unemployment; a greater equalization of incomes through taxation; the equalization of bargaining power and the outlawing of necessitous bargains; the prohibition of monopolies, restriction on holding companies, and supervision of profits and investments. Yet Mr. Lippmann was not yet ready to enroll under the banners of the New Deal, brightly as they glistened in the sunlight of the new day. For though he approved of most of its program, he disapproved of its methods and techniques. Reforms were imperative, but they must come through the ordinary operations of the common law, not through administrative fiat. "Liberalism," he said, "seeks to govern primarily by applying and perfecting reciprocal relations; whereas authoritarianism governs primarily by the handing down of decrees." The means, in short, were as important as the ends, for in the long run the means determine the ends. And any system of government which used man as a means to an end, however noble, would inevitably find the end, achieved at the cost of the degradation of man, ignoble.

In the nice balance between hopes and fears, confidence and caution, tradition and progress, Lippmann well represented what was best in the American spirit of the twentieth century. Confronted by the ancient but ever new problem of liberty and order, he had taken refuge neither in a liberty so comprehensive that it threatened order nor in an order so authoritative that it threatened liberty, but had attempted, rather, to prove all things and hold fast to that which was good in the American heritage. He had attempted to clarify fundamental issues for his generation as Lester Ward had clarified them for an earlier generation. Clarification, however, was not solution, and some whose hopes had been high were disheartened that Americans seemed no nearer a science of society at the end than at the beginning of the period.

Yet, if there had ben no formulation of a social science in the sense that Lester Ward had imagined, there had been, perhaps, some progress toward that end. Men everywhere had abandoned the paralyzing doctrine that society was governed by fixed and immutable laws and had embraced instead the principle that men were, to some degree, masters of their own destiny. Social statics had given way to social dynamics. The stubborn laissez faire of Sumner was discredited, and even those who still yearned for it found it politic to restate it with embellishments designed to hide its spiritual nakedness. If Americans were no longer confident of the sovereignty of Reason, neither had they embraced, in politics or social science, the cult of Unreason. The notion that mind was a factor in evolution, that evolution might be intelligently directed, and that government was one of the normal agencies of direction, was all but universally acknowledged. The concept of planning was widely accepted and even implemented, and it was no longer easy to frighten Americans with words like bureaucracy, regimentation, or socialism. Thanks to the labors of scores of descriptive sociologists, Americans knew more about their society than ever before, and descriptive sociology was gradually being translated into applied.

And if as yet scholars had found no science of society, who could say that the search had been in vain? Who could deny that, though the goal which once had seemed so near had not been won, society had avoided dangers which threatened to destroy even that which had been won? Liberty had been threatened but had not succumbed, and on any Benthamite principle the restrictions on the individual liberty of the few were more than compensated for by the expansion of effective liberty for the many. Order had been menaced—by vast technological changes, by the unregulated growth of industry, by the exhaustion of natural resources, by business cycles and class struggles, and finally by the most cataclysmic of wars—yet society had not disintegrated. Men still had a standing law to live by, and the gravest threats of arbitrary power, at home and abroad, had been repelled. If the bright hopes of Ward had not been fulfilled, neither had the dire prophecies of Sumner; if Americans had not yet fashioned the Good Society, neither had they taken the Road to Serfdom.

CHAPTER XI

Thorstein Veblen and the New Economics

I

TO THOSE WHO thought in terms of centuries, the temptation to fashion a science of society was almost irresistible; to those concerned with the problems of the present, the formulation and application of a new economic theory was far more urgent. For American economy was changing even more rapidly, and more extensively, than American society. It would be extravagant to speak of a social revolution in late nineteenth-century America, but almost moderate to speak of an economic revolution.

The control and exploitation of natural resources by private individuals or corporations was concentrating wealth and power in the hands of the few. Science and invention brought incomparable benefits to society, but their immediate impact upon economy was to redistribute wealth and to forfeit many of those skills which were labor's chief possession. A technological revolution was bringing in massive new industries, built upon discoveries in engineering, chemistry, and electricity. Giant corporations, built up by such business captains as Rockefeller, Carnegie, and James J. Hill, were thrusting small business into a hopelessly subordinate position. Finance capitalism, in the hands of men like J. P. Morgan, George F. Baker, and Jacob Schiff, was shifting the control of industry from the builders to the bankers and converting the directorates of many corporations into a tightly knit structure; the findings of the Pujo Committee of 1912 went far to justify the popular term "money trust." The farmer, selling in a world market and buying in a protected one, and confronted by far-reaching scientific and technological changes, was being forced to the wall. For the new economic world that rose above the horizon at the end of the century, the old orthodox economic theory was as irrelevant as the old orthodox theological theory for the new world of science. A new economics was called for—or a return to that far older and almost pastoral economics that had not sharply distinguished between economy and ethics.

In economics, as in sociology, the principles of natural law formulated during the eighteenth century were sovereign throughout the nineteenth and not entirely discredited in the twentieth. As propounded by its most authoritative interpreters, economics was a deductive rather than an inductive science. It assumed a natural order working through immutable and unerring laws to achieve a perfect competitive system, and a normal economic man responding automatically to those laws in accordance with hedonistic impulses. From these presuppositions it deduced with skill and learning the right principles of economic conduct, and it did not fail to assign to the term "right" a moral character. It was no accident that instruction in political economy was so long commonly assigned to the department of moral philosophy, that so many of its most commanding expositors—McVickar, Wayland, Colton, Bascomb, Perry, Clark, Sumner—were recruited from the ministry and that as late as 1896 the issue of free silver was fought so largely on moral grounds.

It might be thought remarkable that economic theories fashioned to fit the needs and rationalize the policies of France and England should have found such general acceptance in the New World, yet with the exception of some of Jefferson's followers and of some of the more obscure come-outers, American economic thinkers revealed no such originality or adaptability as did the political, and though the economic conditions of the New World diverged more sharply from those of the Old than the political, economic theories diverged less. Because economists started with the doctrines of Quesnay and Adam Smith, Malthus and Ricardo, instead of with American resources and society, they attempted to fit American policy into the framework of received laws instead of deriving their laws from the lessons of American experience. However acrimonious the disagreement on the application of economic laws to particular problems, mercantilists and agrarians, protectionists and free traders, agreed readily enough on the authority of those laws and on the importance of such fundamental truths as the sanctity of private property. The compulsive force of self-love or, as Charles Peirce called it, greed mercantilism, allied with the rising capitalist system, found it convenient to support a policy of government subsidies but inconvenient to accept the logical corollary of government control. Agrarianism became tangled up with slavery, and the proslavery argument required from it an increased emphasis on the necessity of government protection to private property and the danger of any tinkering with the status quo, which made its practical conclusions not too inharmonious with those of mercantilism. Thus, however profoundly they differed on the issue of state versus federal authority or protection versus free trade, statesmen like Webster and Calhoun, jurists like Story and Taney, economists like Wayland and Carey were one in their zeal for the defense of private property against the assaults of heretics and demagogues.

That the sanctity of private property was ordained by natural law was assumed by economists in Europe and America alike; in America alone that assumption was transfigured into a doctrine of constitutional law. This achievement was largely the work of those two stalwarts, Marshall and Story. It can be read in a score of famous decisions—the Yazoo land case, the Fairfax land case, the New York bankruptcy case, the Kentucky land cases, the Dartmouth College case—and in Story's magisterial *Commentaries* on the Constitution. Taney challenged it in that famous Charles River Bridge decision from which Story so vigorously dissented, but the challenge came to seem fortuitous, for in *Dred Scott* vs. *Sanford* he reaffirmed the sanctity of private property as a doctrine binding on the Congress as well as on the states and embracing property in slaves as well as in land or banks. The due process clause of the Fourteenth Amendment formalized what had heretofore rested largely on judicial intuition and in fact, notwithstanding Justice Holmes's protest, enacted Herbert Spencer's *Social Statics* into a constitutional dogma. Justice Field—so largely responsible for its development—might well be considered the most influential economist of the postwar generation.

Evolution affected economic less than sociological or juridical thought. Economists adopted a new vocabulary but only as a clothing for familiar ideas, and Wayland and Bascomb, Cooper and Lieber were merely brought up to date by Wells and Walker, Sumner and Perry. An evolutionary economics would have recognized the changing character of property dictated by the widespread use of the corporate device, but postwar economists united with jurists to insist that the laws applicable in the past to real property were no less valid for intangible property. Evolutionary economics would have adjusted itself to the realities of competition between great corporations and individual workingmen, but economists maintained the fiction of perfect competition. Evolutionary economics would have articulated its doctrines to the facts of the industrial and technological revolution, of the transfer of power from industrialists to financiers, and of the shift in emphasis from industrial productivity to pecuniary profits, but economists attempted instead to articulate these phenomena to their classical doctrines. Evolutionary economics would have confessed the irrelevance of laissez faire to the realities of modern industrial society, but economists persisted in regarding the state as a necessary evil. Evolutionary economics would have abandoned the attempt to apply fixed standards of right and wrong to economic conduct, but the economists of this postwar generation were fundamentalists. In short, the economists, like the sociologists, achieved the symmetry and beauty of their pattern by discarding experience, annulling history, and ignoring man.

The devotion to classical and hostility to evolutionary concepts of economics can be read in all the major academic economists of the eighties and the nineties. "Rightly viewed," wrote General Francis A. Walker, most distinguished and probably most respected of them all, "perfect competition would seem to be the order of the economic universe, as truly as gravity is the order of the physical universe, and to be not less harmonious and beneficent in operation." Competition was the ideal, too, of David A. Wells, advisor to a whole generation of statesmen. Inequality of wealth, he pointed out, "seems to many to constitute the greatest of all social evils. But, great as may be the evils that are attendant on such a condition of things, the evils resulting from an equality of wealth would undoubtedly be much greater. Dissatisfaction with one's condition is the motive power of all human progress, and there is no such incentive for individual exertion as the apprehension of prospective want." Any attempt to mitigate these inequalities by legislative intervention, he added, was dangerous, for "no special legislation can invalidate the economic axiom 'less work, less pay' without destroying the rights of property, and with it, civilization itself." Sumner's hostility to state intervention in the economic process is familiar enough. Like Wells, he identified inequality with civilization. "Let it be understood," he wrote, "that we cannot go outside of this alternative: liberty, inequality, survival of the fittest; non-liberty, equality, survival of the unfittest. The former carries society forwards and favors all of its best members; the latter carries society downwards and favors all its worst members." Professor Arthur L. Perry of Williams College, whose *Elements of Political Economy* was the most widely used text during the last quarter of the century, maintained that legislative interference with wages and hours was an economic abomination and that strikes were "false in theory and pernicious in practice," but he consoled workingmen with the reflection that "each human being is as much constituted by Nature to receive services as to render them, and each is naturally able to become a capitalist; economic laws present no obstacles to all men becoming rich."

These doctrines, so authoritatively promulgated by the high priests of the faith, reappeared in even more dogmatic if less subtle form in popular literature. They could be read in such books as *Natural Law in the Business World* and *The Political Economy of Natural Law* by Henry Wood, the Friedrich von Hayek of his day. They were celebrated in Andrew Carnegie's lyrical *Triumphant Democracy* and in the widely read articles in which the ironmaster paid tribute to the economic system which permitted the accumulation of vast wealth and the social philosophy which dictated its redistribution through the channels of philanthropy. They were given moral sanction by Bishop Lawrence, who announced that "in the long run it is only to the man of morality that wealth comes," and by the Reverend Russell Conwell, whose "Acres of Diamonds" dazzled larger audiences than even Bryan's "Prince of Peace." They were vulgarized into simple precepts for success by Orison Swett Marden, whose pap, purveyed in scores of volumes, gave an illusory nourishment to millions of frustrated and ambitious men and women, and by Elbert Hubbard who rejoiced in the name of Philistine and whose flamboyant "Message to Garcia" made him the idol of the business community. They reached their widest audience through the hundred-odd stories by Horatio Alger of poor boys who made good, each one preaching the same moral in language so simple that even the most immature mind could not fail to grasp it: opportunities lie all about you; success is material and is the reward of virtue and of work. They reached perhaps their extreme, in the twentieth century, in the propaganda of the National Association of Manufacturers and the practices of advertisers who exalted the worst manifestations of individualism, pandered to the worst instincts of jealousy, snobbery, and fear, and reduced competition to its most primitive form.

2

"Soon a flash and a quick peal will shake economists out of their complacency," wrote Charles S. Peirce in 1893. Even as he wrote the western skies flashed and pealed, but the Cambridge philosopher had underestimated the toughness of economic complacency. After all, that complacency had survived generations of dissent, from the days of Tom Paine, whose economics was as egalitarian as his politics and as heretical as his theology, to those of the Grangers and the Greenbackers, and it was to survive the Populist and the Progressive movements of the future. The tradition of economic protest was as deeply rooted and tenacious as of social and political protest: the persistence of economic inequalities into an era of political democracy was not so much a confession of the inadequacy of the protest as a tribute to the formidable character of the defenses against which it beat.

There had always been rebels and heretics, fanatics and iconoclasts, world-seekers and world-forsakers, who rejected the smooth rationalizations and neat apologies that justified slavery, privilege, monopoly, inequality, and who saw in the ship of state

> The great slave-driven bark,
> Full oared upon the dark,
> With gilded figurehead,
> With fetters for the crew
> And spices for the few.
>   (S. V. Benét, *John Brown's Body*)

They were the champions of paper money, the land reformers, the labor leaders, the come-outers and Fourierists and Utopians, the socialists and philosophical anarchists, who refused to be fobbed off with pseudoscientific laws that legalized the predatory practices of the rich and condemned the rest of society to poverty. They were always ready with some curious panacea of their own: some Utopian community or Fourierist phalanx, some scheme for equating value to time, for abolishing banks, for emancipating man from the despotism of money or of property, for outlawing inheritance, for redistributing land, for raising wages and shortening hours of labor, for cooperative buying and selling, for using greenbacks or silver or paper notes instead of gold, for land-bank and subtreasury and social security systems. There were Robert Owen and Frances Wright, trying to substitute a New Harmony for the old discord and indulging in a score of fresh heresies; there was Edward Kellogg who anticipated the learned Brooks Adams in his assault upon usury, and Thomas Skidmore who would put an end to the inheritance of estates, cancel all debts, and auction off all property, and Joseph Warren who tried to base all values on the time required to produce them and who was scorned by Americans and admired by John Stuart Mill. There were come-outers like George Ripley, Fourierists like Albert Brisbane, common-wealthers like the venerable Hosea Ballou, and founders of curious colonies like John Humphrey Noyes of Oneida. There was the "great American preacher," Theodore Parker, who excoriated the merchant class from his mighty pulpit, and his friend Wendell Phillips, who for half a century championed the underprivileged and at the end defended nihilism to Harvard's intellectual elite. The Gilded Age raised new regiments of rebels. There were Greenbackers like staunch old Peter Cooper whose wealth did not blind him to the seamy side of the economic system, and James Baird Weaver who grew old leading lost causes, and Populists like the ebullient Ignatius Donnelly who prophesied the march of *Caesar's Columns,* and the sad-eyed Mary Lease who advised Kansas farmers to "raise less corn and more hell." There was Henry George with his single tax which the lordly Francis Walker dismissed as "a project steeped in infamy," and Daniel De Leon, intellectual leader of the Socialists, and Eugene Debs, no intellectual but a passionate champion of the rights of workingmen, and Edward Bellamy whose *Looking Backward* started a movement and almost a party and whose *Equality* translated into the vernacular Lester Ward's assault on the competitive system. There were rank amateurs who intruded brashly into the domain of the professional economists and the businessmen—like "Coin" Harvey who taught the ABC's of the money question to bankers and statesman and who was put in his place by that stalwart Professor Lawrence Laughlin who had not feared to expurgate criticism of laissez faire out of John Stuart Mill's *Political Economy;* like "General" Jacob Coxey who named his son Legal Tender and advocated a program of government spending during depressions that came almost half a century too early; like Henry Demarest Lloyd who attacked the Standard Oil Company twenty years before the muckraking era and dramatized the coal miners' plight as a "strike of millionaires against miners." There were the Christian Socialists: Graham Taylor who founded the famous Chicago Commons and inaugurated the first chair of Christian sociology in the country; "Golden Rule" Jones who as mayor of Toledo tried to do what Charles Sheldon had proposed in the famous *In His Steps;* the Rev. W. S. Rainsford, minister of the aristocratic St. George's Church in New York, who defied the mighty Pierpont Morgan by bringing workingmen into the vestry.

There were a hundred others, men ignored and contemned, men consigned by their betters to infamy or to Bedlam, men forgotten now by history, who wore out their lives pleading the cause of the underdog, fighting for justice as they saw it, seeking, sometimes in curious ways, to fulfill the promise of American life.

In the eighties came reinforcement for these heretics from the ranks of the more respectable economists. Lester Ward had repudiated classical economics, but he left to his disciples the task of elaborating and applying his positive program. He had not long to wait. Just two years after the publication of *Dynamic Sociology* a group of younger economists, including Richard T. Ely, Henry C. Adams, Simon N. Patten, Edmund J. James, the Rev. Washington Gladden, and—rather curiously—Woodrow Wilson, met at Saratoga Springs to organize the American Economic Association and draft what proved to be a declaration of independence from Manchester.

"We regard the state as an educational and ethical agency," wrote young Ely, "whose positive aid is an indispensable condition of human progress. While we recognize the necessity of individual initiative in industrial life, we hold that the doctrine of laissez faire is unsafe in politics and unsound in morals, and that it suggests an inadequate explanation of the relations between the state and the citizens." This, to be sure, was modified before it was accepted as a formal platform, but even in modified form it challenged the whole body of accepted economic thinking about the relations of the state to the economy. Other resolutions were equally critical of orthodox economics. "We believe that political economy as a science is still in an early stage of its development . . . and we look not so much to speculation as to the historical and statistical study of actual conditions of economic life for the satisfactory accomplishment of this development."

Here were the three major principles of that new economic thought which was to become the orthodoxy of the twentieth century: recognition that economics was an inductive and pragmatic science; appreciation of the relevance of ethical as well as scientific considerations; and acknowledgment of the necessity of state intervention in the economic processes. The first of these principles led to the Pittsburgh Survey, to Veblen's *Theory of Business Enterprise,* Commons' *History of Labor in the United States,* Brandeis' *Other People's Money,* Mitchell's study of *Business Cycles,* Douglas' analysis of *Real Wages in the United States,* the Lynds' *Middletown,* Berle and Means's *Modern Corporation and Private Property,* and Walton Hamilton's penetrating analyses of the economic realities behind the facade of legal fictions. It justified, too, the scientific study of statistics and that long series of Congressional investigations into the anatomy and pathology of American economy of which the reports of the Industrial Commission of 1902, the Immigration Commission of 1911, the Pujo Committee of 1912, and the Commission on Industrial Relations of 1915 are perhaps the best examples. The second principle found expression in the hopeful and not wholly futile effort to Christianize and humanize the social order which enlisted the efforts of such men as Washington Gladden, Walter Rauschenbusch, Richard T. Ely, Simon Patten, and Father John A. Ryan, and of that large and straggling body of reformers from Henry George to Henry Wallace who sought to subordinate economic to social ends. The third principle, authoritatively required by Lester Ward, was promptly elaborated by Henry C. Adams, who in 1886 published a *Study of the Principles that Should Control the Interference of the State in Industries* whose very title was a challenge. Thereafter the program of state intervention became the theme of a substantial part of the economic and political literature of the next half-century, celebrated by publicists like Herbert Croly, Walter Weyl, Louis Brandeis, and Walter Lippmann, and by scholars like Frank Goodnow, Ernest Freund, and John R. Commons.

The whole focus of economic interest shifted; its animus directed inquiry into new channels and required the use of new techniques. From the contemplation of economic laws, students turned to the analysis of economic institutions, and that social science which should have been the most realistic but which had, in fact, been the most abstract belatedly concerned itself with life. It was life as actually lived, not as fondly imagined by scholars in their studies or businessmen in their well-appointed offices—life with all its ambitions and frustrations, its vagaries and follies. The liberals of the nineties had pointed the way, but even they could not wholly emancipate themselves from the inherited pattern of logic and rationality— witness Lester Ward's naïve notion of trained and impartial legislators. It remained for a scholar ostentatiously withdrawn from the life about him to look beneath the full-dress pretenses of the economic order to the naked realities of greed, pretense, and passion, to see behind the workings of the economic machinery the genuine impulses of economic conduct.

3

"The eighteenth century," wrote John M. Clark, son of the John Bates Clark whose *Philosophy of Wealth* allied him uncertainly with the classical economists, "took the ultimate results of the social order for granted, consciously and devoutly. The nineteenth century took a sufficiency of underlying beneficences for granted, more than half unconsciously. . . . The twentieth century, in its most characteristic moods of thought, takes nothing for granted, questions everything, and is altogether merciless." The final generalization might have been a description of Thorstein Veblen, whose *Theory of the Leisure Class* appeared just a few months before the opening of the new century and who died just as the great crash of 1929 dramatized the failure of that pecuniary economy against whose ostentatious pretentions he had directed his most mordant criticism.

Certainly Veblen took nothing for granted, questioned everything, and was merciless, though his mood was only indirectly characteristic of the new century. Inscrutable and sardonic, he stood aloof from most of the currents of thought that swirled about him. Repudiating the classical economists, he refused to associate himself with the pragmatic; at war with the conservatives, he was not an ally of the radicals but cherished throughout his life a position of independent belligerency. His rebellion went so deep that it confounded even dissenters; his heresies were so profane that they baffled orthodoxy and heterodoxy alike. He invoked not only a new philosophy but a new vocabulary. He had always gone his own way, this Norwegian farm boy whose alienation was so much more than a matter of language or race—at Carleton College where John Bates Clark had failed, at Yale where Noah Porter and William G. Sumner had taught in vain, at Cornell where J. Lawrence Laughlin had stooped to conquer and been frustrated, even at Chicago where President Harper had assured him that he was not an asset to the University, and at Stanford where toleration could not extend to his personal idiosyncrasies. To the end of his life, even when he had become a legend, he was alone and imperturbable, seeking truth along the byways, in the fens or the bogs, rather than in the cultivated fields of scholarship. What he wrote of The Jew was autobiographical: "The first requisite for constructive work in modern science, and indeed for any work of inquiry that shall bring enduring results, is a skeptical frame of mind. The enterprising skeptic alone can be counted on to further the increase of knowledge in any substantial fashion. . . . He becomes a disturber of the intellectual peace, but only at the cost of becoming an intellectual wayfaring man, a wanderer in the intellectual no-man's land, seeking another place to rest, farther along the road, somewhere over the horizon." It was characteristic of him that he never voted or joined a party, that he stood aside from all those eager reform movements that were so deeply indebted to him, that his wartime book on *Imperial Germany and the Industrial Revolution* should be used by the Creel Committee for propaganda and denounced by the postal authorities as subversive, that his greatest fame should have come in the decade which most decisively rejected him, and that he should have provided that no memorial or epitaph should commemorate a life whose truest memorial was, in the end, the catastrophe he had predicted and the ruin he had divined.

Although Veblen was aloof, he was not isolated. Historians have emphasized his Norwegian inheritance, but Ole Rølvaag had a similar inheritance and was not flawed. The environment was more important—the Middle Border that produced in his generation Lester Ward and Frederick Turner, Vernon Parrington and Charles Beard, Simon Patten and John R. Commons, and so many others who broke through the neat patterns of thought which the wise men of the East had designed for them. He grew up in the Minnesota of Ignatius Donnelly and the Granger movement, and he shambled through life like some figure out of Hamlin Garland or Ole Rølvaag; had Hollywood decided to film *Main Travelled Roads* or *Giants in the Earth,* it could have cast Veblen for almost any part. For all his sophistication, his esoteric learning, his muffled echoes of Marx, he can be understood better in terms of agrarian radicalism than of eastern progressivism or of the revolutionary economics of central Europe, and it may be doubted that he learned as much economics at Yale or Cornell as he did on his hard-scrabble Iowa farm.

Many of those economic insights and theories which mystified a generation of academic students were familiar and even elementary to Middle Border farmers, though it is not to be imagined that they ever read the tortured pages in which those theories were traced. They did not need to. Veblen's distinction between the engineer and the businessman might have been made by any Kansas Populist comparing the constructive work of building the transcontinentals with the destructive work of exploiting them—comparing, let us say, the contributions of Gen. Grenville Dodge and Jay Gould. His doctrine of business sabotage could be documented by farmers who saw wheat cornered on the exchange or corn used for fuel because high freight rates made it unprofitable to ship it to market. His assertion that depressions are inherent in the price system, not the economic system, had been anticipated by the Populist platform of 1892 and was the theme of Bryan's first crusade. Western farmers, who contemplated the millions of acres of public lands granted to the railways and the legal chicanery whereby some of the most worthless of these were exchanged for timber and mineral lands, could appreciate his definition of a vested interest as the legal right to get something for nothing. His description of the spirit of American business—"a spirit of quietism, caution, compromise, collusion, and chicane"—put succinctly what every midwestern farmer paying twelve per cent to an eastern mortgage company knew from experience. And his description of the Country Town—"the perfect flower of self-help and cupidity"—might have served as a title to many of Garland's stories.

Veblen's uncompromisingly pragmatic approach to economic institutions and his skeptical attitude toward economic dogma were rooted in his own experience. He who had been buffeted by fortune, and whose alienation from the prosperous and respectable elements of American society was so pronounced, was not to be fobbed off with a set of neat principles concocted as rationalizations for an acquisitive economy. Where others saw that economy as a self-balancing mechanism working efficiently to beneficent ends, he, who had experienced its breakdown, saw merely a "cumulatively unfolding process" responding to "cumulatively unfolding exigencies." "The standpoint of the classical economists," he wrote, "may not inaptly be called the standpoint of ceremonial adequacy. The ultimate laws and principles which they formulated were laws of the normal or the natural, according to a preconception regarding the ends to which, in the nature of things, all things tended. In the end this preconception . . . is a projection of the accepted ideal of conduct."

Where others saw progress, Veblen saw merely change. Like Henry Adams he was fascinated by the spectacle of the response of history to force, but where, to Adams, force was impersonal and mechanical, to Veblen it was personal and psychological. He early proposed "an inquiry into the life history of material civilization," and that inquiry looked consistently to the operation of its machinery rather than to its grand design. The most realistic of American economists, he never failed to ask of the institutions which he examined: how do they work? This question he asked explicitly; it is relevant to add that he asked only implicitly: how should they work? He was a diagnostician, not a healer, an iconoclast, not an architect, and he shared with the classicists an indifference to ethical considerations.

Veblen's most important contribution was his demonstration of the antagonism between industry and business or, to use the title of one of his most notable books, of the engineers and the price system. The object of industry, or of the engineers, was the production of goods; the object of business was pecuniary gain. Sometimes the two coincided, but often they conflicted, and when they did production gave way to gain:

The realities of the technician's world are mechanistic realities, matters of material fact. And the responsibilities of the technician, as such, are responsibilities of workmanship only. . . . On the other hand the arts of business are arts of bargaining, effrontery, salesmanship, make-believe, and are directed to the gain of the business man at the cost of the community, at large and in detail. Neither tangible performance nor the common good is a business proposition. Any material use which his traffic may serve is quite beside the business man's purpose, except indirectly, in so far as it may serve to influence his clientele to his advantage.

A common sense economy, Veblen argued, would make money to facilitate the production and distribution of goods; an acquisitive pecuniary economy subordinated production to the making of money. While machines were inordinately productive, businessmen were required to articulate production to profit. This adjustment of supply to financial rather than to economic demand, of output to possible profits rather than to potential consumption, Veblen characterized as a "conscientious withdrawal of efficiency" or, in a more famous phrase, as "capitalistic sabotage."

Veblen's assault upon the businessmen responsible for the application of these perverted economic standards, though couched in an anthropological vocabulary that seemed dispassionate and scientific, was virulent: beside his malicious effronteries, the barbs and shafts of Populists and Progressives seemed almost innocuous. For he did not, like these, single out any particular abuses or particular "malefactors of great wealth" for excoriation but argued that the pecuniary economy was itself an abuse and that its beneficiaries were a predatory class. Thus:

The tendency of the pecuniary life is, in a general way, to conserve the barbarian temperament, but with the substitution of fraud and prudence, or administrative ability, in place of that predilection for physical damage that characterises the early barbarian. This substitution of chicane in place of devastation takes place only in an uncertain degree. . . . The discipline of modern life in the consumption of time and goods does not act unequivocally to eliminate the aristocratic virtues or to foster the bourgeois virtues. . . . From what has been said, it appears that the leisure-class life and the leisure-class scheme of life should further the conservation of the barbarian temperament; chiefly of the quasi-peaceable, or bourgeois, variant, but also in some measure of the predatory variant. In the absence of disturbing factors, therefore, it should be possible to trace a difference of temperament between the classes of society. The aristocratic and the bourgeois virtues—that is to say the destructive and pecuniary traits—should be found chiefly among the upper classes, and the industrial virtues—that is to say the peaceable traits—chiefly among the classes given to mechanical industry. (*Theory of the Leisure Class,* pp. 240-241)

To the "ideal pecuniary man," heir of the predatory barbarian, Veblen ascribed qualities customarily associated with very different types. Comparing the "pecuniarily successful upper-class" and the industrial class, he observed that:

Tenacity of purpose may be said to distinguish both these classes from two others: the shiftless ne'er-do-well and the lower-class delinquent. In point of natural endowment the pecuniary man compares with the delinquent in much the same way as the industrial man compares with the good-natured shiftless dependent. The ideal pecuniary man is like the ideal delinquent in his unscrupulous conversion of goods and persons to his own ends, and in a callous disregard of the feelings and wishes of others and of the remoter effects of his actions; but he is unlike him in possessing a keener sense of status, and in working more consistently and far-sightedly to a remoter end. The kinship of the two types of temperament is further shown in a proclivity to "sport" and gambling, and a relish of aimless emulation. . . . The delinquent is very commonly of a superstitious habit of mind; he is a great believer in luck, spells, divination and destiny, and in omens and shamanistic ceremony. . . . At this point the temperament of the delinquent has more in common with the pecuniary and leisure classes than with the industrial man or with the class of shiftless dependents. (*Theory of the Leisure Class,* pp. 237–238)

Because Veblen was sociologist and anthropologist as well as economist, he saw that the distinction between the industrial and the pecuniary economies was far more than economic merely, that it extended to the realms of habits, methods, standards, and values as well, and he elaborated this argument in his *Theory of Business Enterprise, The Instinct of Workmanship,* and *Absentee Ownership.* Those engaged in industry, he submitted, were tied down to facts and realities, to physical and measurable phenomena, to mechanical cause and effect; they adapted themselves to the discipline of the machine and were impatient with doctrine, precedent, tradition, and convention; they had, in short, the scientific attitude of mind. Those engaged in business were given to "anthropomorphism, to explanation of phenomena in terms of human relations, discretion, choice, and precedent, to de jure rather than de facto arguments"; they tended to make facts conform to law, to accept "custom-made rule as something real," to exalt tradition and precedent and take refuge in abstractions—especially such abstractions as Natural Rights. And what was most interesting was that Americans, who were as machine minded as any other people, were psychologically habituated to the standards and ways of thought of the pecuniary rather than

the technological economy; the dichotomy explained both the ie
current economic crises and the inability to resolve them.

The logical conclusion of Veblen's argument was an economy in
which technicians and engineers were at the levers of control and
the instinct of workmanship given full play regardless of the supposed needs of the market. Whether from that same circumspection
which had dictated an impersonal, anthropological approach to the
analysis of modern economy or from a reluctance to indulge in constructive suggestions, Veblen did not commit himself to this logical
conclusion until he had cut loose his academic traces. *The Engineers
and the Price System,* published at the beginning of that decade
which saw the efflorescence of the pecuniary economy, did clearly
recommend the control of economy by technicians. The notion,
which seemed merely whimsical at the time, was subsequently taken
up by the technocrats, who made a great stir but no progress. It was
adopted, unsystematically and almost surreptitiously, by the United
States Government during the second World War with spectacular
success. If engineers were not put in control of the nation's economy
during this crisis, they were at least given a free hand; if profits were
not eliminated—far from it—they were not permitted to dictate production. Yet the most illuminating aspect of this capitulation to the
exigencies of war was not the spectacular success with which the technicians organized the economic resources of the nation for victory
but the decisiveness with which the experiment was abandoned and
its lessons repudiated once victory had been achieved. If the engineers
were in at least partial control during the war, the price system was
triumphantly restored as soon as the Manhattan Project had demonstrated the validity of Veblen's thesis.

Veblen himself would have appreciated the irony of this demonstration and of its repudiation. For he brought to the study of economic institutions and conduct not only history and anthropology
but philosophy and psychology. He realized how deeply rooted in
habit and custom were the economic mores of any society, and his
Theory of the Leisure Class was the most penetrating commentary
on the psychological bases of economic institutions that had yet been
made. All his life he had studied how people act, not how they should
act, and he who had proved that human nature did not conform
to a set of imaginary laws was not to be confounded by an exhibition
of illogic. Nor would he have thought it remarkable that a society

psychologically habituated to pecuniary standards should summarily reject any experiment which challenged the validity of those standards. "By settled habit," he wrote,

the American population are quite unable to see their way to entrust any appreciable responsibility to any other than business men; at the same time that such a move of overturn (control of the economy by a Soviet of engineers) can hope to succeed only if it excludes the business men from all positions of responsibility. This sentimental deference of the American people to the sagacity of its business men is massive, profound, and alert.

It was Veblen's misfortune that the society to which he addressed his heresies could tolerate them only as long as they seemed whimsical and that any authentication of his theories was bound to lead to their prompt repudiation. It can scarcely be doubted that he would have regarded this paradox with that same malign humor with which he regarded life itself.

4

The report of the Industrial Commission of 1902, which furnished Veblen material for his *Theory of Business Enterprise,* contributed richly to the education of another economist, one who was far more representative of the major trends in American economic thought than the saturnine Norwegian—John R. Commons of Wisconsin. The two had much in common. Like Veblen, Commons was a son of the Middle Border; like him, familiar with hardship and manual labor; like him, too, a victim of academic timidity, buffeted from college to college, constantly under fire from trustees who confused liberalism with communism. Both, too, drew their economic theories from observation and experience, from the actual propensities and desires of workingmen, tradesmen, investors, and industrialists; both were skeptical of the shibboleths of classical economics.

Yet in temperament the two were wholly unlike: imagine Veblen writing, at the end of his career, "this is a beautiful world after all"! Commons' was a buoyant spirit; whatever vicissitudes he experienced, cheerfulness always broke through. His roots were deep in the American past. He shared with the Hoosier school—Riley, Tarkington, Nicholson, and others—the conviction that the Valley of Democracy was the most American part of America, and he was never wholly happy away from the Middle West; when he turned from New York to Wisconsin, he exulted that he was "born again." In character, too, he seemed thoroughly American, resilient, adaptable, and shrewd, not easily discouraged, alert to land on his feet and chalk up to experience his disappointments and defeats; he was critical but not disillusioned, and his humor never soured into cynicism.

Better perhaps than any other economist of his generation, unless it was his master, Ely, Commons subscribed to and acted on those principles that were to distinguish American economic thought in the new century: humanitarianism, pragmatism, and the reaction from private to public control. The ethical note was a product of both inheritance and training. "Liberty, equality, and defiance of the Fugitive Slave Law were my birthright," he later recalled, "and Hoosierdom my education." From his Quaker mother, whom he revered, he derived much of his passion for righteousness, his faith in the ultimate triumph of virtue and reason. Oberlin College reinforced the teachings of the home—Oberlin which for half a century had triumphantly combined orthodoxy in religion with radicalism in politics and social relationships, and where a lively social conscience was a prerequisite to graduation. At the Hopkins, where he tried in vain to win a degree, Professor Ely taught him that economics was but a subdivision of ethics and put him on case work for the Baltimore Charity Organization Society. He was early caught up in the movement for Christian Socialism, attended the World's Parliament of Religions at Chicago, founded a Christian Socialist society at the University of Indiana, lectured at Chautauqua, and served on the editorial board of George Herron's radical religious magazine, *The Kingdom,* and in 1894 he published a series of essays on *Social Reform and the Church*. In his later work the religious note is muted, but the ethical persists; it is the one thing that marks him off most sharply from both Veblen and the classicists.

If Commons' ethical approach was a matter of inheritance and schooling, his ardent pragmatism derived from experience. "I had always supposed economics was a deductive science," he wrote of his youth, but a little study quickly disillusioned him. The disillusionment might have passed had he settled down, like so many others, into some comfortable academic berth, but a persistent inability to pass examinations or to keep jobs, together with a prying curiosity, threw him again and again into nonacademic work. In his youth he had set type in a newspaper office—to the end of his life he was a member of the

Typographer's Union—and thereafter he was rarely absent for long from the workaday world. His teaching, his voluminous books and reports, his philosophy, all came out of experience. He compiled what was perhaps the first commodity price index for the Democratic National Committee; when it showed an embarrassing tendency to go up instead of down, the Committee dispensed with his services, and it was grist for his literary mill. He investigated conditions in sweatshops and coal mines for the Industrial Commission, and the investigation furnished him material for *Races and Classes in America*. Many of the introductions to his voluminous *Documentary History of American Industrial Society,* and those chapters which he wrote in the *History of Labor in the United States,* were hewed out of the same quarry of experience, and so, too, the weighty chapters of his *Legal Foundations of Capitalism.*

These two principles, the ethical and the pragmatic, came easily and naturally; the third, the principle of government control, though likewise a product of experience rather than of ratiocination, was of slower growth. Ely had brought Commons to Wisconsin to write the history of American labor, and the younger economist, a bit wearied with government work, had welcomed a career of teaching and scholarship. He had that career, to be sure—few economists trained a more remarkable group of students, and none had his name on the title-pages of more books. But his career was public rather than academic, and from the beginning he helped the elder LaFollette make Wisconsin a laboratory of democracy. He drafted a civil service law; organized an Industrial Commission which formulated codes of fair practice a quarter-century before the NRA rediscovered them; helped reorganize the municipal government of Victor Berger's Milwaukee and found nothing shocking in socialism; went on an official junket to study municipal ownership of utilities in Britain and concluded—it was the day of the Shame of the Cities—that though the British could do it, Americans couldn't. Later he served on President Wilson's Industrial Relations Commission where he earned the enmity of labor and got more notes for his *Institutional Economics*. All of his conclusions about race relations, labor legislation, housing, banking practices, and rate regulation came out of these experiences.

He was the least doctrinaire of economists, distrusted all general principles, even his own, took nothing on trust, and always had to find out for himself. He could not be persuaded that government regulation was a violation of economic laws—especially as he was skeptical about the existence of such laws—but neither was he ready to go to the other extreme and advocate government operation or ownership as virtues in themselves. He saw social security work in Wisconsin but was by no means convinced that it would work in less fortunate states. He accepted the necessity of collective bargaining and drafted machinery to administer it, but experience led him to suspect the wisdom of compulsory arbitration. He and his fellow-intellectuals at Madison, men like Ely and Andrews and Perlman, had done much to explain labor to capital and to advance labor's well-being, but he early learned to share Gompers' distrust of intellectuals in the labor movement. He knew that wealth was unfairly distributed and was familiar enough with Veblen's animadversions on captains of industry, but whenever he needed money to finance some particularly bold investigation he turned with assurance to some friendly millionaire.

In his pragmatism, his opportunism, his talent for compromise and for common sense, his shrewdness and curiosity, his humor and simplicity, his suspicion of theory and of theorists, his versatility and industry, and his idealism, Commons was one of the representative men of his generation. If he contributed little to economic theory, he contributed much to economic practice; if he opened up no new continents to economic investigation, he surveyed those already discovered and took them under the jurisdiction of a more enlightened and humane economic scholarship.

CHAPTER XII

The Literature of Revolt

I

AMERICAN SOCIETY of Veblen's generation may have been habituated to money standards, but it found few literary spokesmen to justify those standards or even to explain them. Who, in the half-century from Cleveland to Franklin Roosevelt, celebrated business enterprise or the acquisitive society—who aside from John Hay, Thomas Bailey Aldrich, Mary Halleck Foote, Booth Tarkington, and a miscellany of contributors to popular magazines whose efforts are now buried in oblivion? Almost all the major writers were critical of those standards, or contemptuous of them; they voted, as it were, for Bryan and the two Roosevelts and sometimes even for Eugene Debs and William Z. Foster rather than for McKinley, Taft, or Hoover. Those authors who repudiated the economic system outright were few; Mark Twain, Henry James, Willa Cather, Ellen Glasgow, and others accepted it tacitly, while such lesser writers as James Lane Allen, George W. Cable, and Sarah Orne Jewett took little thought of economic affairs. But the dominant trend in literature was critical: most authors portrayed an economic system disorderly and ruthless, wasteful and inhumane, unjust alike to workingmen, investors, and consumers, politically corrupt and morally corrupting.

This all but unanimous repudiation of the accepted economic order by its literary representatives is one of the curious phenomena of American culture. The tradition of protest and revolt had been dominant in American literature since Emerson and Thoreau, but the protestants had by no means monopolized the stage, and their protests had been, for the most part, political or social rather than economic. Never before in American literature and rarely in the literature of any country had the major writers been so sharply estranged from the society which nourished them and the economy which sustained them as during the half-century between the *Rise of Silas Lapham* and *Grapes of Wrath*. The explanation is elusive. It can scarcely be maintained that novelists from Howells to Steinbeck were unfamiliar with the scene they portrayed. Yet their findings did not correspond with those of more popular novelists and journalists, or, later, of Hollywood producers, radio script-writers, and advertisers—most of whom pictured a society that was prosperous, vigorous, harmonious, and contented. To suggest, however, that the novelists misrepresented their society presents difficulties equally perplexing; assuredly the society that cherished and rewarded them did not regard them as alien or false.

Whatever the explanation, the facts are incontrovertible. From the mid-eighties to the second World War the literary protest paralleled the political, and both were directed toward the economic malaise. The parallel was so close as to suggest subservience, yet we know that literature was not only an echo but often—as with *The Jungle*—a trumpet and an alarm. During the Populist era it was Howells and Garland, Norris and Frederic, who set the literary tone: those who were not championing the cause of the farmer were pleading the rights of labor or designing Utopias—some fifty of them altogether during these years—to show what felicity man might achieve if only economic competition were banished. In the early years of the new century, the novelists stood with T. R. at Armageddon and battled for the Lord: William Allen White was there, and Winston Churchill and Ernest Poole and David Graham Phillips and Brand Whitlock and, somewhat uneasily in such company, Upton Sinclair. They exposed the iniquities of business, romanticized labor, lamented the slums, and denounced corruption, and they were as sure as Roosevelt himself that the promise of American life would be fulfilled if virtuous men supplanted malefactors of great wealth. Volume for volume, they echoed the muckrakers, and if the whole of that body of evidence were to be lost, it could be reconstructed from the findings of the novelists. For Jane Addams' *New Conscience and an Ancient Evil*, substitute Phillips' *Susan Lenox;* for Lawson's *Frenzied Finance*, Norris' *The Pit;* for Phillips' *Treason of the Senate*, Robert Herrick's *Memoirs of an American Citizen;* for Russell's *Greatest Trust in the World*, Upton Sinclair's *The Jungle;* for Steffens' *The Shame of the Cities*, one of Winston Churchill's New Hampshire novels; for Judge Lindsey's *The Beast*, Brand Whitlock's *Turn of the Bal-*

ance; for Ross's *Sin and Society,* Theodore Dreiser's *The Titan.* The list could be extended interminably.

The twenties brought cynicism and disillusionment, and the novelists faithfully reflected the new mood. With Sinclair Lewis they were revolted by the shabby meanness of the small town or the dullness of the businessman; with Scott Fitzgerald they found riches, love, and liquor still this side of paradise; with Ring Lardner they exposed the irremediable depravity of the ordinary man; with Cabell and Wilder and Hergesheimer and Elinor Wylie they fled from it all. They shared the aversion to Mammon and Mrs. Grundy that had animated their predecessors, the revolt from the farm and the revolt against the city, the distaste for the standards of the market place and the country club, but they shared little else. They were zealous to disassociate themselves from these things rather than to change them. They did not, like Garland, suffer with the farmers and villagers but, like Lewis, from them. They did not, like Churchill, Whitlock, and White, crusade for progress but seemed to repudiate the concept. They did not, like Howells, Sinclair, and Phillips, champion the cause of labor and the middle class but ignored the first and discovered that the second was a *bourgeoisie.* Too sure of their own superiority to be greatly troubled by the lot of the average man and woman, their hatred of injustice was not nearly so lively as their hatred of vulgarity. Where the novelists of the Bryan-Roosevelt era had found it intolerable that a virtuous people should suffer, the literary rebels of the twenties found it intolerable that virtue should be so dull.

The depression discovered the cheapness of this pose and its sterility, and novelists abandoned their attitude of anguished superiority and addressed themselves with sincerity and passion to fundamental problems. Dreiser came belatedly into his own, and *Main Travelled Roads* seemed less dated than *Main Street.* The literature of the thirties pulsed with anger and pity—anger against an economy that wasted the resources, paralyzed the energies, and corrupted the spirits of the people, pity for the victims of that economy. The indictment was explicit in Farrell's brutal pictures of life among the Chicago Irish, in Faulkner's convulsive rejection of the plantation tradition, in Caldwell's recreation of the Jukeses and the Kallikaks of the present-day South, in Wolfe's desperate search for a spiritual refuge, in Dos Passos' nightmare survey of the whole *USA,* in Steinbeck's tragic history of the Salinas Valley from the pioneers to the Okies. The minor novelists echoed the major: Grace Lumpkin and Josephine Herbst, Robert Cantwell and Fielding Burke, John O'Hara and Richard Wright, and a score of others lamented with their greatest poet,

> the long monstrousness of life
> that most have suffered and a few have been crowned for.
>
> (E. A. Robinnson, *King Jasper*)

All confessed that sense of outraged bewilderment at

> Blight—not on the grain
> Drought—not in the spring
> Rot—not from the rain
>
> (Archibald MacLeish, *Panic*)

that was perhaps the dominant note of the depression years.

Prosperity returned, self-confidence was restored, the war inspired a new sense of national pride, and writers found fresh fields for their imagination. Bernard De Voto insisted that the novelists, victim of a literary fallacy, had libeled their country and their generation, and with the second World War they did rediscover the American past and find much of it admirable. Yet few came to give a different version of the modern economic order or to revise the judgment which had been passed upon the acquisitive society. The advertisers exalted the rich, magazines celebrated them, the movies and the radio stood ready to immortalize them, and Congressmen identified their achievements with Americanism. Yet the novelists remained irreconcilable. When readers turned wearily from the literature of war to the literature of peace they were offered *The Hucksters* or *B. F.'s Daughter,* and Sinclair Lewis' Dodsworth and Marquand's Charles Gray were the only successors to Silas Lapham who shared any of his more amiable traits.

2

The creator of Silas Lapham made not only the most authentic transcript of American society but the most penetrating analysis of American economy in the transition years from the Civil to the Spanish War. That analysis is for the most part implicit: only in the two

Utopian romances, *A Traveler from Altruria* and *Through the Eye of the Needle,* does it become explicit; implicit or explicit, it is consistently critical. What Howells recounted in his long series of economic novels was, to a large extent, his own experience, and that experience, it is well to remember, was somewhat wider than the editorial offices of the *Atlantic* and *Harper's,* the summer resort veranda, and the deck of the Atlantic steamer. He who had known the pastoral simplicity, the egalitarian democracy, of a Boys Town, could never quite reconcile himself to the new commercialism, so destructive of moral standards, the new industrialism that exploded in the Haymarket riot and the Homestead strike. Nor could he cut himself off from responsibility, confine himself to those charming social vignettes, those amusing theatricals, those delightful travelogues which brought him assured popularity. He had a Quaker conscience, and his wife's uncle had founded the Oneida community; his reading of Tolstoy, his friendship with Garland and Bellamy, the move from Boston to New York, the Haymarket executions, the Socialist and the Populist movements—all these brought him face to face with "the riddle of the painful earth"; and in a long series of novels—*The Minister's Charge, The Quality of Mercy, Annie Kilburn, The World of Chance, A Hazard of New Fortunes, The Son of Royal Langbrith,* and the two Utopian romances—he tried to solve it. "There's something in the air that won't allow you to live in the old way if you've got a grain of conscience or of humanity," he wrote, and if he did not change his way of life, he changed his literary argument, which was more important.

Howells' criticism of the economic order of the eighties and nineties was fundamental yet expressed, for the most part, with such indirection that it lost its cutting edge. Only in his Utopian novels did he try a head-on attack, and they were perhaps his least successful. Yet the indictment is there, no less telling for the suavity with which it is presented. He did not fall into the error of idealizing the poor or scarifying the rich or of personifying the system which he abhorred in a series of villains: the amiable Silas Lapham is a millionaire, and Mr. Homo gets along very well with his hosts. There are, indeed, few villains in Howells and few heroes: life, as he saw it, was too complex for such simplifications, and he was too faithful a reporter to ignore the complexities. Even for those who are dubiously cast in the role of villain, Howells has more pity than contempt—

Dryfoos with his millions, old, frustrated, and defeated; Northwick, dying in distant Quebec, gloating over the money he has embezzled but knowing, too, that he has missed what he wanted. All alike are defeated by the economic system they do not understand and cannot control—the wicked and the virtuous, the greedy and the generous, Silas Lapham who loses all save honor, Ansel Denton who ends in suicide, Julius Peck who abandons the ministry for work among the poor. They are defeated, as society itself is defeated, by the competitive spirit which brings out the worst in men, by commercialism which perverts values, by the World of Chance of modern business. It is Howells who speaks through his favorite character, Basil March:

What I object to is this economic chance-world in which we live, and which we men seem to have created. It ought to be law as inflexible in human affairs as the order of day and night in the physical world, that if a man will work he shall both rest and eat, and shall not be harassed with any question as to how his repose and his provision shall come. Nothing less ideal than this satisfies the reason. But in our state of things no one is secure of this. No one is sure of finding work; no one is sure of not losing it. . . . And so we go on, pushing and pulling, climbing and crawling, thrusting aside and trampling underfoot; lying, cheating, stealing; and when we get to the end, covered with blood and dirt and sin and shame, and look back over the way we've come to a palace of our own, or to the poor-house, which is about the only possession we can claim in common with our brother-men, I don't think the retrospect can be pleasing. (*Hazard of New Fortunes,* II, 252–253)

Certainly the retrospect was not pleasing to Howells, and his supersensitive conscience sometimes charged him with vicarious guilt and admonished him to atone by some gesture of withdrawal and sacrifice. "Elinor and I both no longer care for the world's life," he wrote at the time of the Haymarket executions, "and would like to be settled somewhere very humbly and simply, where we could be socially identified with the principles of progress and sympathy for the struggling mass." Meantime, as he wrote wryly to Henry James, "I wear a fur-lined overcoat and live in all the luxury my money can buy." His dilemma was characteristic and reappeared in his novels. He knew that charity was no substitute for justice, but he did not know what would assure justice in the modern order or what was better than charity. He knew that competition stained all who engaged in it, but his substitute for competition worked only in Altruria.

He knew that women had lost almost as much through emancipation as they had gained, but he would not undertake a frank treatment of sex or countenance it in others.

Profound as was Howells' revulsion from the economic order, it was, in its literary form, curiously unreal and ineffective. For Howells never understood the order which he hated as he understood the order which he had loved, never understood his economy as he understood his society. When he described society his art was as authentic as that of Jane Austen or Flaubert; when conscience drove him to economic issues he was vague and mystical. He did not know the world of the rich as Henry James knew it; he did not know the world of the poor as Dreiser knew it. He knew his middle-class, northern, feminine world better than any one else who has ever described it, and he knew what happened to the inhabitants of that world when they won unexpected riches or suffered unmerited poverty. He could explain what money did to old Dryfoos, what social ambitions did to Silas Lapham's daughters, how community opinion pressed on Adeline and Suzette Northwick, but he could not be similarly realistic when he tried to explain monopoly or the competitive system. His moral revulsion from the iniquities of urban life was far deeper than that of Jack London, but compare, for example, *London Films* with the contemporary *People of the Abyss*. His economic arguments remained pale abstractions. "Competition," says David Hughes,

is the Afreet that the forces of civilization have bottled up after a desperate struggle, and he is always making fine promises of what he will do for you if you will let him out. The fact is he will do nothing but mischief, because that is his nature. He is Beelzebub, he is Satan; in the Miltonic fable he attempted to compete with the Almighty for the rule of heaven, and the fallen angels have been taking the consequence ever since. Monopoly is the only prosperity. Where competition is there can be finally nothing but disaster and defeat for one side or another. . . . Competition enslaves, monopoly liberates. We must, therefore, have the greatest possible monopoly; one that includes the whole people economically as they are now included politically. Try to think of competition in the political administration as we now have it in the industrial. It isn't thinkable . . . (*The World of Chance*, pp. 118–119)

Howells was against the economic system without knowing much about business, as his friends, Lowell and Norton and Gilder, were against the spoils system without knowing much about practical politics. If, in the end, he accepted it, he was never reconciled to it, as these guardians of the genteel tradition were reconciled to a political system that at least shielded them from the dangers of populism and free silver. It is this unregenerate quality in Howells that is most illuminating, that fixes the pattern, as it were, for the literary interpretations of American economy during the next half-century.

The most distinguished of Howells' successors, Robert Herrick, was similarly unregenerate. His theme was essentially that which Howells elaborated in the novels of his middle period—the corrupting influence of material standards—but he presented it in a more modern style, the attack upon economic injustice more direct, the exposure of political implications more specific, the recognition of the effect upon the relations of the sexes more candid, the vocabulary more passionate. He began where Howells left off, and more than style and setting distinguish the portraits of Van Harrington from those of Silas Lapham and the elder Dryfoos. Although Herrick owed much to Henry George and Bellamy—witness *Clark's Field* and the Utopian *Sometime*—he belonged to the muckrake rather than to the earlier, and perhaps more innocent, protestant movement.

He was a transplanted New Englander, fastidious, severe, and consistently censorious. The brutal, brawling city on the shore of Lake Michigan—the city of the Haymarket riot and the Pullman strike, of Yerkes and Marshall Field, of the stockyards and the railroads —exercised the same horrid fascination for him as for Henry Fuller and Frank Norris, Upton Sinclair and Theodore Dreiser, and he could neither reconcile himself to it nor escape from it. He was one of that remarkable group of University of Chicago radicals—Thorstein Veblen, W. I. Thomas, Albion Small, Shailer Mathews, Graham Taylor, John Dewey, Ernst Freund, Robert Morss Lovett, and William Vaughn Moody were among them—who for a time gave that institution a significance in the reform movement comparable to that held by the University of Wisconsin. There was something of Veblen in Herrick's interpretation of the leisure class, something of Thomas, perhaps, in his recognition of the role of sex in the social and economic struggle, but in many ways he was closer to William Vaughn Moody than to any other colleague, and his novels may be considered an extended commentary upon "Gloucester Moors" or "The Menagerie."

It was a simple story which Herrick rehearsed in a dozen novels—the story of the crumbling of the old integrities, the integrity of professional skill, of business honesty, of political morality, of love itself, before the insidious demands of modern business. The moral, too, was simple and familiar: that the search for material rewards—money, power, social position—leads inevitably to disintegration and corruption. In *The Common Lot,* the architect who uses shoddy and permits jerry-building sees the luckless inmates of his "fireproof" tenement burn before his eyes; in *Clark's Field,* unearned increment on a Boston block infects all who profit or hope to profit from it; in *The Man Who Wins,* social rather than financial ambition thwarts the idealism of a physician; and in *Waste,* it is an engineer whose vaulting plans for a better society are similarly frustrated. Most thorough in its exploration of the pathology of modern business, most merciless in its findings, is *The Memoirs of an American Citizen,* the story of a self-made man who in his progress to power and wealth demoralized honest business associates, bribed judges, corrupted legislatures, and destroyed his family and his marriage. "No business in this modern world," says Van Harrington, contrasting his methods, with those of his wife,

could be done on her plan of life. That beautiful scheme of things which the fathers of our country drew up in the stage-coach days had proved itself inadequate in a short century. We had to get along with it as best we could. But we men who did the work of the world, who developed the country, who were the life and force of the times, could not be held back by the swaddling clothes of any political or moral theory. Results we must have: good results, and we worked with the tools we found at hand. (*The Memoirs of an American Citizen,* Macmillan)

It is this novel which illustrates most sharply the shift in animus from Howells to Herrick; not only in its portrait of the self-made man but in its philosophy of determinism, it anticipates the Dreiser of *The Financier* and *The Titan.*

If Herrick owed much to Henry George and Thorstein Veblen, his more popular contemporary, Winston Churchill, was inspired by the effervescent Theodore Roosevelt, and his books confess the character as well as the source of the inspiration. Like Roosevelt, Churchill found health in the pioneer virtues, blended romanticism with progressivism, came late to the realization of the corrupt alliance of business and politics, and learned publicly the facts of political life. Like Roosevelt, too, he was a romantic turned reformer by circumstances—his own career in New Hampshire politics had something to do with it—a historian who celebrated the past and deplored the present but who viewed past and present alike through the glasses of sentiment. And—again like T. R.—he was a follower rather than a leader, a sensitive sounding board for the voice of public opinion. When imperialism and the Spanish War stimulated interest in the American past, he furnished what were perhaps the best of the historical novels of his day—*Richard Carvel, The Crossing,* and *The Crisis.* When it became not too audacious to discuss the new woman, he embroidered on that theme in *A Modern Chronicle,* and the widespread interest in the socialization of Christianity brought the immensely popular *Inside of the Cup.* His political novels—*Coniston* and *Mr. Crewe's Career*—coincided with the Progressive movement, and when progressivism, under the pressure of men like Stephens, Brandeis, and LaFollette, took on an economic character, he responded with *A Far Country* and *The Dwelling Place of Light.*

Not without convictions, Churchill was without passion; there is no spiritual travail in *Mr. Crewe's Career* or *A Far Country* as there is in *The Common Lot* or *Clark's Field:* the moral seems to be a form of scaffolding rather than an integral part of the structure. Churchill subscribed to admirable ideals but to nothing that can be called a philosophy, and the ideals were sicklied over with sentimentalism. His insights were shrewd rather than profound, his moral judgments facile rather than conclusive. His villains had hearts of gold, he could not forego the happy ending, and—notwithstanding his own experience in New Hampshire politics—he retained to the end faith in the healing power of the democratic dogma. It is precisely because he was so sensitive a seismograph that his record of the impact of Darwinian ethics upon the older morality has more than an antiquarian interest. He is the perfect historian of the Rooseveltian phase of progressivism. That so popular a storyteller should abandon historical romances for muckraking and that his most mature work should deal with economic rather than with political corruption was itself significant. If he did not see as deeply as did Howells and Herrick into the nature of that corruption, neither did he explain it away as did Booth Tarkington as an amusing eccentricity of the middle-class American.

Like so many novelists of his generation Churchill was concerned with the pervasive immorality of modern business—the passing of professional integrity, the transfer of economic power from those who were builders and creators to those who dealt with paper, the growth of an interlocking directorate of industrialists, lawyers, bankers, and politicians, the perversion of older social and moral values to a search for prestige and power, the sacrifice to Mammon of love, honor, obedience, troops of friends. All this is most explicit in *A Far Country*—Churchill's major assault upon that alliance of business, politics, and law which was becoming so familiar a feature of the American landscape. It is a novelized version of *The Shame of the Cities* and a commentary on the blighting influence of the Darwinian and Nietzschian philosophies as applied to business practices. Hugh Paret who—like Van Harrington in *The Memoirs of an American Citizen*—tells his own story, is a product and a mouthpiece of these half-baked philosophies. Repudiating the professional standards that his father had maintained inviolate, he was early initiated into the new moral code:

I learned that not the least of the functions of these representatives of the people was . . . to facilitate the handing over of the Republic's resources to those in a position to develop them. The emphasis was laid on development, or rather on the resulting prosperity for the country: that was the justification, and it was taken for granted as supreme. I listened with increased fascination to these gentlemen in evening clothes calmly treating the United States as a melon patch that existed largely for the purpose of being divided up amongst a limited and favoured number of persons. (*A Far Country*, pp. 111–112.)

All this was hard to reconcile to traditional ethics, but ethics seemed increasingly irrelevant to modern life. "It was impossible," Paret explained carefully to the friend he was about to rob,

to apply to business an individual code of ethics—the two were incompatible, and the sooner one recognized that the better: the whole structure of business was built up on natural, as opposed to ethical law. We had arrived at an era of frankness—that was the truth—and the sooner we faced this truth the better for our peace of mind. (*A Far Country*, p. 34)

The whole panel of lesser novelists of the Roosevelt-Wilson era, however they differed in background and training, united with Howells and Herrick and Churchill in pronouncing a verdict of guilty against American business and businessmen of this generation. It is the verdict to be read in *Coniston* and *Mr. Crewe's Career,* confused as they are with recommendations of mercy; it is the verdict that emerges from Phillips' numerous journalistic exposures—*The Master Rogue, The Plum Tree, Light-Fingered Gentry, The Second Generation*—the very titles suggest a mistrial; it is the verdict passed by William Allen White, who compromised less in *A Certain Rich Man* and *In the Heart of a Fool* than in practical politics; it is the verdict affirmed by the experienced Brand Whitlock in *The Thirteenth District* and *The Turn of the Balance;* it is the verdict delivered in Ernest Poole's *The Harbor* and in Abraham Cahan's *Rise of David Levinsky.* These judges were all, in their way, clement, all willing to accept sentimental confessions or romantic atonements or death-bed repentances. What they affirmed, with no little indirection, was argued with more brutal insistence by Theodore Dreiser and Upton Sinclair.

These two major critics of American society differed profoundly in philosophy but not in analysis or diagnosis. Where Sinclair was animated by love for his fellow-men, Dreiser regarded them with dispassionate objectivity; where Sinclair was a propagandist, Dreiser was a scientific observer; where Sinclair was a moralist, Dreiser pretended to amorality; where Sinclair was melioristic, Dreiser was desperate; where Sinclair regarded the titans of industry with loathing, Dreiser confessed a sneaking admiration for those who came to the top in the struggle for existence. But however deep these differences, the two novelists agreed in describing the economic order as inhumane and corrupt. Philosophically *The Jungle* and *Sister Carrie, The Metropolis* and *The Financier, Boston* and *An American Tragedy* belong in different categories, but as indictments of American economy in the first quarter of the twentieth century they are interchangeable.

Even the tender and compassionate Henry James, who had withdrawn physically but could not withdraw spiritually from the American scene had, in the end, some apprehension of the pervasive corruptions of those riches which, in the past, he had accepted as less malign than the social and spiritual impurities of the Old World, hopelessly tainted as it was by hereditary evil. He had indeed, for the most part, portrayed with amiable toleration, even with affection, the American rich, vulgar rather than wicked, flaunting their money like children flaunting their toys, fundamentally innocent in their ambitions and in their assumption that there was nothing that money could not buy, generous, simple, kindly, romantic, virtuous, so often and so poignantly misunderstood, as Daisy Miller, as Bessie Alden were misunderstood. Yet in his one American novel of the later period, *The Ivory Tower,* James pictured the acquisitive society, parading its pretenses and its vices in that Newport which he had once loved "too much for description or definition"—that society which no other American author except Edith Wharton had really known—not as brashly vulgar but as morally blighted and corrupt. Here is a gallery of rich who do not so much do evil as suggest evil, rich ravaged not so much by ostentatious greed as by some corrosive infirmity which prevents them from thinking except in terms of millions and over whom hangs a miasmic air that recalls the atmosphere of the *Turn of the Screw:* the dreadful Mr. Gaw, dying of twenty millions—"to say that he was surrounded by the desert was almost to flatter the void into which he invited one to step"; Uncle Betterman, imperious and pertinacious, who proposed to train his nephew to "the awful game of grab"; Gussy Bradham, who was "naturally never so the vulgar rich woman able to afford herself all luxuries as when she was most stupid about the right enjoyment of these and most brutally systematic—for some inferior and desecrating use of them"; and the glittering Horton Vint, spiritually blighted, morally rotten, incapable of love or friendship. And against these are the two pure spirits scarcely come to life as living persons—the gentle Gray, guileless and childlike but with the most delicate perceptions, the subtlest sense of honor, the deepest integrity, and the large but enchanting Rosanna, unfortunate heir to millions—who would cut themselves off, as a gesture of disavowal, from their wealth and from all its commitments so reprehensible to their spirits, resigning their money to "its natural associations."

An interest founded on the mere beastly fact of his pecuniary luck, what was that but an ugly thing to see, from the moment his circle, since a circle he was apparently to have, shouldn't be moved to some decent reaction from it? How was he going himself to like breathing an air in which the reaction didn't break out, how was he going not to get sick of finding so large a part played, over the place, by the mere *constatation,* in a single voice, a huge monotone restlessly and untiringly directed, but otherwise without application, of the state of being worth dollars to inordinate amounts? (*The Ivory Tower,* pp. 258–259)

It was, in fact, James himself who made the sad gesture of disassociation, and for all its inconclusiveness, it was as effective, in its way, and as decisive as the more ostentatious gestures of Howells and Herrick.

3

In the mid-twenties a distinguished historian described American civilization as "almost wholly a businessman's civilization." Perhaps the generalization had been valid since Appomattox, but its validity was more readily conceded in a decade when the president announced that the business of America was business and when a political campaign could substitute the promise of two cars in every garage for the more modest full dinner-pail of an earlier generation. The advertisers, the radio, the movies, popular journals and newspapers, even churchmen, hastened to welcome the "new era," and colleges and universities were zealous to confer their honorary degrees upon corporation lawyers and stockbrokers. A chorus of praise for what was now, in despite of Jefferson, called the American system ascended to the skies. No major novelist joined in the chorus: the novelists remained unreconciled and unregenerate.

Yet the direct assault of the Populist-Progressive era was abandoned. Muckraking had been played out, and there were no successors to *The Arena* or *McClure's* or *Hamptons,* or to Herrick and Churchill and Phillips and Whitlock. It was partly that, as William Allen White later recalled, "the whole liberal movement . . . which had risen so proudly under Bryan and Roosevelt and LaFollette, was tired. The spirits of the liberals . . . were bewildered." It was partly that the public, lulled into complacency by prosperity and disillusioned by the abortive crusade to make the world safe for democracy, was no longer interested in exposures. It was chiefly that the triumph of business was so spectacular and its battlements were so formidable, that it seemed invulnerable to direct assault. Protest persisted, but the attack, in so far as that term may be used, was oblique and insidious. It took the form of satire and of repudiation, and satire and repudiation are confessions of defeat.

The confession is written large in the literature of the twenties. For as the novelists contemplated the business civilization which reached its apogee in that decade they were uncomfortable rather than indignant, derisive rather than rebellious; their protest was personal and their estrangement private. They looked with disapproval, even scorn, upon the contemporary scene, but they confessed no sense of shock, only a desire to shock. And what was perhaps most striking about the fiction which they wrote was not its overtones of satire and its undertones of antipathy and repudiation, but that the satire should be directed toward the middle classes rather than toward the rich, that the antipathy should be reserved for the social rather than the economic manifestations of the new era, and that the repudiation should be private rather than public. What these novelists lacked was what their predecessors so conspicuously had—sympathy, dignity, and purpose. They were not deeply moved by wrong because they had so little pity for the victims of wrong. They were not outraged by the violation of moral standards because they themselves were so unsure of their standards. They did not embark upon crusades because they had no program, only an attitude. They did not stand at Armageddon and battle for the Lord—how could they when they did not believe in the Lord?—but fled to Greenwich Village or to the Left Bank and thumbed their noses at the middle classes or at Puritanism or at the small town. Their greatest ambition was *épater la bourgeoisie,* their greatest triumph when the bourgeoisie acknowledged the shock.

Yet that triumph was brittle and evanescent. The economic hide was too thick for the barbs of the satirists, and the ultimate evidence of the futility of the attack was the enthusiasm with which it was welcomed by its victims. How completely mere satire failed of its purpose was made clear in the case of Sinclair Lewis, for when the public swarmed to buy his novels, when Main Street became a national shrine and Babbitt a folk hero, when the Pulitzer Committee found that *Arrowsmith* reflected the "wholesome atmosphere of American life," the joke was surely on Lewis himself rather than on Gopher Prairie or Zenith. Others who took refuge in satire or in malice suffered a comparable fate: the mordant Ring Lardner was regarded as a first-rate sports writer; the profoundly disillusioned Fitzgerald was acclaimed the spokesman for gilded youth; James Branch Cabell, whose repudiation of contemporary life was complete, achieved popularity because Jurgen contained passages esoterically erotic; Mencken, whose hatred of democracy was morbid, was embraced by all the young liberals; *The New Yorker* was welcomed as merely a humorous magazine, the fortunate successor to *Life* and *Judge*.

Of all the novelists of the twenties, it was Sinclair Lewis who gave the most elaborate report on his society and whose scenes and characters came most nearly to symbolize its meaning to the future. *Main Street* was published the year of Howells' death, and its author was, as much as any one could be, Howells' successor. Yet the contrasts between Howells and Lewis are more striking than the similarities. Both were observant and shrewd, both ranged widely over the national scene though rarely outside the middle classes they knew so well, both were realists and critics. Both were historians of the commonplace, but where Howells had rejoiced in the commonplace, Lewis found it intolerable. Both were interested primarily in character, but where Howells was concerned with its inner compulsions, Lewis was content with its outward manifestations. Both looked with skepticism upon the conventions of their day, but where Howells acquiesced in order to achieve intellectual freedom, Lewis battered so frantically against convention that he had no energy left to enjoy the freedom he won. Where Howells was urbane, Lewis was raucous; where he was judicious, Lewis was dogmatic; where he was affectionate—or at least compassionate—Lewis was scornful. Yet Howells' quarrel with his society was deeper than Lewis', his repudiation more fundamental.

For in this, too, Lewis mirrored his age, that he was content with surface effects, with photographs that were merely candid, with passion that was merely verbal. He belonged to that school of historians content with description and not curious to know the causes of things. Sooner or later he turned his searchlight on almost every aspect of American society and on almost every problem that engaged public attention, but a searchlight illumines only the surface of what it touches. He left few areas of American life unexplored but none surveyed, few issues unprobed but none explained: how futile, after all, were Babbitt's gestures toward emancipation, how irrelevant to the problem of religion the chronicle of Elmer Gantry's sleazy antics, how inconclusive the struggle of Arrowsmith for professional integrity. Like so much of the liberalism of the twenties, Lewis' protest was literally inconsequential.

Although it is clear that Lewis disapproved of the society and economy of his day, it is never quite clear what kind of society or economy would command his approval. He was in revolt, but his revolt was against bad manners rather than bad morals, and we feel that he found bigotry intolerable not so much because it maimed its victims as because it was an outward manifestation of smugness. His mimicry was devastating, his rage immense, but he never found an object wholly worthy of so much passion, and the rare victories his characters win over their mean environment—some brief emancipation, some glimpse of beauty, some lapse into decency—move us as little as the defeats and humiliations they suffer. He is for the most part the historian of defeat, yet if there are few happy endings in his books, there are few that are tragic, for he does not allow his characters the dignity of tragedy. Though he differed wholly from H. L. Mencken in philosophy, he was, like Mencken, engaged in guerrilla warfare against the *boobus Americanus,* and his novels were an extended gloss on those American Creeds that drag their dreary way through the pages of the old *American Mercury.*

It is in *Babbitt* that we find the most extensive report on society in the twenties, and the contrast between Howells and Lewis can best be appreciated when we compare Silas Lapham with George Babbitt. Silas Lapham, for all his vanity, his weakness, his vacillation, his confusion, is a hero. He has dignity, integrity, and character. The battles he fights are real, like the Civil War battles in which he was wounded the battle for his farm, for his factory, for his family, for his own integrity; the victories he wins, the defeats he suffers, are meaningful. Nor is the society in which he moves negligible, or the delicate issues of class relationships, business honesty, friendship and love. But what shall be said of Babbitt—that "walking corpse" as Parrington calls him—content with his dull life, his dull family, his dull house, his dull business, his dull town, his dull ideas, his dull virtues and duller vices, mouthing the platitudes of the Rotary Club and the Republican platform as if they were gospel? What but that he is not only a success, but the very symbol of Success, the symbol of the New Era. Babbitt is a caricature who came to life; here, as so often, nature conformed to art.

With the passing of years Gopher Prairie and Zenith took on something of the charm of period pieces and—by comparison with the Grand Republic of *Cass Timberlane* and *Kingsblood Royal*—a certain dignity. The society described in *Main Street* and *Babbitt* is shabby but rarely vicious, numbered a few honest men and women, and recognized some standards of morality. Not so that reconstructed by Ring Lardner. He, too, transcribed the American dream of success, but with him the dream was a nightmare. The dreadful specimens who haunt his pages are both shabby and vicious: the hopeless provincials who yearn for the Big Town, the moronic baseball players headed for the bush leagues, the sadistic prize fighters ready to sell out, the dopes and chumps, the crooks and chiselers and their gullible victims, the drummers with their appalling stories, the ham actors who dream of Broadway, the golfers who cheat and the caddies who lie, the illiterates who think they can earn a fortune writing poetry for the papers, the butter-and-egg men whose love nests are charnel houses, the "Mr. and Mrs." always suspicious, always quarreling, always avaricious. Lardner sears them all with impartial hatred.

A universal avarice corrodes and consumes all his victims: it is their one positive trait. They know neither love nor passion nor tenderness; they have no interests, no ideas, no conversation, even. They are interested only in Success, and Success is money, not earned but chiseled. They know all the tricks for getting ahead: how to meet the right people, who are always the wrong people; how to make a good impression, which inevitably is a fatal one; how to get on the inside of a good thing, which invariably turns out to be a bad thing. They lie and cheat, gamble and swindle, bilk their associates and double-cross their wives and husbands. And always in vain.

For Lardner is above all the historian of frustration—of courtships that go on the rocks or, what is worse, end in marriage; of honeymoons that fizzle out, of marriages that turn sour; of plays that flop, prize fights that are fixed, games that blow up; of beauty that is skin deep, affection that is phony, talent that is meretricious. Thus his account of "How to Write Short Stories" closes with the recommendation that ambitious writers

take up the life of a mule in the Grand Canyon. The mule watches the trains come in from the east, he watches the trains come in from the west, and keeps wondering who is going to ride him. But she never finds out.

The mule is a symbol for all Lardner's characters: they wait, and nothing happens, nor do they ever find out.

Nothing happens, nothing ever pans out; life is infinite boredom, futility, and frustration. It is the theme, too, of Scott Fitzgerald, the most gifted of all the novelists of the twenties, the incomparable historian of gilded youth, of the jazz age, of the rich and the near rich, of the great prosperity and the great disillusionment. His characters are, for the most part, extravagantly rich, but they differ from those of Lewis and Lardner chiefly in circumstances, not in aspirations: it is when we contrast Fitzgerald's playboys and demimondaines with their equivalents in Edith Wharton or Henry James that the comparison is qualitative. Nor do West Egg or the Riviera or Hollywood differ greatly from Gopher Prairie or Zenith or the Big Town, except that their inhabitants live what the hapless denizens of the sticks dream and thus reveal the tawdriness of the dream. Amory Blaine, penniless and jobless, his Rosaline deserting him for a richer man; Anthony Patch, heir to thirty millions, but broken by excesses and unbalanced by anxiety; the great Jay Gatsby bereft and murdered; the marionettes of *Tender Is the Night* indulging in aimless infidelities along the Riviera; Monroe Stahr smashed in an airplane before he could produce the kind of pictures he wanted—or call off the murder he had planned—how do they differ from George Babbitt or Jack Keefe except in the poignancy of their disillusionment?

First implicitly in *This Side of Paradise,* then more explicitly in *The Beautiful and the Damned, The Great Gatsby,* and *Tender Is the Night,* and finally in the wonderful fragment of *The Last Tycoon,* Fitzgerald laid bare the pathology of that generation which Gertrude Stein had called "lost," and it is relevant to remember that pathology derives from pathos. His theme—as surely as that of Dos Passos—was the Big Money, and he showed, not with malice but with compassion, what money did to his generation, how its standards conditioned life, dictated habits, condemned to futility, and led, in the end, to that "crack-up" which he himself experienced. He is the chronicler of the Beautiful but especially of the Damned, of All the Sad Young Men, of the golden bowl of riches that was so fatally flawed.

Of all Fitzgerald's novels, *The Great Gatsby* best mirrors not so much the economy as the economic fantasies of the twenties. Here, in the curious blend of Jay Gatsby's fancies and attainments, was the dream life: education at Oxford (which college was it, now?); a tour of "all the capitals of Europe—Paris, Venice, Rome, collecting jewels, chiefly rubies, hunting big game, painting a little"; a majority in the Army; decorations from every Allied government, "even little Montenegro"; and then a business in New York (what matter if it was disorderly?) and an estate on Long Island. Here was the dream mansion at West Egg: its feudal silhouette, its marble steps, its "Marie Antoinette music rooms and Restoration salons, its period bedrooms swathed in rose and lavender silk and vivid with new flowers, dressing rooms and poolrooms, and bathrooms with sunken baths," its bars stocked with Scotch and rye, its swimming pool and private beach and private plane. Here was the dream car: "rich cream color, bright with nickel, swollen here and there in its monstrous length with triumphant hat-boxes and supper-boxes and tool-boxes, and terraced with a labyrinth of windshields that mirrored a dozen suns . . . a sort of green leather conservatory." *The Great Gatsby* is one of the saddest novels in American literature. It is not that, in the end, Gatsby lies dead in the symbolic swimming pool and the rooms of the fabulous mansion are silent; it is rather that while he lived he realized all his ambitions.

4

There was, it must be admitted, something a little plaintive about all this, just as there was something plaintive about the whole self-conscious postwar generation. "Lost, and forever writing the history of their loss," as Alfred Kazin observes, "they became specialists in anguish. They had the charm of the specially damned." The satire in which Lewis and Lardner indulged, the bright depravity of Fitzgerald, the whimsy of Van Vechten, the flight from reality of Hergesheimer and Thornton Wilder and Elinor Wylie, were like one of those nervous breakdowns these novelists so often recorded—a luxury denied to farmers or washwomen and reserved for the sophisticated and the rich. There was, even at the time, something precious about their repudiation of a society whose dullness and meanness they exploited so successfully and which rewarded them so well: Fitzgerald himself admitted of his Jazz Age that he

looked back to it with nostalgia. It bore him up, flattered him and gave him more money than he had dreamed of, simply for telling people that he felt as they did, that something had to be done with all the nervous energy stored up and unexpended in the war. . . . It all seems rosy and romantic to us who were young then. (*Echoes of the Jazz Age*)

The depression changed this, made everything that was merely plaintive and precious and whimsical seem dated. It tore the novelists away from satire that was often an expression of superciliousness, and disillusionment that was often too personal, and brought them back to the main current of protest and reform. The situations that had titillated, the crises that had agitated, even the hothouse tragedies that had stirred the readers of *Babbitt* and *The Beautiful and the Damned* seemed brittle and exotic at a time when hunger stalked the land. And as F. D. Roosevelt was closer to Bryan than to Coolidge, or even to Wilson, so the novelists of the thirties had more in common with Garland and Sinclair than with Lardner or Fitzgerald. At least they were no longer embarrassed, as Hemingway confessed himself embarrassed, "by the words sacred, glorious, sacrifice, and the expression in vain . . . There were many words that you could not stand to hear and finally only the names of places had dignity."

Hemingway, Dos Passos, and Wolfe had all emerged in the twenties as Fitzgerald's Sad Young Men, as self-conscious members of the lost generation. Hemingway had, indeed, all but copyrighted the lineaments of that generation in *The Sun Also Rises;* Dos Passos had elegized it in *Three Soldiers* and *Streets of the Night;* Wolfe, a late-comer to the Babylonian scene, had discovered it independently of Paris and Gertrude Stein, as it were, and thus given it a flavor of homespun authenticity. In the thirties, when they reached maturity, they changed in varying degrees the focus of their interest, addressed themselves not so much to the tragedy of their own lost souls but to the tragedy of man's inhumanity to man: Hemingway who at last found a theme worthy of his talent, Dos Passos who discovered that the script of a symphony blown in the wind would never ravish the soul, Wolfe who at the close of his life struggled toward a recognition of something larger than himself. And they were joined by two new-comers: John Steinbeck who worked his way from Sir Henry Morgan's quest for gold to the Joads' search for security, and James Farrell who was sired, as it were, by Dreiser and whose whole attitude toward his own day was expressed in the bitter title of one of his novels —*A World I Never Made.*

Of them all, Thomas Wolfe's quarrel with his society remained the most personal and the most nearly artistic; more consistently than any other major novelist, he wrote autobiography. *Look Homeward, Angel, Of Time and the River,* and *The Web and the Rock* all indict the society in which Wolfe was so conscientiously and so articulately uncomfortable, yet it is difficult to escape the feeling that what was chiefly wrong with that society was that it was hard on a young man from North Carolina in search of his soul. Thus he tells us, in *The Web and the Rock,* of the boyhood memories that tortured his nights:

These memories and many others now came back to him and the result was a nightmare vision of man's cruelty, vileness, defeat and cowardice so unendurable that he writhed upon his cot, ripping the sheets between convulsive hands, and cursing with a twisted mouth and finally smashing his bloody knuckles at the wall as the black horror of man's cruelty and fear writhed like a nest of vipers in his brain.

Not until the close of his tragically short life did Wolfe show an awareness of the impact of inhumanity on others than himself. *The Story of a Novel* recalls that

Everywhere around me, during these years, I saw the evidence of an incalculable ruin and suffering. My own people, the members of my own family, had been ruined, had lost all the material wealth and accumulation of a lifetime in what was called "the depression." . . . In this endless quest and prowling of the night through the great web and jungle of the city, I saw, lived, felt, and experienced the full weight of that horrible human calamity . . . I saw acts of sickening violence and cruelty, the menace of brute privilege, a cruel and corrupt authority trampling ruthlessly below its feet the lives of the poor, the weak, the wretched, and defenceless of the earth.

And the staggering impact of this black picture of man's inhumanity to his fellow man, the unending repercussions of these scenes of suffering, violence, oppression, hunger, cold, and filth and poverty going on unheeded in a world in which the rich were still rotten with their wealth left a scar upon my life, a conviction in my soul which I shall never lose.

Yet even this was personal and, in a curious way, fortuitous or so broadly philosophical that its force was dissipated. The credo of *You Can't Go Home Again* addressed itself not to the "ruin and suffering of these years," but to original sin:

I do not think the enemy was born yesterday or that he grew to manhood forty years ago, or that he suffered sickness and collapsed in 1929, or that we began without the enemy, and that our vision faltered, that we lost the way, and suddenly were in his camp. I think the enemy is old as Time and evil as Hell, and that he has been here with us from the beginning.

It was Dos Passos and Steinbeck who addressed themselves most specifically and directly to the economic collapse of the thirties and the spiritual illness that lay behind it. Dos Passos was the most social minded of the major novelists, and it is appropriate that we are interested not in his characters but in what they portend and symbolize. As early as 1922 he had written of the Spaniard Baroja that "his mission is to put the acid test to existing institutions, and to strip the veils off them," and the insight was autobiographical. He is, as Max Lerner acutely observes, the Veblen of American fiction, his business to strip the veils of illusion from institutions: certainly that was the mission of *1919, The Forty-Second Parallel,* and *The Big Money.* Yet the comparison breaks down at a crucial point: where Veblen was objective and aloof, Dos Passos is passionate and involved. In him we find again something of that indignation against social injustice, the exploitation of the workers, the corruption of a commercialized civilization, that seared the pages of books like *The Octopus, The Jungle,* or *The Thirteenth District.*

The *U.S.A.* trilogy is the most extensive commentary on American economy of the war and the boom years that has yet been written, and the most nearly desperate. It is a kind of Domesday Book, a Calendar of Sin, an Index Expurgatorius of economic malpractices. Here is everything that Lewis satirized, that Fitzgerald lamented, that Lardner scarified, and a great deal more, for it is the most elaborately documented of books. It is not the whole of our business civilization, for Dos Passos is a relentless partisan and infallibly selects what is worst, but it is the whole of its cruelty and hyprocrisy and waste. The USA which Dos Passos surveys is indeed a Waste Land, the characters he creates are Hollow Men, their voices

> quiet and meaningless
> As wind in dry grass
> Or rats' feet over broken glass
> In our dry cellar
>   (T. S. Eliot, *The Hollow Men*)

Sex haunts them all, and drink—these are the narcotics of the day—and they stagger from speak-easy to speak-easy and from brothel to brothel. They drink, but only to escape reality; they make love, but only for pay; they marry, but only for money; they join clubs and make friends, but only to get ahead; in the end, they all crack up.

And does their world end with a bang or a whimper?—Charley Anderson smashed up in an automobile wreck, the physical smash-up merely a symbol of the moral; Margo Dowling buying her way to stardom in Hollywood and then disintegrating; Joe Williams killed in a drunken brawl in St. Nazaire; Mary French abandoned; Ben Compton jailed for his radicalism; Dick Savage degenerate; J. Ward Moorehouse a nervous wreck; "ideas, plans, stockquotations unrolling in endless tickertape in his head"; the homeless Vag thumbing a ride on the Lincoln Highway, the planes overhead filled with the hollow men who "think contracts, profits, power, wires humming dollars," while he

waits on the side of the road; the plane had gone; thumb moves in a small arc when a car tears hissing past. . . . Head swims, belly tightens, wants crawl over his skin like ants:

went to school, books said opportunity, ads promised speed, own your home, shine bigger than your neighbor, the radiocrooner whispered girls, ghosts of platinum girls coaxed from the screen, millions in winnings were chalked up on the boards in the offices, paychecks were for hands willing to work, the cleared desk of an executive with three telephones on it;

waits with swimming head, needs knot the belly, idle hands numb, beside the speeding traffic. (*The Big Money,* pp. 560–561)

If it is illuminating to compare Silas Lapham with George Babbitt, it is no less than startling to contract Van Harrington, Hugh Paret, and Frank Cowperwood with Dos Passos' representatives of Big Business, J. Ward Moorehouse and Charley Anderson. For those earlier titans of finance and of industry are amoral and ruthless, but they are never contemptible or obscene. They have certain standards of decency and some sense of. honor, and they formulate what appears to them satisfactory philosophical rationalizations for their conduct; each, in his twisted way, thinks that he is serving some larger end of progress. Nor can their authors wholly abandon them or repudiate them: Van Harrington and Paret, we feel, may yet be saved, and as for the fabulous Cowperwood, Dreiser can scarcely conceal his admiration for the man who was, after all, merely obeying those laws of nature which Darwin and Nietzsche had deciphered. But Anderson and Moorehouse have no redeeming qualities, nor is their creator troubled for a moment by any twinges of sympathy for them. They inspire disgust and justify it. They are Ring Lardner characters who, according to their ruined standards, make good, and their success is the blighted success of Lardner's dopes.

Dos Passos shows us businessmen far more corrupt than any who crowd the pages of Howells or Norris or Churchill or Herrick—depraved as these authors, who came to maturity in the afterglow of the Victorian era, could scarcely imagine depravity. Yet the object of his antipathy is not, as with these earlier critics, the bad man. It is the system, and he is the first major novelist after Upton Sinclair to condemn capitalism itself. It is not a little curious that those novelists whose resentment was focused most sharply on malefactors of great wealth should have displayed them with certain redeeming qualities, while Dos Passos (as indeed Wolfe and Steinbeck and Farrell), who made clear that the malefactors are merely the creatures of their environment, should give us villains of unmitigated wickedness. The acquisitive society of the twenties was scarred and pitted with evil, but it was not wholly, not even mainly, bad, and we may well ask what it had done to deserve a portrait done entirely in black.

If Dos Passos derives from Veblen, John Steinbeck derives from Henry George. His theme, like that of the great California radical, is the contrast between *Progress and Poverty,* and the calamitous consequences of the exploitation of the land. More clearly than any other critic or crusader of the thirties, he carries on the tradition of revolt and reform established by Hamlin Garland and Frank Norris, and of the nostalgia for the generation of the builders and impatience with the generation of the exploiters that is implicit in so much of Willa Cather. The connection with Garland and Norris is obvious; the debt to the Willa Cather of *My Ántonia* and *O Pioneers* and *A Lost Lady* not so obvious but significant. It is a long way from the Sweetwater to the Salinas Valley, but the triumph of Ivy Peters over old Captain Forrester anticipates the triumph of the banks and the great California fruit-growers over those who had won the land and belonged to it. It was the moral, too, of *Grapes of Wrath,* and if the Joads are far from "great-hearted adventurers," they are not much more shiftless than the farmers of Miss Cather's Hanover or Black Hawk, Nebraska, while "Ma" Joad has something of that fortitude and dignity that Miss Cather found so admirable in Alexandra Bergson and Ántonia Shimerda.

Grapes of Wrath is more than the story of the flight of the Okies from the dust bowl to golden California. It is an indictment of the economy that drove them into flight, that took the land from those who had tilled it and handed it over to the banks, that permitted hunger in the land of plenty and lawlessness in the name of law and made a mockery of the principles of justice and democracy.

The banks worked at their own doom, and they did not know it. The fields were fruitful, and starving men moved on the roads. The granaries were full, and the children of the poor grew up rachitic, and the pustules of pellagra swelled on their sides. The great companies did not know that the line between hunger and anger is a thin line. And money that might have gone for wages went for gas, for guns, for agents and spies, for blacklists, for drilling. On the highways the people moved like ants and searched for work, and food. (*Grapes of Wrath*, pp. 387–388)

Of all the novels of the decade, *Grapes of Wrath* etched most sharply the remembered contours of the depression, re-created most vividly the atmosphere of the days of crisis, of unemployment and starvation, of the dust bowl and the triple-A program, of relief and reform, spoke most authentically the voice of the New Deal. It was just such an indictment as Franklin Roosevelt himself might have drawn:

Burn coffee for fuel in the ships. Burn corn to keep warm, it makes a hot fire. Dump potatoes in the river and place guards along the banks to keep the hungry people from fishing them out. Slaughter the pigs and bury them, and let the putrescence drop down into the earth.

There is a crime here that goes beyond denunciation. There is a sorrow here that weeping cannot symbolize. There is a failure here that topples all our success. The fertile earth, the straight tree rows, the sturdy trunks, and the ripe fruit. And children dying of pellagra must die because a profit cannot be taken from an orange. And coroners must fill in the certificates—died of malnutrition—because the food must rot, must be forced to rot.

The people come with nets to fish for potatoes in the river and the guards hold them back; they come in rattling cars to get the dumped oranges, but the kerosene is sprayed. And they stand still and watch the potatoes float by, listen to the screaming pigs being killed in a ditch and covered with quicklime, watch the mountains of oranges slop down to a putrefying ooze; and in the eyes of the people there is a failure, and in the eyes of the hungry there is a growing wrath. In the souls of the people the grapes of wrath are filling and growing heavy, growing heavy for the vintage. (*Grapes of Wrath,* pp. 476–477)

It was a tract for the times, a campaign document, as *U.S.A.* could never be, like *Uncle Tom's Cabin,* like *Looking Backward,* like *The Jungle.* What linked it so surely with the economic novels of the earlier generation was not merely its eloquence or its partisanship or even its dramatic qualities but its affirmative note. It was a long time since that note had been sounded with any confidence by a major novelist. *Grapes of Wrath* painted a hideous picture of cruelty and want, but it preached faith, hope, and charity. It portrayed a society so confused that it placed the protection of property before the preservation of human values, but it unblushingly proclaimed the existence and asserted the priority of those values, and implied that if men could only be brought to understand them, they would not only survive but triumph. It admitted, with Lowell, that right was forever on the scaffold, wrong forever on the throne, but affirmed, too, his conclusion that

> That scaffold sways the future and behind the dim unknown
> Standeth God within the shadow keeping watch above his own.

In its sentimentalism, its moral fervor, its air of challenge and defiance, its undismayed confidence in the integrity of the human spirit, *Grapes of Wrath* goes back to the morality of an earlier day. With it the novel of protest and reform came full circle.

5

Surveying the literature of the twenties, one of the most astute critics, Bernard De Voto, charged that the major novelists were victims of a literary fallacy—the fallacy that what they saw was the whole of America and that their report on it was faithful:

The repudiation of American life by American literature during the 1920's signified that writers were isolated or insulated from the common culture. There is something intrinsically absurd in the image of a literary man informing a hundred and twenty million people that their ideals are base, their beliefs unworthy, their ideas vulgar, their institutions corrupt, and, in sum, their civilization too trivial to engage that literary man's respect. That absurdity is arrogant but also it is naive and most of all it is ignorant. For the repudiation was the end-product of systems of thinking, and the systems arose in an ignorance that extended to practically everything but imaginative literature and critical comment on it. (*The Literary Fallacy,* p. 150)

Mr. De Voto, in short, was pained that the novelists did so badly by American civilization, that they emphasized its harrowing aspects and ignored its admirable. He wrote in 1944 when Americans, confronted with the greatest crisis of their history, had revealed qualities not wholly ignoble, and he asked how it happened that the walking shadows who strutted and fretted their hours through the pages of Lewis and Fitzgerald and Dos Passos were able to meet that crisis.

And it was, in fact, remarkable, a reflection on the accuracy of the literary interpretation. Yet Mr. De Voto's charge is a point of departure rather than a conclusion. No major critic denied that the novelists of the twenties and the thirties were alienated from their society: it is the theme of much of the writing of Edmund Wilson, of Lewis Mumford, of Maxwell Geismar and Alfred Kazin. What is important is to ask how this situation came about. How did it happen that novelists from Lewis to Steinbeck were uniformly critical of America's business civilization? How did it happen that, after Silas Lapham, almost the only respectable businessmen in American fiction are Booth Tarkington's Plutocrat—the dubious Earl Tinker— and Sinclair Lewis' equally dubious Sam Dodsworth? Mr. De Voto is inclined to blame the novelists, and his resentment against what appears to be calculated misrepresentation is not hard to understand. Yet it is difficult to believe that all the novelists were blind except those who wrote for the popular magazines, that two generations of writers could have been led astray. It is, after all, a serious reflection on the business civilization that it was unable to commend itself to artists who were, on the whole, men of good will.

The problem is even more intriguing when we compare American with English literature of the same period. British writers from Hardy to Forster were critical enough of the class-ridden society and the raddled economy which they portrayed, but except for a few of them, like D. H. Lawrence, they confessed no such alienation from their society as Americans revealed. There is poverty and meanness in De Morgan's Hackney and in Bennett's Five Towns as in Wells's middle-class London, and Galsworthy's patricians are scarcely more admirable than Mrs. Wharton's. Yet with what tenderness does De

Morgan re-create the world of Joseph Vance, with what romance does Bennett invest the life of Edwin Clayhanger, how irresistible Wells finds his Mr. Polly, with what dignity does Galsworthy surround the austere Soames Forsyte. These writers had come to terms with their society and their economy, and when they criticized, it was like a family quarrel. Just as American literature lacks the amiable satire of the small town that we find in an E. F. Benson or an E. H. Young, the humorous attitude toward class distinctions of a P. G. Wodehouse or a George Birmingham or a Humphrey Pakington, the affection for the metropolis that permeates everything that Bennett and Wells and Priestley and Swinnerton wrote, so it lacks the quality of taking the acquisitive economy for granted and dealing with it on its own terms that is implicit in the work of such varied writers as Galsworthy and Brett Young, Forster and Priestley, Swinnerton and Walpole.

Was American society, then, so much less admirable than the British in its economic manifestations? Was its cupidity more ostentatious, its irresponsibility more reckless, its cruelty more revolting? Was it afflicted with some singular depravity, ravished by some unique immorality? No one familiar with the economic history of the two countries would so argue. Indeed the most perspicacious British observers, from Bryce to Brogan, agreed that the American economy offered fairer rewards to the average man than any other in the world, and immigration statistics suggested that this opinion was widespread.

What then is the explanation of the minority report which imaginative writers filed on the American economy? It explains nothing to say that they were out of touch with reality: they had taken out a patent on realism. Perhaps it was that American economy had developed so rapidly and so spasmodically that it left little room for the amenities and the artist was more sensitive than others to ugliness. Perhaps it was that the transformation of a rural to an urban economy had been too abrupt and the artist, whose roots in the past were intellectual as well as personal, had failed to make the readjustment. Perhaps it was that the novelists were, almost by nature, protestants: those who were content rarely bothered to write novels to advertise their felicity. Perhaps it was that the novelists, after all, were idealists, that they took seriously the promise of American life, expected to realize the American dream. They were not put off by the shibboleth of free enterprise, for they knew that the great tradition was the tradition of free men. "We must strike once more for freedom," wrote the youthful Dos Passos, "for the sake of the dignity of man." And that was what concerned most of those who addressed themselves to social and economic issues—not, perhaps, Faulkner or Caldwell or Lardner but the major figures from Howells to Steinbeck—freedom and the dignity of man. Thomas Wolfe spoke for them all in almost the last thing that he wrote:

I believe that we are lost here in America, but I believe we shall be found. . . . I think the true discovery of America is before us. I think the true fulfillment of our spirit, of our people, of our mighty and immortal land, is yet to come. I think the true discovery of our own democracy is still before us. And I think that all these things are certain as the morning, as inevitable as noon. I think I speak for most men living when I say that our America is Here, is Now, and beckons on before us, and that this glorious assurance is not only our living hope, but our dream to be accomplished. (*You Can't Go Home Again*)

CHAPTER XIII

The Transition in Historical Literature

I

HISTORY AND POLITICS, like sociology and economics, were making strenuous efforts to become sciences at the very time that law, long regarded as a science, condescended to become more social. All three abandoned a priori principles and adopted the scientific method; yet, aware that modern science made appropriate concessions to the vagaries of human nature, they did not feel compelled to reach definite conclusions or to generate sovereign laws. All felt the impact of evolution, acknowledged the validity of pragmatic tests, and found an economic interpretation congenial. Barriers between the social sciences were shattered: historians submitted to instruction in economics, and the good social scientist was expected to be at home in anthropology, geography, biology, psychology, and philosophy. To this utopia of omniscience many were called but few were chosen. For neither pantology nor synthesis came easily to a generation exposed to more, and more complex, facts than had ever before been available. So along with the leveling of artificial barriers went an increasing fragmentation of the whole field of the social sciences. However eloquently philosophers might denounce the dangers of specialization or commencement orators extol the virtues of catholicity, no sound student of political theory was expected to understand administration, while any historian who pretended to expert knowledge in more than one field of history was suspected of superficiality. While everyone recognized that society was a unit and clamored for broad philosophical treatises which would disclose that unity, the characteristic form of scholarly literature of this generation was the monograph.

As the doctrine that history is past politics fell into well-merited disrepute, politics forgot history: only a generation ignorant or contemptuous of history could have been guilty of the reckless errors that characterized American foreign policy from 1919 to 1938. As the aridity of much of the political theory of the past was exposed, scholars and statesmen alike felt that they could safely dispense with philosophy: no political debate of the twentieth century was conducted on so high a level as the debate over the ratification of the Constitution or the Compromise of 1850. The degree of Doctor of Philosophy was imported to America just as scholarship cut loose from its philosophical moorings; certainly the creation of over two thousand Ph.D.'s in 1938 did not guarantee that philosophers were more numerous than in Aristotle's Athens or, for that matter, in Jefferson's Williamsburg. The half-century after 1890 was dedicated to reform and reconstruction, yet neither the Progressive movement nor the New Deal had the firm philosophical basis of the reform movement of the mid-nineteenth century, and a generation that fought two wars to preserve democracy added nothing significant to the definitions of democracy which Thomas Jefferson had formulated.

Henry Adams was doubtless perverse when he insisted that any nine pages of his *Esther* were worth more than the nine volumes of his great *History*—especially as *Esther* was so bad a novel—but the underlying implication of his whimsy was clear enough. Even he knew that the *History of the Administrations of Jefferson and Madison* was good history—but what was it good for? What, indeed, was any history good for, any study of politics or law? The generation that had rejoiced in the stately histories by Bancroft, Motley, Prescott, and Parkman had not been troubled by this question. It had been content with the richness of the narrative, the symmetry of the pattern, the felicity of the style that was to be found in all these magisterial volumes. If it looked for more, it could find philosophy, too, unobtrusive but unequivocal: a vindication of the principles of democracy and liberty and order, a demonstration of the triumph of right over wrong. Just so Joseph Story and Francis Lieber had written their legal and political treatises in the grand tradition, sure of their ground and of the ultimate validity of their work, never puzzled or discouraged, never doubting that the Law, the State, and the Constitution could be defined and described in shipshape manner. Their nationalism was absolute, and they conceived of Law, Reason, and Justice a interchangeable terms. But Justice Holmes, who belonged philosophically to the new era, preferred to define the law as something the courts would enforce and truth as the majority vote of that nation that could lick all others. He had early learned, he liked to recall, that he was not God.

It was the lesson that most of the historians and jurists who came to maturity in the decade of the nineties were required to learn. As they could no longer reveal Law or construct Systems, they turned resolutely to more urgent if less grandiose tasks. For if they were not God, or His spokesmen, they could be men and play a man's part in the reconstruction of the social order which they observed and analyzed. Exposed to the hot noontime glare of public events, ravaged by public opinion, levied on by politicians and businessmen, they discovered a new realism and displayed an anxious interest in facts rather than theories and a secular concern with the practical implications of their findings. It was perhaps fortuitous that two historians, Theodore Roosevelt and Wilson, should go to the White House, but it was not an accident that leading students of political science such as Frank Goodnow, Henry Jones Ford, Charles Beard, and Charles E. Merriam should be as familiar with legislative chambers as with Aristotle or that such distinguished jurisprudents as Louis Brandeis, Walton Hamilton, and Thurman Arnold should be equally at home in law and economics.

If scholarship confessed the impact of politics, politics in turn yielded to the importunities of scholarship. Such academic immunity as scholars had enjoyed they now surrendered and plunged headlong into the swift currents of public controversy, cheerfully taking sides and fashioning the weapons of battle. Some enlisted openly in the armies of the heretics and the rebels, fought under the tattered banners of the Populists or the Socialists, and shamelessly permitted their books to vote for Bryan or Roosevelt or Wilson. Others—Rhodes among historians, for example, or Burgess among political scientists—ranged themselves stoutly alongside the embattled defenders of the status quo and invoked the past to justify the present and reassure the future. Historians, called upon to explain the agrarian revolt or the exploitation of the South, emerged not only with explanations but with remedies. Students of politics, required to account for corruption, the boss, the failure of municipal government, or the ineptitude of Congress, devised techniques to meliorate these evils and make democracy more effective. Jurisprudents, confronted with the practical consequences of the income tax decision or the bakeshop labor case could no longer validate judicial review by repeating the simple arguments of *Marbury* vs. *Madison* but were forced to devise safeguards against those partisan and economic preconceptions of judges which so often dictated the character of judicial legislation. It was no longer convenient to draw a sharp line between scholarship and pamphleteering; to a people whose most notable contribution to the literature of politics was *The Federalist* the distinction could not be thought important.

There were exceptions, to be sure; the humanists of the twenties sought to escape from rather than to improve a society they thought vulgar, and scholarship confessed its humanists as well as literature. As late as 1940 Archibald MacLeish denounced scholarly recluses as *The Irresponsibles,* and Van Wyck Brooks, whose reconstruction of the literary past had seemed to some critics almost archeological, supported the attack in his essay *On Literature Today.*

By then, to be sure, the crisis had come; the drum beats

> Through the windows—through doors—burst like a ruthless force
> Into the school where the scholar is studying.

Academic insularity was no longer tolerable; those problems to which scholars had addressed themselves during the transition decades came to seem almost reassuring, and a generation that had been troubled by the simple issues of laissez faire or civil service reform or judicial review took on a quality of almost Arcadian innocence.

For the second quarter of the century confronted history, politics, and law with the most prodigious challenge these disciplines had known since they laid claim to the term science. Heretofore, and since the beginnings of the Republic, history, politics, and law had flourished within the framework of an orderly universe, and a sympathetic one, and had been sustained by the conviction that Man was rational and that the conclusions of Reason had authority. Only crackpots had challenged the basic assumptions of government and law—that government existed to serve society as a whole and that law was designed to insure justice—and only Henry Adams the theory that history recorded progress rather than retrogression and that those who contemplated it might grow in wisdom. However acrimonious the controversies that raged between political or juristic schools of thought, these controversies had concerned themselves, in America at least, with means rather than with ultimate ends. Hamilton and Jefferson, after all, had cooperated to make a nation, and when Confederate leaders broke it up they reproduced its Constitution; even in the twentieth century the differences between rival parties were esoteric.

The notion that government might logically be anarchical, that law might be lawless, that history might be reduced to an obituary notice, was too outrageous to be tolerated. Yet in the second quarter of the century, scholars and statesmen were required to contemplate these possibilities if only to refute them. The appeal to unreason could not be ignored when it served as an instrument—we can scarcely say a philosophy—to establish Nazi dominion over a score of ancient states and threatened to convulse even the New World, heretofore immune from such convulsions. The crisis in politics and law was more acute than in history, for history, after all, could fall back upon the past for reassurance and could console itself with the long view, while government and law could not escape the present.

The iron compulsion of events forced, temporarily, a reconsideration of basic assumptions, a restatement of traditional doctrines, and a revival of philosophical inquiries. History searched out the nature of democracy and the mainsprings of the American national character in an effort to invoke the virtues of the past to justify the defense of the present. Political science investigated the psychological and emotional wellsprings of conduct to explain even the temporary triumph of an order which by all the principles of ethics and all the teachings of history should never have attained sufficient power to constitute even a threat. Law, confronted with the most formidable challenge, refused to concede the futility of the efforts of jurists and statesmen from Grotius to Franklin Roosevelt to compel nations to conform to standards required of individuals and had the satisfaction of seeing its firmness vindicated. Whatever the technical validity of the rules it invoked, the Nuremberg Court represented the triumph of eighteenth-century doctrines of rationalism over twentieth-century manifestations of anarchy.

Yet even this prodigious cataclysm, which shook the very structure of society to its foundations and threatened the moral order of the western world, while it directed attention to fundamentals, did not change them. Defeat might have produced such a reconstruction, and even such costly success as Britain won led to modifications, but victory appeared to ratify the American position and to justify a return to prewar principles and practices. Certainly the popular mind leaped swiftly to the conclusion that the defeat of the enemy was equivalent to the solution of the problem, and twelve months after Hiroshima and Nagasaki the American public returned to warmed-over issues which had failed to provide intellectual nourishment even in their original form a quarter-century earlier. Scholars who yielded to no such glib illogic were eager enough to discuss fundamentals but not clear about the nature of the discussion. No great philosophical work emerged from the war—not even in the field of imaginative literature—no new concepts of law and few new techniques of democracy, and many signs indicated that Americans generally were as concerned to return to the past as to advance into the future. Where the past was so secure and the future so uncertain this was not astonishing, and insofar as the past retained moral validity it was not regrettable. To the student concerned for the future of history and politics, the crucial question was whether Americans were capable of distinguishing between the glittering past of Harding and Coolidge or the spacious past of Hamilton and Jefferson.

2

Economics and sociology, politics and law, ministered to secular needs and contributed, so it was thought, to order and prosperity. Alone of the social sciences, history could not—or did not—claim to be utilitarian, and if the American character was, as its critics never wearied of reiterating, a hopelessly practical one, history should have suffered from its disability. Yet historical literature was conceded to be more distinguished than any other except perhaps legal, and European critics who depreciated American contributions to imaginative literature acknowledged the genius of her historians. Although the immediate usefulness of history was not clear, it was a tribute to its eminence that, like the classics, it was not required to show its credentials; it was sufficient that it had instructed the Fathers in wisdom and virtue, nurtured statesmen in their high art, inspired poets and novelists, and furnished ready allusions to orators, theologians, and pedagogues. Nor had historians been denied the liveliest appreciation. The Rev. Jared Sparks had achieved both prosperity and the presidency of Harvard College through his historical rather than his theological contributions; Prescott and Motley were as widely read as Hawthorne and Simms; and George Bancroft, once his youthful political heresies were forgiven, was widely regarded as the first citizen of the land. The calculated insolence of Henry Adams' letter to young Cabot Lodge, advising him to follow history as a profession, could not conceal the appositeness of the advice:

The question is whether the historico-literary line is practically worth following, not whether it will amuse or improve you. Can you make it *pay?* either in money, reputation, or any other solid value? If you will think for a moment of the most respectable and respected products of our own town of Boston, I think you will see at once that this profession does pay. No one has done better and won more in any business or pursuit, than has been acquired by men like Prescott, Motley, Frank Parkman, Bancroft, and so on in historical writing. (*Letters of Henry Adams, 1858–1891,* p. 228, Houghton Mifflin Co.)

It is significant that Lodge followed this advice and that only when he abandoned history for politics did he lose that respect with which Adams tempted him.

The American interest in history is not difficult to understand, but the American achievement poses a more complex problem. Every educated American read Gibbon, but none conceded the relevancy to the American experience of his melancholy conclusion that history is "little more than the register of the crimes, follies, and misfortunes of mankind." That this interpretation was relevant enough to the Old World had been noted by Benjamin Franklin who at one time offered to provide Gibbon with material for a history of the decline and fall of the British Empire, but the New World function of history was a happier one. History, here, was the record of a nation which was, in the felicitous words of Jefferson, "advancing rapidly to destinies beyond the reach of mortal eye." The story of that triumphant advance had to be recorded, for the edification of Europe, for the gratification of posterity. Americans knew that they were engaged in a unique experiment and were conscious of the duty to chronicle that experiment. "Wee hope to plant a nation, where none before hath stood," wrote the author of *Newes from Virginia* in 1610, and from John Smith and Bradford to Bancroft and Palfrey the record was largely a self-conscious one. The sense of a peculiar destiny, and of responsibility for explaining it, persisted into the twentieth century where it can be read in Turner's "Contributions of the West to American Democracy" or in James Truslow Adams' *Epic of America,* or in Stephen Vincent Benét's *Western Star,* with its proud boast

> We've done what never men did before.

A people so aware that they were making history were conscious of their duty to record it. A people sure that they were beating out paths for other nations to follow were sensible of the obligation to mark those paths well. A people whose institutions were continually under scrutiny were zealous to explain and defend them. A people so proud of their achievements and so uncontaminated by modesty were eager to celebrate their triumphs. A people made up of such conglomerate elements and with so little racial or religious or even geographical unity were at pains to emphasize their common historical experience and validate their historical unity. A people whose collective memory was so short were inclined to cherish what they remembered and to romanticize it. A people living in the present were conscious of the necessity of connecting that present with the past, of furnishing for themselves a historical genealogy.

The historical achievement was no less impressive than the enthusiasm. The subject was ready at hand—whether it was the miraculous growth of America and the wonder-working Providence that had guided its destinies, or the vicissitudes of liberty in the Old World and its triumph in the New, or the contrasts of Old and New World civilization. The record was, in fact, a stirring one and did not need to be inflated by national pride or distorted by chauvinism: no mere mythology could compete with the reality. A people so conscious of their rectitude and their felicity could even afford to confess occasional indiscretions toward Indian and Negro.

Because America built upon the past and inherited the experience and learning of the western world, her historians were not embarrassed by her youthfulness or by any want of background in themselves. They had inherited the same literary traditions as Macaulay and Froude; if they contributed less than their British contemporaries to the history of the ancient world, they were perhaps more aware of the role of France, Spain, and Holland in the modern, and it was not wholly by chance that the best histories of Spain and the Netherlands should come from their hands. Cultural geography, too, played a part. After Irving and Cooper, New England monopolized the writing of history. Here was a society conscious of its traditions and of its role in creating the American tradition and its responsibility for preserving it; here prosperity had developed a leisure class, Harvard College furnished an intellectual center, a maritime tradition broadened horizons, a relatively homogeneous society gave cultural stability, and slavery did not impose an apologetic or defensive pattern on thought; here the Puritan respect for learning encouraged scholarship, and theology no longer conscripted the ablest scholars, while Puritan distrust of mere literature lingered on to make fiction suspect and to direct the talents of men of letters into history and law.

The mid-nineteenth century was the golden age of American historical literature. In the two decades from 1840 to 1860 appeared Irving's *Washington*, Prescott's *Mexico* and *Peru*, Ticknor's *Spanish Literature*, six volumes of Bancroft's monumental *History*, Motley's *Dutch Republic* and *United Netherlands*, Schoolcraft's *Indian Tribes*, Parkman's *Pontiac*, the first volume of Palfrey's tribute to New England, Hildreth's *History*, Parton's *Jackson* and Gayarré's *Louisiana*. By the seventies, though Parkman was still in his prime, the twilight had set in, and the venerable Bancroft was busy on his author's last revision. The historical contributions of Moses Coit Tyler, John Fiske, and Henry Adams were still to come: though trained in the literary and steeped in the moral traditions of the nineteenth century, these younger scholars were the vanguard of the scientific school rather than the rearguard of the romantic.

It would be too much to say that all these historians, from Irving to Adams, constituted a school, yet, for all the differences in the subjects they chose and the interpretations they advanced, they had much in common. They selected great and ample subjects, painted a broad and crowded canvas, and—with the exceptions of Hildreth and Adams—preferred color to chiaroscuro. Untroubled by the question whether history was science or art, they were pre-eminently literary and enjoyed a popularity denied to their more scientific successors in the next century. They belonged with the English and French schools of history rather than with the German, with Macaulay and Froude, Michelet and Guizot, rather than with Ranke, Sybel, and Waitz. They were nationalistic without being chauvinistic; they were romantic, but their romanticism did not—as with Carlyle —take the form of reaction; they were not pedagogues but men of letters and of public affairs. With the exception of Irving, and of such minor figures as Schoolcraft, Parton, and Gayarré, they were all New Englanders. The romantic school was to pass, the literary and amateur spirit give way to the scientific and professional, the political narrative yield to the economic analysis, but the New England dominion was to linger on into the new era.

3

As the golden age passed, the iron age set in. Bancroft died in 1891; there was no successor to write so confidently or to combine, as he had, the writing and the making of history. Two years later, and noble Francis Parkman had finished his half-century of conflict and no longer walked the streets of his familiar Boston. Already John Fiske had turned from philosophy to history, venturing upon that ambitious plan to fit American history into the grand design of social evolution which was never to be completed; already young Frederick Jackson Turner was challenging the Freeman formula of history as past politics by insisting upon the significance of the frontier in the development of American institutions. In 1890 Captain Mahan brought out the remarkable *Influence of Sea Power upon History* which was destined to have greater practical importance than any other historical work in our literature. The next year came the first of James Ford Rhodes's many volumes on the history of the United States since 1850, and with its publication northern writers took that road to reunion with the South which Southerners were more reluctant to follow. And in that year, too, Henry Adams completed his masterly survey of the history of the administrations of Jefferson and Madison and turned from the composition of orthodox history to the search for such historical laws as might explain the futility of orthodoxy.

The laws which he formulated were, to be sure, irrelevant to American history, for it could not be expected that a nation so energetic would entertain seriously the doctrine of the dissipation and ultimate exhaustion of energy. Nor did the events of the next half-century require a more favorable verdict on the validity of Adams' conclusions. But with Henry Adams, as with his brother Brooks, the conclusions were less significant than the argument. For however whimsical the application of the second law of thermodynamics, or however mistaken the notion that the New World was to share the apparent exhaustion of the Old, neither the data nor the reasoning could be brushed aside.

The nineteenth-century historians, from Irving to Parkman, had celebrated the individual and honored moral virtues; the Adams of the great *History* and the authoritative *Gallatin* had not failed to praise famous men or to pay tribute to honor, faith, and courage. But now he was finished with all this; now he substituted impersonal force for individual achievement, and his philosophy had no place for morality. The historians' business, he submitted, was "to follow the track of energy." For, satisfied that "the sequence of men led to nothing and that the sequence of their society could lead no further, while the mere sequence of time was artificial and the sequence of thought was chaos, he turned at last to the sequence of force."

With "The Rule of Phase Applied to History," that sequence was neatly worked out. There was first the era of instinct, a long epoch in which men were controlled by purely automatic drives. The era of instinct was succeeded, after thousands of years, by the era of religion—and it was religious force that Adams was to celebrate in the most moving of his books, *Mont-Saint-Michel and Chartres*. As the power of religion waned, man's fate came to be controlled increasingly by mechanical forces, and the mechanical period was succeeded, in turn, by the electrical, whose symbol was the dynamo. With the twentieth century—more specifically with the discovery of radium—came the impact of "supersensual forces":

Power leaped from every atom, and enough of it to supply the stellar universe showed itself running to waste at every pore of matter. Man could no longer hold it off. Forces grasped his wrist and flung him about as though he had hold of a live wire or a runaway automobile.

"Man could no longer hold it off"—that was the point. Men were, after all, but creatures of force, and the conflicts that agitated peoples were no longer between men but between the motors that drive men. Nor were men competent to control the forces which they had unleashed. "It is my belief," Adams confessed in 1902, "that science is to wreck us, and that we are like monkeys monkeying with a loaded shell. . . . It is mathematically certain to me that another thirty years of energy-development at the rate of the last century must reach an *impasse*." The prophecy missed Hiroshima by thirteen years, but where the sequence of time was artificial the miscalculation was pardonable.

Brooks Adams, like his brother Henry, was committed to the theory that impersonal forces determined the course of history. "If men move in a given direction," he wrote, "they do so in obedience to an impulsion as automatic as is the impulsion of gravitation," and he was not thinking of that upward evolution which solaced John Fiske. Like Henry, too, he concluded that as far as they affected man's fate the forces were malignant—if indeed anything so impersonal as force can be called malignant—for he had read history only to find that all our yesterdays had but lighted fools their way to dusty death. Where Henry fell back upon dubious physics and questionable mathematics, Brooks yielded to the arguments of economics, and he was happy to find in these confirmation of his most grievous fears. He traced the vicissitudes of civilization through its martial and spiritual and to its economic phase, and of all its manifestations he thought the economic the least admirable and the least vigorous and the most vulnerable to the forces of fragmentation. With the nineteenth century, he asserted, the last stage of concentration had been reached, and in this

the economic, and, perhaps, the scientific intellect is propagated, while the imagination fades, and the emotional, the martial, and the artistic types of manhood decay. When a social velocity has been attained at which the waste of energetic material is so great that the martial and imaginative stocks fail to reproduce themselves, intensifying competition appears to generate two extreme economic types—the usurer in his most formidable aspect, and the peasant whose nervous system is best adapted to thrive on scanty nutriment. At length a point must be reached where pressure can go no further, and then, perhaps, one of two results may follow: A stationary period may supervene, which may last until ended by war, by exhaustion, or by both combined, as seems to have been the case with Eastern Europe; or, as in the Western, disintegration may set in, the civilized population may perish, and a reversion may take place to a primitive form of organism. (*The Law of Civilization and Decay*, 1896 ed., Preface)

Henry Adams could stand aside and view the inexorable processes of history dispassionately; he could even imagine a return—in 1938, of all years!—to "a world that sensitive and timid natures could regard without a shudder." There is no evidence that Brooks was sensitive, and conclusive evidence that he was not timid. Unlike

Henry—who, we may believe, had his tongue in his cheek when he formulated his rule of phase—Brooks took himself and his ideas seriously. Because he was convinced that the law of history was the law of concentration of force, he was concerned that his country adapt its policies to that law and thereby achieve supremacy. As the military were superior to the industrial virtues, it behooved the United States to cultivate the military, and Adams became a chauvinist. As supremacy depended upon the control of the sources of power, it was essential that the United States seize power, and he became the first of American geopoliticians. As nations which failed to meet the challenge of competition—or of nature—declined, it was necessary for the United States to respond to the challenge of force, and Adams anticipated Arnold Toynbee's theory of the rise and decline of civilizations. As "political principles are but a conventional dial on whose face the hands revolve which mark the movement of the mechanism within," the American Government could safely ignore principles of democracy or idealism, and Adams anticipated those doctrines later associated with fascism.

Historians could scarcely be expected to accept the gray conclusions of this brace of Adamses, for these conclusions, as Henry Adams saw with characteristic clarity, would have made the writing of history both superfluous and futile. Nor, for that matter, was there any compulsive temptation to accept evidence so capricious and logic so ruinous. Yet the substitution of physical for spiritual force, of determinism for free will, upon which the Adamses insisted, was prophetic. For history did, in the end, bow to the doctrine of force, and of all forces which it was willing to recognize, the economic was the most compelling. In the half-century after Henry Adams published *The Tendency of History* and Brooks Adams the *Law of Civilization and Decay,* every major American historian subscribed, with varying degrees of enthusiasm, to an economic interpretation of history. Evolution was not repudiated, but the emphasis was on environment rather than on heredity: the sifted-grain theory lost much of its authority, and it was no longer clear that those who proved fittest to survive the dangerous environment of the new age were necessarily the vehicles of progress. Progress itself came to be regarded, somewhat wistfully, as an ideal rather than a manifest destiny. Morality was not forgotten, nor ethics ignored, but they came increasingly to seem peculiar rather than universal and fortuitous rather than necessary. Thus morality became historically interesting as an American phenomenon rather than America as a moral phenomenon, and historians, who were entirely willing to concede the historical fact that Americans had long recognized God, no longer insisted upon God's special recognition of America.

The historians of the new century, then, concerned themselves more largely with forces than with persons. They abandoned ethics for science, drama for photography, and narrative for analysis. Nothing was left to God and not much to chance, and such fortuity as had to be admitted was ascribed rather to the inadequacy of the historian than to the vagaries of history. All the past seemed to flow out of the interaction of great impersonal forces—economic, geographical, social, scientific, psychological: only the psychological were regarded as aberrations, and this suggested that men were supposed to conform to nature and to history rather than nature and history to men. Almost every historian of that generation, as Henry Adams observed in his presidential address to the American Historical Association, felt that he was on the verge of some discovery that should do for history what Darwin had done for Nature. Thirty years later Adams' successor in the presidential chair, Edward P. Cheyney, submitted six laws of history and looked forward confidently to future meetings of the Association,

when the search for the laws of history and their application will have become the principal part of its procedure. . . . The most conspicuous place on the programme will be assigned to some gifted young historical thinker who quite properly, disregarding the early and crude efforts of his predecessors, will propound and demonstrate to the satisfaction of all his colleagues some new and far reaching law or laws of history. (*Law in History,* p. 28, A. A. Knopf)

Yet society stubbornly refused to fit into the neat framework of impersonal forces so painstakingly constructed for it, and history remained a shambles. Not only were historians unable to predict future wars, they were unable to explain past ones, and half a century of emphasis on economic and social forces left Americans more confused about the causes of the Civil War than were those who fought it. Schoolbooks which had ceased to be either anecdotal or edifying and had reduced history to a series of problems, all impersonal, left children with a baffled feeling that history was a series of formulas that could never be used for reaching conclusions. Their more sophisticated elders could nurse the suspicion that the formulas were inaccurate or the apprehension that there were no conclusions.

Each generation sees the past in terms of its own interests, and this first twentieth-century generation was no exception. As its interests were material, it saw the past as economics; as its interests were democratic, it created social history; as its interests were liberal, it made the past plead the cause of reform; as its interests were scientific, it eschewed morals and stressed technics and mechanics; as its interests were social, it discounted the personal and the dramatic: while the popular mind wove legends around Washington and Lincoln, historians busied themselves with explaining instead the forces that produced and sustained them.

It was in this "scientific" spirit that the history of the nation was rewritten, and the term "revisionist," so popular in the new century, generally suggested an economic interpretation. The impulses behind the expansion of Europe to the New World were seen to be economic rather than religious or political and the triumph of the English over the French to come from geographical and economic factors. Puritanism was discounted, but where allowed it was animated with economic significance. Colonial administration was studied as a commercial rather than a political phenomenon, and the term "tyranny," which had once explained so much, was given an economic instead of political meaning. Revolutionary heroes were denied both their halos and their oratorical flights, while their constitutional arguments, once so persuasive, were catalogued as propaganda; students concentrated instead on such matters as land policy, trade, currency, and debts. An internal revolution was disclosed and recorded in terms of a class struggle. The palpable failure of the Articles of Confederation was ascribed rather to economic conditions than to political arrangements, the Constitution itself became an economic document, and the struggle for ratification was analyzed in terms that Karl Marx would have approved. Even Jefferson, long immune from the diagnosis of materialism, yielded to an economic interpretation. Frederick Jackson Turner discovered that the frontier was the most American part of America and interpreted the growth of democracy largely in environmental terms. The history of the law and the judiciary was rewritten to prove that they had always been the instruments of class rule. Slavery, heretofore the darling of

the moralists, was viewed chiefly as an economic institution, Southerners pictured as victims of social and economic forces over which
they had no effective control, and even abolitionism was subjected
to dubious economic analysis. War is, by its very nature, force, and
no new interpretation was required to make clear that the government which commanded the largest armies and the richest natural
resources won the Civil War; what perplexed historians was rather
that the Confederacy should have fought so long and so well and
that the outcome should have been so close a thing. Where the constitutional dialectic of states' rights, secession, war, and reconstruction could not be ignored, it was studied as a rationalization of social
and economic realities.

The new fields of history, opened up with bewildering rapidity,
were almost all in the arena of economics, and the ideal historian of
the new day was one as much at home in the history of transportation, banking, labor, agriculture, and business as in politics. New
schools emerged devoted to these aspects of history, once considered
marginal or even unscholarly, and none now apologized for his preoccupation with the history of business as Thomas Madox had
apologized for his *History of the Exchequer,* that "its Subject is Low."
Aesthetics fought a losing battle with sociology and economics even in
the interpretation of literature, art, and architecture.

It is easy to exaggerate all this, and it would be misleading to suggest that history became a mere handmaiden to what had long been
called the dismal science. It came close to that in those academic
circles which, during most of the new century, all but monopolized
the interpretation of history, but outside the universities wider experience encouraged a more catholic view of society and public life
a livelier interest in character. It is illuminating to observe that while
the academicians dredged up the essential source material and reconstructed the history of institutions, most of the notable biographies
were written by nonacademic scholars: witness Nicolay and Hay's
Lincoln, William Roscoe Thayer's *Cavour,* Albert Bigelow Paine's
Mark Twain, Albert Beveridge's *Marshall,* Claude Bowers' *Jefferson,*
Marquis James's *Jackson,* Carl Van Doren's *Franklin,* Carl Sandburg's
Lincoln, and Douglas Freeman's *Lee.* And from Winston Churchill
and Mary Johnston to Kenneth Roberts and Esther Forbes, the
novelists who commanded the widest audience continued to exploit history for its drama and to praise famous men.

CHAPTER XIV

Innovators in Historical Interpretation: Turner, Parrington, Beard

I

NEITHER THE GRIM anticipations of Henry Adams nor the modest hopes of Edward Cheyney were destined to be fulfilled. The new century discovered no grand historical laws to which men were compelled to subscribe, and twentieth-century history could boast neither a Newton nor a Darwin nor even a Comte. Yet though no dominant figure emerged to do for history what Ward did for sociology or Veblen for economics or Holmes for law, there were three scholars who did stamp their personality indelibly upon history and whose formulas commanded wide support and exercised an influence far beyond the realms of historical scholarship: Frederick Jackson Turner, Vernon Louis Parrington, and Charles A. Beard.

Superficially the three seemed very different, in character and in interests. Turner—homespun, erudite, cautious, the historians' historian as Veblen was the economists' economist—wrote fragmentarily of the frontier and sectionalism and enlisted an army of disciples who conquered the whole of American history for the frontier formula. Parrington—affluent, fastidious, aristocratic, and remote, a moralist who saw history as a struggle between the forces of darkness and light —erected during his lifetime one noble monument, its lines harmoniously balanced, its ornament intricate and rich, its colors radiant and splendid. Beard—incisive, searching, magisterial, and imperious, his inquisitive intelligence trained on almost every field of historical inquiry, his cascading energy breaking through the boundaries of the social sciences and flooding out over broad areas of public affairs— in the end repudiated the concept of a historical science and took refuge in a kind of neotranscendentalism.

Yet these three scholars had intellectually much in common. All came from that same Middle Border which nourished Ward and Veblen and Commons and Patten and Pound and so many other seminal thinkers of the new century. All were caught up, in youth, in the swift currents of liberalism and reform, though where the views of Turner and Parrington were colored by the agrarian radicalism of the nineties, those of Beard were illuminated by English and European radicalism and, eventually, by German historical philosophy. All three accepted the doctrine of evolution but as continuity rather than progress; all agreed in awarding environment a more influential role than heredity and in assigning to economy the dominant role in environment.

Of the three, Turner was first on the scene, and he remains in many respects the most influential. Himself relatively unproductive, he inspired a larger volume of historical writing than any other scholar of his generation. The most modest of men, he was most ambitious in his claims and the most successful in establishing them. The least chauvinistic of scholars, he was the most aggressively American, the most insistent upon the unique value of the American historical experience. Alert to the dangers inherent in unregulated individualism and with a tender social conscience, through his celebration of the pioneer virtues he gave aid and comfort to the champions of rugged individualism in the post-frontier era. Not primarily a philosophical historian, his influence was philosophical, for he was concerned with a point of view rather than with the view itself.

That point of view was the frontier, moving inexorably across the continent. Yet Turner was not the historian of the frontier—that he left to others—but the historian of America, who took his vantage point along the frontier. To this vantage point he had made his way, originally, not so much with the aid of the historians' surveying instruments as by instinct. The frontier, indeed, was in his blood. He had grown up in a Wisconsin not far removed from the wilderness stage. As a boy he had watched in fascination while the city fathers of Portage uncovered the graves of early French pioneers; from the old settlers he had heard stories of frontier days, and he was on the first train that puffed its way into the northern woods. His brief experience at the Johns Hopkins did not abate his zeal for the study of the West, and when he returned to Wisconsin, it was to the university that housed the great Draper collection of western history, that encouraged the pioneer work of Reuben Gold Thwaites, and that boasted such scholars as Ely, Commons, and Ross. Here he saw a pioneer democracy adjust itself to the realities of modern industrial capitalism; here he watched Robert LaFollette battle against corporate greed and exploitation; here he formulated his ideas about the significance of the frontier and of sectionalism. He was never really happy outside his Middle West, and for all his broad Americanism, for all his later years in Cambridge and in California, he was almost parochial in his conviction that the Mississippi Valley had somehow taken out a patent on democracy and on Americanism.

Turner's epoch-making paper on the "Significance of the Frontier in American History" appeared the year of Parkman's death. Turner was, in a sense, Parkman's successor, and there could be no better illustration of the difference between the old history and the new than that afforded by the work of these two historians of the West. Parkman's narrative was spacious, poetic, varicolored, and bold, its pages vibrant with life and with heroic deeds, tense with conspiracy and politics and war. Turner was incapable of narrative, eschewed color, ignored individuals except where they served as types, shunned heroism and drama except the heroism of unnamed pioneers and the drama of social evolution, and contented himself with analysis. The stately forests and glistening lakes and rushing waters, the frowning mountains and sweeping plains, which had served as a magnificent backdrop to Parkman's history, with Turner moved into the foreground and became the very stuff of history; but the romantic characters—the black-robed priests and plumed warriors and *couriers-de-bois* and painted savages—vanished from the scene, their place usurped by impersonal institutions. Of all the fifty-some essays which Turner wrote, not one was biographical, and it is not a little curious that a historian so zealous to celebrate individualism should so consistently have ignored the individual.

Yet in this Turner was consistent enough. It was the frontier, after all, that was the hero of his story, the frontier that had molded the great individuals, the frontier that had distinguished American from Old World history and thus given meaning to its story:

The wilderness masters the colonist. It finds him a European in dress, industries, tools, modes of travel, and thought. It takes him from the railroad car and puts him in the birch canoe. It strips off the garments of civilization and arrays him in the hunting shirt and the moccasin. It puts him in the log cabin of the Cherokee and the Iroquois and runs an Indian palisade around him. Before long he has gone to planting Indian corn and plowing with a sharp stick; he shouts the war cry and takes the scalp in orthodox Indian fashion. In short, at the frontier the environment is at first too strong for the man. . . . Little by little he transforms the wilderness, but the outcome is not the old Europe, not simply the development of Germanic germs, any more than the first phenomenon was a case of reversion to the Germanic mark. The fact is, that here is a new product that is American. . . . The advance of the frontier has meant a steady movement away from the influence of Europe, a steady growth of independence on American lines. And to study this advance, the men who grew up under these conditions, and the political, economic, and social results of it, is to study the really American part of our history. (*Significance of the Frontier in American History*)

All this was clearly in the evolutionary stream—an effort to explain the development of institutions from the simple to the complex—but it was just as clearly not the kind of evolution that John Fiske was teaching. For where Fiske emphasized inheritance, Turner emphasized environment; where Fiske liked to find the genesis of the New England town in the *folkgemot* of primitive Germany, or of liberty in Magna Carta, or of federalism in the leagues of the Greek city-states, Turner insisted that the American environment accounted sufficiently for these and for most other American institutions:

American democracy is fundamentally the outcome of the experiences of the American people in dealing with the West. Western democracy through the whole of its earlier period tended to the production of a society of which the most distinctive fact was the freedom of the individual to rise under conditions of social mobility, and whose ambition was the freedom and well-being of the masses. . . . American democracy was born of no theorist's dream; it was not carried in the *Susan Constant* to Virginia, nor in the *Mayflower* to Plymouth. It came out of the American forest, and it gained new strength each time it touched a new frontier. Not the constitution, but free land, and an abundance of natural resources open to a fit people, made the democratic type of society in America for three centuries. (*Frontier in American History*, pp. 266, 293)

It was inevitable that such a formula should appeal to a people who felt instinctively that they had created more than they had inherited and that they owed little to the Old World. It was a nationalistic formula, for it suggested that democracy and freedom and the institutions that gave them meaning were largely American inventions; insofar as it did not inquire into the experience of other peoples with their frontiers, it was almost parochial. It was a democratic formula, for it presented American history as a creative act and one in which all had participated, the humble and obscure as well as the famous. It gave to each new generation an equal chance, made every American a contributor, and made the contribution a continuous one. It fitted the individualistic temper of the time, revealing what had been achieved in the past by individual enterprise and fortitude, yet it gave some support to the forces of progressivism for it made clear that the individualism of the pioneer had necessarily been accommodated to the security and prosperity of the community. It fitted the pragmatic mood, for it submitted American institutions and ideals to the test of experience and accepted as American what had come out of the crucible of experience. It appeared to be a scientific formula, for it rejected all a priori notions and discovered the nature of the American character and of American institutions by laboratory tests, and for all its celebration of individualism it made clear that the processes of history were controlled by grand, impersonal forces. It justified optimism, for if out of such rude and awkward beginnings Nature and man had fashioned a great civilization, what might not be achieved in the future? Nor did the emphasis on the role of environment detract in any way from the satisfaction felt for the American achievement; it was, after all, as gratifying to discover that America had molded Washington as that Washington had fathered America, that America had created Lincoln as that Lincoln had preserved America.

It was ominous, to be sure, to be reminded that the frontier had gone, for with it much of the old America seemed to have vanished, the America of freedom and individualism, the America of the second chance. Sectionalism rather than the frontier held the key to the future, and if American sections were comparable to European nations, as Turner insisted, could America hope to avoid the rivalries and wars that had for so long plagued the Old World? Turner assessed soberly enough the problems that confronted twentieth-century America—urbanization, industrialism, class conflicts, the rise of the giant corporation—but his deep-rooted optimism did not permit discouragement, and his study of "Sections and the Nation" ended on a lyrical note which revealed how transcendental the new scientific history could be:

There are American ideals. . . . It is inconceivable that we should follow the evil path of Europe, and place our reliance upon triumphant force. We shall not become cynical, and convinced that sections, like European nations, must dominate their neighbors and strike first and hardest. However profound the economic changes, we shall not give up our American ideals and our hopes for man, which had their origin in our own pioneering experience, in favor of any mechanical solution offered by doctrinaires educated in Old World grievances. Rather, we shall find strength to build from our past a nobler structure, in which each section will find its place as a fit room in a worthy house. We shall courageously maintain the American system expressed by nation-wide parties, acting under sectional and class compromises. We shall continue to present to our sister continent of Europe the underlying ideas of America as a better way of solving difficulties. We shall point to the *Pax Americana* and seek the path of peace on earth to men of good will. (*Sections in American History*, p. 339, Holt)

2

Parrington, like Turner, was sure that there were American ideals and, what is more, he was zealous to champion them. But he was by no means sure that those ideals had their origin in the American environment and experience, nor was he confident of their power to resist Old World influences. Like Turner he had been born and raised on the Middle Border, and he had early committed himself to that most characteristic manifestation of the Middle Border spirit —the Populist revolt—nor did he ever wholly abandon the youthful enthusiasm with which he had embraced the radicalism of the nineties. A political cyclone had blown him from Oklahoma to the Pacific coast, and there he passed the mature years of his life, working quietly and confidently on the book which was to insure him such immortality as scholars can attain. He knew—what Easterners so often forgot—that Cambridge was as far from Seattle as Seattle from Cambridge, and much of his work, as he cheerfully confessed, was a calculated revolt against the intellectual dominion so long exercised by Harvard College. Yet for all his seeming provincialism, for all his identity with and loyalty to the Middle and Far West, Parrington was in every way a more sophisticated and cultivated scholar than the homespun historian of the frontier. Familiar not only with the whole course of American thought and literature but with English and Continental as well, he was as deeply read in philosophy and art, sociology and economics as in history and literature, and he never fell into the error of interpreting American intellectual development in a vacuum. He was the historian of ideas, and he knew that, however creative the frontier might be of habits, practices, and institutions, ideas have a long genealogy; however the frontier might resist political or economic pressures, ideas are carried with the wind.

Parrington was a professor of literature, and the *Main Currents in American Thought* which he charted were, for the most part, literary currents. Yet it is as mistaken to label him a historian of literature as to label Turner a historian of the frontier. From the vantage point of literature, Parrington surveyed the whole sweep of American history. His concept of literature was a catholic one, embracing theology, economics, law, politics, and journalism as well as belles-lettres; he saw it as a product of the total experience of a people and read it as a faithful expression of that experience. In literature he saw mirrored the mind of America, and he addressed himself valiantly to the greatest subject which can challenge the understanding of a historian—the mind and character of a people.

Deeply influenced by Hippolyte Taine and Georg Brandes, Parrington interpreted American literature as these distinguished critics had interpreted English and European, and his performance was neither less scholarly nor less brilliant than theirs. Yet he was no mere imitator; his work was original and bold, fitted to the pattern of American history and consistent with the American character. More sensitive than any other major historian to the interplay of European and American thought, he was as concerned with the Americanization of imported ideas as with the impact of those ideas on the American mind. His interest in ideas was not genealogical but consequential. That Americans had inherited or imported much of their philosophy was clear; what was important was to understand the principle of natural selection and the consequence of transplantation. For,

transplanted to American soil these vigorous seedlings from old world nurseries took root and flourished in such spots as proved congenial, stimulating American thought, suggesting programs for fresh Utopian ventures, providing an intellectual sanction for new experiments in government. Profoundly liberalising in their influences, they gave impulse and form to our native idealisms, and contributed largely to the outcome of our social experience. The child of two continents, America can be explained in its significant traits by neither alone.

He had a strong sense of the continuity of history, rejected wholly Henry Adams' conclusion that the sequence of thought was chaos, and believed that the main currents of thought, like some Gulf Stream or Black Stream, flowed on, undiverted, from generation to generation. "The principle of religious toleration that was involved in the movement of Independency," he wrote, "was the ecclesiastical form of a struggle which, shifting later to the field of politics, and then to economics, is still raging about us."

One of the few American historians who had matured a philosophy of history, Parrington's whole work was a repudiation of those notions, which owed their inspiration to von Ranke, that the historian's task was limited to the accumulation of data and that this edifying task could be performed with complete impartiality. A generation earlier, Moses Coit Tyler had written of his own admirable history of American literature during the colonial era, "it is a very grave judicial responsibility that the author is forced to assume; it is also a very sacred responsibility," and his work had been a miracle of impartiality. Parrington did not regard his task as a judicial one or pretend to be objective, impartial, or aloof. He interpreted American intellectual history as a struggle between the forces of freedom and of privilege, and he deliberately took sides in that struggle.

Indeed this fastidious scholar, himself so aloof from controversy, so remote from the hurly-burly of public affairs, lived all his life in the midst of battle. His splendid pages pulse and glow with passion and excitement, resound with the clash of arms and echo with the rallying cries of chieftains. He was a veritable Creasy, and all the decisive battles of American history were fought out anew in his volumes: the struggle between theocracy and Independency, Old World tyranny and New World liberty, federalism and republicanism, slavery and freedom, frontier and seaboard, agrarianism and capitalism, labor and industry. All his heroes were warriors; those who somehow did not fit into the neat scheme were passed over or made to do service in a civilian capacity, as it were.

What emerged from all this was an identification of democracy with Americanism. The great tradition of American thought, Parrington insisted, was the tradition of liberalism and revolt; and they were the most American who spoke with the accent of radicalism— the word he originally used instead of the weaker "liberalism." His heroes, some famous, some forgotten, are, all of them, popular champions—Roger Williams and Sam Adams, Jefferson and Paine, Theodore Parker and Ellery Channing, Jackson and Lincoln, Wendell Phillips and Peter Cooper, Henry George and Edward Bellamy, and a host of other world-movers and world-shakers—and when he writes of them his prose leaps and soars. Listen to his tribute to Roger Williams:

A great thinker and a bold innovator, the repository of the generous liberalisms of a vigorous age, he brought with him the fine wheat of long years of English tillage to sow in the American wilderness. . . . The shadow of Massachusetts Bay still too much obscures the large proportions of one who was certainly the most generous, most open-minded, most lovable of the Puritan emigrants—the truest Christian among many who sincerely desired to be Christian. He believed in men and in their native justice, and he spent his life freely in the cause of humanity. Neither race nor creed sundered him from his fellows; the Indian was his brother equally with the Englishman. He was a Leveler because he was convinced that society with its caste institutions dealt unjustly with the common man; he was a democrat because he believed that the end and object of the political state was the common well-being; he was an iconoclast because he was convinced that the time had come when a new social order must be erected on the decay of the old. (*Main Currents,* I, 74–75)

Or to Jefferson, whom he admired above all other Americans:

To all who profess faith in the democratic ideal Jefferson is a perennial inspiration. A free soul, he loved freedom enough to deny it to none; an idealist, he believed that the welfare of the whole, and not the prosperity of any group, is the single end of government. He was our first great leader to erect a political philosophy native to the economics and experience of America, as he was the first to break consciously with the past. His life was dedicated to the service of freedom, and later generations may well recall his words "I have sworn upon the altar of God eternal hostility against every form of tyranny over the mind of man."

Or to that sturdy keeper of the conscience of his generation, Theodore Parker:

More completely than perhaps any other representative, he gathered up and expressed the major revolutionary impulses of his time and world: the idealistic theism implicit in the Unitarian reaction from Calvinism; the transcendental individualism latent in the doctrine of divine immanence; and the passion for righteousness, to make the will of God prevail in a world where the devil quite openly kept his ledgers. He was an eager and thorough iconoclast, impatient to break the false images—the God of John Calvin with its slanders of human nature, and the God of State Street with its contempt for justice—which New England, he believed, had worshipped too long, forgetting the ideals of the Revolutionary fathers. The mind and conscience of Boston seemed to him stifled by the strait-jacket of respectability. . . . As a free soul loving freedom, and a righteous man loving righteousness, he believed a duty was laid on him to cut away the strait-jacket, to shame the Boston that had sold the poor in the gates for a pair of shoes. He must labor to set free the mind and conscience of Boston that they might go forth purified to work a beneficent work in a world that was God's and not the Devil's. (*Main Currents*, II, 415–416)

As these passages make clear, Parrington was not only the historian of the tradition of American liberalism but himself heir to that tradition, transmitting it from the age that was past to the age that was waiting before. His work was not merely a record of battle but a summons to battle. And it was a summons that, for all its stately style, was yet harmonious with the idiom of the time. Parrington had begun to write his great work the year that Beard published *An Economic Interpretation of the Constitution* and Wilson went to the White House, and he remained a belated Populist, an unreconstructed Progressive. He was one of that younger group of liberals —Weyl, Croly, Lippmann, Bourne, Steffens, Simons, Beard—who were busy rescuing liberalism from the dead hand of Godkin and the neo-Manchesterians. Like them he understood the economic bases of politics, and alone of the group he was able to place American thought in its economic context in a systematic and comprehensive fashion. Time and the war had scattered or disintegrated that group, and when, a decade after the collapse of Wilsonian idealism, *Main Currents* appeared, many younger intellectuals were turning for inspiration to Marx and Lenin. Parrington was familiar enough with Marx and Lenin and, for that matter, with older and more esoteric radicalisms, but he knew what so many of the young intellectuals had never learned, that America had its own tough-minded radicalism on which protestants and rebels could confidently draw. He taught them that, properly read, Jefferson and Emerson were more relevant to the problems of twentieth-century America than anything that they could import, and he taught them how to read properly. His book was a contribution to philosophy, history, and politics; it was a monument to all that had been pledged and sacrificed that America might continue to mean liberty and democracy; it was a magnificent tract calling upon Americans to be true to their past and worthy of their destiny.

3

It can be said, with some exaggeration, that Turner's fame derives from a single essay and, with none, that Parrington's depends upon a single book. The fame and influence of Charles A. Beard rest, in no inconsiderable part, upon the very volume of his writings. His industry was prodigious, his curiosity insatiable, and the range of his interests was wider than that of any other major American historian except Henry Adams. Textbooks, from the most elementary to the most sophisticated, popular and semipopular histories, collections of readings and editorial surveys of society and culture, monographs on politics, administration, economics, and foreign policy, studies in English and European as well as in American history, a steady stream of articles, letters, communications, documents, and committee reports flowed from his facile pen. He was ubiquitous and he seemed omniscient; he ranged, almost blithely, from dry investigations of municipal administration to ventures in philosophy. He was not only historian but commentator and critic, an objective—if he would let us use the word—recorder of the past, a vigorous participant in the present, a pamphleteer and polemicist, a veritable Voltaire let loose in the complex world of the twentieth century, with something of Voltaire's wit, irony, and philosophy, and something, too, of his passion.

The most philosophical of modern American historians, Beard never formulated a philosophy of history unless it was—in the end—the negative conclusion that no philosophy of history could be formulated. Probing mercilessly beneath the surface appearance to underlying realities, searching tirelessly for the meaning to be found in apparently casual manifestations, he repudiated the possibility of ascertaining true reality or ultimate meaning. Zealous to fix the role of economics in history and largely responsible for the widespread acceptance of economic determinism by younger scholars, he was

himself the foe of any form of determinism. Rejecting contemptu-
ously the "devil theory" of history and persistently warning against
the application of the moral standards of the present to the events of
the past, his findings provided ammunition for those who saw conspiracy and even deviltry in the making of the Constitution, the fabri-
cation of the Fourteenth Amendment, and American participation
in World War II. The most cosmopolitan of scholars, versed in European as in American history, at home in philosophy, law, economics, sociology, and literature, he became the intellectual leader
of the isolationists and consorted with those whose views were bound
by the Atlantic and the Pacific and whose sympathies were narrow
and provincial.

"Any selection and arrangement of facts," said Beard, in his presidential address to the American Historical Association, "pertaining
to any large area of history, either local or world, race or class, is controlled inexorably by the frame of reference in the mind of the
selector and arranger." His own frame of reference changed, but
originally it would seem to have been the Progressive movement,
with its insistence upon the economic bases of politics, its attack
upon privilege, its passion for reform. Born in Indiana in 1874, he
came to maturity during the Populist and Progressive crusades; he
early associated himself with the British labor movement, and was
not untouched by Fabianism with its zest for the concrete and the
functional and its realistic practicality. In a letter to his fellow-
historians in 1935 he quoted with approval Andrew D. White's admonition that "historical scholars . . . ought to contribute powerfully to the opening up of a better political and social future for the
nation at large," and his own career, particularly before the 1930's,
was a fulfillment of that admonition. Certainly from the days he
helped found Ruskin College at Oxford to the time, over a generation later, when he became the spokesman of the isolationists, he
was never aloof from public affairs. Ceaselessly active in the political
and economic arenas, temporary advisor to the governments of Japan
and Yugoslavia, counselor to a host of left-wing movements, one of
the founders of the New School of Social Research, his penetrating
mind and unflagging energy carried him into all the major political
movements of his generation, and his vigorous personality stamped
itself upon the whole reform movement of the first quarter of the
new century. A student of politics as of history, he did much to im-

prove municipal government, advance the initiative and referendum, illuminate the preconceptions of lawyers and courts, expose the malpractices of big business, sustain civil liberties, and rally scholars to public affairs. Only John Dewey, among later American scholars, played a comparable role or exercised a comparable influence.

In all this, Beard, like Parrington, belonged to the Progressive era, but it was the progressivism of LaFollette and Brandeis—toughminded, competent, and empirical—rather than that of Theodore Roosevelt and Woodrow Wilson. Like LaFollette and Brandeis, Beard had profited from acquaintance with British and Continental social thought, and like them, too, he was economic minded. He was, almost by instinct, a muckraker and an iconoclast, though his exposures of the malpractices of the past were couched in impeccable historical terms. He was closer to Veblen and Brooks Adams— whom he later revived—than to the more opportunistic muckrakers of the Roosevelt era such as Russell or Hendrick or Tarbell; he was incurably skeptical, and he applied to all pretensions toward idealism and disinterestedness in economic and political history the same skepticism which he was later to apply to the pretensions of his colleagues to historical objectivity.

This background of progressivism goes far to explain that emphasis upon the economic basis of politics and the economic interpretation of history with which Beard's fame is associated. That the major issues of politics were economic; that its essence was acquisition and exploitation; that party platforms, campaign oratory, Congressional debates, made sense only in terms of class and interest groups—all this was to Populists and Progressives the common sense of the matter. What Beard did was to apply to earlier chapters of American history the same tests that contemporaries like LaFollette and Altgeld and Lloyd and Tom Johnson applied to trusts, railroads, the tariff, and the currency. Like them he cut through the rhetoric of patriotism, the clichés of campaign oratory, the cabalistic pronouncements of the courts, to underlying economic realities.

That he was by no means the first in the field is irrelevant; he was assuredly the most influential. Over a decade before the appearance of *An Economic Interpretation of the Constitution,* Beard's colleague, E. R. A. Seligman, had announced that "to economic causes . . . must be traced in last instance those transformations in the structure of society which themselves condition the relation of the social classes and the various manifestations of social life," and six years later Parrington's friend, J. Allen Smith, had described the Constitution as a mechanism calculated to frustrate democracy. Beard's carefully documented analysis had two signal advantages over previous economic interpretations: its method and its timing. It was not so much a polemic as a case study, and a generation more susceptible to scientific evidence than to argument found it all but irresistible. It appeared just as the Progressive movement reached its climax, suggested that the technique of the Pujo Committee was as relevant to the eighteenth as to the twentieth century, and seemed to give historical perspective to the assaults of Roosevelt and Wilson upon privilege and exploitation. As Justice Holmes said of John Marshall, it was "a strategic point in the campaign of history," and part of its greatness consisted "in being there."

It is irrelevant to inquire here into the validity of the *Economic Interpretation of the Constitution* or the *Economic Interpretation of Jeffersonian Democracy,* Beard's earliest important books and, in many ways, his best. If these interpretations were open to criticism, it was not so much because they assigned to economics a decisive place in history as because they excluded history from a controlling place in economics. They were more concerned with cause than consequence. They might be accepted as definitive but could not be regarded as conclusive, for economic motivation was not a conclusion but a point of departure. What was primarily important was not, after all, the motivation of the men who made the Constitution and formulated the policies of Jeffersonian democracy but the consequences of their work. The search for the recondite led, as it so often does, to the neglect of the obvious, and a generation familiar with the economic influences at work in the Federal Convention was inclined to ignore the fact that the Convention had created a Federal Constitution.

Beard himself was subsequently to moderate his historical materialism and to emphasize pluralism in historical causation, and his advance to moderation and qualification can be read even in the magisterial *Rise of American Civilization.* Meantime the doctrines which he had preached were accepted as gospel by enthusiastic disciples, and for a time almost every student who hoped to share the spoils of history enlisted under his banner. There was nothing disloyal about this: the new loyalty did not require any betrayal of older faiths. Turner and his school had been ready enough to acknowledge the role of economics in history, and so, too, McMaster and the social historians; and the antecedents of the economic interpretation were, as Beard pointed out, both native and respectable.

The economic interpretation was actually as moral—or as amoral —as the political or religious, but for reasons intriguing to the psychologist and illuminating to the historian, it carried connotations of guilt. In this character it suited admirably the temper of the second and third decades of the century. To a generation of materialists, it made clear that the stuff of history was material. To a generation disillusioned by the exploitation and ruthlessness of big business, it discovered that the past, too, had been ravaged by exploitation and greed. To a generation that looked with fishy eyes on the claims of Wilsonian idealism and all but rejoiced in their frustration, it suggested that each generation had made similar claims and that all earlier idealisms had been similarly flawed by selfishness and hypocrisy.

Beard himself was skeptical rather than partisan and, for all his repudiation of the possibility of objectivity, more nearly objective than the run of historians. Where Parrington, for example, was frankly partisan and Bowers and Beveridge less openly so, Beard seemed to be above the battle. Yet if it was difficult to discover his sympathies, it was not difficult to discover his antipathies. Few chapters of American history commended themselves to him, few idealisms escaped his skepticism, few characters his irony. He seemed to delight in puncturing popular illusions and exposing the fallacies of accepted historical interpretations. History, as it unrolled in chapter after chapter of his monumental volumes, appeared less splendid than many had supposed, its gilt tarnished, its grand passions frayed. Here was realism, and it was the realism of Dreiser rather than of Howells.

Beard's animus was, to be sure, patriotic and devout rather than censorious: it was because he believed the United States to be the best of all countries and the Americans the most virtuous of peoples that he was so impatient with imperfections. He was, in fact, dissembling his love, even as he kicked his historical characters down the stairs. But this was not always clear. Many readers came from his books with the impression that at last the veil of illusion had been torn aside and they were privileged to look at history divested of its heroics, and heroes of their halos. An age which itself made no great plans found malign satisfaction in the invariable miscarriage of the great plans of the past; an age eager to tear the stuffing out of all shirts was delighted to find that the emperors of the past had no clothes. To his students and disciples, Beard communicated something of his own passionate concern for such truth as could be recovered from the ruins of history. But in those who knew him only through his writings, he encouraged an attitude of iconoclasm and, often, of cynicism.

As Beard grew older, he became fascinated by the metaphysics and epistemology of history. Although no other historian of his time had submitted more facts to an avid public or done more to fix in its mind a pattern of the past, he became, in the thirties, weighed down with the consciousness of the illusiveness of all facts and the subjectivity of all patterns. If he did not, like Henry Adams, repudiate his own handiwork, he did repudiate its controlling formula and, indeed, the propriety of all formulas. Written history, he concluded, was not a science but an "act of faith"; the historian could not know the past; he could only reconstruct such fragments of it as were fortuitously available to him according to some incoherent plan which reflected the inescapable limitations of his own mind. The historian, he felt, was like Newton, who had described himself as "a boy playing on the sea shore, and diverting myself now and then finding a smoother pebble or a prettier shell than ordinary, whilst the great ocean of truth lay all undiscovered before me"; and he subscribed to the implication that truth was indeed as changing and elusive as the waves of the ocean. The scientific method, "bequeathed by Ranke and embroidered by a thousand hands," was, Beard insisted, bankrupt, its champions confounded and bewildered.

Slowly it dawned upon them that the human mind and the method employed were not competent to the appointed task, that omniscience was not vouchsafed to mortals. Moreover it was finally realized that if all human affairs were reduced to law, to a kind of terrestrial mechanics, a chief end of the quest, that is, human control over human occurrences and actions, would itself become meaningless. Should mankind discover the law of its total historical unfolding, then it would be imprisoned in its own fate, and powerless to change it; the past, present, and future would be revealed as fixed and beyond the reach of human choice and will. Men and women would be chained to their destiny as the stars and tides are to their routine. The difference between human beings and purely physical objects would lie in their poignant knowledge of their doom and of their helplessness in its presence. (*Open Door at Home*, pp. 13, 14, Macmillan)

There was virtue in admonishing historians to be conscious of the assumptions that controlled their inquiries and the subjectivity that permeated their findings; there was value in making clear that history was no more a science than economics or sociology and that the hopes and faiths of the Victorians were doomed to frustration. Yet to a large extent Beard was attacking men of straw. "It is almost a confession of inexpiable sin to admit, in academic circles," he wrote, "that one is not a man of science working in a scientific manner with things open to deterministic and inexorable treatment, to admit that one is more or less a guesser in this vale of tears." But this was a palpable exaggeration. Few historians pretended to more than a scientific method; few claimed finality for their findings. Even the doughty champion of historical orthodoxy against whom Beard directed his sharpest barbs submitted only that scientific history was a "noble dream": Beard could quarrel logically only with the adjective.

The real objection to Beard's historism was not that it repudiated certainty but that it was sterile and, in a literal sense, inconsequential. The doctrine of subjectivity and uncertainty, like the doctrine of economic motivation, was not a conclusion but a point of departure, and everything depended on the route and the destination. That history was subjective, fragmentary, and inconclusive—like almost everything in life—would be readily acknowledged, but if history were to be written at all it was necessary to go on from there. And no more than Henry Adams did Beard appear able to go on and make his philosophy a constructive instrument. Most of those who conned Beard's own writings in the decade of the forties were inclined to feel that the demonstration of the subjectivity of history could be carried too far and that Beard had in fact carried it too far. Though denied the consolations of science, they could find satisfaction in recalling the words of Socrates:

That we shall be better and braver and less helpless if we think we ought to enquire, than we should have been if we indulged in the idle fancy that there was no knowing and no use in seeking to know what we do not know;—that is a theme upon which I am ready to fight in word and deed to the utmost of my power.

CHAPTER XV

Toward a New Science of Politics

I

NO PEOPLE were more fertile of political inventions than the American, more ingenious, more resourceful, or more practical. It was the practical contribution that was most consequential and most characteristic. They had invented the constitutional convention which, by institutionalizing the principle that men make government, had, as old John Adams put it, "realized the theories of the wisest writers." They had all but copyrighted the written Constitution which had brought the Laws of Nature and Nature's God out of the realms of abstraction and made them secular realities. They had solved the problem of imperial organization on which the old British Empire had foundered, and constructed a federal system which became a model for the western world. They had formulated a colonial policy which, by recognizing colonies as equals and incorporating them into the mother country, had dissipated the traditional antagonisms between colony and metropolis and which had worked so smoothly that most Americans were unaware that their country had ever had either a colonial problem or a colonial policy —or even colonies. They had implemented the theory of checks and balances and devised, in judicial review, the most effective of all mechanical restraints on the pretensions of government. They had, in short, gone far toward solving the oldest and most vexatious problem in the realm of politics—the reconciliation of liberty and order.

All this, to be sure, was the achievement of the Founding Fathers, and subsequent generations had nothing to show of comparable importance. Yet if new inventions were lacking, that was a tribute to the effectiveness of the old, and ingenuity and resourcefulness persisted into the nineteenth century. Americans had been the first people to make democracy work. They had established that system of universal education which Jefferson rightly held essential to the success of democratic government. They had adapted a Constitution, based on seventeenth-century notions of the relations of men to government, to the exigencies of a rapidly growing industrial society. They had expanded from sixteen to more than forty states without doing violence to the original constitutional fabric. They had gone far toward insuring that the melting pot not only melted but fused. They had developed the political party as an instrument of popular government and justified the two-party system. They had proved that the liberties of men could be safe, even in the greatest of civil wars.

There was no comparable body of theory to match these nineteenth-century inventions and practices. Political thought since Jefferson had been repetitive and sterile. The one contrivance which inspired the most elaborate theoretical analysis, judicial review, was the most artificial and the least characteristic of American political inventions; the one major speculative political philosopher, John C. Calhoun, was also the one whose speculations were the most irrelevant to American experience; the one magisterial analysis of the principle of democracy came from the Frenchman, Tocqueville. Story's exposition of the Constitution was innocent of theory, unless the dogmas of nationalism can be called theory, and those who read the ponderous treatises by Lieber, Brownson, Hurd, Pomeroy, and Woolsey found little to nourish the mind and less to elevate the spirit.

Most Americans, if they were aware of this situation, regarded it with equanimity, for they rightly assumed that the bankruptcy of political theory was a product of the prosperity of political practice. As long as the institutions established by the Fathers and the principles expounded by Jefferson worked well, there was no felt need for theoretical justification: success was its own justification. That they did work well was long acknowledged: "Our government," said the lordly Edward Everett, "is in its theory perfect, and in its operation it is perfect also," and he spoke for his generation and even his century. Even where the system appeared to fail, the failure was ascribed to the folly of statesmen rather than to its own imperfections: Lincoln and Jefferson Davis alike invoked the principles of 1787. It was little wonder that in the realm of politics the nineteenth-century American was complacent, conservative, and orthodox, for to tamper with the institutions and principles of the Founding Fathers seemed almost like tampering with the Ten Commandments or the Laws of Nature.

The analogy is not strained. The political theory to which the Fathers had subscribed, and which the nineteenth century inherited, was Newtonian. The universe, as they saw it, was a perfectly contrived mechanism, and it was the duty of man to articulate all human institutions—among them government and law—to its predestined operations. "Look around the world," wrote David Hume,

contemplate the whole and every part of it: You will find it to be nothing but one great machine, subdivided into an infinite number of lesser machines, which again admit of subdivisions, to a degree beyond what human senses and faculties can trace and explain. All these various machines, and even their most minute parts, are adjusted to each other with an accuracy which ravishes into admiration all men who have ever contemplated them.

It was the Laws of Nature that entitled Americans to assume a separate and equal station among the powers of the earth, and the great truths of equality and of unalienable rights were labeled self-evident. Even Hamilton acquiesced in this interpretation. We do not need to rummage in the dusty parchments of the past, he said, for our natural rights, "they are written as with a sunbeam in the whole volume of human nature, by the hand of Divinity itself, and can never be erased or obscured by mortal power." Constitutions were but transcripts of natural law, and the ideal toward which all rational lawmakers aspired was a government which should reduce the merely human factor to a minimum—a government of laws and not of men. Law was, in fact, pre-existent and fundamental; it was not the function of men to make it but to discover and publish it: the power of Parliament, as James Otis said, is *jus dicere; jus dare* belongs only to God. Thus, government which was bound by natural law could no more transgress that law than the tides could reverse themselves or the stars depart from their fixed courses; if it did so, it would, in the words of Samuel Adams, "subvert its own foundations." The techniques adopted to restrain government within its proper bounds were mechanical: separation of powers, checks and balances, fixed elections, judicial review. The very vocabulary of the time was eloquent of mechanistic concepts: state of nature, natural law, social compact, inalienable rights, immutable laws, eternal principles of justice, a standing law to live by, and the other phrases that even now linger on in judicial opinions and Fourth of July orations.

These artificial principles might have given way to concepts more harmonious with the realities of American experience had it not been that, alone among modern peoples, Americans transformed natural into constitutional law. Thus a written Constitution, long immune to change, assured them permanence. The success of the American experiment was most easily ascribed to the perfection of that Constitution, and its purely mechanical features shared the sanctity which enveloped the whole. And by reading natural-law concepts into the Constitution, year after year, the courts animated them with new life and endowed them with new authority.

The Newtonian doctrine of a government of laws and not of men inevitably directed attention to the laws rather than to men and assumed that men would conform to laws rather than laws to men. Students who came to maturity during the period of political rationalism—men like Lieber, Woolsey, Brownson, and even Burgess—addressed themselves to the analysis of impersonal institutions rather than of social practices. They were vastly concerned with Sovereignty, or States' Rights, or the distinctions between People, Nation, and Government, with the Judicial Function or the Executive Power, with theories of Territorial Authority or of Reconstruction. They drew up admirable definitions of the Political Party whose resemblance to any actual political party was purely coincidental; they indulged in learned analyses of the nature of Law without bothering to trace the law in its actual operation; they made sweeping assumptions about federalism, the separation of powers, or judicial review which had little perceptible relation to their functioning. Their methods were deductive, their concepts static, their erudition—and their sympathies—embraced almost everything but man. As the Spencerian sociologists had ignored the psychic factors in civilization and the Manchester economists the business cycle, so these authoritative political theorists made no provision for the spoils system, political pluralism, inertia, emotionalism, or irrationality. Thus, with the passing of time, political theory which had once faithfully expressed the objectives and practices of the American people got more and more out of harmony with realities.

2

A theory that was out of harmony with reality could be indulged as long as it did not interfere with the business of government, much as esoteric refinements of theology could be indulged as long as they did not interfere with religion. The real difficulty—and one that became oppressive only after the Civil War—was that the Fathers had designed constitutions which faithfully reflected and legal machinery which effectively implemented these seventeenth- and eighteenth-century political theories. It was not only theory but the constitutional instrument itself that was at variance with practices and needs. An obvious example was the constitutional provision for choosing the chief executive. This broke down almost at once; yet nothing was more illuminating than the failure of the Twelfth Amendment to harmonize the electoral provisions with the realities of democracy and of parties: the amendment retained all the mechanical features of the original provision. A no less obvious example was the original failure of the Constitution, and the subsequent refusal of the law, to recognize the political party; not until the twentieth century did American law so much as acknowledge the existence of its most important political institution.

The gap between the eighteenth-century constitutional pattern and nineteenth-century political practice widened steadily. Constitutional theory and machinery separated legislative, executive, and judicial functions, but in fact all three were interdependent and interlocking parts of the business of government, and political parties had to break down the artificial barriers. Theory and machinery provided for the election of a president by an independent electoral college, but in fact the president was nominated by party caucuses and conventions and chosen by popular vote. Theory and machinery made Congressmen spokesmen for particular territorial subdivisions, but in fact they became spokesmen for political parties and for pressure groups. Theory and machinery confined the judiciary to deciding upon litigation, but in fact courts, through judicial review, participated in the legislative process. Theory and machinery designed a federal system in which states regulated all ordinary economic and social activities such as education, labor, industry, but in fact the state lines were for many purposes artificial, and the national government stepped into these fields. Theory and machinery limited the authority and enumerated the powers of the national government, but in fact that government was called upon increasingly to operate as a welfare state. Theory and machinery assumed that the liberties of men could be most safely entrusted to the states and that the dangers to be apprehended were from the central government, but in fact it was the states that most frequently impaired and the central government that most zealously safeguarded those liberties. Theory and machinery left the states as laboratories for far-reaching political and economic experiments, but in fact few such experiments were inaugurated and these were required to run the gauntlet of judicial scrutiny. Theory and machinery assumed an exalted standard of disinterested public service, but in fact spoilsmen served and business exploited the government for selfish purposes.

Thus with the profound change in society, economy, and technology that came in the latter half of the nineteenth century, the traditional constitutional theories became inapplicable to and the constitutional framework incompatible with realities. The dichotomy between static constitution and dynamic politics became increasingly apparent and the difficulty of administering a welfare state with a constitution designed to confine government to its narrowest limits more and more embarrassing.

Nor was the difficulty confined to the constitutional instrument itself; it extended to the whole realm of politics. With the passing years, the resemblance between the government designed on paper and the government which functioned in legislative halls and lobbies, in political conventions and party caucuses, in police courts and club rooms, grew ever more remote. Mr. Homo from Altruria, if given a copy of the Constitution and asked to re-create from it the government of the United States, would have gone as far astray as if he had attempted to describe the character and activities of the Episcopal church from a contemplation of the Thirty-Nine Articles or the business and other activities of the Standard Oil Company from an examination of its charter.

Yet it was scarcely to be expected that a people as sentimental and as conservative as the Americans would give up their traditional principles or that a people as ingenious and adaptable as the Americans would abandon their necessary practices. They were neither to be frightened away from their symbols nor reasoned out of their habits. Confronted with what moralists and other theorists alleged was a choice between official and unofficial governments, they very sensibly chose both, keeping one for ceremonial purposes, as it were, and one for workaday purposes. The first received obeisance on the Fourth of July and state occasions, in Presidential messages, Supreme Court opinions, and Congressional speeches designed for home consumption; the authority of the second was acknowledged by businessmen, lawyers, and political bosses on most other occasions. The first was the concern of statesmen, the second that of politicians, and though the term statesman was an honorific one and the term politician one of opprobrium, businessmen who wanted things done went to Mark Hanna rather than to William McKinley.

Thus Americans clung tenaciously to their Constitution, and just as tenaciously, though less ostentatiously, to their bosses, caucuses, and lobbies. Politics, as imagined by the scholar, was a science; politics, as indulged in by the people, was a game; politics, as practiced by the politician, was a business. To fit these different needs, all legitimate enough, there came into existence alongside the formal government and the informal pageantry, what Elihu Root called the Invisible Government. "We talk about the government of the Constitution," he said in the New York Constitutional Convention of 1915,

We have spent many days in discussing the powers of this and that and the other officer. What is the government of this State? What has it been during the forty years of my acquaintance with it? The government of the Constitution? Oh, no; not half the time, or half way. . . . From the days of Fenton, and Conkling, and Arthur and Cornell, and Platt, from the days of David B. Hill, down to the present time the government of the State has presented two different lines of activity, one of the constitutional and statutory officers of the State, and the other of the party leaders. . . . They call the system . . . invisible government. For I don't know how many years Mr. Conkling was the supreme ruler in this State; the Governor did not count, the legislatures did not count; comptrollers and secretaries of state and what not, did not count. . . . Then Mr. Platt ruled the State; for nigh upon twenty years he ruled it. It was not the Governor; it was not the Legislature; it was not any elected officers; it was Mr. Platt. And the capitol was not here; it was at 49 Broadway: Mr. Platt and his lieutenants. . . . The ruler of the State during the greater part of the forty years of my acquaintance with the State government has not been any man authorized by the Constitution or by the law.

By the 1890's the constitutional and political machinery was creaking at the joints, its inadequacies palpable and troublesome. That government which had long been regarded as the best on earth was apparently incompetent to cope with the most elementary problems of modern economy. Yet the basic assumptions of democracy remained unimpaired, and there was the greatest reluctance to admit any imperfections in the constitutional system. It was far easier to fall back on what may be called the devil theory of politics—to explain away the imperfections as fortuitous and ascribe the breakdown of the political machinery to the incompetence or the depravity of those who operated it.

Incompetence could be excused as the price paid by democracy for the principle of rotation in office, but corruption presented a more serious problem. That a people whose private morals were, according to the testimony of foreign observers, singularly pure, should have tolerated a public immorality as flagrant as almost any to be found in the Old World was one of the most puzzling features of American life. Yet there was nothing new about this political corruption except its magnitude, its pervasiveness, and its ostentation: the growth of business afforded it new opportunities, the expansion of the bureaucracy opened the way to widespread infection, and the decline of the aristocratic tradition in politics facilitated its conquests. Certainly, though Tocqueville and Bryce agreed on many aspects of American life, there was nothing in *Democracy in America* comparable to the grim chapters on corruption in *The American Commonwealth,* nor had the celebration of the fiftieth anniversary of American independence evoked from contemporary poets anything like Lowell's disillusioned Centennial Ode:

> Show your new bleaching process, cheap and brief,
> To wit; a jury chosen by the thief;
> Show your State Legislatures; show your Rings;
> And challenge Europe to produce such things
> As high officials sitting half in sight
> To share the plunder and to fix things right;
> If that don't fetch her, why you only need
> To show your latest style in martyrs-Tweed:
> She'll find it hard to hide her spiteful tears
> At such advance in one poor hundred years.

Yet if the increase in corruption was remarkable, so, too, was the strength and the zeal of the crusade against it. No issue of this character had shattered an old party or created a new one before the Civil War, but after the war reform inspired the Liberal Republican movement, kept Grant from a third term and Blaine from a first, sent

Cleveland to the White House, and created that political phenomenon known to its critics as a Mugwump and to its friends as an Independent.

The remedy for corruption was so obvious that it scarcely requisitioned political theory—the purification of politics, more commonly called civil service reform. It was a remedy at once simple and moral; everyone could understand it, and everyone must of necessity subscribe to it. It was not only the easiest intellectual solution, it seemed the easiest practical one. It raised no awkward questions of constitutional reform, required no dangerous tinkering with political machinery, and involved no shift in the balance of economic power.

This panacea recommended itself irresistibly to such publicists as E. L. Godkin and G. W. Curtis and to their followers and disciples —men like Norton, Atkinson, Eliot, and Moorfield Storey in Boston; like Gilder, Low, Eaton, and Cutting in New York; to elder statesmen like Carl Schurz and George F. Hoar, and younger ones like Theodore Roosevelt and Woodrow Wilson. They were, indubitably, a distinguished group, and if the impression they made on American politics was, in the end, less lasting than they had anticipated, that was perhaps an illustration of the passing of the genteel tradition rather than a reflection upon their sincerity or their talents. They had gone to the best schools—one sometimes feels that a college degree was a prerequisite to admission to their club—associated with the best people, belonged to the Century or Harvard Club, read *The Nation* and *The Independent,* and knew politics, for the most part, at second hand. They recognized few evils that learning could not diagnose and honesty could not cure. They had the same abiding faith in the efficacy of moral sentiments that H. G. Wells ascribes to the English liberals of the period in his *New Machiavelli,* and the English example was constantly in their minds. Good government, they believed, would follow axiomatically from the merit system and the participation of gentlemen in politics, and when they thought of gentlemen they thought of each other. Thus Godkin, who conveniently forgot that Henry Cabot Lodge graduated from Harvard and Chauncey Depew from Yale, could write of "The Duty of Educated Men in a Democracy" that

We should probably, in a college-graduate government, witness the disappearance from legislation of nearly all acts and resolutions which are passed for what is called "politics"; that is, for the purpose of pleasing certain bodies of voters, without any reference to their real value as contributions to the work of government.

They could deplore corruption but they could not explain it, for they understood neither its motivations nor its implications nor, for that matter, its consequences. They looked upon the spoils system or bribery or the pollution of the ballot box as moral delinquencies—which indeed they were—and they were reluctant to associate with bosses. But they did not understand that corruption was more than a personal manifestation of depravity, and when confronted, as they so often were, with the spectacle of the rich and the well-born engaged in political malpractices, they were confused. A journalist like Lincoln Steffens, a sociologist like E. A. Ross, an economist like Veblen came closer to understanding the real nature of the spoils system than this whole phalanx of reformers.

It is unfair, however, to characterize those men as doctrinaires or to dismiss them as superficial. All of them were upright and intelligent, some of them were shrewd, and a few were genuinely open minded. Curtis and Storey, Eaton and Low, for example, had experienced the hurly-burly of politics, and Roosevelt learned early and Wilson late to distrust the insulated intellectual. Yet they were, for the most part, prisoners of their own class and philosophical limitations. They had no real faith in democracy, quoted Tocqueville on the tyranny of the majority, and distrusted the political party; it will be remembered that the young Roosevelt thought Tom Paine a "dirty little atheist" and that the young Wilson excluded Thomas Jefferson from his Calendar of Great Americans. They had no interest in the agrarian crusade and little sympathy for organized labor, and they considered panaceas like the single tax or nationalism as eccentric as Mormonism. Free silver they thought simple dishonesty, and outbreaks like the Haymarket riot and the Pullman strike filled them with horror. They were equally fearful of socialism, communism, and anarchism and inclined to place any economic heresy indiscriminately in one of these categories. They were, in short, incapable of understanding the real nature of the fight that was going on about them. They seemed constantly to be engaged, heroically enough, in minor skirmishes while the real battles for the control of the government raged elsewhere. An aura of unreality hangs over their history, and their enterprises seem chimerical.

3

'The moral approach of the civil service reformers was clearly bank-rupt. "Before you can begin to think about politics at all," wrote the young Walter Lippmann in 1914, "you have to abandon the notion that there is a war between good men and bad men. . . . For if politics is merely a guerrilla war between the bribed and the unbribed, then statecraft is not a human service but a moral testing ground." Resting as it did upon Newtonian concepts, the moral approach had promised the very perfection of liberty and order if men were but reasonable enough to recognize those concepts and virtuous enough to conform to them. The promise had not been fulfilled, not even for the wise and the good, for though the reformers had cried, "Lord, Lord," the gates of heaven had not opened for them. "It is our desperate adherence to an old method," Mr. Lippmann added,

that has produced the confusion of political life. Because we have insisted upon looking at government as a frame and governing as a routine, because in short we have been static in our theories, politics has such an unreal relation to actual conditions. Feckless—that is what our politics is. It is literally eccentric: it has been centered mechanically instead of vitally. We have been seduced by a fictitious analogy: we have hoped for machine regularity when we needed human initiative and leadership, when life was crying that its inventive abilities should be freed. (*Preface to Politics,* p. 23)

Our political thinking, he concluded, "needs the infusion of contemporary insights."

The infusion had, in fact, already taken place. The revolution which was to transform political science from static to dynamic, from analytical to instrumental, from abstract to concrete, was already under way. What destroyed the Newtonian concepts in the realm of politics, and of law, were the same philosophical and scientific considerations that made them an anachronism in economics and sociology: evolution, pragmatism, the recognition of the economic forces and the psychic factors.

Evolution gave a scientific foundation to what some of the wisest of the Fathers had known almost intuitively and to what Marshall and Story had from time to time pronounced, but what scholars had forgotten and what the public, so easily contented with political shibboleths, had never fully learned—that the Constitution was not static but dynamic. The historical approach, accepted on the Continent since von Ranke and Savigny, explained much heretofore taken as sacrosanct, as a mere accident, or—if that is too deprecatory —as a product of history. Thus it made clear that the tripartite separation of governmental powers was not something fixed in the cosmic system but a product of two secular considerations: a temporary and perhaps regrettable misconception of the British constitutional system, and a fear of governmental tyranny. And it suggested that with the passing of these considerations there might well be a readjustment of this mechanical feature of the constitutional system to the realities of politics. It made clear that the profound fear of government which inspired the system of checks and balances—John Adams enumerated with pride "eight complicated refinements of balance" —was not a reflection of natural law but of conditions peculiar to a time when the moral of history seemed to be that "government, like dress, is the badge of lost innocence." The conclusion was inescapable that the expansion of governmental activities was not a violation of the moral code—as it was sometimes assumed to be even in the mid-twentieth century—but a logical shift in the use of the Constitution from symbol to instrument, a logical response to the conclusion that government was made for man, not man for government. It made clear that the distribution of powers in the federal system was not a revelation of the divine inspiration of the Framers—as Jefferson Davis thought as late as 1881 when he wrote his *Rise and Fall of the Confederate States*—but an outgrowth of experience in the British Empire, and it indicated that new experience might justify continuous modifications of that original distribution.

Evolution indeed placed the whole problem of states' rights and nationalism in a new light, outmoded much that Calhoun had argued, made irrelevant much that Davis had proved, gave new justification to the arguments of Story and Webster and the intuitions of Lincoln. For it revealed that a nation was not the conclusion of a syllogism or the discovery of political theorists but a product of history and could not be argued out of existence by all the refined metaphysics of Calhoun or the dialectic of Alexander Stephens. It was no accident that though Calhoun continued to be regarded as the greatest of political theorists he was, in the twentieth century, universally unread or that the problem of sovereignty which had engaged his most anxious attention should have ceased to command serious interest. Evolution did not so much repudiate the older doctrines of sovereignty as shelve them ("we do not nowadays refute our predecessors," wrote Santayana, "we pleasantly bid them good-bye"), and by 1908 the learned Arthur Bentley could write of sovereignty that "as soon it gets out of the pages of a lawbook or the political pamphlet it is a piteous, threadbare joke." It gave new impetus to the study of government as it actually developed rather than as it was originally contrived. It cleared the ground of the debris of the past and made possible a fresh start on the problems of politics—one which could regard change as normal rather than as immoral, accept it cheerfully rather than surreptitiously, and look to the reform of the constitutional system itself rather than merely to the men who administered it.

4

Woodrow Wilson was neither the first nor the most learned scholar to recognize the impact of evolution on politics, but he remains the most interesting. Nor is this interest wholly dependent on the accident of his subsequent career. That he had a unique opportunity to put his principles into practice doubtless gives a certain retroactive significance to those principles, for it is rare in America that scholars are called upon to test their conclusions by experience. But the contributions of Wilson to political thought, fragmentary and almost haphazard as they seem, have an importance of their own. For he revealed early that sensitiveness to the intellectual atmosphere, that talent for absorbing ideas, which was to distinguish his public career, and early, too, that capacity for putting so eloquently the ideas of others that they become his by a sort of prescriptive right. Not an original thinker— he readily acknowledged his debt to Burke and Bagehot and even Burgess—he had flashes of intuition that beggared mere originality. Not exhaustive or profound, he was provocative and brilliant. There is a tantalizing quality to almost everything he wrote, for he left most of his insights undeveloped, his suggestions unfulfilled, and his slender essays seem singularly unimpressive beside the massive volumes by contemporaries like Woolsey, Willoughby, and Burgess. Yet his political career was to reveal that he had sufficiently explored the arena of political science to know what track he preferred to follow and how to reach his destination with a minimum of confusion.

No one familiar with Wilson's literary career should have been surprised by his political. He came to the presidency with a fully matured philosophy, and he recognized no incompatibility between his philosophical principles and the exigencies of practical politics. More boldly than any other major statesman of his generation, except possibly Robert LaFollette, he was ready to break with the past, adapt himself to the present, anticipate the future. A lifetime of study had prepared him to reject the mechanical interpretation of the Constitution, insist that both liberty and democracy were dynamic concepts, hurdle the artificial barriers between departments, to assume presidential and party leadership, modernize the federal system, adjust the whole machinery of government to the needs of a twentieth-century economy and use government as a social service agency.

From the beginning he adopted, almost by instinct, the evolutionary approach to politics. It is implicit in his essay on "Cabinet Government in the United States," written while he was still in college, explicit in the *Old Master* essays, and it forms the central theme of his justly neglected textbook on *The State*. With his lectures on *Constitutional Government in the United States,* the rejection of Newtonian for Darwinian principles became specific and applied—applied with such boldness that had George Harvey really read them he could scarcely have adopted Wilson as the hope of the conservatives.

The government of the United States was constructed upon the Whig theory of political dynamics, which was a sort of unconscious copy of the Newtonian theory of the universe. . . . The trouble with the theory is that government is not a machine, but a living thing. It falls, not under the theory of the universe, but under the theory of organic life. It is accountable to Darwin, not to Newton. It is modified by its environment, necessitated by its tasks, shaped to its functions by the sheer pressure of life. No living thing can have its organs offset against each other as checks and live. On the contrary its life is dependent upon their quick cooperation, their ready response to the commands of instinct or intelligence, their amicable community of purpose. Government is not a body of blind forces; it is a body of men. . . . Living political constitutions must be Darwinian in structure and in practice. (*Constitutional Government in the United States,* pp. 56–57)

More specifically Wilson subscribed to the evolutionary view with respect to those three broad fields of interpretation which so concerned his generation: the structure of government, the functions and powers of government, and the nature of the federal system. He early perceived that the government which had actually evolved had little structural resemblance to that designed by the Fathers, and he advocated a recognition of realities in order to encourage efficiency and fix responsibility in government. He saw that the separation of powers had in fact broken down and advised that "we think less of checks and balances and more of coordinated power" and that we achieve that coordinated power through the encouragement of presidential leadership. Indeed, long before he was called upon to exhibit them he had formulated those principles of presidential leadership toward which the American constitutional system has been tending over the last half-century.

He had early arrived, too, at the conclusion that fear of government was illogical in a democracy and that there was nothing either immoral or illegal in a welfare state—a conclusion less trite at that time, when Cleveland was president, than at a later date. "The State a Beneficent Organ of Society," read one of the headings in his analysis of 1889, and the idea was spelled out:

We ought all to regard ourselves and to act as socialists, believers in the wholesomeness and beneficence of the body politic. . . . Every means by which society may be perfected through the instrumentality of government, every means by which individual rights can be fitly adjusted and harmonized with public duties, by which individual self-development may be made at once to serve and to supplement social development, ought certainly to be diligently sought and sedulously fostered by every friend of society. (*The State,* pp. 631–632)

And when he came to analyze *Constitutional Government in the United States* he anticipated his even more audacious successor. "The Constitution," he said, in words that Franklin Roosevelt was to echo, "is not a mere lawyers' document; it is a vehicle of life, and its spirit is always the spirit of the age." It

was not meant to hold the government back to the time of horses and wagons, the time when postboys carried every communication. . . . The United States have clearly from generation to generation been taking on more and more of the characteristics of a community; more and more have their economic interests come to seem common interests.

Notwithstanding his southern inheritance, he was ready to acknowledge that a nation had evolved and that the Constitution must be read in the light of that evolution. As the economy of the nation had become centralized, so must the power of government to regulate that economy. What are the general commercial, economic, and financial interests, he said,

is a question of fact . . . and case by case we are inevitably drawn on to include under the established definition of law matters new and unforseen, which seem in their very magnitude to give to the powers of Congress a sweep and vigor certainly never conceived possible by earlier generations of statesmen, sometimes even revolutionary in our own eyes.

There were elements of pragmatism, too, in Wilson's philosophy, of the recognition that the proper study of politics was not deductive but inductive and that the proper place to pursue that study was not the library but "the streets, the counting-house, the drawing room, the club-house, the administrative offices, the halls and the lobbies of legislatures." Yet the functional approach was essentially alien to Wilson's mind. He did not, in fact, frequent either clubhouses or lobbies. He preferred interpretation to description, and neither in his academic nor his political career did he suffer facts gladly.

5

The second major factor which operated to justify the claim of politics to be a science was pragmatism. All over the western world in the latter part of the nineteenth century the pragmatic analysis of political phenomena was gaining ground. Sir Henry Maine and Walter Bagehot led the way in England, Kohler and Roscher in Germany; and soon Austin and Hegel were neglected, if not wholly repudiated, even in their own countries. France established the École Libre des Sciences Politiques not long after the Franco-Prussian War; American counterparts presently arose in The Johns Hopkins University and the Columbia University faculty of Political Science, and in due time the London School of Economics was launched. The pragmatic approach had more direct and immediate consequences even than the evolutionary. For where evolution was a philosophical attitude, pragmatism was a technique; where evolution furnished a point of departure, pragmatism required analysis and solution. It looked not to the theory of political institutions but to their machinery; it sought the causes of corruption, inefficiency, and governmental impotence not in the realm of morals but in administration, economics, and psychology.

With the shift from the Newtonian to the Darwinian philosophy came the abandonment of efforts to fit men to some preconceived pattern of political conduct. Students turned instead to the analysis of government as it actually operated, addressing themselves not to the original blueprint but to the living structure. They devoted themselves to diagnosis rather than to homilies or incantations. Their method was frankly opportunistic, for "more and more," as their leader Frank J. Goodnow pointed out, "students are recognizing that a policy of opportunism is the policy most likely to be followed by desirable results and that adherence to general theories which are to be applied at all times and under all conditions is productive of harm rather than good." They did for the study of politics what James and Dewey were doing for the study of philosophy, Veblen and Commons for the study of economics, Ward and Ross for the study of sociology, Freund and Pound for the study of law.

It would be merely confusing to rehearse their investigations and their findings. One by one they called all political institutions into their laboratories and subjected them to scientific tests. They were as interested in the unwritten as in the written constitution and in the administration as well as in the enactment of laws; they carried on their studies, as Wilson had suggested, in the lobbies as well as in the legislative halls, and they went—where Wilson did not think to go until he became president—into the offices of banks and corporations as well. With Ostrogorski and Merriam they examined the political party, not in terms of Burke's famous and misguided definition but in terms of the parties themselves. With Brooks Adams and J. Allen Smith they analyzed judicial review, not as the dictum of some brooding omniscience in the sky but as the product of particular economic and political preconceptions to be studied on its own merits. With Frank Goodnow and W. F. Willoughby they reconsidered the whole problem of the separation of powers, not with a view to pressing actual government into the mold contrived by the Framers but of adapting that mold to the felt needs of government. With a minimum of moral preconceptions they studied the emotional and irrational elements in politics: the nature of party organization and of party loyalty; the function of the spoils system; the character and conduct of bosses; the role of pressure groups in politics; the relations, carnal and platonic, between business and government; the considerations that persuaded men to vote or not to vote. Equally important, if less original, was the attention which the instrumentalists directed to the study of administration, state and local as well as national, and the contributions which they made to modernizing the machinery of government.

Their work was not so much facilitated as made possible by the rapidly growing body of statistical data and the developing science of statistics. It is perhaps the use of such data that most sharply distinguishes the work of the pragmatists from traditional political science. The masters of an earlier generation—Calhoun and Lieber, for example—were ready enough to submit "facts" but rarely found it necessary to bolster their "facts" with "figures." It was the government itself which furnished most of the figures which the new political scientists used. First, of course, was the Census Bureau, reformed and revitalized by General Walker in 1880 and placed on a permanent basis in 1902; and in the twentieth century, income tax and Army statistics illuminated aspects of finance and of public health and psychology heretofore neglected. In addition there were continuous landslides of statistical material from a vast number of government departments, bureaus, and commissions—the Department of Agriculture, the Labor and Commerce Departments, the Smithsonian Institution, the Federal Trade and the Interstate Commerce Commission—as well as from *ad hoc* commissions such as that on immigration which deposited no less than forty volumes of statistical data on the desks of overburdened scholars. States and municipal bodies were responsible for tributary streams, and from private business—the insurance companies, for example—came further trickles. A technique for the use of statistical data was developed only in the twentieth century. Although Continental economists like Quetelet, Knies, and Le Play, and the neglected American Lemuel Shattuck, had built up a science of statistics early in the nineteenth century, little attention was paid to the subject in the United States before the publication of Richmond Mayo-Smith's *Science of Statistics* in 1895. Thereafter progress was rapid, and exploitation of statistical material by political scientists ruthless.

The pragmatists did not so much constitute a school as a whole educational system. Their leaders were, for the most part, men who had had practical experience in public affairs. A. Lawrence Lowell, for example, had practiced law for two decades and written his masterly

Government and Parties in Continental Europe before he joined the faculty of Harvard University. Henry Jones Ford, whose *Rise and Growth of American Politics* was one of the earliest analyses of the relation of parties to government, was called by Woodrow Wilson to Princeton University from a newspaper desk and later served with conspicuous success on the Interstate Commerce Commission. Charles E. Merriam, who turned from the study of sovereignty to the analysis of parties and voting, was all his life active in municipal politics. W. F. Willoughby, who did so much to train students for the profession of administration, was an expert in the Department of Labor and had long experience in colonial administration. Frank Goodnow, pioneer and leading spirit in the development of administrative studies, was not only a university president but a member of government commissions on administrative efficiency and advisor to foreign governments. The list could be extended almost indefinitely: those who did not come to the study of "actual government" from the arena of public affairs were speedily drawn into that arena by government bureaus which learned to appreciate their services.

So completely did the pragmatists dominate the field of politics that the study of political theory fell into abeyance. It is suggestive that the scholarly tribute to William A. Dunning, long a leading figure in the study of political theory, took the form of a series of essays in history and practical politics innocent of theory, and that when Charles E. Merriam, dean of political scientists, came to write his *Systematic Politics* he addressed himself to "the intimate study of the political process, dealing with interest groups and power relations, with skills and understandings, forms of communication, and personalities."

6

The third major factor in modernizing the study of politics was precisely the recognition of "interest groups and power relations." There was nothing new about this recognition of the economic basis of politics. Hamilton and Madison had not failed to appreciate it, Jefferson built a political party upon its foundation, and John Taylor of Caroline, whom Charles Beard regarded as the last major political thinker, made it the core of his philosophy. It had, however, fallen into academic neglect. The ponderous treatises by Woolsey and

Brownson and Pomeroy and Burgess were innocent of economic underpinning, and even Wilson, for all his perspicacity, did not learn until his governorship that most political issues involved questions of "interest groups and power relations." And as late as 1913 Beard's *Economic Interpretation of the Constitution* was regarded in polite circles as either bad manners or blasphemy.

The economic interpretation came with most persuasive force, not unexpectedly, from politicians and journalists. Spokesmen for groups and parties excluded from what Parrington called "the great barbecue" could scarcely ignore the economic basis of politics; and the Grangers, the Greenbackers, the Single Taxers, the Nationalists, the Populists, and the Progressives, who disagreed on so many matters, agreed in assigning to economic influences the bankruptcy of the older parties and the incompetence of the government. The lesson was written large in the history of tariff, currency, railroad, and land legislation; it was spelled out in words of one syllable, as it were, in state legislatures from Maine to California, and every schoolboy knew that the Standard Oil had refined everything in Pennsylvania but the legislature. It is not supposed that William Sylvis or Terence Powderly, William Peffer or Ignatius Donnelly, or, for that matter, William Jennings Bryan or Robert LaFollette were familiar with "Number Ten" of the *Federalist* or with *An Inquiry into the Principles and Policy of the Government,* but they had no need of historical scholarship to reveal to them the moral that had been so clear to Madison and Taylor.

Few dissident political leaders, however, had the time or the competence to formulate systematic interpretations of the economic bases of politics. That was the work first of the muckrakers, then of the scholars who found themselves, sometimes to their astonishment, in the muckrake camp. Of the muckrakers, not only the first but one of the most active was Henry Demarest Lloyd, a rich and respectable editor who early threw in his fortunes with the poor and oppressed. *Wealth against Commonwealth,* the one book for which he is remembered, was an attack upon the malpractices of the Standard Oil and other corporations, not always accurate and as far from judicious as, say, Carnegie's *Triumphant Democracy.* Yet it had qualities which give it an importance transcending the immediate circumstances of its publication. It was an exposure of the processes by which business exploited government for private ends, an elementary lesson in what corporation directors of the nineties knew almost by instinct but what platform framers conveniently ignored.

Two classes [wrote Lloyd] study and practise politics and government: place hunters and privilege hunters. America has grown so big—and the tickets to be voted, and the powers of government, and the duties of citizens, and the profits of personal use of public functions have all grown so big— that the average citizen has broken down. No man can half understand or half operate . . . it . . . except the place hunter and the privilege hunter. Government, therefore—municipal, State, national—is passing into the hands of these two classes. The power of citizenship is relinquished by those who have a livelihood to make to those who make politics their livelihood. These specialists of the ward club, the primary, the campaign, the election, and office unite, by a law as irresistible as that of the sexes, with those who want all the goods of government—charters, contracts, rulings, permits. . . . There might come a time when the policeman and the railroad president would equally show that they cared nothing for the citizen, individually or collectively, because aware that they and not he were the government. (*Wealth Against Commonwealth,* pp. 355–356)

Lloyd's book was permeated by moral fervor, but it was not merely a homily, and he was one of the first students to see the bankruptcy of the merely moral approach. "The world is too full," he wrote,

of amateurs who can play the golden rule as an aria with variations. All the runs and trills and transpositions have been done to death. . . . Titillation of our sympathies has become a dissipation. . . . "Regenerate the individual" is a half-truth; the reorganization of the society which he makes and which makes him is the other half. . . . Change of heart is no more redemption than hunger is dinner. We must have honesty, love, justice in the heart of the business world, but for these we must also have the forms which will fit them. (*Wealth Against Commonwealth,* pp. 357–358)

Where Lloyd led the way a host of muckrakers followed—a decade later. Their achievement is familiar enough but not, perhaps, its moral. For whether they examined, with Steffens, the *Shame of the Cities,* or with Lawson *Frenzied Finance,* or with Russell *The Greatest Trust in the World,* or with Gustavus Meyers the *History of Great American Fortunes,* or with Phillips "The Treason of the Senate," their central thesis was the same—the corrupt alliance of business and politics, with business usually the corruptor. Their exposures were, in reality, elementary treatises on modern civics.

Of them all, Lincoln Steffens was the most astute, and the most influential. His findings are to be read in the sensational *Shame of the Cities,* but it is the sober and disillusioned *Autobiography* that best presents his conclusions. It is a book in the tradition of Machiavelli's *Prince,* a cold-blooded analysis of how the political system actually works. Together with such autobiographies as Tom Johnson's *My Story* and Brand Whitlock's *Forty Years of It,* it swept away the whole case of the civil service reformers of the Progressive era, for it made inescapably clear that political corruption stemmed from commercial, that bosses were the creatures of big business and the spoils system the natural product of a predatory economy, and that the moral approach to politics was not only inadequate but foredoomed to frustration. A case study of political machinery and political corruption, it was worth a library of formal histories of parties or full-dress biographies of statesmen.

The more academic analysis of the economic bases of politics owed much to the muckrakers but more to the pioneer work of Lester Ward, Thorstein Veblen, and the skeptical Brooks Adams. Arthur F. Bentley, whose profound *Process of Government* is a study of the function of government as umpire between conflicting interest groups, was clearly influenced by Veblen—even, regrettably, in the matter of style—and Charles A. Beard later confessed his debt to Brooks Adams' remarkable studies of *The Law of Civilization and Decay* and *America's Economic Supremacy.* The most notable scholarly contributions came, however, from what may be called the Wisconsin group—Van Hise, Ely, Commons, and Ross—and it was not wholly by chance that what these taught in the classroom LaFollette was announcing from the rostrum and the gubernatorial chair. None of them was primarily concerned with politics; all of them illuminated the role that business played in government and law: Van Hise with his study of the processes of concentration and control of natural resources, Ely with his masterly analysis of *Property and Contract in Their Relation to the Distribution of Wealth,* Commons with his astute investigation of the *Legal Foundations of Capitalism,* and E. A. Ross with his acute and original interpretation of *Sin and Society.*

Sin and Society, published when Theodore Roosevelt was in the White House and read by him with explosive enthusiasm, illustrates not only the new appreciation of the place of economics in politics but the role of what we may call, for want of a better term, psychology. The American awareness of "Human Nature in Politics" is often

traced to English and Continental scholars—to Le Bon who discovered *The Crowd,* to Tarde who analyzed the psychological factors
in jurisprudence and the *Laws of Imitation,* to Durkheim who
studied the group mind, to William McDougall who allied political
to *Social Psychology,* and to the brilliant Graham Wallas who took
out a copyright on the term itself. But there is an American tradition
of appreciation of social psychology in politics—a tradition logical
enough in a democracy and long cultivated by those political bosses
who could have told Le Bon and Tarde things never dreamed of in
their philosophy. Lester Ward, who deeply influenced Ross, emphasized the "psychic factors"; Veblen was as much psychologist as economist; and Bentley dealt exhaustively with psychological forces only
to deny them a controlling place in his scheme of the political process.

Writing in 1893 of the malevolence of the industrial order, Ward
had pointed out that,

These are great and serious evils, compared with which all the crimes
recognized as such, that would be committed if no government existed,
would be as trifles. The underpaid labor, the prolonged and groveling
drudgery, the wasted strength, the misery and squalor, the diseases resulting and the premature deaths that would be prevented by a just distribution of the products of labor, would in a single year outweigh all the so-
called crime of a century. . . . It is utterly illogical to say that aggrandizement by physical force should be forbidden, while aggrandizement by
mental force or legal fiction should be permitted. It is absurd to claim that
injustice committed by muscle should be regulated, while that committed
by brain should be unrestrained. (*Psychic Factors in Civilization,* pp. 320,
322)

Economists had devoted sufficient attention to the tragedy of unemployment and poverty, and moralists had called for amelioration by
government of the lot of the poor and the weak. It remained for Ross
to explain why the analyses of the economists and the pleas of the reformers had alike failed to achieve effective governmental action, to
put his finger on the economic confusions and the psychological inhibitions that combined to frustrate reform.

The difficulty, Ross submitted, was primarily psychological. The
American mind and American law were equipped to recognize and
to deal with the old familiar personal sins—theft, embezzlement, assault, drunkenness, murder; confronted by new, impersonal, social
sin, they were confused. The moral and legal codes inherited from the

eighteenth century were adequate to detect and punish cruelty to children or misappropriation of funds or poisoning; they were incompetent to detect and punish child labor, stock watering, and the adulteration of foods. Modern sin lacked "the familiar tokens of guilt"; the modern sinners were, for the most part, upright and well-intentioned gentlemen who "sinned with calm countenance and a serene soul." They were caught in the meshes of a business system which had not yet developed a moral code adequate to its own needs and to which the old codes were irrelevant. "How idle in our new situation," Ross concluded, "to intone the old litanies."

For the new social sin was impersonal and without evil intent. It outraged none of the habitual moral attitudes, inspired no sense of personal guilt. The explanation of this curious situation was to be found largely in the nature and operation of the corporate device. It was the essence of the corporation, Ross pointed out, that it was a person for legal but not for moral purposes. The corporation could manufacture shoddy products, exploit child labor, hire labor spies, bribe legislators, bargain for rebates, violate safety laws—and neither the stockholders nor the directors nor the agents themselves feel any personal responsibility in the matter. For "the corporation is an entity that transmits the greed of investors, but not their conscience, that returns them profit, but not unpopularity." Corporation employers were responsible to the management, the management was responsible to the directors, the directors were responsible to the stockholders, and the stockholders were too far removed from the business to exercise any control over its ethics even had they been inclined to do so.

Yet nothing was to be gained by denouncing the corporation or lamenting the diffusion of responsibility. The real difficulty was, in last analysis, with the victims themselves. For the victims, if they but knew it, were in control: the corporation was, after all, but the creature of the law and at all times subject to the law. Modern sin could be outlawed if public opinion could only be brought to recognize it and to visit upon it the same obloquy heretofore reserved for vice.

But what was public opinion? There was the rub. Ross assumed, as Ward had before him, that it was rational, that it could be organized and directed. But was it in fact rational? Was it susceptible of organization and direction? Man, said Pascal, is but a reed, but he is a thinking reed, and that aphorism had consoled generations of political idealists. Was this, too, one of those "intellectualisms" against which

Graham Wallas warned his contemporaries? "Whoever sets himself to base his political thinking on a re-examination of the working of human nature," Wallas had written, "must begin by trying to overcome his own tendency to exaggerate the intellectuality of mankind." Had the political theorists of the past—the reformers especially— gone astray through an exaggeration of the rational element in public opinion? This was the inquiry to which Walter Lippmann directed his attention in the most important of his early books, *Public Opinion*. "The existence of a force called Public Opinion," he wrote,

is in the main taken for granted, and American political writers have been most interested either in finding out how to make government express the common will, or in how to prevent the common will from subverting the purposes for which they believe the government exists. According to their traditions they have wished either to tame opinion or to obey it. (*Public Opinion*, 1947 ed., p. 191)

Practicing politicians had doubtless understood the true nature of public opinion, but scholars and publicists had assumed that it was rational and reliable. It was not, Lippmann submitted, either rational or reliable but an incoherent, fickle, and evanescent thing, an amalgam of stereotypes, prejudices, and inferences, a creature of habits and associations, moved by impulses of fear and greed and imitation, exalted by tags and symbols, distracted by the personal and sensational, seduced by bombast and flattery, impressed by repetition, played on by propaganda, victimized by pressure groups.

This was the thesis that LeBon and Tarde had popularized on the Continent and that the German Michels and the Italian Pareto had pushed to what seemed a logical conclusion—that man in the mass was never to be trusted. Continental theory used the term "mass" as one of opprobrium, regarded the crowd as the repository of all evil and sinister instincts, and took refuge either in despair or in the exaltation of the Führer principle. It was an analysis based on history and justified, it seemed to the pessimistic, by the events of the thirties and the forties. But American history afforded no ground for findings so dismal or conclusions so desperate. America had never known the mob in the European sense, nor had irrationality held sway in American politics as it had so commonly in European.

So neither Lippmann nor Thurman Arnold, who in the decade of the thirties analyzed the symbols of government and the folklore of economics, was moved to despair. For though the vagaries of public opinion defied the axioms of rationalism, it by no means followed that reason had no place in politics or that a philosophy based on the assumption that men in the mass were virtuous and enlightened was bankrupt. It was characteristic of the American political temper that Lippmann and Arnold should, for all their appreciation of emotion, appeal in the end not to emotion but to reason. *Public Opinion* celebrated the work of experts, called for intelligence services to be attached to each department of the government and concluded, significantly, with an "Appeal to Reason." We can take our stand on reason and faith, Lippmann wrote, in words as applicable to 1950 as to 1922, and,

We can do all this the better if we do not allow frightfulness and fanaticism to impress us so deeply that we throw up our hands peevishly, and lose interest in the longer run of time because we have lost faith in the future of man. There is no ground for this despair, because all the *ifs* on which, as James said, our destiny hangs, are as pregnant as they ever were. What we have seen of brutality, we have seen, and because it was strange, it was not conclusive. . . . The more realistically men have faced out the brutality and the hysteria, the more they have earned the right to say that it is not foolish for men to believe, because another great war took place, that intelligence, courage and effort cannot ever contrive a good life for all men. (*Public Opinion,* 1947 ed., p. 315)

Nor was Thurman Arnold, for all his superficial cynicism, ready to abandon faith in political intelligence. He exposed the "mystery of jurisprudence" but celebrated the "greatness of the law"; he laid bare the paradox of faith in private enterprise that was incompetent and inhumane and mistrust of public enterprise that was efficient and humanitarian, but he did not conclude that the paradox was beyond resolution. "The wages of pessimism," he wrote, "are futility. The writer has faith that a new public attitude towards the ideals of law and economics is slowly appearing to create an atmosphere where the fanatical alignments between opposing political principles may disappear, and a competent, practical, opportunistic governing class may raise to power."

CHAPTER XVI

The Applications of Political Theory

I

I T WAS NOT a governing class that America needed—that ideal cherished by the Federalists and revived by the civil service reformers—but a people intelligent enough to use government to prosper the commonwealth, realistic enough to recognize the economic bases of politics, moderate enough to exercise self-restraint, bold enough to countenance experiments, mature enough to distinguish between statesmanship and demagoguery, farsighted enough to plan for their children and their children's children. All this was, to be sure, a large order, and only perfectionists could be disappointed that it was not filled. Yet if Americans remained politically immature, they revealed as great a competence in the art and science of politics as any other people, and rather more than most. They were reluctant to modernize their machinery of government, yet though it needed constant care it never wholly broke down as it often did in the Old World. They tolerated corruption, yet their political standards were as high as their business standards, and the contrast between the conduct of the Civil War and the second World War suggests some progress in political morality. They clung to the vocabulary of laissez faire, yet faithfully supplied the money and the personnel for vastly expanded governmental activities. They frightened themselves with bogies of bureaucracy, regimentation, and dictatorship, but in fact remained singularly free from bureaucracy in the Old World sense, avoided political regimentation, and never knew the meaning of dictatorship as so many peoples in Europe, Latin America, and the East knew it.

For in defiance of the conclusions of European students of the masses, Americans revealed themselves susceptible not so much to propaganda as to political instruction, or at least to political experience. No one who contemplated the course of American politics during the half-century after 1890 could doubt that the teachings of evolution and pragmatism had practical consequences. That half-century was remarkable quantitatively for the expansion of governmental activities and qualitatively for reform, and the direction of the one and the zeal for the other required an enlightened electorate.

It was the West that first showed itself receptive to new political ideas—the West of Henry George, Lloyd, Ross, Veblen, Steffens, and William Allen White—and it was the Populists who most nearly anticipated the course that American politics was to follow in the twentieth century. What first Weaver and Donnelly, then Bryan and LaFollette, espoused—the adaptation of the constitutional system to the exigencies of a modern society, the regulation of the economic by the political authority, the development of new techniques of administration—Theodore Roosevelt and Woodrow Wilson effected. After the lapse of a decade and a half, Franklin Roosevelt took up once more the program of the Populists and the Progressives and carried it to its logical conclusion.

Notwithstanding irrelevant differences in party allegiance, superficial differences in political methods, and deep differences in character, these five great leaders of American democracy in the twentieth century, Bryan, LaFollette, Wilson, Theodore and Franklin Roosevelt, had much in common. All were children of the Enlightenment, as it were, inspired by new insights and equipped with new tools. All were evolutionists—even Bryan, for all his religious fundamentalism. All were pragmatists, more concerned with the machinery of government than with its façade. All recognized, though with varying degrees of perception, the economic bases of politics and the role of pressure groups in the formulation of policy. All understood the nature of public opinion and how to inspire and to guide it.

The most illuminating test of their conversion to the evolutionary and pragmatic philosophy was their attitude toward that symbol of traditionalism, the judiciary. As they looked upon the Constitution as a tool rather than a symbol, so they regarded the Court not as a Delphic oracle but as a political institution. Bryan campaigned in 1896 against the judicial nullification of the income tax—which he had helped write—and the use of the injunction in labor disputes. Roosevelt, who denounced him for this heresy, came himself to advocate the recall of judicial decisions, and for his own heresy forfeited the support of stalwarts like Henry Cabot Lodge and Elihu Root. LaFollette, who saw the courts frustrate public policy for a quarter-century, ran for the presidency on a platform that branded judicial conduct a "plain violation of the Constitution." Wilson, who never faced a judicial crisis—except perhaps in that impudent nullification of the Child Labor Law which remains one of the scandals of American constitutional history—confessed his position boldly enough by his appointment to the Supreme Court of the greatest of sociological jurisprudents, Louis Brandeis, and of the liberal John H. Clarke. And Franklin Roosevelt's response to the attempt of the judiciary to fasten a strait jacket about the government took the form of the boldest program for judicial reform that had ever been attempted by an American president.

What populism and progressivism, the New Freedom and the New Deal, meant in terms of political philosophy was the final repudiation of laissez faire and the explicit recognition of government as a social welfare agency. What it meant in terms of constitutional theory was the unqualified triumph of the doctrine of broad construction. The pernicious notion that there was some inevitable conflict between man and the state had long embarrassed American politics. Distrust of government, inherited from the Revolutionary era, approved by Jefferson, endowed with perverse rationalization by Herbert Spencer, gave way at last to the realization that the government was man organized politically, and that vigilance—still the price of liberty—was not synonymous with paralysis. The "necessary evil" of Thomas Paine had become so necessary that it was no longer an evil.

Less spectacular than the crusade for a dynamic democracy, but scarcely less important, was that improvement of old and development of new techniques in government which may be called the pragmatic attack on politics. If the first quarter of the new century does not compare in creative inventiveness with the first quarter-century of the history of the Republic, it was more resourceful and fruitful than any other comparable period in our history. Under pressure from dissident groups, and under the leadership of scholars like Frank Goodnow and W. F. Willoughby and Joseph Chamberlain, Americans embarked on far-reaching experiments with governmental machinery. Some of these were designed to expand democracy itself— woman suffrage, for example, the initiative and the referendum, the Australian ballot, the direct primaries, the popular election of Senators. Others looked not so much to political as to administrative reforms. These were applied not only in the federal but in the neglected areas of state, county, and local government: within a generation they had largely transformed the whole machinery of American politics.

What were the results of the new experimental attitude toward administration? First, it broke through the rigid tripartite separation of powers not only by the formal recognition of the unifying function of the political party but by the creation of a fourth department—the independent commission, whose authority was quasi-executive, quasi-legislative, and quasi-judicial and whose duties were primarily administrative. The Interstate Commerce Commission was the first of these, and it was for long the model. By the time of the second World War there were some forty or fifty of these commissions, functioning independently of politics or spoils, doing a large part of the actual governing, and accepted by the courts. Second, it required an enormous enlargement of governmental structure and personnel to take care of the new functions and responsibilities assigned to public administration. Within a generation, single departments of the government, like the Agricultural, grew to proportions where they required the services of thousands of experts, and in the forty years from the opening of the century to the eve of the second World War the number of federal employees increased four times as fast as the population. If the government was to enjoy the services of technicians, these had to be selected regardless of party considerations and assured permanence of tenure. It was practical rather than moral considerations that brought the triumph of civil service reform, in state as in national politics.

A third major contribution of the study of public administration was in the realm of government finances. This realm had traditionally been the happy hunting ground for spoilsmen and pressure groups while fiscal policies—witness the agitation of the silver issue—had long been a moral rather than a scientific preoccupation. As the annual expenditures of a single city like New York mounted toward a billion dollars, and as the annual appropriations of the federal government, even in the peaceful twenties, rose to three or four times the total for the first fifty years of the history of the Republic, the study of finance moved into a central position. Public finance could never, to be sure, be divorced from considerations of political policy nor—witness the depression and the world wars—from the accidents of world events, but it could at least be divorced from practical politics and its administration placed on a scientific basis. This was achieved, in part, by the establishment of bureaus of the budget, the improvement in methods of government financing, the development and exploitation of new sources of taxation, the elimination of overlapping and waste, and the imposition of rigorous auditing standards.

The study of finance as well as of other practical aspects of administration owed a great deal to the many new agencies for governmental research—municipal reference bureaus, legislative reference libraries, the Institute for Government Research which W. F. Willoughby long directed, and the many graduate schools of public administration attached to universities—and the establishment and maintenance of these was likewise one of the triumphs of the new experimental attitude. These research organizations were more effective in municipal than in national affairs, and it was in large part owing to their unspectacular work that the government of American cities ceased to be that one conspicuous failure of democracy which Bryce had described and became, under the leadership of men like Newton D. Baker in Cleveland, Emil Seidel in Milwaukee, and the colorful Fiorello La Guardia in New York, models of efficient administration. Finally the pragmatic attitude encouraged scientific planning in and by governments. Long suspect because associated with notions of regimentation and of socialism, some form of planning was nevertheless imposed on governments by the growing complexity of modern economy and by the fragmentation of administration in the United States. Its effective beginnings may be traced to the various conservation boards and conferences of the Theodore Roosevelt administration; it was stimulated by the first World War; it was given respectability by Herbert Hoover, who brought to problems of politics the attitude if not the achievements of the engineer; it reached its fullest peacetime development in the large-scale regional plans for the Rio Grande Valley, the Great Plains, and the Tennessee Valley and with the establishment of the short-lived National Resources Planning Board.

Along with the expansion of governmental activities to fit the needs of the welfare state went a growing appreciation of the realities behind the formalities of political, civil, and personal rights. This owed something to the new awareness of the economic bases of politics something to the rigorous study of public opinion, and more perhaps to the depression at home and the rise of totalitarianism abroad. The nineteenth century, in its felicity, had thought sufficient the guaran tees of the Constitution and the Bill of Rights. The actual content and incidence of these guarantees—what they meant to the industrial worker, the immigrant, the Negro—received little consideration: certainly we look in vain in the treatises of the commentators from Story to Burgess for any analysis of political and civil rights that went behind the glittering promises to the commonplace actualities. Men had come to repeat the familiar phrases of the Declaration of Independence and the Bill of Rights, thoughtlessly and automatically, as they intoned the Apostles' Creed or college songs.

Perhaps the most important product of the new political realism was a livelier apprehension of the interdependence of liberty and security. What did the right to vote mean to a Mississippi Negro; what did the privileges and immunities clause mean to Steinbeck's Okies; what did the rights of free speech and assembly mean to CIO organizers in Jersey City? Of what value was the guarantee of due process of law to a Negro confronted by a white jury in a case involving the honor of a white woman? What was the price of freedom of worship to Jews who paid for orthodoxy by social ostracism? What did freedom of contract mean to a charwoman, except that she was permitted to work ten hours instead of eight and saved from the dangerous regimentation implicit in a minimum wage? Clearly it was necessary to clothe ancient rights in modern garments, to supplement traditional freedoms adequate to the pastoral society of the eighteenth century with new ones efficacious in the industrial society of the twentieth.

Realization of the gap between formal promises and actual fulfillment was nothing new: it could be found in the literature of abolition and reform in the 1840's, in the socialist and single-tax arguments of the eighties, in the program of the Populists at the end of the old century and of the Progressives at the beginning of the new. Theodore Roosevelt expressed it when he denounced judicial nullification of tenement house, hours of labor, and workmen's compensation laws and when he compared the abstract doctrine of equality of bargaining with the actualities of a bargain between an immigrant steelworker and the United States Steel Corporation. It was implicit in much of the New Freedom, and explicit in Woodrow Wilson's inaugural address. But it was the New Deal that most openly acknowledged the gap and energetically attempted to bridge it. It was characteristic that the sponsor of the first national social security legislation should have given freedom from want and freedom from fear an equal dignity with freedom of speech and freedom of worship.

It was not merely domestic considerations that hastened this recognition of the interdependence of political and economic freedom. Events abroad, all through the twenties and the thirties, dramatized the danger of relying too heavily on merely formal rights to the neglect of that security which people so desperately wanted and which tyrants were so ready to promise. In speech after speech President Roosevelt pointed the moral of contemporary European history— that given a choice between liberty and bread, men will choose bread —and warned against permitting such pernicious alternatives to be submitted to the American people:

Democracy has disappeared in several other great nations—not because the people of those nations disliked democracy, but because they had grown tired of unemployment and insecurity, of seeing their children hungry, while they sat helpless in the face of government confusion and government weakness through lack of leadership in government. Finally, in desperation, they chose to sacrifice liberty in the hope of getting something to eat. We in America know that our own democratic institutions can be preserved and made to work. But in order to preserve them we need . . . to prove that the practical operation of democratic government is equal to the task of protecting the security of the people. ("Fireside Chat" of April 14, 1938)

2

One example is worth a wilderness of abstractions. The extent to which the new philosophical concepts had worked a transformation in American political thought and conduct is perhaps best illustrated by the history of the Tennessee Valley Authority. For the TVA was a philosophical and historical as well as a political and social laboratory. It was the first major attempt by government to use what John Dewey had proposed, "plural and experimental methods in securing and maintaining an ever-increasing release of the powers of human nature in service of a freedom which is cooperative and a cooperation which is voluntary," and it foreshadowed a series of attempts only less notable. It was the proving ground, as it were, of a dynamic democracy. Here were tested the broad construction of the Constitution, large-scale planning, the recasting of federalism along regional lines, new techniques of administration and new standards of civil service, the alliance of science and politics, and the revitalization of democracy through a calculated program of economic and social reconstruction. There was nothing new about any one of these—broad construction dates back to the First Bank of the United States, science and politics were wedded in the work of the Smithsonian Institution and the Geological Survey, political regionalism was acknowledged in the Federal Reserve Bank System—but the TVA was the first institution to combine all of them in one tremendous experiment.

The whole history of the TVA is wonderfully illuminating. It began, modestly enough, in the early twenties when the indomitable George Norris of Nebraska, himself a symbol of the new democracy, proposed that the Government take over and operate the hydroelectric dams at Muscle Shoals which the Government had built as a war measure. This proposal, with its remote suggestion of government participation in business, challenged the shibboleths of private enterprise and inspired a frantic opposition which revived every argument of laissez faire that had been hackneyed for two generations. A first Muscle Shoals bill encountered a not unexpected but quite uninstructive veto from President Coolidge. More illuminating was the reaction of President Hoover to the refurbished bill of 1931. As a civil engineer—the first ever to reach the White House—Hoover was better equipped than any other contemporary statesman to appreciate the technological possibilities of the Tennessee River project; as a disciple of William Graham Sumner he was unable to divorce his appreciation of its technological merits from his repugnance to its political implications. When the issue came squarely before him, he vindicated Veblen's analysis of the triumph of commercial over engineering considerations. "For the Federal government deliberately to go out to build up and expand an occasion to the major purpose of a power and manufacturing business," said Mr. Hoover in a message which was to be a classic example of the folly of political prophecy,

to break down the initiative and enterprise of the American people; it is destruction of equality of opportunity of our people; it is the negation of the ideals upon which our civilization has been based. . . . I hesitate to contemplate the future of our institutions, of our country, if the preoccupation of its officials is to be no longer the promotion of justice and equal opportunity, but is to be devoted to barter in the markets. That is not liberalism, it is degeneration.

However misguided this argument, however fallacious its analysis and ruinous its logic, it had at least the merit of dramatizing the contrast between the old and the new ways of thinking about political problems: the old way of starting with a series of abstract principles and deducing from them some ideal course of action—or of inaction—and the new way of starting with a concrete situation and seeking pragmatically some workable solution.

Implicit in the Coolidge and Hoover vetoes of the Muscle Shoals bills was the assumption that there was more here than met the eye. There was indeed. The Tennessee Valley Act of 1933, imaginatively reconstructed by President Roosevelt himself, went far beyond the modest plan that Senator Norris had originally sponsored to embrace a vast and varied scheme for "the economic and social well-being of the people" of the entire Tennessee Valley, and Roosevelt's first directive provided that the Authority should be "clothed with the power of government but possessed of the flexibility and initiative of a private enterprise." The new Authority was not to be limited to the generation of hydroelectric power or the manufacture of fertilizer but was instructed to undertake conservation, reforestation, and agricultural rehabilitation looking to the "fuller and better balanced development of the resources of the region"—a region embracing parts of seven states, with an area as large as England and Scotland and a population of over five million.

The success of the TVA was such a triumph as even its original proponents had scarcely dared to anticipate. It was not only that within a decade or so it had constructed sixteen giant dams—a construction which equaled the total railroad construction in the United States for a century—eliminated floods, made 650 miles of streams navigable, created a series of inland lakes and hundreds of thousands of acres of parks and recreation grounds, planted some two hundred million trees, generated power for homes and factories throughout the whole region and for the Manhattan Project, wiped out malaria, restored to fertility soil once condemned to sterility, vastly improved agriculture, revived old and created new industries, stimulated education and cultural developments, accelerated the progress of the whole region by perhaps half a century, and furnished a model for comparable projects in the Columbia and Missouri River

Valleys and in other countries. It was not only that it commanded the approval, on constitutional grounds, of the unreformed Supreme Court and won the support of almost all those whose lives it touched —notable exceptions were one Senator who was intellectually, and one Boss who was morally, bankrupt. All this was a great achievement—probably the greatest peacetime achievement of twentieth-century America. But the student of politics was concerned not only with the material achievement but with the principle, and foreign observers confirmed the American conviction that TVA opened new possibilities in the realm of government.

It was planning, but planning not superimposed from above but worked out cooperatively by those who were involved. It was socialization, but socialization that prospered rather than impaired private industry—even the power industry of the region found itself embarrassed by its unwonted prosperity. It was centralization, but centralization that operated through local communities and that actually strengthened both the states and the communities where it operated. It recognized that the divisions in America were geographical rather than political, and its regionalism cut across artificial state lines to offer a new solution to the old problem of federalism. It triumphantly allied science and politics, not merely for special and limited purposes, as with the Geological Survey or the Agricultural Experiment Stations, but in an integrated and coordinated plan for the whole life of the region, as a great university allies teaching and research. It was politics, but in the Aristotelian sense of the word, its standards of civil service so high that maintaining them almost cost its chairman his political life. It was the justification of Lester Ward's thesis that public intelligence can operate most effectively through government and that government can be more efficient than business. It was a shining example of William James's moral equivalent of war and enlisted the loyalty and enthusiasm of those engaged in it just as an army did, or a military campaign. And—what was perhaps most instructive—the whole experiment was carried through, as Chairman David E. Lilienthal wrote, "under the existing rules of the game of American life."

3

Throughout most of the history of the Republic, the major political philosophers had been statesmen, not savants or academicians.

Neither Hamilton nor Jefferson, Story nor Calhoun, had lived sheltered lives, and in the great crisis of the history of the Republic the people of the North looked to Lincoln, not Lieber, to express their deepest feelings, while Southerners remembered not so much what Calhoun had written in the privacy of his study as what he had said and done in the halls of Congress. The generation that separated Lincoln from Bryan constituted an exception to this generalization and an illuminating one. This period, so barren of political thought, was likewise the ebb tide of statesmanship; political philosophy became the peculiar province of the academicians, rather because there were no other claimants than because the justice or propriety of the claim was acknowledged. With the twentieth century came a return to the true tradition of American politics: the work of Bryan and Theodore Roosevelt, of Wilson and Franklin Roosevelt, was one of restoration.

William Jennings Bryan was not a political philosopher, and many would deny his title to statesmanship. Yet his political creed was born of an instinctive understanding of the meaning of American history, and he pioneered in the advocacy of more and more important legislation than any other politician of his generation. The most representative American of his time, he represented what was, on the whole, soundest and most wholesome in the American character. His democracy was intuitive but none the less rationalized for that; his moral earnestness grew out of religious convictions; his economic radicalism was a product of experience familiar enough to those born and raised along the Middle Border. He spoke for the God-fearing, Protestant, evangelical America, for the rural America that was giving way to the urban, for the South and the West whose resources were being exploited to profit the East, for the homespun, egalitarian America dismayed at the emergence of social classes and exotic standards, and he spoke with the tongue of angels. Less sophisticated than Theodore Roosevelt, less profound than Wilson, not so hardheaded as LaFollette, he was neither the simpleton nor the demagogue that his critics pictured and that a later generation, misled by Dayton and Coral Gables, imagined. Without any profound grasp of economics, he knew as much about the tariff or the money question as most contemporary politicians—and rather more than Mark Hanna or the silver-plated McKinley—and as his instincts were sound he managed to penetrate to the nature, though not to the solution, of the economic problems that harassed his followers. Lacking in critical acumen, he had nevertheless a firm grasp on political and economic realities, and, though he clothed all his arguments in trailing clouds of rhetoric, the arguments themselves were logical enough. He was the first major political figure to give articulate expression to the rumblings of discontent that were sweeping the nation, the first to understand that the problems of politics were primarily economic, the first to formulate a broad program designed to translate the hopes of the nineteenth-century democracy into policies relevant to the practical needs of the twentieth. The most astute politician of his day, he never compromised his integrity; the most ambitious, he never sacrificed principle to ambition; three times rejected by the American people, he never wavered in his faith in their virtue or in the essential soundness of their judgment, and he gloried in the name, "The Great Commoner." He had an understanding of the psychology of his own kind that has never been surpassed and inspired such devotion in them as few other American statesmen have been able to command.

Of the new forces transforming American political thought—evolution, pragmatism, economics, and psychology—he was wanting in comprehension of only the second. He knew, none better, that the Constitution had to be adjusted to the needs of a twentieth-century society, and for two decades he led the fight on laissez faire; all his political campaigns were economic—though it was an economics curiously blended with morals; his understanding of popular psychology was shrewd and enlightened. But, unlike his contemporaries, La-Follette, Theodore Roosevelt, and Wilson, he was wholly lacking in the scientific habit of mind, and for the expert he had only distrust— a distrust which was generously reciprocated. He is the connecting link between the nineteenth and the twentieth centuries, embodying the best of the American character that was rapidly becoming archaic, anticipating the political program designed to adjust that character to the complex demands of the new day. The people whose battles he so gallantly fought have all but forgotten him; the causes he championed were to be vindicated under new leaders; his reputation has been buried among the ruins of his own triumphs.

Only by using the term in its broadest sense could Theodore Roosevelt be called a political philosopher: had McKinley lived, it is improbable that students would read anything that Roosevelt wrote except the *Winning of the West* or the *Naval War of 1812* or that they would remember any of the simple sermonizing in which he indulged under the delusion that it was political wisdom. But, as Justice Holmes said of John Marshall, a great man represents a stragetic point in the campaign of history, and part of his greatness consists in being there. Roosevelt was the instrument chosen by destiny for the implementation of a reform movement whose origins he scarcely knew, whose character he but dimly understood, whose objectives he failed to appreciate, and whose consequences he often deplored. Like Bryan, he carried on his education in public and, as with so many such educations, at public expense; yet no one who contemplates the monotonous administrations of his immediate predecessors, unrelieved as they are either by conspicuous virtue or by conspicuous vice, can doubt that the public got something back on its investment if only in entertainment. His mind was neither original nor profound but sensitive and receptive, and as long as he breathed the atmosphere of progressivism he was a progressive. If he did not generate ideas, he generated enthusiasm for them, and his exalted position gave a certain respectability to principles long regarded as heterodox. His broad construction of the Constitution—and particularly of Article II of that document— was not, as with Wilson, a reasoned conclusion from the study of politics but an expression of ardent nationalism and of a touching confidence in himself as the most fit instrument for achieving the ends of the positive state. He had something of Bryan's intuitive appreciation of mass psychology—though the mass to which he appealed was urban rather than rural—and, if his political magnetism seems at times cultivated and faintly artificial, its power was undeniable. He had been part of that moral crusade which crystallized in the civil service reform movement, and had come in time to recognize its weakness and to prefer a practical to a moral approach to politics. Yet the lesson which he had learned as Civil Service Commissioner, and in the New York Police Department, was only a partial one. Too shrewd to use moral weapons against spoilsmen like Mark Hanna, Tom Platt, Nelson Aldrich, or Speaker Cannon, he was entirely prepared to rely upon them in the economic arena against malefactors of great wealth. Thus while his political battles—and victories—were real, his economics were largely sham, and it was a matter for embarrassment rather than for surprise when some of the malefactors, like George Perkins or Frank Munsey, financed his campaign in 1912. His most important achievement was practical and personal—the use of the executive power to advance the cause of conservation, build the Panama Canal, and make American power felt in world affairs; his significance was not philosophical but symbolic—that he came to represent an ideal of progressivism which, under leadership more sincere and more heroic, might be realized.

Like Bryan and Theodore Roosevelt, Wilson was a moral crusader, a democrat, and a progressive. Because his morality was more critical, his democracy more calculated, his progressivism more pragmatic than that of either of these contemporaries, he was more effective. He was a student of politics, familiar with the great literature of the subject from Aristotle to Bagehot, on easy terms with both history and theory, and he brought to the practical tasks of statesmanship a mind more distinguished and fastidious than that of any chief executive since the days of Jefferson and the two Adamses. It was by sheer force of intellect—as well as by chance—that he came to be the leader of a protest movement of which he had never been a part: where Bryan and Roosevelt and LaFollette fought their way up from the ranks, he started, as it were, as a general officer. It was in part because he had been for so long isolated from the hurly-burly of politics that he lacked the common touch—lacked Bryan's obvious identification with the plain people, Roosevelt's ability to appeal to the average intelligence, LaFollette's robust sympathy with farmers and workingmen. His experience was literary and derivative; his enthusiasms and indignations were intellectual. He loved humanity in the abstract rather than in the particular, and though he had ardent disciples he had few friends. His superiority was both intellectual and moral, and in both realms it was obtrusive: he did not suffer fools or Congressmen gladly, and the distrust with which the average politician regarded him went deeper than the exigencies of partisanship required. Where most politicians were content to retain their integrity, he was never unconscious of his rectitude.

Of the four major statesmen of his generation, Wilson was most aware of the dynamic character of modern democracy and displayed the boldest readiness to accommodate traditional constitutional dogma to new social needs; the generalization might have been less valid had LaFollette reached the White House. Wilson gave new meaning to the general welfare clause, supplied executive leadership to Congress and to his party, fought privilege, confronted most of the issues that Roosevelt had evaded and set them on the road to solution, and pushed through the most impressive body of legislation that any president had sponsored since Polk. His response to the other major political influences of his generation was less effective. He recognized the role of pragmatism in politics, the influence of economics, and the necessity of mastering public opinion, but the recognition was never unqualified and was sometimes grudging. He had applauded the work of the expert in government but did not use him to any large extent, regarding himself, perhaps, as sufficiently expert for most purposes, and it is not clear that his presidency will be remembered for innovations or improvements in administration. More mature economically than Theodore Roosevelt, he could sponsor far-reaching economic measures like the Federal Reserve Act or the Federal Farm Loan Act or the Clayton Act; yet he never fully understood the economic interests and pressures that motivated men and nations. In economic as in political philosophy he was the expounder of sound principles rather than the contriver of effective mechanisms: the distinction can be read in the contrast between the generalities of *The New Freedom* and the particularities of Brandeis' *Other Peoples' Money,* which appeared at the same time and were addressed to the same theme. Finally, Wilson understood public opinion but understood its nobler rather than its more ignoble manifestations. His idealism was penetrating, but it penetrated to possibilities rather than to actualities. He was familiar enough with the doctrine of original sin, but even sin was to him something of an abstraction: he could contend with it when it assumed the guise of German "frightfulness," but not when it took more prosaic form as public apathy or political chicanery. His knowledge of human nature was rather that of a Unitarian divine than that of a Catholic priest.

For Wilson the American people had a deep and enduring respect, but little affection. They revered him as a symbol of their better nature, but his appeal was intellectual rather than emotional, and he inspired the kind of enthusiasm excited by a noble poem rather than that aroused by a national anthem. It is suggestive that while thousands of parents named their sons—and even their daughters—after William Jennings Bryan, there was no comparable crop of Thomas Woodrows, and that while Bryan, Roosevelt, and LaFollette all earned familiar appellations, no one thought of calling Wilson the Great Commoner, or W. W., or Fighting Tom.

Bryan, Roosevelt, and Wilson all had their intellectual roots deep in nineteenth-century America. Their sense of a constitution adequate to the exigencies of a changing society derived from Marshall; their appreciation of the economic realities behind the ornamented façade of politics had antecedents in Hamilton and Jefferson; their understanding and mastery of public opinion was more informed rather than shrewder than that of Clay or Lincoln. Had they strayed, by some mischance, into the early nineteenth century they would not have been ill at ease: Wilson and Madison would have understood each other; Bryan could have consorted happily enough with Thomas Hart Benton; Roosevelt would have echoed, with enthusiasm, Webster's "Reply to Hayne"—and his "Seventh of March" speech. Their modernity was a matter of degree rather than of kind, and the impact of the new philosophical tendencies on their political thought confirmed and strengthened rather than changed inherited attitudes.

Alone of the four, Robert LaFollette would have been an obvious misfit in that earlier age, his manners awkward, his vocabulary strange, his point of view exotic. It would, to be sure, be a mistake to suggest that he owed nothing to the past or that his intellectual antecedents were not respectable. Hamilton would have understood him, or tough John Adams, and would have regarded him as a worthy opponent. Yet alone of the four major statesmen who represented American politics at the turn of the century, he belongs unmistakably to the new day. Alone of them, he had, unreservedly, the scientific habit of mind and the pragmatic temper.

He is remembered as "Fighting Bob," and the adjective is just enough, but it was not his courage that was unique—all the other major leaders had that—but his realism, his disillusioned skepticism, his fierce zeal for facts. What he symbolized, most conspicuously, was the principle of efficiency in government—not just the impersonal efficiency of the accountant or even of the engineer but the more enlightened efficiency of the great architect who combines beauty with utility. The principles to which he subscribed were those that aroused the enthusiasm of Bryan, Roosevelt, and Wilson; and his objective, like theirs, was social and economic democracy. But he alone of these four realized fully that means determine ends as often, and as decisively, as ends determine means; he alone had a passionate sense of the concrete. Like the architect Frank Lloyd Wright (was it an accident that Wright found refuge in Wisconsin?) he knew that function determines form, and he concentrated on function.

It was in the laboratory of the state that LaFollette operated most effectively, not because his pragmatic technique was inapplicable to the national arena but because there he was denied a constructive role and restricted to criticism. It is suggestive that he was not as successful in dissent as Bryan who, like him, wandered for years in the wilderness before he saw the promised land: the idealist can operate more effectively in dissent than the technician, for idealism flourishes on unemployment but technology rusts. LaFollette was never given the opportunity to apply the scientific method to the affairs of the national government, but he did make an experimental laboratory of his own state, and almost a decade before Woodrow Wilson diverted New Jersey temporarily toward democracy, the "Wisconsin idea" was born. Under LaFollette's guidance, or inspiration, that state pioneered in the effective regulation of public utilities, conservation, scientific agriculture, income and inheritance taxes, workmen's compensation, social security, and a dozen other measures that were later to emerge as part of the New Freedom or the New Deal. There was no political magic in all this. The methods that LaFollette used were those that scholars like Ely, Ross, Commons, and Van Hise were formulating at his own state university, and he was the first statesman since Jefferson to see the possibilities of the state university as a powerhouse to generate social and economic programs. His approach to every problem was practical and pragmatic rather than moral and theoretical. It consisted of investigation, the collection of statistics, the application of scientific principles by impartial boards and commissions, and the encouragement of what Lester Ward had called "social invention." It was the method of the Brandeis brief applied to tasks of statesmanship, and of all contemporary statesmen LaFollette was closest in spirit and in method to the great Boston lawyer who in one cause after another was the people's counsel. Like Brandeis he showed what was possible when humanitarian passion was allied with scientific curiosity, and like him he justified the faith that law and politics might in time become both an art and a science.

4

The task that confronted Franklin Roosevelt when he came to the presidency in the dark days of the spring of 1933 was one that taxed statesmanship to the utmost. But it was, or appeared to be, practical rather than philosophical. The contributions of Bryan and Roosevelt, LaFollette and Wilson, were a matter of history, and in intelligent circles the principles which they had so ably espoused had ceased to be controversial. No student of politics, outside the judiciary, questioned the propriety of the evolutionary interpretation of the Constitution or of the application of pragmatic methods to administration, and Wilson's successors, by turning the government itself over to business, admitted not only the importance but the priority of economic considerations. Roosevelt's task, therefore, was not to formulate new principles but to apply those already accepted and long familiar.

It was not an easy task, for the opposition was stubborn and unregenerate. Yet it was not the stubborn character of that opposition which was illuminating to the student of American political thought but the anachronistic. For a decade it confronted the New Deal not with a reasoned hostility to its political principles or even with a practical challenge to the application of those principles but with a potpourri of the shibboleths and aphorisms of Spencerian economics. The exigencies of partisanship explained much of this and the paralysis of the conservative imagination—which, after all, had been numbed since the days of Hamilton—but much was to be debited to the power and persistence of political stereotypes. Undismayed by either history or statistics, critics of the New Deal denounced presidential leadership as dictatorship, Government regulation as regimentation, the welfare state as socialism, and every expansion of political enterprise or authority as a calculated defiance of the Framers. They identified the misleading phrase "private enterprise" with the vague concept "American system," and this triumph of ambiguity won the votes of all those who preferred to take refuge in formulas rather than to face facts. Nor, notwithstanding the long record of civil service reform, the contributions of scholars, the findings of public service commissions, the accomplishments of progressive states, did the pragmatic method in government go unchallenged. The protest against the "brain trust," the contempt for professors in politics, the hostility to scientific undertakings like the TVA, came precisely from those elements in the community who prided themselves on their intelligence, habitually sent their sons and daughters to sit at the feet of professors, and found it cause for personal satisfaction that they lived in a scientific age. If the political history of the New Deal is a tribute to the prophetic visions of a Lester Ward, a Henry D. Lloyd, a Frank Good-

now, the history of the opposition constitutes a triumphant vindication of the more sardonic insights of a Thorstein Veblen, a Walter
Lippmann, or a Thurman Arnold. Every student of the American
mind must give weight to the fact that Franklin Roosevelt's philosophy of government was four times endorsed by thumping majorities,
but no student can fail to be impressed with the consideration that on
each occasion the majority of the wise, the rich, and the well-born
voted the other way.

It is in Franklin Roosevelt as spokesman for American political
ideas rather than as president that we are chiefly interested, and it
would be difficult to find a more representative figure or one who
combined more harmoniously all those attitudes and principles which
distinguished twentieth-century political thought. He had the emotionalism of Bryan without his intellectual flabbiness, the magnetism
of Theodore Roosevelt without his economic immaturity or his fatal
tendency to compromise on essentials, the pragmatic hardheadedness
of LaFollette without his inflexibility or his harshness, the idealism of
Wilson without his doctrinaire intellectualism. With a rationalized
philosophy of government he combined an instinct for practical politics: more fully than any president since Jefferson he saw government
as both an art and a science. Like his four great liberal predecessors he
was a moral crusader, and as with them his moral objectives were
directed to practical ends. No one was more adept at translating a general principle into a particular policy, and his talent for transforming
the generalities of party platforms into statutes excited the indignation
of those who had become accustomed to regard platforms as merely
ceremonial. A democrat by conviction as well as by training, his
background of Groton and Harvard, of family and money, did not
make him self-conscious about his democracy or embarrass his intercourse with people of all kinds. He was deeply rooted in the American
tradition and deeply versed in American history. A radical, he knew
that that tradition was one of protest and reform, and that much of
the meaning of American history was to be found in the steady enlargement of the concept of liberty and the expansion of self-government. All his major experiments derived from native antecedents,
for he found in the American past a sufficient arsenal of democracy.
A conservative, his policies were designed to strengthen liberty with a
foundation of security, to protect property by a distribution so wide
that all would have a stake in it, and to maintain order by subordinat-

ing all private and feudal authorities to the authority of the state. A lawyer himself, he knew that the Constitution was a "layman's document, and not a lawyer's contract," and remembered what even judges sometimes forgot, that government regulation antedated laissez faire, that the procedural meaning of "due process" was older than the substantive, and that "liberty of contract" was a figment of the modern legal mind. History may record that he did more to advance democracy than any president since Lincoln and as much to strengthen capitalism as any statesman since Hamilton.

As Roosevelt's philosophy of government was affirmative, his statesmanship was constructive, and he used government boldly to advance the common wealth. Buoyant and optimistic himself, he was alive to the potentialities rather than the limitations of democracy and based his policies on hopes rather than on regrets, on faith rather than fear. The mandate he received at his first election was congenial to his temper, and that temper, in turn, helped persuade the American people to reaffirm the mandate—a reciprocal process which threatened to continue indefinitely. A thoroughgoing evolutionist, he repudiated the Newtonian concepts of constitutionalism which still found support among a limited class of beneficiaries and with some Supreme Court justices, asserting instead the responsibility "to perfect, to improve, to alter when necessary, but in all cases to go forward." Perfection was scarcely to be expected in politics, but supporters and critics alike agreed that the New Deal represented alteration and change. Whether it represented improvement was a question that lingered, briefly, in the realm of politics, but a glancing reference to the Republican platforms of 1940 and 1944 suggests that it commended itself, in time, even to the opposition.

It was the manifestation of his empirical attitude toward politics that distinguished Roosevelt most sharply from his predecessors in the White House. As pragmatic as LaFollette, he was ready to experiment with new techniques in government and to levy upon the intelligence of experts, and the New Deal attracted more first-rate minds to government service than had any previous administration since Theodore Roosevelt. "Brain trust" was a term of derision, but the difference between that term and the term "Kitchen Cabinet" was in itself a tribute to the caliber of men upon whom the President relied. Roosevelt's experience in New York State had taught him the necessity of scientific administration, and he attempted, though not very successfully, to introduce scientific methods into the executive branch of the Government and to raise the level of the civil service. Long familiar with city and state planning, he applied planning to the national scene—witness the recommendations of the National Resources Planning Board—and, unavoidably perhaps, to the conduct of war. Endlessly resourceful, always ready to experiment within permissible bounds, respectful of precedents only when they commended themselves on their own merits, something of an opportunist and something of a gambler, he displayed an ingenuity and boldness typical of the traditional American character. Resourcefulness gave the country major enterprises like the TVA and minor ones like the Federal Writers' Project; it dictated the precedent-shattering third term; it prescribed, perhaps regrettably, the particular character of the Supreme Court reform bill; it was ultimately responsible for that Office of Scientific Research and Development whose achievements contrasted so sharply with those of the National Research Council of World War I; it authorized the gamble on the Manhattan Project.

Like Wilson, Roosevelt subscribed to the principle of executive leadership and like him knew that this required, to be effective, party leadership, and he went beyond Wilson in his effort toward enforcement. It was the part of realism to recognize that parties operate through local machines and to require, and reward, cooperation from those machines: only those who ignored the close party division on such measures as lend-lease and conscription could feel that the association did an unqualified disservice to the nation. It was the part of wisdom to base leadership not on party allegiance alone but on the broadest possible popular support, and Roosevelt's talent for rallying that support was the despair of his opponents. Nature gave him a personality that won crowds and enchanted individuals, an impressive physical presence, an infectious grin, and a reassuring voice, and the radio and the airplane made it easy for him to exploit these gifts. To a political astuteness that seemed instinctive he added an intimate knowledge of politics that was the result of laborious study. No president since the first Roosevelt had understood so well the mysteries of public opinion nor appealed to it so successfully. He developed his own technique and machinery for charting the temperature of that opinion, and the thousands of letters that poured into the White House daily— it took a staff of 150 to keep track of them—afforded him an insight into the popular mind that no previous executive had enjoyed. The radio had been available since 1920, but Roosevelt invented the "Fireside Chat"; the press had bedeviled many previous administrations, but though three-fourths of the newspapers of the country were hostile to his administration, his numerous press conferences were a series of minor triumphs. To fight the stereotypes of his critics he created stereotypes of his own, and not even the first Roosevelt had displayed a comparable talent for coining words and phrases that caught the public imagination: New Deal, good-neighbor policy, lend-lease, Four Freedoms, arsenal of democracy, and a dozen others.

It was in the domestic arena that Roosevelt first revealed the scope and depth, the adaptability and resilience, of his political philosophy. The demands of the world scene differed quantitatively rather than qualitatively from those of the domestic, and it was because public opinion recognized this that it held Roosevelt to his post for a third and a fourth term. In dealing with both the philosophical and the overt challenge of totalitarianism, he displayed those same qualities of idealism and resourcefulness, that same mastery of politics and of public opinion, that same sense of the limitless potentialities of a dynamic democracy, that same inventiveness, that had marked his war on the depression. The idealism owed much to Wilson, under whom he had served for eight years, but the hardheaded realism and the imaginative audacity that recognized danger and prepared to meet it, that organized industry and science to the demands of war, that contrived the destroyer-bases deal and lend-lease, that anticipated military requirements by peacetime conscription, that directed the building of the largest navy and the best-equipped army in all history, was largely personal. Yet it was personal only in the sense that the president represents the moral and intellectual resources and symbolizes the character of the people. In a larger sense the greater political acumen with which the American people fought the second than the first World War is a measure of the triumph of those political principles and techniques which for almost half a century had been soliciting their approval.

If American political thought and conduct were to be judged by the history of the Roosevelt administrations, the verdict must of necessity be favorable. Confronted by two major crises, the depression and war, the American people showed themselves resourceful, mature, and magnanimous. They were not persuaded by economic disaster to abandon traditional principles in favor of plausible expedients, nor did the exigencies of war seduce them into fundamental alteration of their governmental system or any serious impairment of those liberties which that system was designed to guard. Faced with the necessity of a rapid expansion of governmental powers and a strengthening of governmental authority, they discovered in their Constitution an unexpected flexibility, and if the result pained a Justice Butler or a Justice McReynolds, it would not have alarmed a Marshall or a Story. During the stress of battle against depression and against foreign enemies, when the first claim on their energies was that of survival, they restored their natural resources and repaired their physical plant, gave security to elements of society heretofore exposed to the vicissitudes of the business cycle, modernized the federal system, improved and perfected the machinery of government, embarked upon far-reaching experiments in social and economic planning, raised standards of living for the people as a whole, expanded democracy, furnished new and more realistic bases to liberty, responded imaginatively to appeals to their generosity and their power, and embraced, willingly enough, new international responsibilities. The principles which inspired and guided this course of conduct were deep rooted and familiar; the successful application of those principles to circumstances that were unfamiliar and complex was an achievement which compared favorably with that of any earlier generation in American history.

CHAPTER XVII

The Evolution of American Law

I

AMERICANS INHERITED their law as they inherited their language and their political institutions. But where, with most institutions, inheritance was speedily modified by environment to produce something characteristically American, law successfully resisted environmental modification. Although in language or religion or the social structure, for example, Americanization meant acceleration of the evolutionary process, liberalization, and democratization, in law it meant arrested evolution and even reaction. Resourceful and ingenious in politics, Americans were content in the legal field to abide by familiar formulas. "It is revolting," Oliver Wendell Holmes was to write in 1897, "to have no better reason for a rule of law than that so it was laid down in the time of Henry IV," but for a century American judges, most of them trained in black-letter law, had found it not revolting but eminently proper. It came in time to seem something of an anomaly that American judges had abandoned so early the powdered wig of the eighteenth century.

In the realm of private law Americans took over the common law, and in the realm of public law the natural law. By the time of American independence the common law, itself the product of a long evolutionary process, had hardened into rigid, intricate, and artificial forms; and the growth of equity, designed to remedy the palpable inadequacies of the common law, was slow. It was no wonder that Federalists like Kent and Story and their successors should have found the common law congenial or that Jefferson should have thought it so pernicious that he fought, successfully, to deny common law jurisdiction to the federal courts and unsuccessfully to exclude Blackstone from his University of Virginia; nor was it remarkable that frontier communities should have regarded it with hostility and departed from it so frequently. "Ignorance is the best of law reformers," Justice Holmes said, and where the force of tradition was weak, professional standards low, and judges and lawyers ignorant, law was often confused with justice or common sense. The advance of civilization into successive frontiers, the weight of tradition, and the improvement of professional standards put an end to this scandal; and legal erudition, guided by such scholars as Nathan Dane and James Kent and Joseph Story, prided itself on preserving intact the anachronisms and mysteries of the common law.

The doctrines of natural law which were transferred to America were those dominant in England and on the Continent throughout the seventeenth and eighteenth centuries and given authoritative form by the great Blackstone. By the close of the eighteenth century, however, they were already suspect, and their sovereignty was shortly to be challenged and overthrown by the school of historical jurisprudence. But, transplanted to America, they took root and flourished; institutionalized in state and federal constitutions, they took on not only sanctity but permanence. Of all the social sciences, law retained longest its Newtonian character, resisted most successfully the impact of evolution and economic realism. The intellectual lag persisted into the twentieth century: as late as the mid-1930's Justice McReynolds could assert that the exercise of sovereign power over money and currency was a violation of natural law and Justice Roberts could subscribe, in the AAA case, to the purely mechanical theory of judicial review, alleging that when a court nullifies an act of Congress all it does is "to lay the article of the Constitution which is invoked beside the statute which is challenged and to decide whether the latter squares with the former."

The strength and persistence of natural law concepts is one of the most arresting phenomena in American intellectual history, but it is not inexplicable. Americans inherited those concepts in the eighteenth century, found them wonderfully useful in the struggle against Parliamentary pretensions, and wove them into their own constitutional fabric as a matter of course. The neat formulas of a ready-made system of law, symmetrical in appearance and mechanical in operation, fitted well enough the simple needs of an eighteenth-century society and furnished a convenient solution to what seemed the most pressing of all constitutional problems—the establishment of effective limitations on government. Their precepts erected into constitutional dogma and their authoritative interpretation entrusted to the least democratic branch of the government, they resisted all but judicial modification and frustrated all but extraconstitutional evolution. Their constitutional form gave them sanctity and invested them with a certain immunity from criticism, and the judicial gloss with which judges annotated them shared something of that sanctity: in time criticism of the natural law doctrines which judges read into the Constitution came to be looked upon as an assault upon the Constitution itself. No system of law was better fitted to restrict government to negative functions, to put property rights on a par with human rights, or to invest existing economic practices with legal sanction; and from the beginning the dominant forces of American economy gravitated to the support of natural law: slavery, corporations, and industrial capitalism. It was no accident that corporations should early take refuge in a natural law interpretation of the contract clause, that slavery should find protection in the natural law limitations of the due process clause, and that, after the Civil War, capitalism—speaking through corporation lawyers—should persuade the Court to read into the Fourteenth Amendment natural law restrictions upon the police power of the States.

Along with conservatism in law went veneration for the Law—a veneration which was enjoyed vicariously by its high priests and oracles and even by its acolytes. Americans alone of western peoples made constitutionalism a religion and the judiciary a religious order and surrounded both with an aura of piety. They made the Constitution supreme law, and placed responsibility for the functioning of the federal system upon courts. The Supreme Court, in time, became the most nearly sacrosanct of American institutions—became to Americans what the Royal Family was to the British, the Army to the Germans, the Church to the Spaniards. Criticism was sometimes acrimonious but rarely disrespectful. In the mid-1930's, when conservatives were exhausting the vocabulary of billingsgate against the chief executive, those who criticized the Supreme Court were regarded as tainted with un-Americanism, and the most instructive lesson to be drawn from Franklin Roosevelt's fight for judicial reform was to be found in the outpouring of quasireligious devotion to the Court which the hearings of the Senate Judiciary Committee evoked.

It was not a little curious that a people reputedly lawless should confess by their attitudes and their conduct the deepest respect for the Law, and that a people who had rejected alike the divine right of Kings and the unlimited power of legislatures should throw over their courts an aura of divinity and permit them the exercise of ultimate authority. The courts are, to be sure, creatures of the political branches, but they are creatures who grew more powerful than their creators; judicial review, required neither by law nor by logic except as a harmonizer of the federal system, was sustained and exalted by public opinion. In the United States alone of western nations the courts became the ultimate arbiters of political questions, and great issues of public policy were exposed to the hazards of private litigation. In the midst of the Civil War, the right of the president to resist disunion and treason was submitted to the judiciary and sustained by only five votes to four; in the midst of one depression, the right to impose income taxes—a right enjoyed by every other sovereign nation—was denied, and in the midst of another, authority to fix minimum wages, to bring order out of the chaos of the coal industry, and to establish a system of social security, all hinged on the outcome of private suits. Nowhere else except in Alice's Wonderland could a comparable situation be found. Yet so great was the respect for Law and for the Courts that public opinion not only tolerated this situation but took it for granted and even found in it cause for gratification. That "the Court will decide" became one of the axioms of American politics, acquiesced in even by legislative bodies who willingly abdicated their constitutional function in deference to the more powerful branch of the government.

Reverence for the law manifested itself in illuminating ways. It found expression in the tendency to substitute constitutional for political considerations in the formulation of policy—to discuss all questions in the vocabulary of the law, enmesh all problems in cobwebs of legal technicalities, and judge legislation by abstract standards of constitutionality rather than by pragmatic standards of wisdom or expediency. It dictated the emphasis placed upon the observation of precedent. *Stare decisis* was defensible on the ground that certainty in the law is more important than justice, but not even in England were precedents studied so religiously or cited so frequently as in the United States, and even in the realm of constitutional law, where the doctrine of *stare decisis* was never formally accepted, the most enlightened judges felt themselves bound by earlier decisions to vote against their own reason. It justified the tolerance for what

Dean Pound has called the etiquette of justice—the delays, the technicalities, the ritual and ceremony, the mysteries of procedure, and the respect for the record. It helped explain the almost lawless passion for lawmaking: only a people confident that the solution to all problems was to be found in laws could enact so many of them, and if Americans no more expected their laws to be enforced than they expected their religion to be applied, it was as comforting to them to know that the laws were on the statute book as to know that the churches were open every Sunday.

The American attitude toward law in general was transferred, somewhat naïvely, to international law. Because the American federal system was, in interesting respects, an international one, the subject had from the beginning commanded American interest, and Wheaton had early made distinguished contributions to the study of international law and Story to the complex problem of conflict of laws. No other people appeared so confident of the power of law to preserve peace or were so zealous in contriving machinery for the control of international relations. The confidence, and the zeal, can be read in the enunciation of the Open Door policy and in the various treaties, declarations, and agreements for the preservation of the integrity of China which proved, in the end, so futile. It can be read in Bryan's numerous cooling-off treaties; in Wilson's policy of non-recognition of governments that rested upon violence, his devotion to the "fine fabric" of international law, and his Fourteen Points; in the Kellogg Peace Pact with its slightly premature renunciation of war as an instrument of national policy; and even in the neutrality legislation of the 1930's whereby Americans tried to talk themselves out of foreign involvements. Faith in the validity and efficacy of legal guarantees was creditable to the American character; when it took the form of gullibility, it was less creditable to the American intelligence. Creditable or discreditable, it was part of the larger pattern of American legal thought.

If it cannot be said that lawyers inspired veneration, it will not be denied that they commanded respect and exercised power. Hostility to lawyers had appeared in every community, at one time or another, and regularly in frontier communities: before the Revolution the Regulators of North Carolina had protested that "lawyers, Clerks, and other pensioners, in place of being obsequious Servants for the Country's use, are become a nuisance," and a generation later Kentucky boasted an anti-Court party. But more remarkable than the persistence of hostility toward lawyers was the regularity with which it was overcome. Where titles to land were unsettled, lawyers were essential; where an agricultural economy was being transformed into a commercial, lawyers were prosperous; where the interpreta· tion of the Constitution was judicial, lawyers were dignified. "In America," wrote the astute Tocqueville in the 1830's, "lawyers form the highest political class and the most cultivated circle of society. . . . If I were asked where I would place the American aristocracy I should reply without hesitation that it is not composed of the rich . . . but that it occupies the judicial bench and bar."

The dignity, prosperity, and influence of the legal profession is one of the most striking phenomena of American culture. Surely in no other country have lawyers occupied a comparable position or played a comparable role. All but some ten American presidents were exposed, in varying degrees, to legal training, and of those customarily thought great only Washington and the first Roosevelt were wholly without benefit of law. In the first century of the history of the Republic, Judge Dillon has estimated, some two thirds of all Senators, over one half of all Representatives, and more than half of all state governors were lawyers. It is not without interest that during the Civil War the Secretary of War was a lawyer and the Secretary of the Navy had studied law; that during World War I the Secretary of War was drawn from the ranks of the law; and that in World War II Secretaries Stimson and Patterson of the War Department and Forrestal of the Navy were all lawyers. A comparison with English cabinet ministers for comparable periods would be illuminating.

Nowhere has the law been more faithfully cultivated, nowhere more assiduously studied. The Law School, like the constitutional lawyer, is an American institution, and no British or Continental university gives the training in law that a score of American universities provide as a matter of course. At a time when Sydney Smith was asking who read an American book, Joseph Story was recognized as the greatest legal scholar in the English-speaking world, and whatever may be the judgment on American scholarship in general, no one familiar with the *Harvard Law Review* and the *Yale Law Journal* can doubt that in those fields of legal scholarship which are not antiquarian America is pre-eminent.

It is a tribute to the position of the lawyer that no other profession has inspired such a literature, or such a mythology, as the legal. Lawyers are legendary characters, their careers and their arguments the very stuff of folklore: who does not know how Marshall invoked his jurisdiction over the whole United States to justify bringing out the Madeira; how Lincoln summoned the moonlight to clear a client from the charge of murder; how Webster outargued the Devil himself? The glories of the law are celebrated in a hundred volumes on the Bench and Bar, but who ever heard of volumes on the clergy or the teachers or the architects of Franklin County?

As lawyers took over politics and, to a large extent, business, so legal ideas and attitudes permeated most aspects of American thought. What Tocqueville observed in the 1830's was equally true a century later:

Scarcely any question arises in the United States which does not become, sooner or later, a subject of judicial debate; hence all parties are obliged to borrow the ideas, and even the language, usual in judicial proceedings in their daily controversies. As most public men are, or have been, legal practitioners, they introduce the customs and technicalities of their profession into the affairs of the country. . . . The language of the law thus becomes, in some measure, a vulgar tongue . . . the spirit of the law gradually penetrates beyond their walls into the bosom of society, where it descends to the lowest classes, so that the whole people contracts the habits and tastes of the magistrate.

This influence, so pervasive and so powerful, was, naturally enough, a force for conservatism, for law is by its very nature conservative, and most of its disciples gladly share its nature. Again the insight of Tocqueville—himself, it should be remembered, a magistrate—was prophetic. "It must not be forgotten," he wrote of lawyers, "that if they prize the free institutions of their country much, they nevertheless value the legality of those institutions far more; they are less afraid of tyranny than of arbitrary power." The invention by the legal fraternity of the fiction of liberty of contract—a fiction designed to safeguard the right of working men and women to contract for any hours, wages, and conditions that they saw fit to accept; the diversion of the Fourteenth Amendment, and especially of its due process clause, from its original purpose of protecting the rights of freedmen to its derivative purpose of protecting the rights of corporations; the hostility of the legal profession to almost every item of social welfare legislation from the income tax and tenement house reform to workmen's compensation and minimum wages, is a familiar story. From the days of Jefferson's "assault on the judiciary" to Franklin Roosevelt's "court-packing" plan, almost every liberal has found it necessary to attack the misuse of the judicial prerogative, and almost every reform movement has included some measure designed to curb judicial pretensions.

2

The doctrines of natural law were deeply rooted, plausible, and tenacious. They derived from Greek and Roman philosophy, were fortified by medieval Christianity, and vindicated by Newtonian science; tested in the crucible of seventeenth-century English and eighteenth-century American revolutions, they appeared to justify themselves. Intellectually their appeal was almost irresistible, for they taught that law was rooted in the very nature of things, articulated to the framework of the universe, and expressive of the will of God, that it operated with the mathematical certainty of the axioms of Euclid, and that conformity to it was a duty of Reason. Emotionally, too, their appeal was persuasive. They offered a formula at once simple and conclusive and asserted the harmony of man with the universe; in a world of change they provided permanence, and in a world of disorder security.

The Fathers of the Revolution and of the Constitution embraced the tenets of natural law as a matter of course. A generation trained on the classics could quote Aristotle's definition of law as "reason unaffected by desire" and Cicero's conclusion that "law is the highest reason implanted in nature, which commands what ought to be and forbids the opposite." A generation which drew inspiration for its own Revolution from the deep wells of seventeenth-century English philosophy was familiar with that long line of argument from Harrington and Coke, Milton and Locke, which held that Nature had set impassable bounds to the ambitions of rulers and that, in the words of Hobbes, though

Princes succeed one another, and one judge passeth, another cometh; nay heaven and earth shall pass, but not one tittle of the law of nature shall pass, for it is the eternal law of God.

A generation still deeply imbued with Puritanism knew that religion itself dictated conformity to the laws of Nature, for, as Jonathan Mayhew put it, "God himself does not govern in an absolutely arbitrary and despotic manner. The power of this Almighty King is limited by law—by the eternal laws of truth, wisdom, and equity, and the everlasting tables of right reason." A generation which read the *Commentaries* of Blackstone recalled that "upon the law of nature and the law of revelation depend all human laws; that is to say, no human laws should be suffered to contradict these," and rejoiced that the laws of England, happily transferred to America, were patterned on the laws of nature. A generation bathed in the Enlightenment pledged its lives, its fortunes, and its sacred honor to the conviction that the laws of Nature and Nature's God required American independence and justified faith in the unalienable rights of life, liberty, and the pursuit of happiness. It was not surprising that Americans wrote natural law into their constitutions, enshrined it in their Bills of Rights, and pronounced it from their judicial tribunals.

According to the philosophy of natural law, laws are discovered, not made. They are deduced from the nature of things rather than patterned on the needs of man. In the first half of the nineteenth century, under the impulse of new forces of nationalism and under the leadership of men like Savigny in Germany and Sir Henry Maine and James Stephen in England, natural law gave way to historical jurisprudence. The change seemed important, but its importance was quantitative rather than qualitative, a shift in the point of departure rather than in the conclusion. For the historical school, too, held that law was discovered, not made. If it no longer found law in the reverent contemplation of nature, it read it, no less reverently, from a contemplation of the past. And if the principles that emerged from this inquiry were no longer held to be of universal validity, their validity for the particular people or nation which had produced them was no less compelling. It is an interesting question whether more was not lost by the abandonment of the principle of universality, however fictitious, than was gained by the capitulation to the forces of particularism, however compulsive.

Historical jurisprudence was evolution applied to law, but it was not an evolution which afforded grounds for a belief in progress or which left room for reform. It was rather like that Spencerian version of evolution which condemned human institutions to the slow and inexorable processes of natural determinism: it merely substituted history for nature. From the sound argument that law was a product of a long historical process the historians drew the unsound conclusion that it could be nothing else. They found law in the slow processes of history and tradition, in the customs and habits of peoples, in the *Volkgeist* and the *Zeitgeist*. Legislation, they held, could at best explain and elaborate law, it could not alter it, and they were inclined to look upon legislators as lay intruders into sacred mysteries. Their evolution was pre-Huxleyan and left no room for the interposition of human intelligence; it was pre-Mendelian and made no allowances for sports. It was not progressive but static and even reactionary.

Instead of being revolted to find the reason for a law that "so it was laid down in the reign of Henry IV," the historians were gratified to find an antecedent so respectable. They delighted in precedents, in the religious observation of old forms and customs, in the study of black-letter law, and they preserved reverentially the barbarous Latin and French terminology and the anachronistic "words and phrases" that baffled the layman and confounded the logician: in the mid-twentieth century, students still looked up labor law under the heading "master and servant." Like the disciples of natural law the historians took refuge in abstractions, only theirs were the abstractions of Society, Custom, and History rather than the Cosmic Processes.

3

So strong was the hold of natural law on the American imagination that historical jurisprudence penetrated only slowly, and when it came it rather merged with natural law than supplanted it. It is suggestive that though in such men as John Adams and James Wilson, John Marshall and Edward Livingston, America produced natural law jurists who compared favorably with their English and Continental contemporaries, there was no American Savigny. Nor did historical jurisprudence, when it came, follow the familiar Continental and British pattern of nationalism. For there was, in fact, no American legal past to explore, no corpus of practices and traditions to mold into customary law: though American legal scholarship has been both profound and prodigious, no Maitland or Holdsworth has yet written a history of American law. Of necessity the American historians turned to the common law, cultivating the rich fields of English rather than the supposedly barren fields of the American past. Except on the frontier, and among radicals like Jefferson, the political break with the Mother Country did not involve even strained relations among the jurists; the law retained its colonial status long after language and literature, religion and education, architecture and painting, had announced their independence.

Joseph Story best illuminated the transition from natural to historical law. He was, no less than Marshall, a product of the age of reason, and he knew that there were "eternal principles of right and justice" which controlled legislative authority and dictated judicial opinions. But he was, too, a man of massive learning, a scholar almost by instinct, an antiquarian by inclination, and he was rarely willing to content himself with those exercises in logic that satisfied his brother Marshall. His monumental opinions were grounded on Nature and constructed of rugged blocks hewn from the quarries of History. Where, for example, in the Dartmouth College case Marshall confined himself to general principles, proceeding imperially from unsound assumptions that seemed plausible to misleading conclusions that seemed irrefutable, Story rested his case on a formidable body of historical antecedents, ransacking history to prove the immunity of charitable foundations from public control. This was not a singular instance of an opinion which was an historical treatise: *De Lovio* vs. *Boit,* for example, was the most exhaustive treatment of admiralty jurisdiction which had been written up to that time. It was entirely natural that the scholar who compiled twenty volumes of *Commentaries* that were like judicial opinions should have written opinions that were like commentaries. Like the Continental historians, Story was both a conservative and a nationalist. His consciousness of the place of precedent, custom, and tradition made for a conservatism which became, in time, mere petulance. But it made, too, for an appreciation of the importance of historical processes which, in the field of politics, was to be profoundly constructive. Conservatism would have triumphed even without Story's contributions, but the triumph of nationalism owes much to his awareness of the creative force of history.

Historical jurisprudence left less scope for public contributions than natural law, for whereas the laws of nature could be read by any reasonable man, the laws of history were to be deciphered only by the initiated. Under its auspices the gap between the layman and the lawyer broadened steadily: law became more scholarly but less philosophical, more specialized but less humane; it became increasingly a private thing, the exclusive province of the jurisprudent, remote from reality, living upon itself and upon its past. The professional view was admirably expressed by E. J. Phelps, in 1879 president of the American Bar Association: the Constitution, he asserted, belonged to the bench and the bar, not to the people. It was not a proper subject for political discussion; it was too sacred to be "hawked about the country, debated in the newspapers, discussed from the stump, elucidated by pot-house politicians and dunghill editors, or by scholars . . . who have never found leisure for the grace of English grammar or the embellishment of correct spelling."

Perhaps the best representative of the school of historical jurisprudence during the transition years of the end of the century was James Coolidge Carter, eminent corporation lawyer and author of a once popular but now universally unread study of *Law, Its Origins, Growth and Function.* Law, Carter held, is a series of rules growing out of customs and experience and found and applied by judges. An esoteric subject, its discovery and application was best left to judges experienced in the business. Writing a decade after Judge Holmes had pointed out that "the very considerations which judges most rarely mention, and always with an apology, are the secret roots from which the law draws all the juices of life. I mean, of course, considerations of what is expedient for the community concerned," Mr. Carter put Holmes in his place. "That the judge cannot make law," he said, "is accepted at the start."

That there is already existing a rule of law by which the case must be determined is not doubted. . . . It is agreed that the true rule must somehow be found. Judge and advocate, all together, engage in the search. Cases more or less nearly approaching the one in controversy are adduced. Analogies are referred to. The customs and habits of men are appealed to. Principles already settled as fundamental are invoked and run out to their consequences; and finally a rule is deduced which is declared to be the one which the existing law requires to be applied to the case. In this the things which are plain and palpable are, 1, that the whole process consists in a *search* to find a rule; 2, that the rule thus sought for is the *just* rule—that is the rule most in accordance with the sense of justice of those engaged in the search; 3, that it is tacitly assumed that the sense of justice is the same in all those who are thus engaged; 4, that the field of search is the habits, customs, business and manners of the people, and those previously declared rules which have sprung out of previous similar inquiries into habits, customs, business, and manners. (Carter, *The Ideal and the Actual in Law,* pp. 10–11)

There was nothing here about considerations of public policy or of expediency but merely a restatement of the hackneyed doctrines of natural law and historical jurisprudence. A somewhat less eminent practitioner of the law, but one who was more familiar with considerations of expediency, put the matter even more succinctly. Writing in 1919, the year before he won a famous victory over the Boston police, Calvin Coolidge pointed out that "Men do not make laws. They do but discover them. That state is most fortunate in its form of government which has the aptest instruments for the discovery of law."

That was the year after *Hammer* vs. *Dagenhart* and the year of *Abrams* vs. *United States,* two cases in which the Supreme Court showed how it operated as "the aptest instrument for the discovery of law." In the first the Court discovered that the commerce clause of the Constitution did not authorize congressional regulation of the shipment of products of child labor in interstate commerce; a quarter-century later the Court discovered that it did. In the second case the Court discovered that the Bill of Rights did not protect an agitator who expressed unorthodox opinions in wartime; with the subsequent adoption of Justice Holmes's clear and present danger test, this discovery, too, was repudiated. It was all very confusing to those who subscribed to Calvin Coolidge's neat theory of mechanical jurisprudence or to James Coolidge Carter's doctrine that there already existed some rule of law which implacably determined what judges were required to decide.

For half a century the courts, under the leadership of jurists like Field and Brewer and Sutherland and of lawyers like Carter and Choate and Depew, abandoned themselves to delusions of mechanical jurisprudence, interpreting the Constitution as a prohibition rather than an instrument, reading into it limitations on the scope of governmental authority which existed only as abstract conclusions of natural law syllogisms. Insisting that they were without discretion and that their functions were purely mechanical and phonographic, judges struck down literally hundreds of state police laws on the theory that they deprived somebody of property or of liberty of contract without due process of law. Two characteristics distinguished most of these decisions. First, they assumed that the provisions of the Constitution were axiomatic, inflexible, and crystal clear, and that the judges were the only persons competent to find those provisions and to apply them to particular cases. Second, they held that whenever social or economic facts conflicted with the theoretical assumptions of natural law, the facts must give way to the assumptions. For though judges acknowledged readily enough that, notwithstanding the alleged clarity of the Constitution, neither property nor liberty nor due process could be defined, they preferred their own Newtonian definitions to the pragmatic definitions of legislative bodies.

The triumph of mechanical concepts in the juristic arena coincided with the triumph of dynamic progressivism in the political. The result was a conflict which increasingly exacerbated the relations between the political and judicial branches of the government and between the various parts of the federal system and all but brought political evolution and experimentation to a standstill. Put in political terms, the conflict was between conservative courts and progressive legislatures with the courts exercising the veto power. Put in legal terms, it was one between the commerce power of the federal government and the police power of the states, on the one hand, and the due process clauses of the Fifth and Fourteenth Amendments, reinforced by some dependence on the Tenth Amendment, on the other, with the judiciary enjoying the privilege of ultimate interpretation.

That the courts exercised that privilege cannot be doubted by anyone familiar with the judicial record from the mid-1880's to the 1930's. For four or five decades the political field was strewn with the corpses of social welfare laws struck down by judicial weapons. The story is too familiar to justify rehearsal in detail and examples are pertinent only as they illustrate the hold that natural law and historical concepts had on the judicial mind. A Pennsylvania act forbidding the payment of workers with orders on company stores was voided as an "infringement on natural inherent rights and an insulting attempt to put the laborer under a legislative tutelage," and the West Virginia court, confronted by a similar act, held that "the evil was in the hands of the employee since he is not compelled to buy from the employer." A New York act fixing the hours of labor of municipal contracts was struck down because it "created a class of statutory laborers," and a Colorado act regulating hours in the smelting industry was voided as an interference with labor's liberty of contract. The New York Supreme Court nullified an act forbidding manufacture in tenement houses because it could not "perceive how the cigarmaker is to be improved in his health or morals by forcing him from his home and its hallowed associations and beneficent influences to ply his trade elsewhere." An Illinois court struck down a statute limiting the hours of labor for women in sweatshops on the ground that women had the same liberty of contract as men, and a New York court, faced with a sixty-hour law for women in industry, held that it was "discriminative against female citizens in denying them equal rights with men in the same pursuit" and "an arbitrary interference with the right of an adult female from working at any time of the day that suits her." An Ohio ordinance providing allowances to the indigent blind was nullified on the ground that "innumerable cases may clamor for similar bounties, and it is doubted that any line could be drawn short of an equal distribution of property." The New York Supreme Court voided a workmen's compensation law because it "did nothing to conserve the health, safety or morals of employees." And it was a New York court, too, which in voiding a sixty-hour week for labor in bakeshops on the ground that bakers were competent to make their own contracts, provoked Justice Holmes's famous retort that "the Fourteenth Amendment does not enact Mr. Herbert Spencer's *Social Statics*." The observation has been frequently quoted, but it has not been sufficiently remarked that at the time he spoke Justice Holmes was obviously wrong.

CHAPTER XVIII

Masters of the New Jurisprudence: Pound and Holmes

I

THE CONFLICT between fixed, mechanical concepts of law and dynamic, progressive ideas in politics could not be resolved save by masters of a new type of jurisprudence. Driven forward by inexorable social and economic forces, the progressive movement could not give way, except temporarily, nor could it fulfill itself without imposing far-reaching readjustments upon the legal mechanics of economy. It was law, therefore, which was required to accept a modified character; and the men who were to be chiefly instrumental in achieving that modification—Oliver Wendell Holmes Roscoe Pound, and Louis Brandeis—were all fully enlisted in the public service by the turn of the century. When on December 5 1902, Holmes alighted from his train in Washington, he had been a judge of the Massachusetts Supreme Judicial Court for almost precisely twenty years. When, three days later, he took the oath a Justice of the Federal Supreme Court, a new chapter opened in the history of that tribunal and—as we can now see—in the history of American constitutional law.

For Holmes recognized, as did Brandeis and Pound, that though natural rights and historical theories of law were entertained by judges who assumed vast responsibilities, the theories themselves were literally irresponsible. Natural law was automatic, mechanical and impersonal and left to jurists only the duty of discovery—in theory, at least, a purely clerical duty. Historical law was determinate and derivative and afforded jurists merely the satisfaction of exercise in erudition. Neither had any logical place for the imagination or for creative activity. By a resort to the principles of natural and historical law, judges could, and did, evade responsibility; and when they voided legislative acts of which they disapproved, they generally accompanied the nullification with the confession that they had no choice in the matter. Thus the most humane judges could strike down laws providing compensation for the victims of industry or prohibiting child labor or a sixty-hour week for women in factories with a clear conscience, reassuring themselves that they were but impersonal agents of an impersonal mechanism. Like the corporate form in business, the natural rights doctrine was a perfect vehicle for concentrating power and dissipating responsibility.

"More than anything else," wrote Roscoe Pound in 1923, "the theory of natural rights and its consequence, the nineteenth century theory of legal rights, served to cover up what the legal order really was and what court and lawmaker and judge really were doing." But it was a fictitious cover, and as with the Emperor's new clothes, the fiction was transparent to the eye of the realist. For law could not permanently lag behind the other social sciences, nor could it be allowed indefinitely to short-circuit the powerhouse of governmental operations. It was, for all its isolation, subject to the same currents of thought that played so boisterously upon such disciplines as economics, sociology, and politics, and if it was immune from political controls it was not immune from intellectual.

The revolt against mechanistic doctrines in law, like that against mechanistic doctrines in the other social sciences, was a revolt from forms to functions, from concepts to activities, from statics to dynamics, from individual ends to social ends, from the satisfaction of intellectual ideals to the satisfaction of human wants. It sought to rescue law from the tyranny of the past and give it to the present, to rescue it from the dead and give it to the living. It asserted that law was made for man and required it to conform to the needs and wants—and even the vagaries—of man. It challenged at once the arrogance and the irresponsibility of jurists who regarded themselves as above the battle and yet, like the gods of Greek mythology, descended from time to time to enter the fray.

The challenge was, in fact, an old one, but not until the turn of the century did it achieve some degree of respectability. Then, as courts played hob with progressive legislation, support to the nonconformists who had grown hoarse in heresy came from a group of brilliant scholars and publicists—the saturnine Thorstein Veblen; the congenital rebel, Brooks Adams; the gifted J. Allen Smith who had inspired Vernon Parrington; the gallant and forgotten Frank Parsons; the vitriolic Gustavus Myers; the learned Richard Ely; and his versatile colleague, John Commons. These attacks, tainted as they were with secularism and inspired more often than not by economic rancor, might be discounted by the high priests of jurisprudence; not so the sober criticism that came from within the temple itself.

In this criticism Oliver Wendell Holmes led the way—Holmes, whose thought was a generation ahead of his time but whose brilliant insights and profound wisdom were so rarely systematized. "The life of the law," he said in 1880—young Louis Brandeis and Brooks Adams in the audience—

has not been logic; it has been experience. The felt necessities of the time, the prevalent moral and political theories, intuitions of public policy, avowed or unconscious, even the prejudices which judges share with their fellow-men, have had a good deal more to do than the syllogism in determining the rules by which men should be governed.

What Holmes announced in the *Common Law* he was shortly to pronounce from the bench. As he conferred not only respectability but distinction on any doctrine, his elegantly phrased heresies were soon echoed by others no less learned and scarcely less illustrious: interestingly enough, they were all but officially adopted by the law school where Joseph Story had taught the doctrines of natural law and Luther Cushing spread the gospel of Savigny. Thus the great James Bradley Thayer, who knew everything there was to know about constitutional law, attacked both the principles and the practice of judicial review and warned that judges were stepping into the shoes of the lawmakers; thus his no less learned colleague, John Chipman Gray—who decided that there was no such thing as constitutional law—said resolutely that "the law is made up of the rules for decision which the Courts lay down," and that the law of the United States is "the opinions of half a dozen old gentlemen." When a third Harvard professor, Joseph H. Beale, went out to organize the University of Chicago law school, he called to its faculty a young scholar trained at Heidelberg and Berlin, Ernst Freund: two years later Freund justified the appointment with a remarkable analysis of *The Police Power* which elaborated and vindicated the intuitions of Holmes.

2

It remained, however, for a son of the Middle Border, a Cantabrigian only by adoption, to formulate systematically that whole body of progressive legal thought which the historians, economists, psychologists, and jurists of the previous generation had advanced in fragmentary—or polemical—form, to augment it with contributions from Continental scholarship, to fortify it with his own prodigious erudition, and to illuminate it with his liberal and catholic spirit. Roscoe Pound grew to maturity in Bryan's Nebraska, and, if he never shared the Great Commoner's fatal tendency to oversimplification of legal as well as political problems, he shared something of his social sympathies and something, too, of his humane realism. He practiced law for a decade before he taught it and knew from experience that the administration and enforcement of the law were as important as the doctrines and philosophies entertained about it. He studied at the Harvard Law School under Thayer and Gray and taught at Northwestern with Wigmore and at Chicago with Freund and Veblen and Dewey. When he went to Harvard to occupy the chair which bore the great Story's name, he carried in his intellectual luggage not only as vast a store of legal learning as any scholar of his generation but a fully matured philosophy of the law, and for almost forty years he elaborated and refined that philosophy in the most original and provocative series of books and essays that have come from the pen of any American jurisprudent. If he did not create sociological jurisprudence—and credit for that belongs properly to Ihering, Durkheim, Duguit, and Ehrlich, and even to Holmes—he took out an American copyright on it and then devoted the copyright to public use. His scholarship uncovered the whole history of American law, explained its persistent colonialism, and justified expectations of ultimate independence; his ardent mind illuminated every aspect of the law, the philosophical, the historical, and the practical; his imagination envisioned a new kind of law that should draw upon both philosophy and the social sciences, that should be both equitable and humane, that should accommodate itself to the needs of a democratic and liberal people, and set new tasks for coming generations. He belongs, with Ward and Veblen and Dewey, among those scholars who by learning, insight, and intellectual gallantry have transformed American institutions.

To make law an efficient instrument for social reconstruction was the task which Pound set himself. It was no simple task. It required not only the repudiation and discrediting of those concepts which had for so long dominated legal thought and paralyzed legal progress but, more important, the formulation and vindication of new legal concepts and of new techniques to translate those concepts into practices. To the philosophy of law which Pound formulated for these purposes he gave the name "sociological jurisprudence." It was a mouth-filling word, but its meaning was clear enough. Pound himself put it succinctly:

The sociological movement in jurisprudence is a movement for pragma·tism as a philosophy of law; for the adjustment of principles and doctrines to the human conditions they are to govern rather than to assume first principles; for putting the human factor in the central place and relegating logic to its true position as an instrument.

Elsewhere he has spoken of it as a method of social engineering, stressing emphatically its constructive aspects. It is, he has said,

a process, an activity, not merely a body of knowledge or a fixed order of construction. It is a doing of things, not a serving as passive instruments through which mathematical formulas and mechanical laws realize themselves in the eternally appointed way. The engineer is judged by what he does. His work is judged by its adequacy to the purposes for which it is done, not by its conformity to some ideal form of a traditional plan. We are beginning . . . to think of jurist and judge and lawmaker in the same way. We are coming to study the legal order instead of debating as to the nature of law. We are thinking of interests, claims, demands, not of rights; of what we have to secure or satisfy, not exclusively of the institutions by which we have sought to secure or satisfy them, as if those institutions were ultimate things existing for themselves. (*Interpretations of Legal History*, p. 152)

Sociological jurisprudence was, like pragmatism, a method—a new way of thinking about law and of applying it. It was a shift from absolutes to relatives, from doctrines to practices, from passive—and therefore pessimistic—determinism to creative—and therefore optimistic—freedom. How revolutionary that method was, how sharply it broke with the methods of natural and historical and analytical law, is best explained by Pound himself. Speaking in the year Holmes warned against the use of the Fourteenth Amendment "to prevent the making of experiments that an important part of the community desires," he said:

In the last century we studied law from within. The jurists of today are studying it from without. The past century sought to develop completely and harmoniously the fundamental principles which jurists discovered by metaphysics or by history. The jurists of today seek to enable and to compel lawmaking and also the interpretation and application of legal rules, to take more account and more intelligent account, of the social facts upon which law must proceed and to which it is to be applied. Where the last century studied law in the abstract, they insist upon study of the actual social effects of legal institutions and legal doctrines. Where the last century prepared for legislation by study of other legislation analytically, they insist upon sociological study in connection with legal study in preparation for legislation. Where the last century held comparative law the best foundation for wise lawmaking, they hold it not enough to compare the laws themselves, but that even more their social operation must be studied and the effects which they produce, if any, when put in action. Where the last century studied only the making of law, they hold it necessary to study as well the means of making legal rules effective. (*The Spirit of the Common Law*, pp. 212–213)

Sociological jurisprudence was, however, more than a method. It had substance, as well, and an affirmative program. It held that the truth of law, like truth in general, was something to be found through experience, that it was relative, and that it could be created. It asserted that good law was what worked best for society, that law was functional and to be understood in terms of ends rather than origins, and that the actual workings of the law were more important than its abstract legal content. It insisted that law was a social science, dependent upon rather than independent of society, that it should be required to conform to social needs and judged by the degree to which it filled those needs. It pointed out that the life of the law was in its administration and enforcement, that law was not only a prediction of what judges would say but what officers would do, and that administration could be studied empirically. It affirmed that the past had exhausted neither the law nor the inventive and creative capacity of men, that law was a continuous social product, that it was susceptible to continuous improvement and a proper subject for social engineering. It confessed that in the making of law judges played a decisive part, but promised to legal scholars and commentators, to statesmen and administrators, a role scarcely less significant. It maintained, finally, that law was as concerned with the collective social good as with the individual good, that the whole range of social interests, needs, and wants came legitimately within its scope, and that it could not protect personal liberty except as part of a larger social security and liberty.

Sociological jurisprudence was pragmatism, and—for all Pound's generous tributes to his Harvard colleague—it was a pragmatism that owed more to Dewey than to James. It had less tolerance for dissent than had James's version of pragmatism, less room, perhaps, for idiosyncrasy, eccentricity, and nonconformity. It saw law not primarily as a concise body of principles regulating the relationship between the individual and his government but as a sprawling body of practices conditioning the conduct of the individual in his society. It used law not as a shield to safeguard personal rights and liberties but as a cooperative instrument to satisfy social needs. It was a legal philosophy fitted to the realities of social life in an urban order, of economic life in an industrial order, and of political life in an egalitarian order.

The impact of sociological jurisprudence was immediate and far reaching and, it should be added, triumphant. It could be traced in the realm of criminal law, where it shifted attention from the criminal to the crime and ultimately to the social background of crime. It could be seen in the field of administration, where it directed attention to the enforcement rather than the making of law. It could be read in the domain of legal scholarship, which for a generation dedicated itself largely to the elaboration of Roscoe Pound's insights. Its most dramatic, and perhaps its most consequential, results were to be found, however, in the arena of constitutional law, and thus of public policy.

There were, to be sure, anticipations and precedents, for Pound was not the first to protest against mechanical, nor did he invent sociological, jurisprudence. What he did, rather, was to create, especially in the legal profession, a climate of opinion favorable to the reception of sociological doctrines. For, notwithstanding the earlier contributions of Miller, Harlan, Bradley, Moody, and even Holmes himself, it is no great exaggeration to say that sociological jurisprudence was formally introduced to the Supreme Court in 1908, when

Louis Brandeis submitted his brief in the case of *Muller* vs. *Oregon,* and that it was officially recognized as part of constitutional law when the Senate reluctantly confirmed Mr. Brandeis' nomination to that Court. That it was, for many years, a minor part, is confessed by the frequency and vigor of Brandeis' dissents; that in the end it became acceptable and even respectable is clear to anyone familiar with the history of the Court, and of constitutional law, in the decades of the thirties and the forties. Illustrations would require us to thread our way through the labyrinths of constitutional law. It is sufficient, perhaps, to refer to the common-sense reinterpretation of the ancient doctrine of reciprocal tax immunity, the pragmatic attitude toward the vexatious problem of the distinction between interstate and intrastate commerce, the abandonment of the once useful but ultimately misleading doctrine of affectation with a public interest, and the willingness to make the due process clause of the Fourteenth Amendment an instrument for the protection of personal and social liberties rather than for conferring exemptions from social responsibility upon property.

Anticipated by Holmes, championed unceasingly by Brandeis, supported by the muscular Harlan Stone and the eloquent Benjamin Cardozo and the learned Felix Frankfurter, sociological jurispudence became, after the great struggle of 1937, the all but official doctrine of the Court. Responsibility for what may, fairly enough, be called a constitutional revolution is widespread, but only those blind to the realization that ideas are weapons would deny that Roscoe Pound shares with such men as Holmes, Brandeis, and Franklin Roosevelt responsibility for that revolution.

3

"If American law were to be represented by a single figure," said Justice Oliver Wendell Holmes in 1901, "sceptic and worshipper alike would agree without dispute that the figure could be one alone, and that one John Marshall." It was the centenary of Marshall's accession to the Chief Justiceship, and something was to be allowed to the compulsions of the occasion; yet few would have quarreled with the generalization, and Theodore Roosevelt, even then pondering Holmes's appointment to the Supreme Court, feared that this tribute to the great Chief Justice was not sufficiently enthusiastic.

But half a century later it would be rather Holmes himself upon

whose pre-eminence skeptic and worshiper alike would agree. Nor
would the acknowledgment of pre-eminence be limited to the juristic field alone. Holmes was indubitably the greatest jurist that the
English-speaking world produced in two generations, but he was, for
all his dedication to the law, more than a jurist, and his greatness in
the law was a product of greatness of mind and of spirit that encom-
passed more than law. "The law is not the place for the artist or
the poet," he once said, yet he himself was artist and poet as well
as jurist and philosopher. That his was the most distinguished mind
of its time was acknowledged, and to a mind flexible, sophisticated,
and spacious, Holmes joined a character humane, affluent, and magnanimous. If a civilization may be judged by its best rather than by
its average, the career and character of Holmes suggest that American civilization had in two centuries achieved a maturity and distinction which few nations of the Old World could match.

He was, in fact, very much an American product; his roots were
deep-struck and tenacious. "All my names," he wrote in 1861, "desig-
nate families from which I am descended," and he was never unaware of his obligation to the "long pedigree" of Olivers and Wendells
and Holmeses, or to the collateral branches for that matter—the
Quincys and Bradstreets and Jacksons—and during the whole of
his early career he was busy escaping the shadow of his famous
father, that Dr. Holmes whose autocracy was so gentle but so pervasive. The granite boulders and barberry bushes, the maples and
elms and firs of New England had gone into the making of his
character along with many intangibles of New England history and
philosophy. He owed something to the traditions of Puritanism—
his industry, his sense of duty, his emotional thriftiness—and something to the unashamed patriotism of the Revolutionary era: he remembered that the house in which his father was born had been
the headquarters of the Boston Committee of Safety and did not
forget that his grandfather's *Annals of America* had celebrated the
founding of his country as the climax of world history.

There was something in him of the Federalist, and something of
the Transcendentalist, and in this staunch conservative who testified
to the abiding influence of Emerson the two proved not wholly incompatible. Harvard College had set its imprint, and even more
the Harvard Law School where all the great names were familiar
and almost neighborly—Story and Greenleaf and Parsons and Sum-

ner and the others. The sense of *noblesse oblige,* the combination of intellectual fastidiousness with humor, the personal conservatism and social liberalism, the independence and integrity, the love of learning and dislike of pedantry, the saltiness of character and economy of speech, the impatience with nonsense, all stamped him as indubitably Yankee. "A man is bound to be parochial in his practice," he said, "and to give his life and, if necessary, his death for the place where he has his roots." He was not, in fact, parochial in practice, he who loved to "twist the tail of the cosmos," but he gave his life to the place where he had his roots, and chanced death—it was a near thing, too—for his nation.

The Civil War was, after everything that family and birthplace and education represented, the second great experience in Holmes's life, and one that confirmed the moral of the first. Like Lester Ward, Holmes fought through most of the war and was wounded three times: where the wounds Ward suffered were spiritual as well as physical, Holmes bore his like a decoration and recalled them as a sacrament. For seventy years the war was to be part of his conscious, or his subconscious, thought. "Accidents," he once confessed,

may call up the events of the war. You see a battery of guns go by at a trot, and for a moment you are back at White Oak Swamp, or Antietam, or on the Jerusalem Road. You hear a few shots fired in the distance, and for an instant your heart stops as you say to yourself, The Skirmishers are at it, and listen for the long roll of fire from the main line. . . . These and a thousand other events we have known are called up, I say, by accident, and apart from accident, they lie forgotten.

But with Holmes nothing of the war was forgotten. "The generation that carried on the war," he asserted with quiet pride, "has been set aside by its experience," and that experience became a permanent part of his philosophy and his conduct of life, colored his thought, his speech, even his judicial opinions. From it he learned the necessity of belonging to something larger than one's self, of being "part of an unimaginable whole," of sharing the passion and action of his time "at the peril of being judged not to have lived." It taught him that "no man can set himself over against the universe as a rival god, to criticize it or to shake his fist at the skies, but that his meaning is its meaning, his only worth is as part of it, as a humble instrument of the universal power." It brought home to him, by rough experience, the realization that "the universe has in it more than we understand, that the private soldier has not been told the plan of campaign, or even that there is one." It made clear that "our comfortable routine is no eternal necessity of things, but merely a little space of calm in the tempestuous streaming of the world," and that men needed war that they might "always be ready for danger." It dramatized the fact that "life is a roar of bargain and of battle," and that "as long as man dwells upon the globe his destiny is battle, and he has to take the chances of war." It taught him the lesson he did not fail to apply from the bench, that "the final test of this energy is battle in some form—actual war—the crush of Arctic ice—the fight for mastery in the market or the court."

After the war came the law, and Holmes's dedication to the law was as whole souled as any on record. For a decade the most desirable of Boston's young men was out of circulation, and it was not only William James who thought the single-mindedness and the passion a bit excessive. He practiced law, but not enthusiastically or even successfully; he edited Kent's *Commentaries,* and, for a time, the *American Law Review;* above all he read law, read it with concentration and insight, with that ability to penetrate to the very heart of it that was to characterize first *The Common Law* and later the great judicial opinions. "Every calling is great when greatly pursued," he admitted, "but what other gives such scope to realize the spontaneous energy of one's soul? In what other does one plunge so deep in the streams of life, so share its passions, its battles, its despairs, its triumphs?" When he spoke of "our mistress, the Law," it was as medieval poets spoke of their mistress, the Virgin. "When I think on this majestic theme, my eyes dazzle," he said, and added that "if we are to speak of the law as our mistress, we know that she is a mistress only to be wooed with sustained and lonely passion, only to be won by straining all the faculties by which man is likest to a god." That was the way he wooed her; that was the way, in the end, he won her.

For win her he did, and his victory was dramatized first by the publication of *The Common Law* and then by his appointment, within a year, to the Supreme Judicial Court of Massachusetts. Later in life he liked to quote the observation that every great man will reveal what greatness he has before he reaches forty, and he was barely forty when he published *The Common Law*. It was in every respect a notable achievement—as scholarship, as literature, as philosophy, and, not least of all, as prophecy. For in the luminous pages of this modest classic was to be found the legal philosophy which was to be associated, peculiarly, with Holmes's judicial career and which was, in time, to permeate American jurisprudence. Here, already, Holmes announced that the life of law was not logic but experience; that judges consulted too often "their own sentiments and prejudices"; that law was not "some brooding omniscience in the sky" but merely "what the courts will enforce"; that the study of the future was to be economics and sociology rather than the black-letter books; that "considerations of what is expedient" were the secret root from which the law drew the juices of life; that "the first requirement of a sound body of law is that it should correspond with the actual feelings and demands of the community, whether right or wrong"; that law, being a practical thing, "must found itself on actual forces," and "explain the observed course of legislation"; that, in short, "the first call of a theory of law is that it should fit the facts."

For twenty years on the Massachusetts bench, and for thirty on the bench of the Supreme Court of the United States, Holmes elaborated these intuitions and conclusions, sometimes in dissents, increasingly in opinions to which his brothers were forced to subscribe. At first a pathbreaker, he became, in the end, a symbol of juridical orthodoxy, but it was an orthodoxy of his own making. His reputation as a heretic was buried beneath the triumph of his own heresies. And the greatest of his heresies became, in time, the very core of juridical orthodoxy: pragmatism.

Holmes counted himself no disciple of William James; indeed the two men, both heirs of the Puritan and the Transcendental experience, carried on for almost half a century a friendly quarrel. To Holmes, James's habit of "turning down the lights so as to give miracle a chance" was antipathetic, while James, in turn, grew impatient with his friend's tendency to "celebrate mere vital excitement as a protest against humdrum solemnity." Neither, it may be said, was quite fair to the other. Certainly however disdainfully Holmes repudiated pragmatism as a philosophy of life, he accepted it as a philosophy of law. He was the first, and remained the greatest, of legal pragmatists. Basic to his philosophy of law was the principle that law is no finished thing, no absolute, but still in the making; that it derives neither from God nor from Nature, less from history than scholars believed and less from logical analysis than jurists supposed, but largely from experience.

As truth, to Holmes, was merely what he couldn't help believing (or, as he put it elsewhere, the majority vote of that nation that could lick all others) and had therefore no cosmic validity, so law was merely what the courts couldn't help deciding and was similarly innocent of cosmic sanctions. Jurists who believed in natural law seemed to him to be in "that naïve state of mind that accepts what has been familiar and accepted by them as something that must be accepted by all men everywhere." That law was an exercise in logic was a fallacy equally pernicious:

The training of lawyers [he wrote] is a training in logic. The processes of analogy, discrimination, and deduction are those in which they are most at home. The language of judicial decisions is mainly the language of logic. And the logical method and form flatter that longing for certainty and for repose which is in every human mind. But certainty generally is an illusion, and repose is not the destiny of man.

And as for history, it was perhaps his own familiarity with legal scholarship, his own erudition, so massive and so exact, that permitted him to "look forward to a time when the part played by history in the explanation of dogma shall be very small, and instead of ingenious research we shall spend our energy on a study of the ends sought to be attained and the reason for desiring them."

It was in this emphasis on ends, rather than on origins or precedents or mechanics, that Holmes most clearly anticipated pragmatism and what came to be known as sociological jurisprudence. "The real justification of a rule of law," he wrote early in his career, "is that it helps bring about a social end which we desire," and elsewhere he phrased it even more sharply:

The true science of the law does not consist mainly in the theological working out of dogma or a logical development, as in mathematics, or only in a study of it as an anthropological document from the outside; an even more important part consists in the establishment of its postulates from within upon accurately measured social desires.

Judges, frightened by the specter of socialism or imposed upon by the authority of Herbert Spencer or perhaps of Thomas Cooley, had failed adequately to recognize their duty of weighing considerations of social advantage. And as for lawyers, if their training led them habitually to consider more definitely and explicitly the social advantage on which the rule they lay down must be justified, they sometimes would hesitate where now they are confident, and see that really they were taking sides upon debatable and often burning questions.

Although no other jurist saw more clearly that judges and lawyers did, in fact, take sides upon debatable questions, or adapted his philosophy more ingeniously to that insight, Holmes was himself the most eminently judicious of all American judges, the one who distinguished most clearly between private beliefs and public decisions, who tolerated most amiably legislation which he thought folly and experiments which he held futile. For though he had no faith in panaceas or in sudden ruin and little in progress, he was as ready as James himself to welcome experimentation: if he would not turn down the lights to give miracle a chance, he was willing enough to dim judicial authority to give legislation a chance. Though he liked to remind reformers that you could cut down in a few minutes the tree which required a century to grow, he was persuaded that some allowance should be made for human folly. There was nothing in the Constitution, he said, that prevented the people from making fools of themselves, nor did he think that duty had fallen to the courts.

It was for this reason, and not because of any weakness for economic panaceas, that Holmes deplored the use of the Fourteenth Amendment to frustrate experiments in the laboratories of the states and that he was equally tolerant of the vagaries of majorities and the protests of minorities. He had the pragmatist's readiness to give every idea an equal vote and every scheme a fighting chance. As he believed that all life was an experiment he would not withdraw law from life, or even the Constitution, but stoutly insisted that these, too, were but experiments. The most eloquent of his dissents reasserted his faith in that principle:

Our Constitution . . . is an experiment, as all life is an experiment. Every year, if not every day, we have to wager our salvation upon some prophecy based upon imperfect knowledge. While that experiment is part of our system, I think that we should be eternally vigilant against any attempts to check the expression of opinions that we loathe and believe to be fraught with death.

Much of Holmes's tolerance was rooted in skepticism, but his philosophy, like his judicial career, was positive and affirmative. This affirmative attitude was, as William James saw, partly instinctive, a reflection of temperament and of physical well-being, of his own experience and the experience of his people, but it was, too, intellectual and calculated. For all his skepticism, Holmes was not skeptical about the nation for whose life he had fought or about the Constitution to whose exposition he dedicated himself or about those freedoms which he held the necessary condition for salvation. To act, he liked to say, is to affirm the worth of an ideal, and where the great issues of national well-being or of personal freedom were at stake he did not hesitate to act.

It is the affirmative note in his judicial pronouncements and constitutional doctrines that is the most impressive. Those doctrines, elaborated in a hundred decisions, can be summarized briefly. Nationalism is a reality, not a legal theory or the conclusion of a syllogism, and the United States is a nation and may do whatever a sovereign nation must do. The state is an organic, not a static, thing, and the Constitution is designed to permit growth, adaptation, and experimentation. Government must have authority adequate to protect the commonwealth and enforce law, and the executive authority should be sustained wherever constitutionally possible. The police power—at best an apologetic phrase—is not narrowly restricted to emergencies of public health or morals but covers all great public needs, and its nature is to be determined by the legislative, not the judicial, branch. There must be play for the joints of the political machine if it is to work, and restrictions should be limited to jurisdiction, not imposed upon administration.

The capital value of the federal system is that it permits experimentation in forty-eight state laboratories, and such experimentation is to be encouraged. Commerce is a general economic process, not a particular business activity, and may be regulated by the national government wherever it flows, or wherever its consequences are felt, across state lines. There is no double standard for business and for labor; each is equally free to combine and seek its ends subject to the restrictions of the law, and the welfare of each is equally the concern of government. Life is a battle in which individuals, classes, and interests engage, and it is not the function of the courts to arbitrate or conclude that battle but merely to see that the rules are observed. Majorities have a right to make mistakes, and there is nothing in the Constitution which forbids them from committing errors of judgment or even from indulging in folly. Limitations on personal liberties should be confined to cases where the exercise of those liberties constitutes a clear and present danger, but on the whole legislatures are the best judges of the matter. Judicial review should be invoked only in exceptional cases and exercised with circumspection: as a harmonizer of the federal system it is indispensable, but as far as federal legislation is concerned it might be abandoned without serious loss. Because there are no ultimate economic or political truths, the best test of economic and political ideas is their ability to get themselves accepted in competition in the open market, and the courts should confine themselves to seeing that the competition is fair and the market open. The Constitution, which has adapted itself to changes in the past, may be confidently trusted to adapt itself to the vicissitudes of the future.

Even in his dissents Holmes was affirmative; indeed, in almost every instance he dissented only to affirm some positive power in government. His dissents were not only affirmative, they were conservative, vindications of the past rather than forays into the future, orthodox rather than original. Where Holmes dissented from the majority, it was the majority who usually dissented from the Constitution. Almost all of his dissents came in time to be accepted as good law: those sustaining the plenary power of Congress over commerce, like *Adair* vs. *United States* and *Hammer* vs. *Dagenhart;* those asserting a broad interpretation of the taxing power, like *Evans* vs. *Gore;* those reading a liberal interpretation into the ambiguous phrase "police power," like *Lochner* vs. *New York* or *Tyson* vs. *Banton;* those vindicating the reality of the Bill of Rights, like the Abrams, the Gitlow, the Macintosh, and the Rosika Schwimmer cases. All of them looked to the vindication of the great principles of federal power, legislative experimentation, and personal freedom. All of them were in the grand tradition of American constitutionalism—the tradition of Marshall and Story and Miller, and of Holmes himself, for already in his lifetime he was part of a tradition.

Because Holmes dissented so often and because he so often joined his brother Brandeis in dissents, a superficial view labeled him a liberal and a reformer. He was a liberal, to be sure, and his association with Brandeis was sympathetic and intimate, but he was no professional reformer, no crusader for righteousness, and he constantly disappointed those who expected him to side, automatically, with the progressives. His dissents were not, like those of Brandeis, inspired by a philosophy of social or economic liberalism—all his inclinations were rather in the other direction. They sprang rather from his belief in experiment, his passion for fair play, and his philosophy of judicial continence. "To have doubted one's own first principles," he had said, "is the mark of a civilized man." He did not in fact doubt his own first principles but merely refused to believe in their cosmic validity or to force them upon others, and he rejected wholly the notion of judicial infallibility. "Judges," he observed, "are apt to be naif, simple-minded men, and they need something of the Mephistopheles." He himself had, along with much that was Olympian, something of the Mephistophelean: in his youth it had been said of him that he believed in no contract "not founded on force or fraud," and in his old age he advised long-winded counsel to cultivate French novels in order to learn the art of innuendo, while some of his opinions—the New York bakeshop, for example, and those sustaining the right of pacifists to naturalization—had in them as much craft as craftsmanship.

"Through our great good fortune," Holmes said of his Civil War years, "in our youth our hearts were touched with fire," and it was not only in youth but throughout a long life that his ardent spirit blazed and glowed. He was eighty when he confessed his ambition "to believe, when the end comes, that one has touched the superlative," and only he would have put it prospectively rather than retrospectively. Ten years later he bade a final farewell to his mistress, the law: "We aim at the infinite," he said, "and when our arrow falls to earth it is in flames." It is relevant to recall Justice Frankfurter's observation that Holmes's specialty was great utterance, but it is well to remember, too, that the greatness of these words reflected faithfully a greatness of spirit. Throughout his life his heart was touched with fire; he aimed at the infinite and his arrow was ever in flames. He was one of those

> Who in their lives fought for life
> Who wore at their hearts the fire's centre.
> Born of the sun they travelled a short while towards the sun,
> And left the vivid air signed with their honour.
>   (Stephen Spender, "I Think Continually of
>   Those Who Were Truly Great")

CHAPTER XIX

Architecture and Society

I

SURVEYING THE PALACES and mansion houses that the new rich were building along the upper reaches of New York's Fifth Avenue and Madison Avenue in the early nineties, Montgomery Schuyler, most perspicacious of architectural critics of his generation, observed that "these are not subjects for architectural criticism; they call for the intervention of an architectural police. They are cases of disorderly conduct done in brick and brown stone." It was of this period, too, that Thomas Beer later recalled, in his re-creation of *The Mauve Decade,* that "architecture was still nothing but a malady." No one familiar with the gimcrack architecture of the Gilded Age—with the "Victorian Cathartic, the Tubercular, the Cataleptic, and the Dropsical," as John Wellborn Root, most promising of the younger architects, designated the popular styles—could doubt the aptness of these judgments. The Centennial Exposition of 1876, responsible for so much bad poetry and oratory, had given an almost official sanction to bad architecture as well—the Michigan State Building was probably the worst public edifice ever erected—but the next decade was to reveal that even the Exposition had not exhausted architectural vulgarity. It was the era of the dumbbell tenement, the brownstone front, and the bogus palace.

It had not always been thus. The early years of the Republic had seen the emergence of a genuine American architecture, one that satisfied the demands both of aesthetics and of utility. Building on traditions of sound craftsmanship, assisted and sometimes inspired by the architects' copybooks imported from England, owing much to the Adam brothers, and working lovingly with native materials, men like McIntire and Bulfinch had built houses of surpassing beauty in Salem and Boston; Manigault and other forgotten builders had made Charleston one of the most beautiful cities in the English-speaking world; while Jefferson, borrowing much but creating much, too, had planned for his University of Virginia the most completely satisfying group of buildings to be erected in the United States. Neither the Federalist architecture of the North nor the Greek revival of the South nor the wholly native architecture of the Bucks County region of Pennsylvania—celebrated in our own day by the artist, Charles Sheeler—were primarily monumental or even leisure-class. The average New England villager and Bucks County farmer lived in houses as comfortable and comely as any that have ever been built, and twentieth-century architects exhausted their ingenuity in copies, while those who could afford it bought the originals in preference to anything that modern art could design or technology build.

It is difficult to say just when or why Americans strayed from the path of architectural rectitude but easy enough to follow them down their gaudy ways. The Greek revival, for all its derivative features, was not wholly archaeological; it bore the imprint of the American environment and character, and its best examples adapted themselves gracefully to the environment of the South and the West. Not so the Gothic revival of the thirties and forties and the subsequent architectural styles—if they can be dignified by that term—such as the Romanesque, the Queen Anne, the Eastlake, the Italian Renaissance, even the Byzantine, which dominated American architecture for most of the next half-century. The error was in passive imitation, in importation without assimilation; it was true of architecture as of painting, literature, philosophy, and social science that where Americans followed their instincts and accepted their environment they were more successful than where they borrowed or imported.

As American architecture blundered from the Gothic to the Eastlake and from the *Néo-Grec* to the Queen Anne—wallowing in turrets, pinnacles, gables, columns, braces, jigsaw brackets, iron balustrades, mansard roofs, stained-glass windows, tortured moldings and fanciful arches—one genuine architect emerged and for a time gave dignity to the architectural scene. It is easy to judge the work but difficult to judge the influence of Henry Hobson Richardson. That he was a great architect may be readily acknowledged; that his influence on American architecture was good remained debatable.

What he built, he built well. He insisted upon good material, honest workmanship, directness, spaciousness, dignity, and—within the limits of the style he chose—originality. That style was the Romanesque. Its simplicity and honesty appealed irresistibly to him, and in an age of industrial feudalism he thought it appropriate enough to provide buildings that symbolized power and permanence.

"The things I want most to design," Richardson said, "are a grain elevator and the interior of a great river steamboat." His mind was, in truth, adventurous and his inclination, in the end, experimental, but he was, in a sense, the victim of his own competence. His Romanesque designs were so admirable that his clients would not let him design in different styles, and soon Romanesque churches, libraries, railway stations, warehouses, and private houses dotted the landscape from Massachusetts to Minnesota; only in some of his summer cottages along the New England coast did he allow himself to experiment with native materials. Trinity Church, Boston, completed in 1877, was his first triumph; the early eighties saw the completion of Austin Hall at Harvard University, the Pittsburgh jail, the wonderful Marshall Field warehouse, and a group of frowning private houses of which the Hay-Adams in Washington was probably the most famous and the Glessner in Chicago the best. These were all built as for the ages, but, almost alone of the buildings of that generation, their ostentatious durability excited no misgivings.

Yet Richardson's work as a whole did excite misgivings, and chiefly because of its very virtues. For Richardson gave respectability to a principle whose falsity was becoming increasingly clear. That was the principle of derivation. Romanesque no more than Gothic or Queen Anne had any real place in America, and the analogy with feudalism was misleading. Romanesque was good enough for warehouses and no worse for churches than Gothic, but it had no perceptible relation to the needs of an industrial society or to the office buildings, schools, or private houses of a democratic society. It is suggestive that though many notable architects—Charles McKim and Stanford White among them—studied with Richardson, he had no successors.

Already, when he died, there were new forces stirring; the struggle between the native and the derivative was to continue, but on a higher plane, as it were, and even with a new vocabulary. Mont-

gomery Schuyler and Russell Sturgis were turning their critical
searchlights on all that was meretricious in architecture; young John
Root, who had studied music at Oxford and Gothic architecture in
the office of James Renwick and then moved west to join forces with
Daniel Burnham, was experimenting with those techniques which
were to produce the incomparable Monadnock building, high tide
of masonry construction in America; Louis Sullivan, most brilliant
and original of all the architects of his generation, was groping his
way toward that philosophy which was to find expression in the
Transportation Building of the Columbian Exposition. Richardson
had died in 1886; his lordly contemporary, Richard Morris Hunt,
who had bestrewn the East with French Renaissance palaces, lived
on to receive the gold medal of the Institute of British Architects for
his imitation of St. Paul's Cathedral at that same Exposition. The
struggle to free American architecture from the dead hand of the
past, as represented by Richardson and Hunt, was under way. It
was doomed to frustration.

2

It was the World's Columbian Exposition of 1893 that condemned
American architecture to the imitative and the derivative for another generation, and it was, perhaps, cause for gratification that the
forces of the past, as represented in that fateful year, spoke with
authority and dignity. "Make no little plans," said Daniel Burnham
who was in charge of the Exposition, and it can be admitted that his
plans were grandiose and that they were fulfilled. His talent was
executive rather than artistic, and though he had helped make Chicago the architectural capital of the nation his attitude toward the
East was that of a colonial. Root, who might have tempered his
archaeological enthusiasms, had died; Sullivan was not yet strong
enough to dampen them. Burnham called in Richard Morris Hunt
and the rising firm of McKim, Mead, and White and along with
them the most distinguished landscape architects, painters, and
sculptors that America could boast. "See here, old boy," Augustus
St. Gaudens said at the first meeting of the group, "do you realize
that this is the greatest meeting of artists since the fifteenth century?"
Perhaps it was: there were Frederick Law Olmsted who had laid
out Central Park, and the sculptors, young Lorado Taft and Frederick Macmonnies and St. Gaudens himself, and among the painters

Alden Weir and Kenyon Cox and Gari Melchers, and Edwin Blashfield who painted murals for the Library of Congress and was busy now with his new edition of Vasari's *Lives of the Painters,* and a dozen others scarcely less famous.

It was a remarkable group, and it created what remains the best planned and designed Exposition of modern times. Hunt's Administration building was almost as good as St. Paul's Cathedral; Atwood's Fine Arts building—the later Field Museum—was perhaps, as Burnham insisted, the most beautiful building since the Parthenon. Everything reminded the visitor of something else, and most of the buildings—Sullivan's was an exception—had all the virtues of the original except originality. The whole Exposition proclaimed in unmistakable terms that there had been little advance since Rome and that it was the first duty of architects to copy.

For what had it all to do with Chicago—the Chicago of the stockyards and steel mills and railroads, young, lusty, brawling, looking to the future rather than to the past, conscious of power, conscious of almost everything but dignity and serenity? What had it to do with the America the four-hundredth anniversary of whose discovery it was designed to commemorate—democratic, equalitarian, industrial, urban, heterogeneous, dynamic America? It was magnificent, but it was a sham. Henry Adams, who knew Old World originals well enough to be unimpressed by copies and knew the New World too and who was already coming to the conclusion that the dynamo was the symbol of the future, put it with characteristic humor:

I revelled in all its fakes and frauds [he wrote], all its wickedness that seemed not to be understood by our innocent natives, and all its genuineness which was understood still less. I labored solemnly through all the great buildings and looked like an owl at the dynamos and the steam-engines. . . . Do you remember Sargent's portrait of Mrs. Hamersly in London this summer? Was it a defiance or an insult to our society, or a rendering in good faith of our civilization . . . or an unconscious revelation of the artist's despair of reconciliation with the female of the gold-bug? . . . Well, the Chicago Fair is precisely an architectural Mrs. Hamersly.

Sullivan, whose Transportation Building excited the greatest admiration from the Continental visitors, was even more severe. "A fraudulent and surreptitious use of historical documents," he said, "however suavely presented, however cleverly plagiarized, however neatly repacked, however shrewdly intrigued, will constitute and will be held to be a betrayal of trust," and he prophesied that "the damage wrought by the World's Fair will last for half a century from its date, if not longer. It has penetrated deep into the constitution of the American mind, effecting there lesions significant of dementia." The criticism was extreme, but the prophecy accurate enough. Burnham had boasted that "the Fair was what the Romans would have wished to create, in permanent form," and under the influence of the great Exposition the classical style spread like a fog over the land, and, where classical did not fit, some other imitation was invoked. Washington adopted the classical as the official style, and the greatest of democracies tried to look like imperial Rome and almost succeeded: poor Horatio Greenough, who just half a century earlier had been rebuked for his figure of George Washington in a toga, was at last vindicated, for logically American statesmen and diplomats should all have worn togas. Banks, post offices, stations, schools, libraries, even private houses presented unblinking classical façades to a public which soon learned to take them for granted and eventually rejoiced that the homespun Lincoln was commemorated in a Memorial more fit for a Caesar. Architects, flushed with triumph, established the American Academy in Rome, in 1894, to train future generations in sound principles, and the firm of McKim, Mead, and White, dedicated to classicism, came to exercise such a monopoly as might have called for the application of a new Sherman Antitrust Law.

Yet there is some exaggeration here. The classicists did not have things all their own way. But there is little exaggeration in saying that the archaeologists did. Churches clung stubbornly to Gothic or Romanesque, and even the Congregational and Unitarian churches occasionally abandoned the lovely white spire for an imitation of Salisbury Cathedral. Some of the rich preferred French chateaux and others yearned for Italian palazzia, and with Hunt and White ready to serve them, both groups were satisfied. Back in the seventies John Fiske had written that Harvard might as well give up any attempt to build in native style—it was the day of the Harvard Memorial, and he could be forgiven—and frankly copy Oxford. Harvard did not heed his advice, but the new University of Chicago did, and when its sons and daughters sang joyfully that

Its battlemented towers shall rise
Beneath the hopeful western skies

only Sullivan asked who was to fight behind the battlements or why a university founded by John D. Rockefeller in the heart of the Middle West should be housed in a reproduction of Magdalen College. Nor was Chicago alone in its passion for Gothic. Princeton abandoned Nassau Hall and Yale long ignored Connecticut Hall, Ralph Adams Cram imposed Gothic on the West Point Military Academy and the new Duke University forgot Jefferson in its passion for Oxford. The architects of the Massachusetts Institute of Technology showed more discernment: as Gothic seemed unsuitable for the purposes of modern technology, they chose the classical instead.

3

We are at that dramatic moment in our national life wherein we tremble evenly between decay and evolution, and our architecture, with its strange fidelity, reflects this equipoise. That the forces of decadence predominate in quantity there can be no doubt; that the creative forces now balance them by virtue of equality, and may eventually overpower them, is a matter of conjecture. That the bulk of our architecture is rotten to the core, is a statement that does not admit of doubt. That there is in our national life, in the genius of our people, a fruitful germ, and that there are some who perceive this, is likewise beyond question.

So said Louis Sullivan in one of those *Kindergarten Chats* whose fame was to await a new and more receptive generation, and there can be no doubt that he thought of himself as one of those—perhaps after the deaths of Richardson and Root the only one—who perceived the germs of health in American architecture and knew how to cultivate them. He may have been right. His own generation did not think so, did him little honor, and—after the World's Fair—gave him few commissions. Yet of all the architects connected with that Fair he was the one best known half a century later.

With Louis Sullivan we come to the most remarkable figure in the history of American architecture between Jefferson and Frank Lloyd Wright—Wright who always referred to him as The Master. His was a curious career and a curious reputation. Neglected in his own day by all but a few of the more astute critics like Schuyler and Sturgis and in the end rejected, he came to be acknowledged the father (or at least the godfather) of modern American architecture. He had studied at all the proper places—at the Massachusetts Institute and the École des Beaux Arts and with that remarkable Le Baron Jenney who built the first real skyscraper in America—and he knew a thing or two about the classical style which had dazzled McKim and the Renaissance which had conquered Hunt and a great deal about the Romanesque: his own Romanesque experiment, if it can properly be called that—the Chicago Auditorium—compared favorably with anything that Richardson himself did. He was the most philosophical of American architects, his philosophy always wordy and even blowzy; he was a disciple of Walt Whitman and sought to make architecture a vehicle for democracy as Whitman had made poetry. Behind all his exuberant verbosity, his posturing, his vanity and arrogance, there was sincerity and integrity. And sincerity and integrity stamp all of his work and his writing as well—the *Kindergarten Chats* and the famous *Autobiography of an Idea*. He seized early upon two fundamental ideas and clung to them throughout his unhappy life: first that form expressed function and function determined form, and second that architecture can have no genuine significance unless it faithfully reflects the life of a people.

It was not an original idea, this principle that form should express function and function determine form; it was rather one of those old ideas that had been forgotten or neglected. Back in the 1840's Horatio Greenough had observed that "the mechanics of the United States have already outstripped the artists and have, by their bold and unflinching adaptation, entered the true track and hold up the light for all who operate for American wants. . . . By beauty I mean the promise of function. By character I mean the record of function." And in a letter to Emerson he set forth the artistic principle at which he had arrived:

Here is my theory of structure: A scientific arrangement of space and forms to functions and to site; an emphasis on features proportioned to their graduated importance in function; color and ornament to be decided and arranged and varied by strictly organic laws, having a distinct reason for each decision; the entire and immediate abandonment of all makeshift and make-believe.

James J. Jarves, too, had recognized something of the relationship between form and function, and Le Baron Jenney, and even Richardson himself. But Sullivan was the first architect to elaborate this principle into a philosophy and the first to apply it consistently in a professional career. He was the first, too, to emphasize social responsibility in architecture, to insist that his profession belonged to the social sciences and the humanities rather than exclusively to the fine arts.

Yet among American architects he was the greatest of artists, and even those who, like Burnham, denied him architectural ability conceded his decorative genius. His splendid and richly colored decorations expressed all his Celtic imagination and sensuousness, elsewhere restrained. "Out of himself," wrote Frank Lloyd Wright, "he devised a complete beautiful language of self expression as complete in itself as Wagner's music or the period ornamentation of any of the great styles which time took so many ages to perfect." In the Transportation Building of the World's Fair, in the great hall of the Chicago Auditorium, in the McVickers Theatre and the Getty tomb, he made decoration an integral part of the structure rather than something laid on as an afterthought. Although a functionalist, he never subscribed to the notion, soon to be so popular with the modernist school, that a house should resemble a machine, but found room for color, emotion, and beauty.

To his philosophical principles, then, Sullivan added a sound technical training and a genius for decoration, imagination, originality, and boldness. He could create a building that was honestly functional and yet a thing of beauty, like the Transportation Building. He could lavish decoration upon an interior and triumph over the difficult problem of acoustics, as in the Auditorium. He could experiment with the use of structural steel in the skyscraper, as in the Wainwright Building in St. Louis, as admirable an example of its type as has ever been built. He could build stores like the remarkable Carson Pirie Scott building in Chicago, perfectly designed to invite light and air and display goods. What he could not do, apparently, was satisfy the demands of those captains of industry who, in architecture as in art, preferred the familiar to the original and the derivative to the native.

He belonged not so much with that Whitman whom he admired inordinately as with William James whom he scarcely knew. For Sullivan was, above all, the pragmatist in architecture—pragmatic in his respect for tools and machinery, in his insistence on marrying style to fact rather than to some a priori theory, in his belief that truth in art, as in philosophy, was something to be achieved rather than something pre-existing. And he belonged, too, with a fellow-Chicagoan, like him neglected and even condemned and like him destined to come into his own after his death: Thorstein Veblen. For he shared Veblen's distaste for a pecuniary economy and preference for an economy run by engineers and technicians. He found himself, he later recalled, "drifting into the engineering point of view, as he began to discern that the engineers were the only men who could face a problem squarely; who knew a problem when they saw it. Their minds were trained to deal with real things, as far as they knew them . . . while the architectural mind lacked this directness, this simplicity, this singleness of purpose."

Frank Lloyd Wright recalls in his *Autobiography* that the mighty Burnham invited him into his office—a glittering invitation for a young man. Wright demurred: "I have been," he said, "too close to Mr. Sullivan." Mr. Burnham dismissed Mr. Sullivan. A great decorator, he admitted, but not an architect, not a man who understood the World's Fair.

The Fair, Frank, is going to have great influence in our country. The American people have seen the Classics on a grand scale for the first time. . . . I can see all America constructed along the lines of the Fair, in noble, dignified, classic style. The Fair should have shown you that Sullivan and Richardson are well enough in their way, but their way won't prevail— architecture is going the other way.

And so it was, for a generation at least. The future belonged to the imitators, and the businessmen, and for fifty years the imitators covered the land with Roman stadia, French or Venetian palaces, Gothic churches, and bogus Elizabethan or "colonial" houses, while the businessmen indulged their passion for size and their sensitiveness to land values by building skyscrapers in a country where land should have been the cheapest of all commodities. "Of such," wrote Sullivan sadly in 1901,

is contemporaneous American architecture. Pitiful in its folly, dying at the top and dead at the core, with here and there a gleam, a little gleam of regret. Functions without forms, forms without functions; details unrelated to masses, and masses unrelated to anything but folly, irresponsible and grossly, callously, ignorant; monuments to the feeble of mind and the shallow of heart; monuments to the mercenary hurly-burly of the hour; the distracted forms of a diseased and distracted function.

The future belonged to the imitators and the businessmen. What the imitators did could shortly be seen in every suburban development, one "colonial," another Spanish, a third Queen Anne, a fourth Georgian; it could be seen in the churches, colleges, banks, and museums which proclaimed so unmistakably the persistence of colonialism, the triumph of archaeology, and the lure of conspicuous waste. Yet whatever their aesthetic qualities, most of these houses and public buildings were well built and comfortable, equipped with numerous labor-saving devices, and with efficient heating, plumbing, and lighting, and socially inoffensive. Only with important qualifications could this be said of the achievement of the businessmen. The skyscraper was, ordinarily, well built, but it would be an exaggeration to say that it was socially inoffensive.

The skyscraper did not so much distinguish as symbolize modern American architecture. It was, properly, assumed to be peculiarly American, and Americans who forgot that Paris and London somehow existed without it took for granted that it was the inevitable and right expression of an urban civilization. Yet, curiously enough, Americans themselves never came to terms with it. Their leading architect, Frank Lloyd Wright, regarded it as an architectural monstrosity; their leading architectural critic, Lewis Mumford, called it an "architecture for angels and aviators"; their foremost city planners looked upon it as a social catastrophe. Yet none could deny that it was a natural product of the passion for business, the worship of the machine, the respect for pecuniary considerations, and the attempt to combine the useful and the beautiful, which characterized the twentieth-century American.

Like so much in American architecture, the skyscraper had its origin in the Chicago of the 1880's. It was the remarkable Le Baron Jenney who, applying to the task of building the engineering techniques he had learned as Chief Engineer of the XV Army Corps, built the Home Insurance Company building in Chicago in the mid-eighties—the first genuine skyscraper. Soon Root and Burnham and Sullivan were experimenting with skeleton steel construction and producing, in such buildings as the Tacoma, the Marquette, and the Carson Pirie Scott, skyscrapers whose beauty and efficiency were not to be surpassed for half a century.

The skyscraper was not the product of the genius of any one man or school: it was the product of an age. It came in response to rising land values; it was made possible by the development of structural steel, floating foundations, and the elevator and, indirectly, by the telephone, pneumatic tubes, the typewriter, and a host of minor inventions. At the hands of architects who understood its function and respected its form and were willing to adapt themselves to the new conditions that it imposed—men like Root and Sullivan and, later, Raymond Hood and George Howe and William Lescaze—it was "a proud and soaring thing." But few architects were content to accept it for what it was. They insisted—witness the Woolworth building or the Flatiron building or the New York Central building, all in New York—on treating it as if it were a stone rather than a steel structure; they plastered it with cornices and cupolas and balustrades, flying buttresses and parapets and spires; they superimposed Gothic or Romanesque ideas on buildings that had no connection either with the Gothic or the Romanesque spirit.

All this offended good taste but presented no serious social problem. The skyscraper itself did, however, present a social problem. Required by financial and not by genuine economic considerations, it gravely accentuated congestion, aggravated already perplexing traffic problems, and engulfed whole areas in darkness. If it was not, as Sullivan called it, "the eloquent peroration of the most bald, most sinister, most forbidding, conditions" of American life, it was—as he elsewhere observed, profoundly antisocial. The set-back design, required first by New York City, did something to solve the problem of light and to improve the appearance of the skyscraper but nothing to relieve congestion or to give spaciousness to great cities or dignity to their inhabitants. It was perhaps more than fortuitous that the skyscraper developed along with the slum and that cities which boasted the ability and wealth to erect the most towering buildings seemed unable to provide decent housing for the men and women who worked in them.

4

Frank Lloyd Wright fought the skyscraper as Sullivan had fought the classicism of the World's Fair. His objections, like those of Sullivan, were not primarily aesthetic but social and even moral. Skyscrapers, he asserted,

have no life of their own—no life to give, receiving none from the nature of construction. They have no relation to their surroundings. Utterly barbaric they rise regardless of special consideration for environment or for each other, except to win the race or get the tenant. Space as a becoming psychic element of the American city is gone. . . . The skyscraper is not ethical, beautiful, or permanent. It is a commercial exploit, a mere expedient. It has no higher ideal of unity than commercial success.

Wright had studied with Sullivan and learned from him the desirability of fitting the structure to the environment, using authentic materials, dispensing with the merely ornamental and the superfluous, and relying upon the technician and the engineer. He had grown up in the Middle West; the environment that he knew, and that he thought characteristically American, was the prairie, and he early developed his preference for the horizontal over the vertical. Indifferent to monumental or public buildings, he concentrated on private houses and on factories where the advantages of a functional treatment were obvious. He was the first major architect since the days of the early Republic to consider the house as a whole, fit it into the ground, blend it into its environment, harmonize style, materials, and furnishings, let in light and air, exploit the findings of technology for plumbing and heating. He was the first, too, to use freely all the resources of modern construction—glass, steel, copper, plastics, tile—and to apply these to interior and to furnishings. And to building after building, for a period of over forty years, he triumphantly applied the principle of functionalism, the technics of engineering, the materials of science, with imagination and audacity: to the Robey house in Chicago and the Falling Waters house near Pittsburgh and the Jacobs house in Madison, Wisconsin; to the famous Imperial Hotel which withstood the great earthquake of 1923 and the romantic Midway Gardens in Chicago; to the Larkin building in Buffalo and the Johnson Wax Company building in Racine, and the daring Guggenheim Museum, still in the blueprint stage.

What Wright did, from the beginning, was original enough to excite suspicion and even hostility at home, and Wright's reputation came back to America from Holland and Austria and Japan and even from conservative Britain where he was awarded the Gold Medal of the Royal Institution. Yet what he did was, in fact, very old, and he belonged properly to the great tradition of American architecture that had flourished during the colonial period and the early years of the Republic and then found refuge in neglected and perhaps less respectable forms of construction. As early as the Jacksonian period, Horatio Greenough had urged his countrymen to study bridges, canals, lighthouses, and clipper ships, and in the Civil War years the great collector and critic, James J. Jarves, had observed that

the American, while adhering closely to his utilitarian and economical principles, has unwittingly . . . developed a degree of beauty in them that no other nation equals. His clipper-ships, fire-engines, locomotives, and some of his machinery and tools combine that equilibrium of lines, proportion and masses, which are among the fundamental causes of abstract beauty. Their success in producing broad general effects out of a few simple elements, and of admirable adaptations of means to ends, as nature evolves beauty out of the common and practical, covers these things with a certain atmosphere of beauty.

It was precisely in the evolution of beauty out of the common and the practical that American craftsmen, designers, and engineers had achieved their greatest triumphs. The really significant achievements, call them architectural or engineering, of the post–Civil War years, were not in monumental buildings, but in railroads, grain elevators, bridges, powerhouses, dams, factories, and, it might be added, elementary and high schools. The distinction persisted into the twentieth century, and few countries could boast more wholly satisfying structures than the Whitestone Bridge in New York, the Brooklyn Army Supply Base, the TVA dams, or the Carl Schurz High School in Chicago.

Where architecture could be functional—where it could escape the paralyzing influence of imitation or the pressure of quick financial gain—it could be beautiful as well. This was the lesson that Sullivan and Wright preached; it was the lesson that Americans had learned, almost unconsciously, when they built with native materials for their use rather than for profit, when they allowed their ingenuity and imagination free play. It was the lesson that emerged, in the 1930's, from Constance Rourke's comprehensive "Index of American Design" and from the Library of Congress collection of prints and plans of old American houses.

The task that confronted American architecture at mid-twentieth century was to recover what was honest, genuine, and humane from the past and apply it to the needs of the present. Architecture was required to abandon its preoccupation with the monumental, the ecclesiastical, and the official, and to create comfortable and comely homes for the masses of the people; to adapt buildings to their environments, use native materials and styles, and utilize all the resources of modern technology; to address itself to the needs of the community as a whole, to considerations of space, light, and air, of health, recreation, freedom of movement, and beauty. This, after all, was what those nameless craftsmen who had built the New England villages of the eighteenth century had done, and it was not too much to expect that professional architects and town-planners and engineers, with all the wealth and resources of the twentieth century at their command, might do as well. The problem, however, was not exclusively architectural or technological. It was economic, social, and moral.

CHAPTER XX

The Twentieth-Century American

I

THE SHIFT in the material circumstances of the American people from the 1890's to the mid-twentieth century was all but convulsive. Yet it is by no means clear that this material change precipitated or even embraced a comparable change in the intellectual outlook or in the national character. Material changes, indeed, seemed at times to have paradoxical consequences, confounding the student tempted to oversimplify the relations between the life of the body and the life of the spirit and dramatizing the danger of all merely material interpretations of history.

In this sixty-year period America changed from rural to urban, but few who knew the conditions of life in the large cities would contend that Americans had come to terms with their cities as their grandparents had come to terms with the countryside: American civilization was urban, but it was not yet an urbane civilization. Americans had conquered leisure for themselves on a scale never before thought possible; yet never before had men seemed so hurried, and when they thought of a leisurely society it was always in terms of a past innocent of labor-saving devices: no twentieth-century statesman accomplished so much as Jefferson, and none enjoyed so much leisure. Mass immigration, particularly from southern and eastern Europe, Latin America, the Caribbean, and French Canada, had accentuated the heterogeneous character of the American population, yet it was the opinion of most foreign observers that Americans tended more and more to conform to a type; certainly the American people of 1950 seemed more standardized than those of 1850. Invention and technology had changed an economy of scarcity to an economy of abundance, but it was the era of abundance that witnessed the greatest and most prolonged depression, and few ordinary middle-class Americans lived so well, in mere matters of food and clothing and shelter, as had their

American grandparents. The new economy had relegated Malthus to the realm of the antiquarian, but Margaret Sanger took his place; and the nation which seemed under least compulsion to limit its population put up barriers on immigration and voluntarily cut down its birth rate. Americans knew more about the mastery of their physical environment than ever before, about saving human lives and natural resources; yet never before had life been so precarious for those who survived infancy, and the resources of the nation vanished with terrifying rapidity. The emancipation of women, birth control, labor-saving devices, prosperity, and education should have made for a happier and healthier family life, but one marriage out of every four ended in divorce, and nervous breakdowns became so common as to be almost unfashionable. Americans had experimented with mass education on a scale never heretofore attempted and its college and university population was as large as that of the rest of the western world combined, but it was not certain that Americans as a whole were either better informed or more intelligent than their nineteenth-century forebears; neither the level of the press nor the standards of literature had improved noticeably, while the popular culture represented by the lyceum or the Chautauqua of earlier generations was more sophisticated than that represented by the radio.

The most important changes were not, in fact, in the purely material but in the philosophical realm, and time had not yet exhausted, had indeed scarcely discovered, their significance. In a general way it could be said that the two generations after 1890 witnessed a transition from certainty to uncertainty, from faith to doubt, from security to insecurity, from seeming order to ostentatious disorder, but the generalization was too loose to cover adequately the diverse manifestations of the American mind and too tentative to justify dogmatic conclusions. First evolution, then scientific determinism, profoundly altered the outlook of most Americans, even of those personally unfamiliar with the specific teachings or even the implications of the new points of view. Americans, who had always accepted change in the material realm, were now prepared to accept it in the intellectual and the moral as well, and they were less confident than formerly of their power to direct or control the change. The temper, though not always the product, of thought was scientific rather than religious: as Henry Adams saw, it was the dynamo rather than the Virgin that the twentieth century worshiped, and, as he suspected, the worship was as irrational. Absolutism was abandoned in every field, even the ethical, though ethical practices continued, for the most part, along traditional lines. Pragmatism triumphed over competing philosophies not so much because of its superior logic as because of its superior relevancy and utility, and a people who made a fetish of individualism socialized philosophy and applied the term social science to history, economics, and politics. Easier communication, urbanization, and the mobility of population combined with a hundred agencies such as the press, the radio, and the motion pictures to produce a greater uniformity of character and habit than had been common in the nineteenth century. The advent of America to world power and two world wars encouraged the abandonment of isolation, and the new internationalism made itself felt in the realm of ideas and of social practices, which became increasingly cosmopolitan. There was a steady democratization, perhaps a vulgarization, of what was called culture.

It would be an exaggeration to suggest that the twentieth-century American was more democratic than his nineteenth-century forebears but accurate enough to say that his democracy, having been more effectively challenged, was more self-conscious and rationalized than at any time since Lincoln. The discrepancy between democratic pretensions and practices had always been considerable; it became notorious, and the notoriety brought reform, particularly in the realms of economics and of race relations. The rich, the middle classes, and the poor came closer to living alike, dressing alike, eating the same food, enjoying the same entertainments, sharing the same advantages, than at any time since the Civil War, and while the disparity in wealth grew, the disparity in what wealth was able to command either in comforts or in security contracted.

These developments, particularly in the field of ideas, were often called a coming of age. Most Americans, in any event, congratulated themselves upon a maturity which they associated with the mere passing of time, while critics were inclined to believe that in the realm of arts and letters America had outgrown her swaddling clothes and even her adolescence and reached years of independence and self-expression. It is not clear that the phrase so commonly used for individual development had any sound application to national, and no one would suppose that the mere passing of time had matured Greece since the days of Plato, or Italy since those of Virgil. Culturally, it was true that America, which had begun with the inheritance of the whole

European past, had never known infancy; it was equally clear that she was not decadent. Beyond these extremes it was difficult to generalize.

That the American mind was more mature in the mid-twentieth than in the mid-nineteenth or even the mid-eighteenth century was by no means clear, and if Compton represented some technical advance over Franklin and Sargent over Copley, it was not certain that architecture had dispensed with Bulfinch or Jefferson, that the *Federalist* papers were of antiquarian interest merely, that the essays of Emerson were less profound than those of Mencken, or that the Lincoln-Douglas debates compared unfavorably with the debates over the League of Nations. All that can be said with certainty is that twentieth-century civilization was more complex than nineteenth and that even partial mastery of it required both intellectual maturity and moral integrity. None familiar with the statistics of crime, of divorce, or of psychiatric aberrations, with the history of depressions or of wars, could plausibly assert that the twentieth-century American's mastery of his environment was more than partial.

2

Whether either the material or the intellectual changes in the half-century after 1890 produced comparable changes in the American character is difficult to determine. The forces that create a national character are as obscure as those that create an individual character, but that both are formed early and change relatively little is almost certain. Those familiar with the English character know that Emerson's analysis of *English Traits* of the mid-nineteenth century is largely adequate a century later, while the persistence of certain traits in the French and the German characters has simplified the task of historians and complicated that of reformers. The American character, as delineated by Tocqueville, Bryce, and Brogan at half-century intervals, seems substantially the same: the differences are quantitative and material rather than qualitative and moral.

Certainly most of those qualities which we noted as characteristic of the nineteenth-century American persisted; with necessary modifications of detail, the earlier portrait would be acceptable on any passport. The American was still optimistic, still took for granted that his was the most favored of all countries, the happiest and most virtuous of all societies, and, though less sure of progress, was still confident that the best was yet to be. Two world wars had not induced in him either a sense of sin or that awareness of evil almost instinctive with most Old World peoples and had but accentuated his own assurance of power and success. His culture was still predominantly material, his thinking quantitative, his genius inventive, experimental, and practical. He remained careless, good natured, casual, generous, and extravagant. War had not taught him discipline or respect for authority. He cherished individualism but was less sure of the virtue of nonconformity. He still boasted his own idiom and his own brand of humor, and he had developed his own art and literature and claimed a native music, while his motion pictures had conquered the world. If class distinctions were sharper than they had been, he retained, by Old World standards, a classless society. Women paid for emancipation by some loss of reverence, but they were still pampered, and the temptation to indulge children was strengthened by the relative decrease in their numbers and by prosperity. The American was amiable and affectionate; though apparently tougher and less romantic than his forebears, his advertisements proclaimed a sentimental strain, as did his music, his motion pictures, his radio, and his domestic relations. He was still suspicious of culture but avid for it; he was still instinctively provincial but had had cosmopolitanism forced upon him. Distrust of the military had been abated by its performances and by the tendency of modern wars to embrace the whole population; but instead of militarizing society, two world wars had rather civilianized the military. If his political antics were often tawdry and the *Congressional Record* often absurd, the American proved himself nevertheless politically mature: he made the two-party system work, achieved reforms by evolution rather than by revolution, produced able leaders in times of crisis, and maintained liberty and republican institutions in times of war.

The persistence of fundamental philosophical beliefs and assumptions was as tenacious as that of practices, habits, and attitudes. Puritanism lingered on, not so much as a search for individual salvation or as a celebration of the virtues of thrift and industry but as a recognition of the dignity of the individual and of his duty to achieve both spiritual and material prosperity. Idealism, in its popular rather than its philosophical form, flourished, for though Americans were by no means so sure of the benevolence of God and of Nature or the perfectibility of man as they had been a century earlier, nothing had as yet persuaded them to acquiesce in a philosophy of despair. For the most part, Americans still believed that such words as honor, virtue, courage, and purity had meaning, and if science had injected some doubts, their standards were confused rather than their conduct. Their patriotism had not become either complicated or sophisticated; they revered the flag and the Constitution, and two decades of debunking did not persuade them to topple Washington, Franklin, Lee, and Lincoln from their pedestals. They still professed faith in democracy, equality, and liberty and practiced that faith as well as any other people. In religion they were less orthodox than their fathers, and perhaps less devout, but the vast majority of them still acknowledged, with Jefferson, "an overruling Providence, which by all its dispensations proves that it delights in the happiness of man here and his greater happiness hereafter."

3

Yet, that changes so profound in the mechanics of living and in the intellectual climate should produce modifications of character was all but inevitable. To suggest that the modifications were either for better or for worse implies the existence of a moral standard; all that can be said with assurance is that the modifications were, in important respects, departures from what had seemed the nineteenth-century norm. Some of the changes were in the realm of ideas, some in habits and practices, some in morals.

Although still persuaded that his was the best of all countries, the American of the mid-twentieth century was by no means so sure that his was the best of all times, and after he entered the atomic age he could not rid himself of the fear that his world might end not with a whimper but with a bang. His optimism, which persisted, was instinctive rather than rationalized, and he was no longer prepared to insist that the good fortune which he enjoyed, in a war-stricken world, was the reward of virtue rather than of mere geographical isolation. He knew that if there was indeed any such thing as progress it would continue to be illustrated by America, but he was less confident of the validity of the concept than at any previous time in his history.

As he was less zealous for the future, he became more concerned with the past: small families and the cultivation of genealogy seemed to go together. He seemed more conscious of his own history than at any time since the Civil War and, after a brief interval of cynicism and disillusionment in the decade of the twenties, found more satisfaction in its contemplation. In everything but manners and morals he was more inclined to let the past set his standards than had been customary. While it would be an exaggeration to say that he regarded America as a finished product, it was demonstrable that he did not welcome change with his earlier enthusiasm or regard the future as a romantic adventure.

The tendency to trust the past rather than the future and the familiar rather than the original reflected an instinct for conformity that revealed itself in countless ways. Businessmen were expected to conform in matters of dress as well as in matters of thought, and the business suit became almost a uniform, while women, who yearned to look different, came to seem turned out almost by machine process, each with the same make-up, the same accessories, and the same patter. A thousand books on etiquette, a thousand courses in manners and speech and parlor acquirements, proclaimed the universal fear of being different. Slang, which represented an effort to get away from conventional language, became as conventional as the speech which Victorian novelists ascribed to their characters. As society put a premium on conformity, individualism declined and eccentricity all but disappeared. Standardization, induced by the press, the moving pictures, the radio, schools, business, urban life, and a hundred other agencies and intangibles, permeated American life. From Maine to Florida, from Delaware to California, almost all country clubs were alike, and with the spread of the chain store, the filling station, motion-picture palaces, and beauty parlors, towns and cities all over the country came to take on a standardized appearance. With advertisements dictating styles and manners, conversation and amusements, the habits of eating and drinking, the conventions of friendship and of business, and the techniques of love and marriage, nature conformed to commercial art.

More serious was the pressure for intellectual conformity and the growing intolerance with independence and dissent. Intolerance had always been an index of the things men thought important and certain: as Justice Holmes put it in *Abrams* vs. *United States,* "If you have no doubt of your premises or your power and want a certain result with all your heart you naturally express your wishes in law and sweep

away all opposition. To allow opposition by speech seems to indicate
. . . that you do not care wholeheartedly for the result, or that you
doubt either your power or your premises." The Puritans who banished Roger Williams and Anne Hutchinson at least took religion
seriously, and the pioneers who chased the Mormons out of Missouri
and Illinois cherished orthodox morality; that the twentieth-century
American, outside the rural sections, was tolerant in matters of religion and morals suggests not so much open mindedness as indifference. That he was increasingly intolerant in matters of politics and
economics indicated that a business civilization was as sensitive to anything threatening prosperity as a religious had been to anything im-
periling salvation, and it was by no means clear that the change in
animus represented progress.

There was, to be sure, nothing new about political intolerance in
America—witness the Alien and Sedition laws—but before the first
World War the incongruity of persecution with the First Amendment
had been generally acknowledged. With the Sedition and Espionage
Acts of that war, the "red hysteria" of the twenties, the Alien Registra-
tion Act of 1940, the loyalty tests and purges of the mid-forties, the
establishment of un-American activities committees, intolerance received, as it were, the stamp of official approval. Loyalty was identified
with conformity, and the American genius, which had been experimental and even rebellious, was required to conform to a pattern.
Congressmen more and more displayed that never-ending audacity
of elected persons which had been thought characteristic of the Old
World and outlawed in the New. No less audacious and equally
shabby was the attempt by corporate business to identify its own version of private enterprise with Americanism.

The new intolerance was distinguished not only by its quasi-official
character but by a certain moral flabbiness, a weakening of intellectual
fiber. The intolerance of the Puritans, or of a Jonathan Edwards, had
been informed, and so, too, in a twisted way, that of the Federalist
die-hards. The proslavery argument was at least a coherent argument,
and in the hands of Calhoun, states' rights had constitutional dignity.
Even the intolerance of Bryan and the Fundamentalists had been sure
of itself and of its ground and had been concerned, sincerely, with
spiritual salvation. The intolerance of the thirties and the forties had
not even the dignity of intelligence or accuracy, or of a moral purpose.
Those who proclaimed undying devotion to the Constitution had not

bothered to read that document, and the Declaration of Independence was similarly terra incognita to them. They arrogated to themselves the guardianship of the American tradition without knowing any more about the American than the Mexican tradition; they were dogmatic about traditional American economic virtues without familiarizing themselves with the most elementary facts of American economic history; they announced as law doctrines that had been consistently repudiated by the Supreme Court.

A simple society whose members could take their social position for granted, or were unaware of its importance, could indulge itself in toleration, but social and economic insecurity led almost inevitably to social and economic intolerance. That intolerance was displayed most aggressively in the realm of race relations. The Negro problem spread to the North, and the Ku Klux Klan of the 1920's was incomparably more sinister than that of the 1860's. The gap between the pretense of equality and the reality of inequality, dramatized by the second World War, shocked public opinion, and the decade of the forties witnessed a sincere effort to bridge it. As race relations deteriorated in the North, prospects for their improvement in the South brightened. The important thing was the acknowledgment of what Gunnar Myrdal called the American Dilemma, and the recognition by state and federal governments of their responsibility to resolve it. Meantime anti-Semitism, which had played so pernicious a role in Germany's history, spread to America, and though novelists and Hollywood united to advertise its perils, it showed, at mid-century, no sign of abating.

Intolerance sprang not only from insecurity but from a mounting, though still hesitant, class consciousness. Social position depended more on race than on family: a well-to-do Nordic who went to the right schools had little need of a family tree, and antiquity of family was itself of no value to a Negro or a Jew or to an immigrant from one of the wrong countries. Class was for the most part, however, economic rather than social; a respectable name was not a disadvantage, but a flourishing bank account was an incalculable asset, and no barriers proved strong enough to resist great wealth.

Class consciousness expressed itself in countless ways. The country club supplanted the church as the center of social life in most towns, and neither its standards nor its practices were equalitarian. Old World practices like tipping were acquiesced in by self-respecting workers whose predecessors, a century earlier, would have rejected gratuities as an affront; and so far had Americans strayed from their earlier principles that few realized that the giving and the accepting of gratuities implied class distinctions. The word "society," when used by city newspapers, came to mean not the whole population but that element of it that was prosperous and Nordic, and while every graduate of Vassar could be sure of having her wedding duly reported in the eastern newspapers, the graduate of a mid-western college knew that her wedding was of no public interest. Private schools took on something of the importance of public schools in England and, with the founding of Groton School in 1884, began openly to imitate the English. Finishing schools continued to emphasize the study of French for reasons not primarily literary or scholarly, and hotels innocent of French cooking to print their bills of fare in that language. As Americans became increasingly self-conscious about family, names became longer, and double-barreled names not uncommon: it was perhaps more than fortuitous that between Washington and Lincoln only three presidents boasted more than one Christian name, but five between Taft and Truman.

Religion was fortunately free of that class connection which characterized it in England, but the socially ambitious tended to attach themselves to the Episcopal church and sometimes referred to it as the Anglican, while church architecture departed increasingly from its American antecedents and imitated English and French. The declining prestige of England put an end to that revival of colonialism so marked in New England at the close of the nineteenth century, but presentation at court still meant the Court of St. James's and was still thought desirable. America had not yet produced either a Debrett or a Burke, but in most communities the Social Register was read more assiduously than Who's Who and carried more weight.

Even morals appeared to take on a class character, though of an unexpected type. Divorce and nervous breakdowns were more easily accessible to the rich than to the poor and, as if in response to Veblen's diagnosis, carried connotations such as had been implied two centuries earlier by mistresses and gout. Even insobriety became respectable if achieved in an expensive night club rather than in a saloon, and the new rich became connoisseurs of cocktails as the gentry of an earlier day had been of wines. Sexual irregularities transcended class distinctions, but a learned investigation of the sex habits of males discovered that while the poor and the unsophisticated strayed more readily and more frequently from the straight and narrow path of virtue, the educated and the well-to-do strayed down more labyrinthine ways.

The most convincing evidence of class consciousness was to be found in advertisements. Advertisers, who presumably knew what they were about, appealed more and more to the snob instinct. They celebrated not the virtues of their product but the social distinction of those who bought it, and keeping up with the Joneses was abandoned for the more titillating task of keeping up with the Biddles. It was supposed to be a guarantee of the merits of a tobacco or a liquor that it appealed to those whose names could be found in the Social Register, while the merits of Mozart and Beethoven were enhanced by the approval of ladies and gentlemen who habitually dressed for dinner.

Along with and not unconnected with class consciousness went what seemed a steady decline of taste. Democracy, here, seemed a matter of leveling down rather than up. Vulgarization could be read in the newspapers, the magazines, the comics, and in much that passed for literature; it could be seen in the moving pictures and heard on the radio. It could be discovered, above all, in advertisements which, during the second quarter of the century, reached the nadir of vulgarity.

American society, as popular advertisements portrayed it, was a nightmare of fear and jealousy, gossip and slander, envy and ambition, greed and lust, where almost any means were justified to attain private and selfish ends, where sentiment was meretricious, ideals tarnished, and virtue debauched. The typical American, as they pictured him, lived in a torment of anxiety and cupidity and regulated his conduct entirely by ulterior considerations. He read books to make conversation, listened to music to establish his social position, chose his clothes for the impression they would make on business associates, entertained his friends in order to get ahead, held the respect of his children and the affection of his wife by continuous bribery. To the advertisers nothing was sacred and nothing private: they levied impartially upon filial devotion, marriage, religion, health, and cleanliness. Love, as they portrayed it, was purely competitive: it went to those who could afford the most lavish gifts and was retained only by incessant attention to externals. Friendship, too, was for sale: to serve inferior liquors or confess to shabby furniture was to forfeit it. Advancement came not through industry, intelligence, or integrity, or any of the old-fashioned virtues but was won by an astute combination of deception, bribery, and blackmail.

All this presented to the student of the American character a most perplexing problem. It was the business of the advertisers to know that character, and their resources enabled them to enlist in its study the aid of the most perspicacious sociologists and psychologists. Yet if their analysis was correct, the American people were decadent and depraved. No other evidence supported this conclusion. Advertisers appealed to fear, snobbery, and self-indulgence, yet no one familiar with the American character would maintain that these were indeed its predominant motivations, and statesmen who knew the American people appealed to higher motives, and not in vain. The problem remained a fascinating one, for if it was clear that the advertisers libeled the American character, it was equally clear that Americans tolerated and even rewarded those who libeled them.

Vulgarization proclaimed itself most blatantly in the passing of reticence. Almost every newspaper published advice to the lovelorn, and one omniscient mother-confessor answered three thousand letters a week. Psychoanalysis went on the air, and troubled women told a gaping audience things their mothers would not have confided to their grandmothers. There was a vast palaver about sex, and books that had once been read covertly behind the barn were distributed by reputable book clubs. Buchmanism enjoyed some popularity in prosperous circles and confession magazines in less prosperous, while other magazines devoted to a rehearsal of the most intimate details of the lives of public figures boasted circulations running into the millions, and every schoolboy knew what kind of soap his favorite actress used in her bath. Publicity came to be regarded as good and even bad publicity as better than none, and the socially elect, who had once taken pride in keeping their names out of newspapers, were now avid to put them in. Reporters, ever notorious for their prying ways, were delighted to find that they could count on the cooperation of their victims, and though Woodrow Wilson had smashed the camera of a newspaper photographer bent on invading the privacy of his family, his successors dealt more amiably with the press. Ivy Lee had taught business the value of good public relations, and soon politicians and film stars had their public relations agents, universities that could not afford adequate teachers' salaries found money for public relations offices, and churches arranged that God should have a good press.

General Sherman had thrown reporters bodily out of his headquarters, but during World War II the Army and Navy thought it advisable to recommend themselves to a public for whose existence they were fighting.

Nothing, perhaps, was more striking than the change in the character of American humor. Old-fashioned comic books all but disappeared—the *Samantha at Saratoga* and *Peck's Bad Boy* type—and while it is easy to imagine Franklin D. Roosevelt regaling his Cabinet with the latest *New Yorker* story it is difficult to suppose him reading to them from Artemus Ward. The nineteenth-century *Life, Judge,* and *Puck* bore a strong family resemblance to *Punch:* the English weekly persisted, through the decades, along its familiar groove, but *The New Yorker* departed radically from its American predecessors. Nineteenth-century humor had been rural, expansive, exaggerated, amiable, and familiar, its purpose, Constance Rourke wrote, "that of creating fresh bonds, a new unity, the semblance of a society and the rounded completion of an American type." That of the twentieth century was urban, pointed, sophisticated, malicious, and startling, designed to wound rather than to entertain, to divide and destroy rather than to unite and complete. The shift from Artemus Ward and Petroleum V. Nasby and Bill Nye to Ring Lardner and Peter Arno and Damon Runyon was a shift from the verbal and gregarious to the literary and private, from the long story and the tall tale to the anecdote and the epigram, from dialect and slapstick to cleverness and subtlety, and from the robust to the morbid; it was almost a shift from good humor to bad. Mark Twain had been disillusioned, but he was careful to keep his disillusionment to himself or to books designed for posthumous publication, but from O. Henry to Ring Lardner, twentieth-century humor was shot through and through with disillusionment. There were exceptions, of course. Donald Ogden Stewart's *Parody Outline of History* was in the Bill Nye tradition; Robert Benchley often indulged in good-natured farce; James Thurber laughed at rather than indulged in disillusionment; E. B. White, along with much kindliness and charm, displayed that indignation against cruelty and meanness that had distinguished Mark Twain.

Yet American humor between the wars was on the whole barbed and malicious. More, it was often sensational, fantastic, and sadistic, and in its preoccupation with sex it came closer to the French than to its English and American antecedents. The "funnies" of an earlier day had attempted comedy; their successors, the "comics," abandoned themselves to violence and fantasy. Literature, too, was no longer content with the exploitation of the homely situations and familiar characters that had sufficed an earlier generation and continued to suffice such English writers as E. F. Benson and George Birmingham and Humphrey Pakington. Of the major literary figures only Steinbeck continued some of the tradition of frontier humor, while Holmes and Howells and Mark Twain had no successors in prose nor James Russell Lowell or Charles Godfrey Leland in poetry. Politics had always been the natural butt of American humor, and though cartoonists and H. L. Mencken continued to exploit it, Mr. Dooley was the last of the commentators whose observations seemed destined to live.

As the comic story disappeared, the humorous poem withered away, and the funnies turned to fantasies, old-fashioned comedy found a successor in the films, and Harold Lloyd, Charlie Chaplin, and Laurel and Hardy were the true heirs of Bill Nye and Josh Billings. But the films showed the same tendency to evolve from simple slapstick to more sophisticated comedy. Thus Chaplin, greatest of the comedians, made his later films vehicles for social criticism, while the Marx brothers indulged in satire. Radio humor, which nightly convulsed its millions, lingered on in the earlier tradition, as did the joke books which so faithfully revived Joe Miller, but both were more obvious and less innocent than the music-hall or the cracker-box humor of the nineteenth century.

The hothouse character of American humor reflected a growing artificiality in American life. It was, perhaps, inevitable that as Americans moved from country to city and embraced a technological civilization they should lose touch with nature, and with its discipline, and come to live at second hand. The change was both physical and psychological. An ordinary snowstorm disrupted the communications, heating, and food supply of a whole city; a telephone strike created nationwide chaos. Labor-saving devices multiplied and largely defeated their own purpose: few Americans of the twentieth century found time to live as spaciously as had their ancestors a century earlier, and every time-saving machine required another to fill the time that had been saved. Automobiles did not in fact expand horizons but merely made it easier to reach them and thus to ignore them, and as Americans ceased to walk they lost familiarity even with their own countryside. Children who studied the geography of China could not name the trees that shaded their own streets, while their parents, who thought nothing of a transcontinental automobile junket, were ignorant of the most elementary facts about the climate and soil of the country they traversed. Workingmen lost much of their craftsmanship, and the nation which lived by cars and radios could not produce mechanics sufficiently skilled or sufficiently honest to repair either. The average woman no longer baked bread or indulged in what had once been called fancywork; men ceased making furniture and boys lost the knack of whittling or of improvising their own games. Dictation and the typewriter all but killed the art of letter writing, and no letters of a twentieth-century statesman yet published compared in literary finish with those written by busy men like Jefferson and Washington. Everyone was literate, but telegraph companies found it profitable to prepare canned messages of sympathy and congratulation. Businessmen, educators, and administrators, who used pieces of paper as counters for real things, came in time to believe that the counters were the real things, and a generation which kept the most elaborate records knew, perhaps, less about human nature than did those innocent of forms and questionnaires. Stockbrokers judged the economic health of the nation not so much by what was grown on farms or made in factories as by what was bet on the stock exchange. No businessman could be sure whether he was rich or poor until he had scanned the stock-market quotations of the day, and school systems that boasted a refined technique of intelligence and aptitude tests seemed unable to teach spelling or geography. Language, too, became artificial and derivative: under the tutelage of advertisers, government bureaucrats, and schools of education, people learned to say simple things in complicated ways, and Latin words crowded out Anglo-Saxon. Recreation came to be enjoyed vicariously. From playing games Americans took to watching them and then to listening to them on the radio. Even enthusiasm ceased to be spontaneous and was artificially organized and evoked by cheer leaders. Men who enjoyed artificial adventures in the pages of mysteries or westerns, and women who acquired artificial complexions, found little difficulty in adopting artificial emotions: they turned to the radio and the movies for excitement and sensation, laughter and tears, and learned about love from the magazines.

There seemed to be, in short, a progressive atrophy of the creative instinct of the average American. Whether this was reflected in what are called the fine arts was more difficult to say. Twentieth-century America boasted a hundred symphony orchestras, but it still imported its conductors and its trios and quartettes, and it had not yet produced a single first-rate composer or even one to rank with Stephen Foster. Art galleries were munificently endowed and well stocked, but it was not clear that any painter of the new century had the talent of a Homer, a Ryder, or an Eakins, and St. Gaudens had no successor in sculpture or La Farge in glass. The resources of technology seemed unable to produce china as lovely as that made in eighteenth-century Britain or nineteenth-century Germany, and furniture-makers could but imitate Hepplewhite or Sheraton. In architecture there was originality and even genius, but Louis Sullivan was unhonored and unemployed, and Frank Lloyd Wright's reputation was made on the European Continent. The skyscraper was a social and architectural catastrophe; academic and ecclesiastical architecture was largely derivative; and neither money nor machinery seemed able to create a domestic architecture as good as that available to almost any New England villager in the eighteenth century. If the creative instinct was to express itself anywhere it might be expected that it would appear in the movies and the radio, yet all the resources of Hollywood seemed unable to compete with the talent of English and French producers, and it was the conclusion of most mid-century critics that American radio had not had a new idea for twenty-five years.

4

Changes in the habits, practices, and morals of the twentieth-century American were, on the whole, consistent with those in the realm of ideas. With the growing emphasis on conformity, eccentricity was no longer so amiably indulged: the passion for creating "characters" which the more popular novelists showed was itself evidence of a felt need. It would be misleading to insist that Americans were less self-reliant than formerly, but certainly society as a whole was far more interdependent, and with interdependence went some impatience with independence. The nineteenth-century farmer and craftsman had not needed to rationalize his enterprise into a philosophy, but the practical disappearance of any enterprise really private brought, as so often, a nostalgic rationalization. Americans had always been gregarious, and even with the inevitable associations of urban life and the growth of self-confidence, the habit did not abate. If lodges and clubs attracted them less, business and professional associations claimed them more insistently, and they could scarcely read a book or listen to music or take a walk except in groups. Life became increasingly regimented. Regimentation was not, as political critics would have it, a product of government regulation or of a Communist conspiracy but of a technological economy, and it was, perhaps, inevitable. The necessity of living in the same kind of houses, doing the same kind of work, using the same machinery, reading the same newspapers, was paralleled by the desire to use the same soap, eat the same breakfast food, laugh at the same radio jokes, admire the same movie stars, and digest the same magazine articles as did everybody else.

Technology and abundance freed men and women from much of the hard physical work that had absorbed the energies of their grandparents. Americans still worked harder than most other peoples, but the work week declined from sixty to forty hours, vacations stretched from one week to a month or more, children were kept out of the labor market until they were eighteen or twenty years old, insurance companies implored men to retire at fifty, and small families, small flats, and labor-saving machinery relieved women from most of the drudgery of housework. For the first time in history leisure became a major problem. Americans, who had all but discovered time, now had so much of it on their hands that they scarcely knew what to do with it, yet they lived energetically rather than leisurely, getting and spending and laying waste their powers. Veblen had discovered in conspicuous leisure the hallmark of class, but where leisure was commonplace it ceased to be conspicuous, and for the professional and the intellectual man it became almost fashionable to work long hours. For the others, the automobile, the movies, and the radio did much to ameliorate the situation; unnecessary travel became necessary to the economy; books rescued some from boredom, and magazines designed to be looked at rather than read multiplied by the hundred. With the passing of the necessity for hard work, the old Puritan idea that work was a virtue and idleness a vice went glimmering, while prosperity, the easy speculative profits of the twenties and the forties, government responsibility for security, high income and inheritance taxes, the vicissitudes of economy and fluctuations in the value of money, all combined to make other Puritan virtues like frugality and thrift seem outmoded. Yet generalization here, as the Lynds discovered in their study of *Middletown,* is dangerous. If work ceased to be a moral virtue it persisted as a habit, and businessmen who could well afford to retire clung tenaciously to their jobs, while rural and small-town Americans still subscribed to the "gospel of hard work." And though thrift was no longer cultivated for moral reasons, insurance and banking statistics showed that Americans continued to provide, as best they could, for the future. If there was a change here from the nineteenth to the twentieth century, it was in the future that was envisioned: where an earlier generation had saved in order to leave an estate, the new generation was inclined to save for more immediate and personal purposes—an automobile, vacations, education, or retirement.

Prosperity and machinery made possible a degree of self-indulgence unknown in a more exacting age, and it was the opinion of many foreign observers that not only the women and children but the men as well were pampered. Certainly there was no asceticism in American life and little self-denial. The second World War imposed but few restrictions and no austerity upon the American people, yet Americans did not, on the whole, react well to such restrictions as were required, and the rationing of such commodities as meat and gasoline was widely evaded. Americans were generous, but a test such as the admission of a few hundred thousand displaced persons—who might possibly compete in the labor market or demand houses or spread alien doctrines—found them inhospitable and grudging. Children took parental support for granted well into their twenties, and it was far more common for young couples to be supported by their parents or even for young men to be supported by their wives than it had been half a century earlier. Most Americans took for granted, too, comforts unknown to all but the rich in other countries. They overheated their houses, insisted upon a car and a radio, consumed incredible quantities of soft drinks, ice cream, candy, and cigarettes, and spent enough annually on liquor and cosmetics to have supported the whole population of less fortunate countries. Luxury and self-indulgence should, perhaps, have led to debility, and those who still subscribed to the Puritan virtues were constantly recalling the latter days of the Roman Empire, but no one familiar with the conduct of American soldiers in the second World War would argue that American youth was soft or effeminate or that America was suffering from a failure of nerve.

Twentieth-century America, even more than nineteenth, seemed to be a woman's country. The supremacy of woman could be read in the statistics of property ownership, insurance, education, or literature, or in the advertisements of any popular magazine. Women ran the schools and the churches, they determined what would appear in the magazines and the movies and what would be heard over the radio. As many girls as boys attended college, and women made their way successfully into almost every profession. There were a hundred magazines designed especially for their entertainment or edification, and among them some with the largest circulation, while most metropolitan newspapers had a page for women and every radio station a series of programs directed exclusively to their supposed needs. As women spent most of the money, the overwhelming body of advertisements was addressed to them, and advertisers found it advisable to introduce the feminine motive even, or especially, where they hoped to attract men. Traditionally women had ruled the home, but only in America did they design it, build it, furnish it, direct its activities, and fix its standards. Most American children knew more of their mothers' than of their fathers' families, and it was the opinion of many observers of World War II that the silver cord bound American youth more firmly than the youth of any other land. It was appropriate enough that an American, Lester Ward, should have propounded the theory of the natural superiority of the female sex which he called gynecocracy, and American experience appeared to validate the theory.

There was a change, almost imperceptible, in the standards of sportsmanship. The professional spirit largely supplanted the amateur, college athletics were invaded by professionalism, football and basketball became big business. Professional sports themselves were marred by one scandal after another, while evasions of the amateur requirements by those who contended for amateur titles became so commonplace as to cease to be a scandal. As the commercial element entered sports, earning power became more important than the game itself, and the game became primarily a spectacle. Colleges and universities hired coaches who were paid as much as their presidents, spent millions on stadia, bought or seduced players, and retained them, as often as not, without any reference to academic qualifications. President Eliot of Harvard had objected to intercollegiate football because he discovered that the attack was directed against the weakest point in the opposition line: the objection was creditable, and was not voiced by his successors. Where English spectators applauded the play, Americans cheered the team, and where English applause was spontaneous, American cheering was organized, and the "cheer leader" was unique to America. Standards of sportsmanship took on something of a class tinge, vindicating the interpretation which Veblen had advanced in his *Theory of the Leisure Class*. Polo, sailing, riding, skiing, and even hunting and fishing were associated with the upper classes and governed by formal rules, and those who indulged in them were expected to observe both a ritual and a ceremonial habit, while baseball, which became the national pastime, ceased to be a major college sport. Yet the habit of fair play was deeply ingrained, and standards of sportsmanship remained high. The phrase "good sport"—all but untranslatable into other languages—still held connotations flattering to the American character. The tendency to regard both politics and business as a game persisted, and if this suggested immaturity, it implied, too, a wholesome willingness to abide by the rules of the game, acquiesce in decisions, and accept defeat cheerfully.

5

More significant, perhaps, than modifications of formal ideas or informal habits, were changes in moral attitudes and practices. The problem of popular morals is infinitely complex, for nothing lends itself less readily to reliable statistical analysis, and in no other realm are judgments so likely to be empirical and subjective. It seems fair to say that while the moral standards of the nineteenth century persisted almost unchanged into the twentieth, moral practices changed sharply, and that though the standards persisted the institutions that had sustained them and the sanctions that had enforced them lost influence and authority. It was this conflict between tradition and practice, this collapse of older sanctions before the creation of new, that accounted in considerable part for the increase in nervous breakdowns and other psychological and moral disorders in the generation after the first World War.

The most striking change was in the realm of religion. Americans were still formally Christian, and increasing numbers of them saw fit to maintain a nominal connection with some church, but few admitted any categorical connection between religion, church, and morals. "It was largely because of the continued strength of religion that the code of morals in most American communities remained extremely rigid," Allan Nevins could write of mid-nineteenth-century America. The churches of that time, he pointed out,

scrutinized behavior sharply. They counselled the drinker, rebuked the swearer, admonished all vice, and expelled any persistent wrongdoer. Employers who were churchmembers usually imposed their moral standards upon subordinates. Most Protestant bodies showed a strong hostility to habitual tippling, and several sternly reprobated the sale and use of liquor in any quantity. They all maintained an unbending code in matters of sex-relationship.

A century later the church, no longer able to satisfy the spiritual needs of the community, had largely forfeited its moral function and assumed, instead, a secular one—that of serving as a social organization. The public school, too, was less concerned with the training of character than with preparation for a job or for college, while private schools and denominational colleges that clung to the old responsibility were rarely sufficiently isolated to fulfill it. And an urbanized America was no longer exposed to the discipline imposed by Nature and by large families. The moral instructors of the new generation were the movies, the radio, and the press, and while they recognized their responsibility—negatively in the form of censorship and positively by precept, advice, and example—their values were meretricious and their standards shabby.

The waning influence of religion could be traced even in literature. The new generation was not familiar with the Bible, as its forebears had been. Religious books poured from the presses, but only theologians appeared to read them, while the layman was familiar neither with theology nor with religious history: when he sought spiritual consolation he was inclined to find it in such a book as Joshua Liebman's *Peace of Mind*. Lloyd Douglas' *The Robe* was in the tradition of *Ben Hur,* but no popular novelist addressed himself to the problem of religion in modern life as had Harold Frederic and Margaret Deland and Winston Churchill a half-century earlier. And in the two decades between the wars only four religious books—a of them dealing with the life and times of Christ—were listed among the "best sellers," while no less than forty books of mystery and detection joined what Frank Luther Mott called the Golden Multitude. The most obvious and the least reliable index to morality was the record of the police courts. Statistically lawlessness was on the increase, but the frowning statistics which, after all, reflected new categories of legal offenses, more effective law enforcement, and improved statistical techniques as much as the state of public morals could be discounted. If the record did indicate that the twentieth-century American was no more law-abiding than the nineteenth, it suggested that he was less given to violence, lynching, and rioting, or to sharpness and chicanery. Yet modern lawlessness, though less violent than that of the nineteenth century, had perhaps more serious consequences: thus, though assault and murder were less common in 1940 than in 1840, the automobile inflicted annually as many casualties as any war in which Americans had ever engaged. Lawlessness, here, seemed rather a matter of self-indulgence and recklessness than of criminality, but the consequences for its victims were no less painful. So, too, with other manifestations of impatience with the restraints of the law or of regulations. There were interesting philosophical reasons why Prohibition was vulnerable, but the reasons why millions of Americans flouted the Volstead Act were not philosophical but hedonistic. Logic and patriotism alike required conformity to the rationing system of World War II, but nonconformity was common and the black market somewhat blacker in America than in Britain. And while the standards of commercial and business honesty had undoubtedly improved over the years, the record of some ten thousand bank failures during the decade of the twenties and the panic years contrasted unhappily with the record of Canadian and British banks during the same period.

No less serious was the persistence of what might be called, paradoxically, official lawlessness. The example was set by federal and state legislators who violated their oaths of office by stubbornly refusing to honor the plain requirements of the Fourteenth and Fifteenth Amendments to the Constitution, who were responsible for the wave of red-baiting laws and for the alien deportations that disgraced the decade of the twenties, and who again and again grossly abused their powers of examination and investigation. There was an open conspiracy, local, state, and national, to reduce Negroes and

Orientals to the status of second-class citizens, and violations of the constitutional rights of Negroes in the South were so much the normal thing that when a Negro in that section actually exercised some of the rights guaranteed him by his Constitution it was news. Police officers, particularly in the cities, were all too often guilty of brutality or of grave violations of the rights of prisoners, and the very term "third degree" achieved unpleasant notoriety as an Americanism.

Yet no one familiar with nineteenth-century American politics could doubt that political morality had improved. Not since Reconstruction, to be sure, had Americans witnessed corruption in high places as shocking as that which dishonored the Harding administration. Yet war presents at once the greatest temptations and the widest opportunities to private greed and chicanery, and neither the first nor, as far as the record is available, the second World War was attended by that venality which stained the pages of the history of the Civil War. That *Shame of the Cities* which Lincoln Steffens described had faded, and Lord Bryce's conclusion that municipal government was the one conspicuous failure of American democracy was not insisted upon by his twentieth-century successors. Nor could any fair historian of the American Senate, after the enactment of the Seventeenth Amendment, charge that body with treason as David Graham Phillips had done at the beginning of the century. If a corrupt alliance between business and politics persisted, it was no longer ostentatious but concealed and apologetic. Civil service reform had gone steadily forward, the great majority of public offices were now removed from the patronage, and the spoils system was no longer the chief lubricant of party politics.

The most conspicuous and probably the most profound change in popular morals was in the realm of family and sex relationships. Marriage came to seem more tentative, virtue more relative, and parental control less authoritative than had been assumed even a generation earlier, and the Seventh Commandment, long the most rigorously enforced, came to be regarded almost as irreverently as the Third and the Fourth. Statistics illuminate but do not explain the change. They show a decline in the birth rate from more than thirty-five per thousand in 1890 to less than twenty in 1945 and change in the size of the average family from over five to less than four; they reveal a sevenfold increase in the divorce rate for th country as a whole and, in the Lynds' *Middletown,* approximately one divorce for every two marriages; they confess a sobering upturn in juvenile deliquency, and especially in the number of juveniles guilty of sex offenses.

No single explanation accounts for the change in family relationships, for the declining size of the family, or the increase in divorces and in juvenile delinquency. A wider knowledge of contraceptives, the emancipation of women, late marriages, an aging population, and the shift from country to city, all contributed, but even combined they leave much unexplained. Birth control is, after all, an effect, not a primary cause; late marriages were accompanied by such improvements in medicine as enabled women to bear children later in life; and anyone familiar with the teeming population of city slums knew that the birth rate was not necessarily dependent upon a rural environment. It is equally difficult to account for the startling increase in divorce. There is no evidence of a comparable increase in cruelty or nonsupport or even marital unfaithfulness, the traditional grounds for divorce, and it is probable that the upswing in the divorce rate was to be explained rather by the greater ease in obtaining divorces, higher standards of marital happiness, and self-indulgence, rather than by any general deterioration of marriage relations.

Nor could the historian confidently draw moral conclusions from his study of vital statistics. Moralists might regard a shrinking birth rate as a shirking of responsibility, but it was by no means clear that society profited from a high birth rate, and a comparison of Denmark and India suggested that there was no necessary correlation between civilization and population. Even some moralists, outside the Catholic church, were ready to agree that divorce was often better than unhappy marriage. And clearly juvenile delinquency was to be explained rather by the impact of depression and of war than by any peculiar depravity in the youth of the new generation.

Sex was still regarded by a large segment of the population as Sin, and the very vocabulary of morality testified to its importance, for such words as virtue, purity, and even morality and immorality carried sexual connotations. Yet both the old taboos and the old integrities were dissolving. Puritanism gave way to hedonism, inhibitions to experiments, and repression to self-expression. Advertisers pandered shamelessly to the erotic instinct, the moving pictures appealed to it, and novelists exploited it, and all used a franker vocabulary than had been customary. The Kinsey report on sex habits made clear that by the mid-twentieth century neither chastity nor continence nor marital fidelity could be taken for granted, and no one familiar with the statistics of the divorce court or the Army Medical Corps or juvenile delinquency could doubt that looseness in sexual morality had serious social consequences.

At the same time neither the new attitude toward sex nor the new code of conduct were necessarily unwholesome. The double standard of morals, never as strong in America as on the European Continent, was relaxed in favor of the single; and, if the single standard meant that women were not expected to be more moral than men rather than that men were expected to be as moral as women, the new realism was preferable to the old hypocrisy. Those antisocial diseases which had so long and so idiotically been called social were now publicly discussed and effectively treated, and medical science held out hope that they might be eliminated in a generation. Morally, immodesty was no worse than false modesty; and censorship boards to the contrary notwithstanding, there was no evidence that the literary treatment of sex impaired the morals of even the most susceptible. Sex education was accepted as a duty of parents and made its way even into some of the more progressive schools and into popular magazines and books, and if much of the romance that had long surrounded sex was dissipated, so too was much of the mystery, and with it the fear and frustration and suffering.

6

It cannot be said that the second World War tested the American character as it did, in different ways, the British, the French, and the German, but it did dramatize that character and, as it were, recapitulate it. Certainly no evaluation of the American character could ignore the fact that the greatest crisis of modern history found American public opinion sensitive to the moral issues involved, that this war united Americans as had no previous war, that it was fought for what seemed unselfish ends, and that Americans generally supported a just peace and a postwar program of unparalleled generosity.

How profoundly five years of war affected American economy and society was clear even during those years; how they affected the American mind and character has yet to be determined. The American was sure of his own superiority and of his invulnerability; did Pearl Harbor and the Battle of the Atlantic give him pause? He had a high sense of fair play, even in war; did his experience with German and Japanese methods of warfare undermine this? He was optimistic about his world and his future; did contact with pessimism and frustration, and the disappointment of high hopes after the war, moderate this optimism? He was adolescent in some of his interests and many of his pleasures; did the grim experience of war mature him? He believed neither in evil nor in the Devil; did Buchenwald and Dachau corrupt him? He was an amateur, distrusting the expert and the specialist; did Manhattan Project convert him? He had been careless of authority and hostile to discipline; did military service persuade him to mend his ways? He had never acknowledged a military caste and rarely rewarded military service with social prestige; did the war make for the creation of a military elite? He had celebrated the virtues of individualism, especially in the economic realm; did the spectacle of what could be achieved by great impersonal organizations, military and economic and administrative, abate his individualism? He had been, on the whole, moral, generous, kindly, and romantic; did exposure to different standards of morality and to opportunities for self-indulgence impair his moral standards? He had known only his own country and was content with its character, its institutions, and its standards; did familiarity with the civilizations of Britain, France, and Italy disturb his satisfaction or suggest other standards and practices?

It is possible to answer these questions tentatively. On the whole the war would seem to have confirmed those traits which we have distinguished as peculiarly American rather than to have changed them. It confirmed Americans in their optimism, their self-confidence, and their sense of superiority, for it ended, after all, in the greatest of victories and one for which they could claim a major part of the credit. They had bet on material power, on machinery and science, on organization and the assembly line, on a citizen army and a democratic system of government—and they had won. They had been sure that America was the best and the happiest of nations, and what they had seen overseas had strengthened this conviction. They were opportunistic and found that their inspired opportunism somehow paid dividends, and few of them realized how much planning and farsightedness went into the conduct of the war. Their army was the most democratic of major armies and it had fought well. They were used to material comforts, and their government supplied them with such comforts as no other armies knew; they took the envy of less fortunate peoples and soldiers as a proper tribute and gave generously of their surplus. They were, most of them, honorable, brave, and idealistic; the war did not force them to abandon honor for treachery, soldiers fought as bravely at Bataan or Okinawa or Bastogne as their forefathers had at Bunker Hill or Gettysburg or the Argonne, and idealism remained not only an individual characteristic but an official policy.

To the extent that all this is true, the war merely deepened certain traits in the American character. Did it change any or introduce new departures? In some respects the American outlook and character may have been affected. Probably Americans overseas were broadened by their experience with other peoples and civilizations, and some assuredly learned that superiority in plumbing did not necessarily mean superiority in all the amenities of life or in moral qualities. Cultural isolationism dissolved, along with economic, political, and military, and the average American of 1950 probably knew more about European society, literature, and politics than had his father or his grandfather. Certainly Americans emerged from the war less self-centered and more conscious of the economic interdependence of all nations and of their responsibilities for the maintenance of sound international economy. The military came to occupy a larger place in the American scene than ever before and to exercise an unprecedented influence on the formulation of political policy, though General Eisenhower's refusal to enter the presidential race of 1948 undoubtedly checked a growing inclination to reward military success with political office. The war dramatized changes in moral standards and conduct. No previous American war had discovered such a breakdown of personal integrity, such looting and destructiveness, such sexual promiscuity. It at once exacerbated race relations and advanced racial equality: the total effect was to bring the whole issue of race out into the open, to expose the gap between the pretense of equality and the reality of inequality, and to force the government to take some action toward bridging that gap. Finally the achievements and responsibilities of the war seemed to have brought along with a sense of power, bewilderment and confusion. Americans knew that theirs had become the most powerful nation on the globe, but they were, for the most part, embarrassed rather than exalted by their position and their power.

7

The decade of the twenties had been one of prosperity, materialism, and cynicism, and it was perhaps cynicism that made the strongest—though not the most permanent—impression on the American mind. Disillusionment, to be sure, was by no means unique to Americans: what was remarkable was that it should have embraced not only the Old World, whose failings had inspired it, but America too—the American past, American culture, American society and economy. The depression, as we have noted, made much of this disillusionment seem unreal or merely literary and made clear that both repudiation and flight were luxuries in which only those indifferent to the fate of the nation could indulge.

Even more emphatic was the impact of war and chaos in the thirties. If the depression tempered impatience with alleged imperfections, the rise of totalitarianism abroad encouraged gratification with undeniable blessings. By contrast with the barbarism that so speedily overwhelmed many ancient nations, American failings came to seem superficial, her sins almost innocent. Theodore Dreiser could write of Tragic America and Archibald MacLeish that "America was Promises," but Americans knew instinctively that it was Europe that was really tragic, and that—the depression notwithstanding—American promises had been as largely fulfilled as any others that had been held out to sanguine men.

Thus, economic convulsions at home and political, social, and moral convulsions abroad brought a reconsideration of the significance of America, a search for what was valid in the American past, sound in the American present, encouraging in the American future. In a world where familiar ideas such as democracy, liberty, equality, the dignity of man, and the rule of law, were callously repudiated, it was no longer possible to take them for granted, and there came, in America, a more scrupulous examination of their meaning and a more exacting test of their efficacy. As had happened in the days of transcendental reform just a century earlier, old institutions and faiths and practices were called before the bar of reason and required to justify themselves.

The search for the meaning of American civilization, given such urgency by the breakdown of European, was stimulated, too, by official policy. Franklin Roosevelt, as richly informed in the history and traditions of his own country as any president since Jefferson, was no less concerned to save the spiritual than the material heritage of the nation, and for the first time in American history artists and writers found themselves beneficiaries of large-scale governmental support along with bankers and industrialists, workingmen and farmers. The Federal Arts Project, to whose manifold activities an enlightened government appropriated altogether some fifty million dollars, was an expression of the principle that literature and art, music and drama, were as essential to the happiness and prosperity of the nation as any merely economic activities and that those who engaged in them were legitimate objects of the patronage of the state. Under its auspices painters depicted the American scene on thousands of canvases and re-created the American past on the walls of countless post offices, courthouses, and libraries scattered over the land. Constance Rourke, biographer of those unmistakably American artists, Audubon and Charles Sheeler, and sympathetic student of many aspects of the American past, directed the great "Index of American Design," a collection which for the first time made known the richness of American folk art—furniture, woodcarving, textiles, embroideries, hardware, and decorations. Archives long moldering in obscurity were dusted off, catalogued, and indexed, and moribund local historical and genealogical societies took a new lease on life. The Federal Writers' Authority prepared that magnificent series of state and local guidebooks which eventually provided Americans with better Baedekers than any other country possessed. And the Library of Congress collection of American prints and photographs of old houses revealed what most Americans had forgotten, the existence of an authentically American tradition in architecture.

Inspired, then, by the depression and by the spectacle of catastrophe abroad and stimulated by governmental patronage, the rediscovery of America took varied and vigorous form. It was in part that what was imperiled seemed doubly dear, that—as Stephen Vincent Benét wrote—

There are certain words,
Our own and others', we're used to—words we've used,
Heard, had to recite, forgotten, . . .
Liberty, equality, fraternity.
To none will we sell, refuse or deny, right or justice.
We hold these truths to be self-evident.

I am merely saying—what if these words pass?
What if they pass and are gone and are no more,
Eviscerated, blotted out of the world? . . .

They were bought with belief and passion, at great cost.
They were bought with the bitter and anonymous blood
Of farmers, teachers, shoemakers and fools
Who broke the old rule, and the pride of kings . . .

It took a long time to buy these words.
It took a long time to buy them, and much pain.*

It was in part, too, that many things heretofore neglected or ignored
took on new significance. A new regional literature, more authentic
and less sentimental than that of the 1880's, celebrated every section of
the country. Rachel Field and Dorothy Canfield were less concerned
with recording the fate of New England spinsters or uncovering evidence of decadence than Alice Brown and Mary Wilkins Freeman
had been and more concerned with suggesting that New England
had not yet exhausted her vitality. T. S. Stribling and Marjorie
Rawlings, Allan Tate and Eudora Welty—to say nothing of Caldwell and Faulkner—wrote less sentimentally about the New South
than James Lane Allen and Thomas Nelson Page had written about
the Old. Louis Bromfield explained Ohio, and Ruth Suckow, Iowa,
and Marie Sandoz, Nebraska, and Frank Dobie, Texas, while Vardis
Fisher and John Steinbeck made clear that the West was no longer
primitive—and not very romantic. No section or state, scarcely a city
or county, was so poor as to lack its literary chronicler, and if most
of this new outpouring of local color was negligible as literature,
it was significant as sociology or psychology. Historical novels, which
had declined in popularity since the days of Winston Churchill and

* From "Nightmare at Noon" in *Selected Works of Stephen Vincent Benét*, published by
Rinehart and Company, Inc. Copyright, 1940, by Stephen Vincent Benét.

Mary Johnston and S. Weir Mitchell, once more found an audience avid to learn history the easy way and conscious of their debt to the past; and competent craftsmen like Kenneth Roberts, Walter Edmonds, Esther Forbes, and Margaret Mitchell exploited this new interest. Those who found reading too difficult or too time-consuming were able to absorb their history through the films, and *Gone With the Wind,* in book and moving-picture form, gave millions of Americans a sense of the grandeur and misery of the Civil War.

Poetry, too, caught the infection; the *Spoon River Anthology* gave way to *The People, Yes* and *The Waste Land* to the *Western Star.* Carl Sandburg, who had immersed himself in Lincoln, prophesied that

> Across the bitter years and the howling winters
> The deathless dream will be the stronger
> The dream of equity will win.

Paul Engle told his countrymen that

> it is time
> To leave this wandering always on the earth
> And take from the hawk his flying wisdom, soar
> On the keen edge of the world's wind, veer and hover
> Until you take the very stars for your eyes.

And Stephen Vincent Benét, who had already written the epic of the Civil War, *John Brown's Body,* and who had "fallen in love with American names," turned at the end of his tragically short life to a poetic re-creation of the migration of those people who followed the Western Star, to celebrate, with almost religious exaltation,

> this dream
> This land unsatisfied by little ways,
> Open to every man who brought good will,
> This peaceless vision, groping for the stars,
> Not as a huge devouring machine
> Rolling and clanking with remorseless force
> Over submitted bodies and the dead
> But as live earth where anything could grow . . .*

Historians, geographers, sociologists, philologists, and many other scholars marched with the novelists and the poets. History abandoned

* From "Listen to the People" in *Selected Works of Stephen Vincent Benét,* published by Rinehart and Company, Inc. Copyright, 1941, by Stephen Vincent Benét.

the debunking so popular in the twenties, and returned to the task of understanding the national character set it by Adams and Turner and Parrington. Scholars like Douglas Freeman, Samuel Eliot Morison, Allan Nevins, and Marquis James re-created the American past, critically, but sympathetically and even affectionately. Historians like Walter Webb, economists like Rupert Vance, sociologists like Howard Odum used the tools of their special technique to illuminate the nature of sectionalism and to integrate sections and the nation. There was an outpouring of books celebrating the American land: the *Rivers of America* series, which traced the advance of white civilization up a hundred river valleys, inaugurated by Constance Lindsay Skinner, herself novelist, historian, and poet; a regional series, a mountain series, a lakes series, and scores of books content with mere pictorial illustration. Even more important were projects to make available the rich material of the American past. Americans had long and gratefully acknowledged their paternity but had known in fact relatively little about the Father of their country: now the writings of Washington were properly edited and published by the government itself, and Douglas Freeman undertook to write a definitive biography. Jefferson had long been acknowledged a veritable arsenal of democratic thought, but not until the Princeton University Press and the *New York Times* combined to publish a definitive edition of his writings under the editorship of Julian Boyd was his full stature appreciated. And when, in 1947, the last restrictions were removed from access to the Lincoln papers, scholars prepared to rescue the Great Emancipator from the realm of legend and present him as he actually was through his own writings and those of his contemporaries.

As early as the twenties, Vernon Parrington had pointed the way to a livelier appreciation of what was American in American literature, and in the next two decades younger critics like Francis Matthiessen and Alfred Kazin repudiated alike the precious isolation of the humanists and the bitter estrangement of the Marxists and interpreted the American past as something to be understood rather than to be fought. Van Wyck Brooks, most distinguished of the rebellious critics of the early years of the century, no longer insisted upon the dichotomy between Edwards and Franklin, between high-brow and low-brow in American culture, but in a series of volumes of exquisite artistry recaptured the flavor of the past and found it both palatable and exciting. Emily Dickinson and Herman Melville and Thoreau had already been restored to their proper places in the gallery of great Americans, and the 1940's saw Henry James rescued from that expatriation which he had imposed upon himself and recaptured for American literature. H. L. Mencken's masterly study of the American language suggested that the English language had had a new birth of freedom in the New World, while the energetic collection of American folklore, folk songs and ballads, and of native American humor all testified to an interest in the American past not only discerning but confident.

Artists, too, turned away from the Beaux Arts tradition to rediscover an American one. That art should have its roots in native soil and should reflect the homely concerns of the common people had been a concept familiar enough in the past, but persistent colonialism, rich but artistically illiterate patronage, the prestige of Düsseldorf, Munich, Barbizon, and the Left Bank, had long obscured the principle in America. Yet from the days of Copley and Peale—to say nothing of Audubon and Wilson—there had been a vigorous native art; and in the early years of the new century, under the inspiration of Eakins and the leadership of such painters as Sloan, Bellows, Luks, Myers, and Prendergast, it attained distinction. It remained for the decades of the thirties and forties to rediscover the genre painting of Eastman and Mount and Bingham, to appreciate the drawings of Russell and Jackson and Remington, to celebrate the great tradition of American cartoons, and to produce a flourishing school of painters whose subject matter and technique were native and who enjoyed both prestige and patronage. Thomas Hart Benton was as authentically American as his distinguished ancestor; John Steuart Curry was equally at home in the plains of Kansas or the cotton fields of the deep South; Grant Wood bathed the rolling hills of Iowa in color and sentiment, and with Dale Nichols and Doris Lee revived something of the Currier and Ives technique; Charles Sheeler found beauty in the farmhouses and barns of the Pennsylvania Germans and the Shakers; Dorset, New Hope, and Taos developed schools dedicated to interpreting the varied beauties of Vermont, the Delaware Valley, and New Mexico. If architects discovered little that had not been implicit in the writings of Horatio Greenough in the mid-nineteenth century and explicit in the teaching of Louis Sullivan and Frank Lloyd Wright at the beginning of the twentieth century, it was interesting that the decades of the thirties and the forties witnessed the belated appreciation of these pioneers in the creation of an American tradition, the masterly studies of American architecture and technology by Lewis Mumford, and the restoration of colonial Williamsburg and of parts of old Salem and Deerfield.

8

"If there is one test of national genius universally accepted," wrote Ralph Waldo Emerson of England in 1847, "it is success." A test invoked by Emerson cannot be ignored nor a material one submitted by a Transcendentalist disparaged. Passionately American as he was, Emerson was constrained to admit that by this test mid-nineteenth-century England was the best of all countries, the one with the greatest store of national genius.

If that test were indeed valid there could be no doubt, a century later, which country in the world possessed the richest resources of national genius. That Americans had been largely successful in what they undertook was undeniable. They had—at least in large measure—formed a more perfect union, established justice, insured domestic tranquility, provided for the common defense, promoted the general welfare, and secured the blessings of liberty for themselves and, it was to be hoped, for their posterity. They had lifted the burdens from the shoulders of men, given to immigrants from the Old World a second chance, cherished the principles and promoted the practices of freedom, advanced social equality, promoted material well-being, furnished a climate favorable for the nourishment of talent, championed the cause of peace, undertaken and largely fulfilled their responsibilities in the community of nations.

It was, in every way, a spectacular achievement and one with few parallels in history. It was not wonderful, perhaps, that America should have achieved mere material success, for no other nation had been more bounteously endowed with natural resources or more fortunate in its inheritance of human. But there seemed no compelling reason why she should have achieved success in the realm of mind and spirit as well. A young nation, with tasks to perform chiefly material, without traditions of church or aristocracy, without learned or even leisure classes, isolated from the main currents of European thought, reverting on every frontier to primitive conditions, her original stock exposed to continuous dilution, her society fluid and her economy unsettled, she seemed condemned from the beginning to that cultural mediocrity of which so many visitors, from Tocqueville to Arnold, complained. That she should have produced a Carnegie, a Rockefeller, a Vanderbilt, a Ford, an Edison, an Eads, a Roebling, a Mahan, or an Eisenhower was natural enough. That she should have produced in half a century a Henry Adams, a William James, a Louis Sullivan, a Thomas Eakins, a John Dewey, an Edwin Arlington Robinson, an Oliver Wendell Holmes, a Vernon Louis Parrington, a Thorstein Veblen, a Willard Gibbs, was more surprising. That within a century and a half of the founding of the Republic she should have taken indisputable lead in science, medicine, law, education, and the social sciences and made contributions of lasting merit to art, architecture, literature, and philosophy was unexpected by all but those who knew best the deep roots of the American character and the fertile soil in which it flourished.

All this was cause for gratification but not for complacency, and the American of the mid-twentieth century was inclined to complacency. Along with spectacular triumphs, physical and intellectual, went frustrations and failures. Americans had failed to preserve and enhance the natural resources with which a benevolent Providence had endowed them. They had failed to realize fully the promise of freedom and equality held out first to immigrants and then to Negroes. They had failed properly to maintain that sanctity of law and inviolability of justice to whose maintenance they were pledged. They had failed to provide adequate education for all children able to profit from it or medical aid for all those who needed it or full security for the weak and the infirm and the perishing classes of society. Although in most respects their civilization was as high as any on the globe, they had failed as yet to create ideal conditions in which a spacious civilization might flourish.

Only a perfectionist would submit these failures as an indictment or hold that a people who had left undone some of those things which it should have done had forfeited its claim to virtue or to greatness. Judged by the standards of the Old World, the American failures were venial; it was something of a tribute to America that in judging her performance new standards were necessarily invoked. And both standards and judgment were, also of necessity, tentative. For it was clear that the American character, notwithstanding its relative maturity, was still in process of development, that the course which that development would take was still open, and that the future promised to be no less interesting than the past. For it was still true, a century and three quarters after Turgot's famous letter to Dr. Price, that this people was the hope of the human race; it was still true, a century after Longfellow had penned the lines, that

> Humanity with all its fears
> With all its hopes of future years
> Is hanging breathless on thy fate.

9

If laws of history were ever to be formulated, Henry Adams had predicted at the beginning of the nineties, they must of necessity be based in large measure on American experience. After the lapse of sixty years whose crowding wars and disasters gave some support to Adams' theory of the collapse of civilization itself, American experience was even more relevant to the formulation of those laws than Adams himself had realized. Both the peoples of the Old World and of the New acknowledged that America would direct, if it did not indeed control, the course of world history in the second half of the twentieth century, and outside Russia and her satellite countries few looked upon this prospect with misgivings. If a future directed by America was not wholly clear, neither was it a blank, and those who knew that nation best were satisfied that it meant intensely and meant good. For the America that would shape the unknown future was an America whose character had been formed in the known past, and if the lineaments of that character had not yet hardened into fixed patterns, they were at least recognizable and familiar. The future was precarious, but it was not an enigma. It presented, perhaps at best, a series of questions, but the very phrasing of those questions, their grammar and vocabulary and frame of reference, was dictated by the American past and the American character and confessed confidence in reasonable answers.

Out of an amalgam of inheritance, environment, and historical experience, Americans had fashioned a distinctive character; could they preserve and develop that character in a changed environment and under the impact of a new set of historical experiences? Adventure, experimentation, and mobility had marked their character; with the frontier gone, immigration dammed up, and resources running low, could they retain their enthusiasm for fresh experience and novel ways, their ingenuity and adventurousness? They were wonderfully inventive in the physical and technological realm; would they prove equally resourceful in the realms of social institutions and of morals? They had achieved the highest standard of living known to history; how would they live? Their society had changed from rural to urban; would they learn to master the city as their forefathers had mastered the country? Immigration had all but ceased; what would be the final product of the interracial melting pot? Fifteen million Negroes confronted one hundred and thirty million whites; would racial conflicts continue to frustrate democracy, or would they find a solution to the racial problem through ultimate amalgamation or through the establishment of such economic and social security as would permit mutual tolerance?

They had created an economy of abundance; could they fashion a political mechanism to assure the equitable distribution of that abundance? They had become the richest people on the globe; would they use their wealth to prosper society or to display power? They were democratic in law; would they be democratic in fact? They were equalitarian by conviction; would they be equalitarian in conduct? They had developed technology to its highest point; would they learn to make technology their servant rather than their master? They were using up their natural resources more rapidly than they were replacing them; would science reverse the process, or would they be forced to a lower standard of living or to economic imperialism? Agreement upon fundamentals had enabled them to maintain a two-party system; would the clashing ideologies of a new age destroy that agreement and fragmentize their politics? They had solved the ancient problem of liberty and order; would they succeed in maintaining order in a war-troubled world without such suppression of liberty as would change the character of their state? They had become increasingly like the peoples of the Old World; could they avoid the clash of doctrine and opinion, the conflict of church and state, of class and party, of race and section, that had for so long rent Europe with dissension and war?

They had inherited a system of law fashioned for the needs of a small, rural society and designed to safeguard the rights of property rather than of persons; could they adapt that law to an urbanized and democratic society which placed human above property rights? Their society had been almost wholly classless; would inequalities of wealth create and divide classes? Their culture had been derivative; could they create a culture of their own? They had the largest educational system in the world; for what would it educate? They enjoyed more leisure than any other western people; how would they use it? They had all but banished God from their affairs; who or what would they put in His place? They had never faced the problem of evil; would the palpable evil of the modern world persuade them to reconsider their idealism? They had begun to question the validity of traditional moral codes; could they formulate new ones as effective as those they were preparing to abandon?

They had relaxed their moral standards and habits; would they preserve themselves from corruption and decadence? They were idealistic; could they make their ideals work? They were pragmatic; could they preserve their pragmatism from vulgarization? They were generous; would their generosity extend to the moral sphere? They were good natured; would their good nature grow to magnanimity? They were intelligent; would their intelligence solve the problems of the future? They cherished a faith in reason but yielded to a philosophy of determinism; would they succeed in reconciling rationalism and determinism as their fathers had reconciled science and religion?

They had made the atomic bomb, would they use it for purposes of civilization or of destruction? They had achieved such power as no other modern nation had ever known; would that passion for peace which Henry Adams had named the chief trait in their character triumph over the temptation to establish a Pax Americana by force? They had fulfilled the responsibilities imposed upon them by the past; would they meet the challenge of the future?

The whole world had an interest in the answers which history would make to these questions.

Acknowledgments

To The Macmillan Company, for permission to quote from *The Collected Poems of E. A. Robinson,* and from Charles A. Beard, *The Open Door at Home.*

To Random House, Inc., for permission to quote from *The Collected Poems of Robinson Jeffers* and *The Double Axe and Other Poems.*

To Farrar, Straus and Company, Inc., for permission to quote from James Branch Cabell, *Beyond Life.*

To Alfred A. Knopf, Inc., for permission to quote from *A Lost Lady* and *Shadows on the Rock* by Willa Cather.

To Houghton Mifflin Co., for permission to quote from *O Pioneers* by Willa Cather; from *The Education of Henry Adams, Mont-Saint-Michel and Chartres, Letters of Henry Adams 1892–1918,* and *Prayer to the Virgin of Chartres.*

To Harcourt, Brace and Company, Inc., for permission to quote from *Main Currents in American Thought* by Vernon L. Parrington.

To Longmans, Green and Co., Inc., for permission to quote from *Pragmatism* by William James, and *Foundations of Belief* by Arthur Balfour.

To Charles Scribner's Sons, for permission to quote from *The Ivory Tower* by Henry James; *The Story of a Novel* by Thomas Wolfe; and *Preludes to Memnon* by Conrad Aiken.

To *Harper's Magazine,* for permission to quote from P. W. Bridgman, "The New Vision of Science" in *Harper's Magazine,* March, 1929.

Bibliography

Part I

CHAPTER I. *The Nineteenth-Century American*
Of all the books dealing with the general subjects of American thought, the most important is Vernon L. Parrington, *Main Currents in American Thought*, 3 vols. Unhappily Parrington did not live to complete the third volume—*The Beginnings of Critical Realism*—which, with the exception of some fragments, peters out with the 1880's. Ralph Gabriel, *The Course of American Democratic Thought* begins in 1815 and is particularly good for the period which Parrington does not cover. Merle Curti, *The Growth of American Thought* is encyclopedic in character and has valuable bibliographies. Of general histories, S. E. Morison and H. S. Commager, *The Growth of the American Republic*, 2 vols., and Charles and Mary Beard, *The Rise of American Civilization*, 2 vols., give particular attention to the interrelations of cultural and social with political and economic history. Interesting briefer interpretations can be found in Vols. I and IX of Henry Adams' great *History of the United States during the Administrations of Jefferson and Madison;* George Santayana, *Character and Opinion in the United States;* Charles W. Eliot, *Five American Contributions to Civilization;* William Orton, *America in Search of Culture;* W. C. Brownell, *Democratic Distinction in America;* F. J. Turner, *The Frontier in American History;* and Ralph Barton Perry, *Characteristically American.*

The most penetrating interpretation of the American character ever penned is Alexis de Tocqueville's *Democracy in America,* available in a critical two-volume edition by Phillips Bradley, and in a one-volume abridgment by H. S. Commager. Denis W. Brogan, *The American Character* is brilliant but concerned largely with the twentieth century. James Truslow Adams, *The American* is particularly good for the colonial and early national periods. Perhaps the most illuminating and certainly the most suggestive material is to be found in the writings of foreign observers and of immigrants. An anthology of foreign interpretations of America from Crèvecoeur to Brogan is H. S. Commager, ed., *America in Perspective.* Allan Nevins, ed., *America through British Eyes* contains valuable introductions and a comprehensive bibliography. Philip Rahv, ed., *The Discovery of Europe,* an anthology of American interpretations of the Old World, illuminates the American almost as much as the European character. Of the hundreds of foreign interpretations of America, the best, in addition to those of Tocqueville and Brogan, mentioned above, are Francis Grund, *The Americans in Their Moral, Social and Political Relations;* Alexander Mackay, *The Western World,* 2 vols.; James Bryce, *The Ameri-*

can Commonwealth, 2 vols.; and Hugo Münsterberg, *The Americans,* and *American Traits.*

Of autobiographical volumes by adopted Americans, the most interesting are: Mary Antin, *The Promised Land;* Jacob Riis, *The Making of an American;* Carl C. Jensen, *An American Saga;* Michael Pupin, *From Immigrant to Inventor;* Edward Bok, *The Americanization of Edward Bok; The Autobiography of Andrew Carnegie; The Reminiscences of Carl Schurz,* Vol. I.

My interpretation of the nineteenth-century American is drawn from a body of historical, biographical, and literary works too large to be listed here. A few special studies illuminate certain aspects of that character. Among the best are Roger Burlingame, *Engines of Democracy;* Arthur M. Schlesinger, *Learning How to Behave;* Ralph Barton Perry, *Puritanism and Democracy;* Dixon Wecter, *The Saga of American Society* and *The Hero in America;* Arthur W. Calhoun, *A Social History of the American Family;* Margaret Mead, *And Keep Your Powder Dry;* Constance Rourke, *American Humor;* Henry L. Mencken, *The American Language;* Constance Rourke, *The Roots of American Culture;* Harvey Minnick, *William Holmes McGuffey and His Readers;* James H. Tufts, *America's Social Morality.* The moral standards held up to children can be read best in William Dean Howells, *A Boy's Town;* Lucy Larcom, *A New England Girlhood;* Hamlin Garland, *A Son of the Middle Border;* and such classics of juvenile literature as *Tom Sawyer, Huckleberry Finn, Little Women,* and *The Story of a Bad Boy.* H. S. Commager, ed., *The St. Nicholas Anthology* gives a sampling of the most beloved of all children's magazines.

Perhaps the best index to the American character is to be found in autobiographical material. The field is so rich that it is difficult to make a selection, but the following are particularly valuable: Samuel G. Goodrich, *Recollections of a Lifetime,* 2 vols.; Mary Northend, *Memories of Old Salem;* Rebecca Felton, *Country Life in Georgia;* Clarence Darrow, *Farmington;* Henry S. Johnson, *The Other Side of Main Street;* Robert T. Coffin, *Portrait of an American;* Mary Ellen Chase, *A Goodly Heritage;* Henry Adams, *The Education of Henry Adams; The Autobiography of Lincoln Steffens; The Autobiography of William Allen White;* Harriet C. Brown, *Grandmother Brown's Hundred Years;* Marquis James, *Cherokee Strip.*

Three convenient collections of material that illustrate various aspects of the American character are H. S. Commager and A. Nevins, *The Heritage of America;* Louis Hacker, *The Shaping of the American Tradition,* 2 vols.; and Willard Thorp, Merle Curti, and Carlos Baker, *American Issues,* 2 vols.

CHAPTER 11. *The Watershed of the Nineties*
Useful general accounts of the transformation of American society and economy in the last decades of the nineteenth century can be found in S. E. Morison and H. S. Commager, *The Growth of the American Republic,* Vol. II, chaps. vi–xv; Ellis P. Oberholtzer, *A History of the American Peo-*

ple Since the Civil War, Vol. V; Arthur M. Schlesinger, *The Rise of the City;* Harold U. Faulkner, *The Quest for Social Justice;* and Matthew Josephson, *The Politicos* and *The President Makers.* The story of the agrarian revolt is told in John D. Hicks, *The Populist Revolt* and Fred Shannon, *The Farmers' Last Frontier;* the passing of the West, in Walter P. Webb, *The Great Plains* and E. S. Osgood, *The Day of the Cattleman;* labor unrest, in Henry David, *History of the Haymarket Affair,* N. J. Ware, *The Labor Movement in the United States 1860–1895,* and John R. Commons and Associates, *History of Labor in the United States,* Vols. III and IV. The rise of nationalism and imperialism can be read in the writings of Admiral Mahan and Theodore Roosevelt and is interpreted in Albert K. Weinberg, *Manifest Destiny.*

There is a wealth of fascinating but undigested material in Mark Sullivan, *Our Times,* especially Vols. I and III, and likewise in Quincy Howe, *A World History of Our Own Times.* Joseph Dorfman, *Thorstein Veblen and His America,* and Elmer Ellis, *Mr. Dooley's America* both set their subjects against a broad background. Thomas Beer, *The Mauve Decade* and Fairfax Downey, *Portrait of an Era as Drawn by C. D. Gibson* emphasize the more frivolous side of the nineties. Of the many autobiographies the best are Hamlin Garland, *A Son of the Middle Border;* Henry S. Canby, *The Age of Confidence;* Henry L. Mencken, *Happy Days* and *Heathen Days; The Education of Henry Adams; The Autobiography of William Allen White;* and *The Autobiography of Lincoln Steffens.*

CHAPTER III. *Transition Years in Literature and Journalism*

Although limited in scope, as its title dictates, Van Wyck Brooks, *New England: Indian Summer* is the best interpretation of the literature of the transition period. The emphasis in Alfred Kazin's brilliant *On Native Grounds* is on the new century, but the chapters on Howells and some of the other transition figures are masterly. Sound judgment rather than brilliance characterizes Percy H. Boynton, *Literature and American Life* and *America in Contemporary Fiction.*

There is a one-volume edition of the *Poems of Sidney Lanier* and a ten-volume collection of his *Writings.* The best biography is that by Aubrey Starke. On William Vaughn Moody, see David Henry, *William Vaughn Moody: A Study.* Hamlin Garland has told his own story in a series of five autobiographical volumes, the most valuable of which are *The Son of the Middle Border* and *Back Trailers of the Middle Border.* For agrarianism in literature, see the chapter in Parrington, *The Beginnings of Critical Realism;* Lucy Hazard, *The Frontier in American Literature;* and Dorothy Dondore, *The Prairie and the Making of Middle America.* Walter F. Taylor, *The Economic Novel in America* confines itself to the period from Reconstruction to 1900, and Edmund Speare, *The Political Novel* is chiefly concerned with English literature. Ellen Glasgow, *A Certain Measure* is a literary creed, and Edith Wharton, *A Backward Glance* an autobiography by no means confined to literature. The literature on Howells is immense:

the most useful studies are those by Oscar W. Firkins and Delmar G. Cooke. Mildred Howells has edited the *Life in Letters of William Dean Howells,* 2 vols. There is an admirable chapter on Howells in Parrington, *Beginnings of Critical Realism* and a more specialized treatment in Walter Taylor, *Economic Novel in America.* Howells' own autobiographical writings are essential: *A Boy's Town, Years of My Youth, Literary Friends and Acquaintances,* and *My Literary Passions.* Five prefaces which he wrote for a contemplated edition of his works have been reprinted in the *New England Quarterly,* Vol. XVII (1944).

There is no substitute for reading the novels themselves. Those particularly recommended are: Hamlin Garland, *Main Travelled Roads, Other Main Travelled Roads, The Rose of Dutcher's Coolly,* and *A Spoil of Office;* Ellen Glasgow, *Virginia, The Voice of the People, The Romance of a Plain Man, The Romantic Comedians, They Stooped to Folly, Barren Ground, The Sheltered Life,* and *Vein of Iron;* Edith Wharton, *The Fruit of the Tree, The House of Mirth, The Custom of the Country, The Age of Innocence, Hudson River Bracketed, Ethan Frome,* and *Summer;* William Dean Howells, *A Modern Instance, The Rise of Silas Lapham, A Hazard of New Fortunes, Annie Kilburn, The Landlord at Lion's Head, Letters Home, The Son of Royal Langbrith,* and *The Leatherwood God.* Van Wyck Brooks, *New England, Indian Summer* is the best account of the literary historians of the New England decline, but see also Francis O. Matthiessen's charming study of *Sarah Orne Jewett.*

Critical comment on most of the writers of this period can be found in Robert E. Spiller, *et. al.,* eds., *Literary History of the United States,* Vol. II; Vol. III of this *History* contains elaborate bibliographies of most of the more important American writers.

The best history of American journalism is by Frank Luther Mott, who has also under way a comprehensive *History of American Magazines,* three volumes of which have been published. W. G. Bleyer, *Main Currents in the History of American Journalism* is useful. Parrington has a critical essay on Godkin in *The Beginnings of Critical Realism,* and Oswald G. Villard a friendly one in *The Disappearing Daily.* Histories of newspapers and biographies of newspapermen are legion, but few of them are good. Among the best are Allan Nevins, *The Evening Post;* Harry Baehr, *The New York Tribune Since the War;* Elmer Davis, *The New York Times;* and Gerald Johnson and others, *The Sun Papers of Baltimore.* Biographies worth consulting are Rollo Ogden, *The Life and Letters of Lawrence E. Godkin;* Gerald Johnson, *An Honorable Titan, a Life of Adolph Ochs;* George Britt, *Forty Years, Forty Millions, a Biography of Frank Munsey;* C. H. Dennis, *Victor Lawson;* Ernest S. Bates and Oliver Carlson, *Hearst, Lord of San Simeon;* and John Tebbel, *George Horace Lorimer and the Saturday Evening Post. The Autobiography of William Allen White* and *The Americanization of Edward Bok* throw a good deal of light on American journalism in the transition period. Oliver Gramling, *AP, the Story of the News* is useful but not critical. Algernon Tassin has a history of *The Magazine in*

America. The sketches of journalists in the *Dictionary of American Biography,* many of them by Allan Nevins and Oswald Garrison Villard, are for the most part first rate.

CHAPTERS IV AND V. *Evolution and Pragmatism*
There is no entirely satisfactory history of American philosophical thought, but there are a number of helpful volumes that contribute to that history. The most readable are Harvey G. Townsend, *Philosophical Ideas in the United States;* Woodbridge Riley, *American Thought, from Puritanism to Pragmatism;* and T. V. Smith, *The Philosophic Way of Life.* Herbert Schneider, *A History of American Philosophy,* written for mature students, is particularly valuable for its comprehensive biographies. George Santayana, *Character and Opinion in the United States,* written with characteristic felicity, contains penetrating essays on Royce and James; no less important are Santayana's essays on "The Intellectual Temper of the Age" and the "Genteel Tradition in American Philosophy" and his "Critique of Pragmatism," all in *Winds of Doctrine.* In *Contemporary American Philosophy,* 2 vols., edited by G. P. Adams and W. P. Montague, leading philosophers expound their own ideas and systems. Morris Cohen has contributed a sketch of recent philosophical thought to the *Cambridge History of American Literature,* Vol. III. Ralph Barton Perry has written on *The Philosophy of the Recent Past* and *The Present Conflict of Ideals;* his study of *Puritanism and Democracy* has much that is relevant to an understanding of recent philosophical thought. Of more general studies of philosophy the most useful for our purposes are John H. Randall, *The Making of the Modern Mind,* Bk. IV; J. T. Merz, *History of European Thought in the 19th Century,* Vol. III; and C. E. M. Joad, *A Guide to Modern Thought.*

The most valuable single study of the implications of Darwinian thought to America is Richard Hofstadter, *Social Darwinism in American Thought,* which covers the whole range of social and economic thought. Philip Wiener, *Evolution and the Founders of Pragmatism* explores the role of the Metaphysical Club on the development of pragmatism. John Dewey, *The Influence of Darwin on Philosophy* is indispensable. Of all Spencer's writings it was *The Man versus the State* that had, perhaps, the widest influence: see especially the 1916 edition by Truxton Beale. For John Fiske, see his own volumes, *Excursions of an Evolutionist, A Century of Science,* and *The Destiny of Man.* John Spencer Clarke has written *Fiske's Life and Letters,* 2 vols., and additional *Letters* have been edited by Fiske's daughter, Ethel Fiske. For interpretation, see the masterly essay in Parrington, *Beginnings of Critical Realism,* and H. S. Commager, "John Fiske," *Proceedings of the Massachusetts Historical Society,* Vol. LXVI (1942). *The Autobiography of Andrew Carnegie* and Henry Holt, *Garrulities of an Octogenarian Editor* are eloquent of the Spencer influence. William Graham Sumner is treated more fully in chap. x.

The literature on William James and on Pragmatism is voluminous. No student should fail to read James's own *Pragmatism, The Will to Believe, and Other Essays,* and *A Pluralistic Universe,* as well as his delightful *Letters,* edited by Henry James. Horace Kallen has edited a convenient selection, *The Philosophy of William James.* Ralph Barton Perry, *The Thought and Character of William James,* 2 vols., is an inexhaustible mine of material on almost every aspect of American thought from the Civil War to James's death in 1910. Perry has also written *In the Spirit of William James* and contributed to the centennial volume, *In Commemoration of William James, 1842-1942.* There are valuable essays by John Dewey and others in another commemoration volume, *William James: The Man and the Thinker.* The French philosopher, Theodore Flournoy, has written a monograph on *The Philosophy of William James.* Josiah Royce has an interpretation of James in his *William James and Other Essays on the Philosophy of Life,* and John Dewey several appreciations in his *Characters and Events,* Vol. I. There is a wealth of material in F. O. Matthiessen, *The James Family.* Herbert W. Schneider, *History of American Philosophy* contains an exhaustive bibliography.

On pragmatism, see also A. C. Lovejoy, "The Thirteen Pragmatisms," *Journal of Philosophy,* Vol. V; John Dewey, "The Development of American Pragmatism," *Studies in the History of Ideas,* Vol. II; G. H. Mead, "The Philosophies of Royce, James, and Dewey in Their American Setting," *International Journal of Ethics,* Vol. XL. There is a severe criticism of pragmatism in Lewis Mumford's *The Golden Day* and a reply by John Dewey, "Philosophy and the Social Order," in *Characters and Events,* Vol. II. W. Y. Elliott, *The Pragmatic Revolt in Politics* is similarly critical of pragmatism for its alleged support to irrationality.

For John Dewey, see his own *Human Nature and Conduct, Reconstruction in Philosophy, Liberalism and Social Action, Problems of Men,* and the miscellaneous essays collected in *Characters and Events,* edited by Joseph Ratner in two volumes. For Dewey's contributions to American thought, see Paul A. Schilpp, ed., *The Philosophy of John Dewey;* William Feldman, *The Philosophy of John Dewey;* and Sidney Hook, *John Dewey, an Intellectual Portrait.*

Santayana's most important philosophical works, *The Life of Reason,* 5 vols., and *The Realms of Being,* 4 vols., are remote from the theme of this book. The best approach to Santayana is through his less academic writings —*Character and Opinion in the United States, Soliloquies in England, Winds of Doctrine,* and *Obiter Scripta;* the two autobiographical volumes, *Persons and Places* and *The Middle Span,* his novel, *The Last Puritan,* and his poetry, conveniently collected in Vol. I of his *Works.* There is a one-volume selection from his writings edited by Irwin Edman. His lively "Brief History of My Opinions" can be found in Adams and Montague, *Contemporary American Philosophy,* Vol. II. George Howgate has a study of *George Santayana* and Van Meter Ames of *Proust and Santayana: The Aesthetic Way of Life,* and there is a popular interpretation in Carl Van Doren, *Many Minds.*

There is a brilliant chapter in Parrington, *Beginnings of Critical Realism* on the impact of determinism on American thought, while the *Education of Henry Adams* reveals how the new physics impressed one of the most thoughtful of Americans. Students should familiarize themselves with the books that were particularly influential at the turn of the century: Karl Pearson, *The Grammar of Science;* Carl Snyder, *The World Machine;* Ernst Haeckel, *The Riddle of the Universe;* and Jacques Loeb, *The Mechanistic Conception of Life.* Later presentations of the problem can be found in C. E. M. Joad, *Guide to Modern Thought;* Arthur Balfour, *Foundations of Belief;* A. S. Eddington, *New Pathways of Science;* Bertrand Russell, *The Scientific Outlook;* and A. N. Whitehead, *Science and the Modern World.*

CHAPTER VI. *Determinism in Literature*

The best general accounts of the literary reflection of the new philosophy are Oscar Cargill, *Intellectual America;* Regis Michaud, *The American Novel Today;* Harlan Hatcher, *Creating the Modern American Novel;* Alfred Kazin, *On Native Grounds;* Ludwig Lewisohn, *Expression in America;* Harry Hartwick, *The Foreground of American Fiction;* and the fragments in Parrington, *Rise of Critical Realism.* Robert E. Spiller, *et al.,* eds., *Literary History of the United States,* 3 vols., contains chapters on most of the significant literary figures of the new day and comprehensive bibliographies.

There are, as yet, few satisfactory biographies of the writers analyzed in these pages, but see, for what they are worth, Charmian London, *The Book of Jack London,* 2 vols.; Irving Stone, *Sailor on Horseback, The Biography of Jack London;* Franklin Walker, *Frank Norris;* Ernest Marchand, *Frank Norris, a Study;* Thomas Beer, *Stephen Crane;* and the introductions to the various volumes of the *Collected Works of Crane,* 12 vols. For Dreiser, see the autobiographical writings, *A Book about Myself, A Hoosier Holiday. Hey Rub-a-Dub-Dub;* and Dorothy Dudley, *Forgotten Frontiers: Theodore Dreiser and the Land of the Free.* Cabell's theories of literature are set forth in his own *Cream of the Jest, Straws and Prayer-Books, These Restless Heads,* and *Beyond Life;* for criticism, see Hugh Walpole, *The Art of James Branch Cabell,* and essays and chapters in Parrington, *Beginnings of Critical Realism,* H. S. Canby, *American Estimates,* Carl Van Doren, *The American Novel,* Percy H. Boynton, *America in Contemporary Criticism,* and Emily Clark, *Innocence Abroad.*

CHAPTER VII. *The Cult of the Irrational*

The cult of irrationality has been elaborately analyzed. Edmund Wilson, *Axel's Castle* is largely a study of the influence of the French symbolists. Houston Peterson, *The Melody of Chaos* is devoted to Conrad Aiken but has wider implications. Frederick J. Hoffman, *Freudianism and the Literary Mind* deals chiefly with English and Continental writers. There is good material in Cargill, Lewisohn, Hartwick, and Michaud, mentioned above.

For the Imagists, see Glenn Hughes, *Imagism and the Imagists* and Amy Lowell's own *Tendencies in Modern American Poetry*. On Amy Lowell, see Winifred Bryher, *Amy Lowell, a Critical Appreciation*. There is interesting material, too, in Sherwood Anderson, *A Story-Teller's Story;* William E. Leonard, *The Locomotive God;* Gertrude Stein, *The Autobiography of Alice B. Toklas;* and Albert Parry, *Garretts and Pretenders, a History of Bohemianism in America*. For Robinson Jeffers, see, in addition to his own poetry, Lawrence C. Powell, *Robinson Jeffers, the Man and His Work;* Rudolph Gilbert, *Shine, Perishing Republic;* Henry Wells, *The American Way of Poetry;* and Alfred Kreymborg, *A History of American Poetry*.

The literature on Henry Adams is large and growing. In addition to his own *Education of Henry Adams* and *Mont-Saint-Michel and Chartres,* students should consult *The Degradation of the Democratic Dogma,* edited by Brooks Adams, the two volumes of *Letters,* edited by Worthington C. Ford, and the volume of miscellaneous letters, *Henry Adams and His Friends,* with a long and interesting introduction by Harold Cater. On Adams and his theories, see James T. Adams, *Henry Adams* and *The Adams Family;* Gamaliel Bradford, *American Portraits;* H. S. Commager, "Henry Adams," in *Jernegan Essays in American Historiography;* Ferner Nuhn, *The Wind Blew from the East;* Van Wyck Brooks, *New England: Indian Summer;* R. P. Blackmur's essays in the *Southern Review,* Vol. V, and the *Kenyon Review,* Vol. II; Paul Elmer More, *Shelburne Essays, Eleventh Series;* and the introduction to Charles A. Beard's edition of Brooks Adams, *The Law of Civilization and Decay*.

CHAPTER VIII. *The Traditionalists*

All the general histories of American literature give some attention to the traditionalists: see, for example, those by Boynton, Pattee, Quinn, Lewisohn, and Carl Van Doren. There are comprehensive bibliographies in Robert E. Spiller, *et. al.,* eds., *A Literary History of the United States*. The novels and poems themselves are, of course, indispensable; none of the traditionalists has been very articulate about literary theories, but see Willa Cather, *Not before Forty;* Ellen Glasgow, *A Certain Measure;* and Twelve Southerners, *I'll Take My Stand*.

For Edith Wharton, see her own *A Backward Glance;* Percy Lubbock, *Portrait of Edith Wharton;* Robert Morss Lovett, *Edith Wharton;* and essays in Henry D. Sedgwick, *The New American Type and Other Essays,* Edwin Bjørkman, *Voices of Tomorrow,* Percy Boynton, *Some Contemporary Americans,* John C. Underwood, *Literature and Insurgency,* and Alfred Kazin, *On Native Grounds*. There are two collections of critical—but not too critical—essays on Ellen Glasgow, one edited by Dorothea L. Mann and the other by Stuart P. Sherman, and there are valuable chapters on her in Nellie E. Monroe, *The Novel and Society* and Kazin, *On Native Grounds*. For Willa Cather, see Maxwell Geismar, *The Last of the Provincials;* Malcolm Cowley, *After the Genteel Tradition;* Regis Michaud, *The American Novel Today;* Elizabeth S. Sergeant, *Fire under the Andes;*

Rebecca West, *The Strange Necessity;* and René Rapin, *Willa Cather.* The literature on Robinson is large. There are biographies by Hermann Hagedorn and Emery Neff; critical studies by Charles Cestre, *An Introduction to E. A. Robinson;* Yvor Winters, *E. A. Robinson;* Robert P. T. Coffin, *New Poetry of New England: Frost and Robinson;* Lloyd Morris, *The Poetry of E. A. Robinson;* and interesting chapters in Henry Wells, *The American Way of Poetry;* Floyd Stovall, *American Idealism;* and Amy Lowell, *Tendencies in Modern American Poetry.* Rollo W. Brown, *Next Door to a Poet: A Friendly Glimpse of E. A. Robinson* deals with the man rather than with his poetry. Estelle Kaplan, *Philosophy in the Poetry of Edwin Arlington Robinson* is inadequate. There is a bibliography of Robinson by Charles B. Horgan.

CHAPTER IX. *Religious Thought and Practice*
There is no satisfactory history of religion or of religious thought in America. The chapters in Tocqueville, *Democracy in America* and in Bryce, *The American Commonwealth* are still unsurpassed. Willard Sperry, *Religion in America* was designed primarily for British consumption but is probably the best survey available. W. W. Sweet, *The Story of Religions in America* peters out in the modern period. Winfred E. Garrison has some valuable chapters on the more recent period in *The March of Faith.* There is much that is interesting, especially pictorially, in Luther Weigle, *American Idealism,* in *The Pageant of America.* Gerald B. Smith, ed., *Religious Thought in the Last Quarter Century* covers the early decades of this century but, like most such collections, is spotty. Probably the best material is to be found in autobiographical and biographical material: William J. Tucker, *My Generation;* James Freeman Clarke, *Autobiography, Diary and Correspondence;* William Lawrence, *Memoirs of a Happy Life;* Cardinal Gibbons, *A Retrospect of Fifty Years;* and *The Recollections of Washington Gladden.* For the socialization of Christianity, C. H. Hopkins, *Rise of the Social Gospel in American Protestantism* and Henry F. May, *The Protestant Churches and Industrial America* are indispensable, and there are admirable chapters in A. M. Schlesinger, *Rise of the City* and Ralph Gabriel, *Course of American Democratic Thought.* W. D. P. Bliss, *Encyclopaedia of Social Reform* furnishes a convenient index to the ideas of the Christian Socialists. The literature of Christian Socialism is voluminous: see, for example, George D. Herron, *The Christian Society;* Henry C. King, *Reconstruction in Theology;* Gerald B. Smith, *Social Idealism and the Changing Theology;* Shailer Mathews, *Social Teachings of Jesus;* Francis Peabody, *Jesus Christ and the Social Question;* S. D. McConnell, *The Church and the Changing Order.* For Gladden, his own delightful *Recollections* are sufficient. Rauschenbusch's philosophy can be found in his *Christianity and the Social Crisis, Christianizing the Social Order,* and *A Theology for the Social Gospel.* There is a biography by D. R. Sharpe. On Fundamentalism, see Grover C. Loud, *Evangelized America* and Stewart G. Cole, *History of Fundamentalism.* Bryan at Day-

ton can be understood best in the sympathetic pages of Wayne Williams, *William Jennings Bryan;* for the opposite view, see Paxton Hibben, *The Peerless Leader* and the famous essay by H. L. Mencken in *Prejudices,* Vol. I. For Modernism, see Frank M. Foster, *The Modern Movement in American Theology* and the writings of such liberals as Harry E. Fosdick and John Haynes Holmes.

The best history of American Catholicism is Theodore Maynard, *The Story of American Catholicism,* and the most helpful biography A. S. Will, *Life of Cardinal Gibbons.* Paul Blanshard, *American Freedom and Catholic Power* is a highly critical analysis of the activities of the Catholic church in publi affairs.

Part II

General

There is no general history of American social thought in the twentieth century, nor are there any histories of any one of the social sciences that are satisfactory. Some information may be gleaned from H. E. Barnes and Howard Becker, *Social Thought, from Lore to Science* and some, too, from such collections as H. E. Barnes, ed., *The History and Prospects of the Social Sciences* and Edward G. Hayes, ed., *Recent Developments in the Social Sciences.* Two studies of American intellectual history contain valuable material on the twentieth century: Merle Curti's indispensable *Growth of American Thought,* and Ralph Gabriel, *Course of American Democratic Thought.* Charles and Mary Beard, *America in Midpassage,* though it has material on such subjects as radio, movies, journalism, and the social sciences, does not compare in depth or learning with the earlier *Rise of American Civilization.* *The American Spirit,* which concludes the Beards' study of American civilization, is an attempt to trace the idea of Americanism rather than to survey its manifestations. Harold Laski's *American Democracy* attempts to do for contemporary America what Tocqueville did for the United States of the 1830's; some of the chapters on social and cultural institutions are perspicacious, but Mr. Laski is so concerned with arguing his thesis that he fails to give a fair or a rounded picture. Lloyd Morris, *Postscript to Yesterday* is unfailingly lively but haphazard and, in parts, superficial. The decades of the twenties and the thirties witnessed a number of collective attempts to interpret American life. The most useful of these are: Harold Stearns ed., *Civilization in the United States,* and *America Now;* Kirby Page, ed., *Recent Gains in American Civilization;* Charles G. Shaw, ed., *Trends of Civilization and Culture;* Charles A. Beard, ed., *Whither Mankind,* and *Towards Civilization;* Fred Ringel, ed., *America As Americans See It.* Foreign Views of America are available in Allan Nevins, ed., *America Through British Eyes;* H. S. Commager, ed., *America in Perspective;* and Oscar Handlin, ed., *This Was America.* In the absence of more substantial or more specialized works, the material in the *Dictionary of American Biography,* 21 vols., and the *Encyclopaedia of the Social Sciences,* 15 vols., is particularly valuable.

CHAPTER x. *Lester Ward and the Science of Society*

Wanting any general history of American sociology, the best introduction is Albion Small, "Fifty Years of Sociology in the United States," *The American Journal of Sociology,* Vol. XVI. E. C. Hayes, ed., *Recent Developments in the Social Sciences* contains chapters by Charles Ellwood on sociology and by Clark Wissler on cultural anthropology. There are chapters on leading American sociologists in Charles H. Page, *Class and American Sociology* and in Howard Odum, ed., *American Masters of Social Science,* and F. N. House, *The Development of Sociology* has some material on American contributions. The chapter in Parrington, *Beginnings of Critical Realism in America,* "Disintegration and Reintegration," deal chiefly with Spencer and Fiske but contains much that is suggestive. Of autobiographical materials, the most helpful are: Richard B. Ely, *The Ground under Our Feet;* E. A. Ross, *Seventy Years of It;* and John R. Commons, *Myself.*

Essential, of course, are the writings of the two great antagonists, Sumner and Ward. Those of Sumner are the more readily available. His *Essays* are collected in a two-volume edition by A. G. Keller and M. R. Davie; an earlier volume, *The Forgotten Man and Other Essays,* contains a careful bibliography by M. R. Davie. While there is as yet no full-dress biography, there is a useful sketch by Harris E. Starr, *William Graham Sumner,* and Sumner's disciple and successor, Albert G. Keller, has given us his *Reminiscences (Mainly Personal) of William Graham Sumner.* A somewhat starry-eyed tribute can be read in John Chamberlain's *Farewell to Reform.* The best analysis of the impact of Spencer and Sumner on American thought is in Richard Hofstadter, *Social Darwinism in America,* but see also Maurice R. Davie, ed., *Sumner Today.*

The most important of Ward's volumes are *Psychic Factors in Civilization, Dynamic Sociology, Pure Sociology,* and *Applied Sociology.* His miscellaneous writings, sociological and scientific, can be found in the six volumes of *Glimpses of the Cosmos,* which include also several autobiographical sketches. *Young Ward's Diary*—the only one of many volumes which has survived—has been edited by B. F. Stern, to whose tireless devotion we owe also excerpts from Ward's correspondence with his fellow-sociologists: see *Social Forces,* Vols. X, XII, XIII, and XV; *The American Sociological Review,* Vols. III and XI, and *The Scientific Monthly,* Vol. XL. The biography of Ward by Samuel Chugerman—somewhat curiously subtitled *The American Aristotle*—is disappointing, as is Emily Cape, *Lester F. Ward, a Personal Sketch.* Fay B. Karpf, *American Social Psychology,* Charles Ellwood, *A History of Social Philosophy,* C. H. Page, *Class and American Sociology,* and H. Odum, ed., *American Masters of Social Science* all contain material on Ward, and E. P. Kimball, *Sociology and Education* is devoted to an analysis of the theories of Spencer and Ward.

The struggle between laissez faire and the welfare state is as old as our history, and every general book on political theory deals with it in one form or another. The persistence of Spencerian notions can best be appreciated by reading the introductions which distinguished Americans such as Elihu Root, Henry Cabot Lodge, William Howard Taft, and Nicholas Murray

Butler contributed to each chapter of Spencer's *The Man versus the State* which Truxton Beale edited in 1916. Two books of particular interest are Jerome Davis, *Capitalism and Its Culture* and Thomas C. Cochran and William Miller, *The Age of Enterprise*. The modern case for laissez faire is presented by Herbert Hoover, *American Individualism, The New Day,* and *The Challenge to Liberty* and by Friedrich von Hayek in his widely read *Road to Serfdom*. The case for the welfare state is put by George Soule, *A Planned Society;* Harry Laidler, *Socializing Our Democracy;* Herbert Finer, *The Road to Reaction;* and George Fainsod and Lincoln Gordon, *Government and the American Economy*. Ralph Barton Perry, *Present Conflict of Ideals,* though originally written as an explanation of the philosophical issues presented by the first World War, contains material valuable for this controversy. For the impact of totalitarianism on the American mind, see Herbert Agar, *A Time for Greatness*.

As a background to Walter Lippmann's philosophy, students should read Graham Wallas, *The Great Society* and *Human Nature in Politics*. Lippmann approached *The Good Society* through a long series of books, of which the most important are *Preface to Politics, Drift and Mastery, Public Opinion, The Phantom Public,* and *A Preface to Morals*.

CHAPTER XI. *Thorstein Veblen and the New Economics*
On the older economics, see C. Gide and C. Rist, *History of Economic Doctrines* and L. H. Haney, *A History of Economic Thought*. Paul T. Homan, *Contemporary Economic Thought* has chapters on John Bates Clark, Veblen, and Mitchell. John M. Clark contributed a long and valuable chapter on economics to E. C. Hayes, ed., *Recent Developments in the Social Sciences*. Joseph Dorfman, *The Economic Mind in American Civilization,* 3 vols., is by far the most thorough analysis of economic thought in our literature; a fourth volume will cover the period from 1918 to the present. Appropriate articles in the *Encyclopaedia of the Social Sciences* are indispensable.

The story of dissent has been told voluminously but nowhere more sympathetically than in the pages of Parrington, *Main Currents in American Thought,* Vols. II and III. See also Lillian Symes and Travers Clement, *Rebel America;* V. F. Calverton, *Where Angels Feared to Tread;* Louis Filler, *Crusaders for American Liberalism;* and the essays in Chester McA. Destler, *American Radicalism, 1865-1901*. Any selection of personal material would include Caro Lloyd, *Henry Demarest Lloyd;* Arthur E. Morgan, *Edward Bellamy* and *The Philosophy of Edward Bellamy;* Louis F. Post, *The Prophet of San Francisco; Personal Memories and Interpretations of Henry George;* Brand Whitlock, *Forty Years of It;* Frederic C. Howe, *Confessions of a Reformer;* Charles E. Russell, *Bare Hands and Stone Walls;* and Tom Johnson, *My Story*. For the emergence of the new economics, see Richard T. Ely, *Ground under Our Feet;* E. A. Ross, *Seventy Years of It;* and John R. Commons, *Myself*. There is a tribute to Henry C. Adams in the *Journal of Political Economy,* April, 1922.

For Veblen the student must turn first to his own writings, difficult as they sometimes are. There are convenient volumes of selections, *What Veblen Taught*, edited with a long and judicious introduction by Wesley Mitchell and *The Portable Veblen*, edited by Max Lerner. The most important of Veblen's books are *The Theory of the Leisure Class, The Theory of Business Enterprise, The Instinct of Workmanship*, and *The Engineers and the Price System*, while his essays have been collected in *The Place of Science in Modern Civilization* and *Essays in Our Changing Order*. Joseph Dorfman, *Thorstein Veblen and His America* is a comprehensive biography; R. L. Duffus, *The Innocents at Cedro*, a charming personal recollection from Veblen's Stanford days. There are interesting critical observations in Max Lerner, *Ideas Are Weapons;* Alfred Kazin, *On Native Ground;* Lloyd Morris, *Postscript to Yesterday;* and Richard V. Teggart, *Thorstein Veblen, a Chapter of American Economic Thought.*

CHAPTER XII. *The Literature of Revolt*

There is no substitute for reading the novels and stories of the writers discussed in the text, and it is superfluous to list them here. There is a good deal of biographical and critical material about some of the authors we have discussed but not much that deals with them primarily as interpreters of the economic scene. Walter F. Taylor, *The Economic Novel in America* unfortunately covers only the period from the Civil War to 1900 and is by no means comprehensive even for those years. Valuable for these transition years are the relevant chapters in Parrington, *Beginnings of Critical Realism* and John Chamberlain, *Farewell to Reform*. Granville Hicks, *The Great Tradition* is an inflexibly left-wing interpretation of American literature that generates more heat than light; John C. Underwood, *Literature and Insurgency* is disappointing. Of the books dealing more specifically with the twentieth century, the most valuable are Alfred Kazin, *On Native Grounds;* Maxwell Geismar, *The Last of the Provincials* and *Writers in Crisis;* Leo Gurko, *The Angry Decade;* Harry Hartwick, *The Foreground of American Fiction;* Harlan Hatcher, *Creating the Modern American Novel;* and Regis Michaud, *The American Novel of Today*. There are few biographies of any value. Of the writers discussed in this chapter, William Dean Howells has been the most fortunate in criticism: see Mildred Howells, ed., *Life in Letters of William Dean Howells;* Oscar Firkins, *William Dean Howells;* and Delmar G. Cooke, *William Dean Howells*. There are, as yet, no satisfactory critical evaluations of Robert Herrick, Winston Churchill, or Upton Sinclair; the literature on Henry James is voluminous, but it is perhaps sufficient to refer to Francis O. Matthiessen, *The James Family* and *Henry James, the Major Phase*. For Sinclair Lewis, see the essay "Our Own Diogenes" in Parrington, *Beginnings of Critical Realism;* Stuart Sherman, *The Significance of Sinclair Lewis;* Carl Van Doren's essay, *Sinclair Lewis;* and the chapter in Percy H. Boynton, *More Contemporary Americans*. The best interpretations of Lardner, Fitzgerald, Wolfe, Dos Passos, and Steinbeck are in the volumes by Kazin, Geismar, and Gurko already listed. See also the introductions to *The Portable Thomas Wolfe* (Geismar), *The Portable Scott Fitzgerald* (John O'Hara), *The Portable Ring Lardner* (Gilbert Seldes), and *The Portable Steinbeck* (Lewis Gannett). For Fitzgerald, see the critical and biographical material in *The Crack Up,* edited by Edmund Wilson. A considerable literature has grown up around Thomas Wolfe: see, especially, *Letters to His Mother, Julia E. Wolfe,* edited by John S. Terry; Herbert J. Muller, *Thomas Wolfe;* and Pamela H. Johnson, *Hungry Gulliver: An English Critical Appraisal of Thomas Wolfe.* Bernard De Voto's protest against the misinterpretation of America by her novelists can be read in his *The Literary Fallacy.*

CHAPTERS XIII AND XIV. *History and Historians*

The most useful general account of American historical writing is Michael Kraus, *A History of American History.* John F. Jameson, *History of Historical Writing in America* deals only with the earlier period and is too brief to be of much value. James Westfall Thompson, *History of Historical Writing,* 2 vols., has nothing on American historians, but Vol. II is useful for the English and European background. Much the same can be said for G. P. Gooch, *History and Historians in the Nineteenth Century.* John Spencer Bassett, *The Middle Group of American Historians* covers the period to the Civil War. For historians since the Civil War, see especially *The Marcus W. Jernegan Essays in American Historiography,* edited by W. T. Hutchinson, which contains essays on twenty-one leading historians. All the volumes of Van Wyck Brooks's history of American literature—*The Flowering of New England, New England: Indian Summer, The World of Washington Irving,* and *The Times of Melville and Whitman*—contain chapters or sections on historians and particularly on those historians whom the academic critics are inclined to neglect. There are biographies of all the leading nineteenth-century historians except Motley —Sparks, Prescott, Bancroft, Parkman, Fiske: see the articles in the *Dictionary of American Biography* for references. No student should neglect the penetrating chapter on history in Tocqueville, *Democracy in America,* Vol. II.

Something of the beginning of the new historical school can be read in John W. Burgess, *Reminiscences of an American Scholar;* Daniel Coit Gilman, *The Launching of a University;* W. Stull Holt, *Historical Scholarship in the United States*—chiefly the work of Herbert B. Adams at The Johns Hopkins and his "The Idea of Scientific History in America," *Journal of the History of Ideas,* I, 1940; S. E. Morison, *The Development of Harvard University since . . . 1869;* and W. A. Dunning, "A Generation of American Historiography," *Annual Report of the American Historical Association,* 1917. For Captain Mahan, see his own autobiography, *From Sail to Steam;* the chapter in Gabriel, *Course of American Democratic Thought;* and the biographies by C. C. Taylor and W. D. Puleston.

The literature on Henry Adams is large and growing. For his philosophy of history, see *The Education of Henry Adams, Mont-Saint-Michel and*

Chartres, and the essays collected and edited, with a fascinating introduction, by his brother Brooks Adams under the title *The Degradation of the Democratic Dogma.* Three volumes of Henry Adams letters have already been published, two edited by Worthington C. Ford and one edited by Harold D. Cater, *Henry Adams and His Friends.* There are evaluations of Adams by Carl Becker in *Everyman His Own Historian;* by Herbert Agar in the introduction to his edition of Adams' *History—The Formative Years;* by H. S. Commager in the *Jernegan Essays;* and by Roy Nichols in *The New England Quarterly,* Vol. VIII. James Truslow Adams has written a short biography of *Henry Adams.* For a caustic criticism of Adams, see Oscar Cargill, *Intellectual America: Ideas on the March.* For Brooks Adams, see C. A. Beard's long introduction to *The Law of Civilization and Decay* and Daniel Aaron, "Brooks Adams, The Unusable Man," *The New England Quarterly,* March, 1949. Cheyney's "Presidential Address" can be found in E. P. Cheyney, *Law in History and Other Essays.*

For the economic interpretation of history, see H. E. Barnes, *The New History and the Social Studies;* E. R. A. Seligman, *The Economic Interpretation of History;* Herbert Heaton, "The Economic Impact on History," in Joseph Strayer, ed., *The Interpretation of History.* For the beginnings of social history in the United States, see Eric Goldman, *John Bach McMaster.*

There are as yet no biographies of Turner, Parrington, or Beard, and the literature on all but the first is scanty. For Turner, besides his own writings, see the introduction by Fulmer Mood, ed., *The Early Writings of Frederick Jackson Turner;* Carl Becker's delightful essay in H. Odum, *American Masters of Social Science;* Avery Craven's penetrating essay in the *Jernegan Essays;* F. L. Paxson, "A Generation of the Frontier Hypothesis," *Pacific Historical Review,* March, 1933; Merle Curti's study of Turner's methodology in S. A. Rice, ed., *Methods in the Social Sciences;* Joseph Schafer's articles in the *Wisconsin Magazine of History,* September, 1931, June, 1932, June, 1933, and June, 1934; and Benjamin Wright's critical "American Democracy and the Frontier," *The Yale Review,* Winter, 1931. E. E. Edwards, *References on the Significance of the Frontier in American History,* published by the U. S. Department of Agriculture, reveals better than any argument how wide was Turner's influence. For Parrington, see the essay by William T. Utter in the *Jernegan Essays* and the brief sketch in the *Dictionary of American Biography.* For an understanding of Beard's philosophy of history the most important of his writings are his Presidential Address, "Written History as an Act of Faith," *American Historical Review,* January, 1934; *A Charter for the Social Sciences; The Idea of National Interest;* and *The Open Door at Home.* There is an astute criticism of Beard's later writings by S. E. Morison in *The Atlantic Monthly,* August, 1948.

CHAPTER XV. *Toward a New Science of Politics*
There is a large literature on nineteenth-century political thought; that dealing with the twentieth century is meagre. William A. Dunning, *History of Political Theories, Ancient and Modern,* 3 vols., is a classic; the

third volume, *Political Theories from Rousseau to Spencer,* touches on the American political scene. Two of Dunning's students, H. E. Barnes and C. E. Merriam, edited a continuation volume, *History of Political Theories, Recent Times.* Merriam himself has written voluminously on American political thought and institutions. His *American Political Theories* and *American Political Ideas, 1865-1917* are the most useful of all the books in the field and contain full bibliographical references. Other general books on political theory are: W. S. Carpenter, *Development of American Political Thought;* R. G. Gettell, *History of American Political Thought;* Edward R. Lewis, *History of American Political Thought from the Civil War to the World War;* F. W. Coker, *Recent Political Thought;* and the minor classic by Ernest Barker, *Political Thought in England from Spencer to the Present Day.*

The older political theory can be best read in such books as W. W. Willoughby, *The Nature of the State;* Theodore Dwight Woolsey, *Political Science or the State, Theoretically and Practically Considered,* 2 vols.; and John W. Burgess, *Political Science and Comparative Constitutional Law,* 2 vols. There is interesting material on the transition to modern political studies in Burgess, *Reminiscences of an American Scholar.*

Two classical accounts of corruption in American politics are James Bryce, *The American Commonwealth,* Vol. II, and M. Ostrogorski, *Democracy and the Organization of Political Parties,* 2 vols. More specific treatment can be found in R. C. Brooks, *Corruption in American Politics and Life;* Arthur T. Hadley, *Standards of Public Morality;* and James H. Tufts, *America's Social Morality.* For the civil service reform movement, students should consult biographies of such leaders as Carl Schurz, E. L. Godkin, George W. Curtis, Abram S. Hewitt, and Theodore Roosevelt: see the *Dictionary of American Biography* for references. Other books of value are William D. Foulke, *Fighting the Spoilsmen;* Charles H. Parkhurst, *Our Fight with Tammany;* Dorman Eaton, *The Government of Municipalities;* Allen H. Eaton, *The Oregon System;* and Claude Bowers, *Beveridge and the Progressive Era.* The attitude of the civil service reformers is perfectly expressed in E. L. Godkin, *Problems of Modern Democracy,* and *Unforeseen Tendencies in American Democracy.* For criticism of the older attitude, see Elihu Root, *Addresses on Government and Citizenship;* E. A. Ross, *Sin and Society; The Autobiography of Lincoln Steffens;* and John Chamberlain, *Farewell to Reform.*

For Wilson's political ideas consult his own academic writings: *Cabinet Government in the United States,* recently republished; *Congressional Government: A Study in American Politics; Constitutional Government in the United States;* and the essays in *An Old Master* and *Mere Literature. The State,* which was scarcely an original work, is not very rewarding. Arthur Link, *Woodrow Wilson: The Road to the White House* is the best study of Wilson's intellectual development before 1912.

The impact of pragmatism on political theory can be followed in Frank Goodnow, *Politics and Administration;* Ernest Freund, *Standards of*

American Legislation; A. Lawrence Lowell, *Essays on Government* and *Public Opinion and Popular Government;* Henry Jones Ford, *Rise and Growth of American Politics;* C. E. Merriam, *New Aspects of Politics* and *Systematic Politics.* For the economic influence, see H. W. Laidler, *History of Socialist Thought;* H. E. Barnes, *Sociology and Political Theory;* E. R. A. Seligman, *Economic Interpretation of History;* J. Allen Smith, *Growth and Decadence of Constitutional Government* and *The Spirit of American Government;* C. A. Beard, *The Economic Basis of Politics* and the two case studies, *An Economic Interpretation of the Constitution* and *An Economic Interpretation of Jeffersonian Democracy.* For irrationalism, see W. Y. Elliott, *The Pragmatic Revolt in Politics,* and Thurman Arnold, *Symbols of Government.*

CHAPTER XVI. *The Applications of Political Theory*

The influence of Populist ideas can be traced in John D. Hicks, *The Populist Revolt.* There is illuminating material, of a more general nature, in H. U. Faulkner, *The Quest for Social Justice;* Matthew Josephson, *The President Makers;* H. T. Peck, *Twenty Years of the Republic;* William Allen White, *Masks in a Pageant;* Claude Bowers, *Beveridge and the Progressive Era;* George Mowry, *Theodore Roosevelt and the Progressive Movement;* Henry F. Pringle, *Theodore Roosevelt* and *William Howard Taft,* 2 vols. Of a different, and more personal, character are such books as Herbert Croly, *The Promise of American Life;* Walter Weyl, *The New Democracy;* Gifford Pinchot, *Breaking New Ground;* and Woodrow Wilson, *The New Freedom.* The story of reforms in government administration can be read in any textbook on American government: one of the best is C. A. Beard, *The American Leviathan.*

For the TVA, see the interpretation by its administrator, David Lilienthal, *Democracy on the March;* Julian Huxley, *TVA, Adventure in Planning;* Wilson Whitman, *God's Valley, People and Power along the Tennessee;* and Charles H. Pritchett, *The Tennessee Valley Authority, a Study in Public Administration.*

Bibliographies for Bryan, Theodore Roosevelt, Wilson, and Franklin D. Roosevelt are superfluous: the literature on the first three is listed in the *Dictionary of American Biography;* the literature on F. D. Roosevelt has already reached torrential and will doubtless reach flood proportions. In each case the best approach is through the writings of the man himself. There has been, as yet, no collection of the writings of Bryan, but his *Speeches* are available in a two-volume edition, and his *Memoirs,* though fragmentary and superficial, are nevertheless illuminating. The writings of Theodore Roosevelt are available in various editions ranging from fifteen to twenty-eight volumes; the *Public Papers* of Wilson have been edited by W. E. Dodd and R. S. Baker in six volumes; and the *Public Papers* of Franklin Roosevelt up to 1940 fill nine volumes. The best single book on Bryan is—for all its grave defects—that by Wayne Williams; the best biography of Theodore Roosevelt, that by Henry Pringle; the best short biography of Wilson is that of Herbert C. Bell. There is as yet no proper biography of Franklin Roosevelt; probably the most revealing of all the books about him are Frances Perkins, *The Roosevelt I Knew* and Robert Sherwood, *Roosevelt and Hopkins.*

CHAPTER XVII. *The Evolution of American Law*

Although American scholarship has nothing to compare with the great histories of English law by Holdsworth and by Pollock and Maitland, the literature on law and jurists is richer than that of almost any other field in the social sciences. For general history, see Charles Warren, *History of the Supreme Court of the United States,* 2 vols., *History of the American Bar,* and *History of the Harvard Law School,* 3 vols. *Two Centuries' Growth of American Law* is a Yale University Bicentennial Publication. Most of the material in *Select Essays in Anglo-American Legal History,* 3 vols., is technical. Roscoe Pound, *The Formative Era of American Law* and *Interpretations of Legal History* are invaluable. Two forthcoming monographs on constitutional interpretation will illuminate a neglected subject: Elizabeth K. Bauer, *Commentaries on the Constitution, 1789–1865* and Charles Larsen, *Commentaries on the Constitution, 1865–1900.* For the period since the Civil War, see E. R. Lewis, *History of American Political Thought,* especially chaps. ii, iii, and vi.

For natural law, see Benjamin F. Wright, *American Interpretations of Natural Law;* C. Grove Haines, *The American Doctrine of Judicial Supremacy* and *The Revival of Natural Law Concepts;* E. S. Corwin, "The Higher Law Background of the American Constitutions," 42 *Harvard Law Review;* and John Dickinson, "The Law Behind the Law" 29 *Columbia Law Review.* There are fascinating chapters on natural law during and after the Revolution in Carl Becker, *The Declaration of Independence,* Pound, *Formative Era,* and Randolph G. Adams, *Political Ideas of the American Revolution.* For the development of higher law doctrines, see especially the biographies of leading jurists: Albert J. Beveridge, *John Marshall,* 4 vols.; William W. Story, *Life and Letters of Joseph Story,* 2 vols.; John T. Horton, *James Kent;* and William B. Hatcher, *Edward Livingston.* The persistence of natural law doctrines into later years can be read in the magisterial *Constitutional Limitations,* 2 vols., by Thomas C. Cooley. See, for interpretation, Morris Cohen, "Jus Naturale Redivium," *Philosophical Review,* Vol. XXV; and H. S. Commager, "The Higher Law and the Constitution," *The Constitution Reconsidered,* edited by Conyers Read.

The best introduction to historical jurisprudence are the chapters in Pound, *Formative Era* and *Interpretations of Legal History.* For the German background, see Kantorowicz, "Savigny and the Historical School of Law," 55 *Law Quarterly Review.* For Carter, see his own *Law: Its Origin, Growth and Functions* and his two essays, "The Provinces of the Written and the Unwritten Law," 24 *American Law Review* and "The Ideal and Actual in Law," *Proceedings of the American Bar Association for 1890.* There is an essay on Carter by George Miller in *Great American Lawyers,*

Vol. VII. Carl Swisher, *Stephen J. Field, Craftsman of the Law* is definitive. There is a remarkable chapter on the aristocracy of the robe in Tocqueville, *Democracy in America*. Warren, *History of the American Bar* is rich in material, and so too, though more indirectly, his *History of the Harvard Law School*. Edward S. Robinson, *Law and the Lawyers* is a psychological study; Benjamin R. Twiss, *Lawyers and the Constitution* emphasizes the relationships between lawyer and judge.

Judicial conservatism and the attack upon it that paved the way for the reforms of the twentieth century can be read in Frank Goodnow, *Social Reform and the Constitution;* Brooks Adams, *The Theory of Social Revolutions* and *Centralization and the Law;* Frank Parsons, *Legal Doctrine and Social Progress;* Thorstein Veblen, *The Theory of Business Enterprise;* J. Allen Smith, *The Spirit of American Government;* and John R. Commons, *Legal Foundations of Capitalism*. More recent criticisms of judicial conservatism can be read in Louis Boudin, *Government by Judiciary,* 2 vols.; H. S. Commager, *Majority Rule and Minority Rights;* E. S. Corwin, *The Twilight of the Supreme Court;* Robert S. Jackson, *The Struggle for Judicial Supremacy;* and Charles P. Curtis, *Lions under the Throne*.

CHAPTER XVIII. *Masters of the New Jurisprudence: Pound and Holmes*
For the beginnings of modern jurisprudence, see especially the two early volumes, John Chipman Gray, *The Nature and Sources of the Law* and Ernst Freund, *Standards of American Legislation*. Samuel Williston, *Some Modern Tendencies in the Law* surveys recent developments. Edwin Patterson, *An Introduction to Jurisprudence* is a comprehensive survey of the subject; unfortunately, it is printed but not published. Morris Cohen, *Law and the Social Order* contains essays by the most legal minded of American philosophers. Jerome Frank, *Law and the Modern Mind* is aggressively modern in its point of view. Much of sociological jurisprudence was derived from German and French sources: see Eugen Erlich, *Fundamental Principles of the Sociology of Law* and Garlan, *Legal Realism and Justice*. Important essays in the field of jurisprudence are reprinted in Jerome Hall, *Readings in Jurisprudence*. Of capital importance for modern legal philosophy are the writings of Holmes's greatest disciple, Justice Benjamin Cardozo; see especially: *The Growth of the Law, Paradoxes of Legal Science, Nature of the Judicial Process,* and *Law and Literature*.

No other American jurist—not even Story—has written so widely as Roscoe Pound. Of his many books, the most important for our purposes are: *The Spirit of the Common Law, The Formative Era of American Law, Law and Morals, Interpretations of Legal History, Introduction to the Philosophy of Law, The Task of the Law,* and *Social Control through Law*. Most of his writings, however, are scattered in legal journals. It is sufficient to list, without further comment, those which illuminate his juristic philosophy: "Mechanical Jurisprudence," 8 *Columbia Law Review;* "Scope and Purpose of Sociological Jurisprudence," 24 and 25 *Harvard Law Review;* "Ideal Element in American Judicial Decisions," 45 *Harvard Law*

Review; "The Call for a Realistic Jurisprudence," 44 *Harvard Law Review;*
"Fifty Years of Jurisprudence," 51 *Harvard Law Review;* "A Survey of Social Interests" and "Law and the State," 57 *Harvard Law Review;* "Liberty
of Contract," 18 *Yale Law Journal;* "The Courts and Legislation," *American Political Science Review,* August, 1913; "Theory of Social Interests,"
Proceedings of the American Sociological Society, 1921; and "The Law
School," in S. E. Morison, *The Development of Harvard University, 1869–
1929.*

The literature by and on Holmes is large and growing. The best introduction to Holmes is through his writings and legal opinions. Of his own
writings, *The Common Law* and *Collected Legal Essays* are the most important. There is a brief collection of his *Representative Opinions,* edited by
Alfred Lief, and a selection from his writings and opinions, *The Mind and
Faith of Justice Holmes,* edited by Max Lerner. Some of his many letters
have been published: *The Holmes-Pollock Correspondence,* edited by
Mark A. DeW. Howe, 2 vols.; and Harry C. Shriver, *Justice Oliver Wendell Holmes, His Book Notes, Uncollected Letters and Papers.* There are
some wonderful Holmes letters in R. B. Perry, *Thought and Character of
William James,* 2 vols. A list of the *Judicial Opinions of Oliver Wendell
Holmes* has been compiled by H. C. Shriver.

A comprehensive biography of Holmes is expected from the pen of Mark
A. DeW. Howe. Meantime, we are fortunate to have a number of valuable
interpretations. Of these, the best are: Felix Frankfurter, *Mr. Justice
Holmes and the Supreme Court;* and Frankfurter, ed., *Mr. Justice Holmes*
—a series of tributes from contemporaries; Francis Biddle, *Mr. Justice
Holmes;* essays by Max Lerner in *Ideas for the Ice Age* and *Ideas are
Weapons;* Silas Bent, *Justice Oliver Wendell Holmes;* Catherine D. Bowen,
Yankee from Olympus; and a valuable study of the contributions of
pragmatism in Philip Wiener, *Evolution and the Founders of Pragmatism.*

CHAPTER XIX. *Architecture and Society*

Of the general surveys of architecture in America, the most helpful are:
Talbot Hamlin, *The American Spirit in Architecture,* Vol. XIII of the
Pageant of America; Fiske Kimball, *American Architecture;* and Thomas
E. Tallmadge, *The Story of Architecture in America.* James Marston Fitch,
American Building: The Forces That Shape It is a general history with
emphasis on the twentieth century and on the more technical aspects of
building. Suzanne LaFollette, *Art in America* successfully integrates archi-
tectural with other artistic developments, and Lewis Mumford, *Sticks and
Stones* interprets American civilization in architectural terms. Oliver Larkin,
Art and Life in America is a masterly survey of the whole field which does
full justice to the place of architecture. Charles H. Whitaker, *Rameses to
Rockefeller* is a general history that gives appropriate attention to American contributions.

For the achievements of early American architecture, see F. Cousins and
P. M. Riley, *Samuel McIntire;* Ellen S. Bulfinch, *Life and Letters of Charles
Bulfinch;* Beatrice St. Julien Ravenel, *Architects of Charleston;* Howard

Major, *The Domestic Architecture of the Early American Republic;* Joseph Jackson, *Development of American Architecture, 1783–1830;* and Constance Rourke, *Roots of American Culture.* Talbot Hamlin, *Greek Revival Architecture in America* is a model of its kind. Lewis Mumford has traced the influence of Jefferson in *The South in Architecture.* For architectural ideas of the period, see James Jackson Jarves, *The Art Idea;* Horatio Greenough, *Talks on Art;* H. M. P. Gallagher, *Robert Mills: Architect of the Washington Monument;* Mrs. Schuyler Van Rensselaer, *Henry Hobson Richardson,* 2 vols.; and Henry R. Hitchcock, *H. H. Richardson.* On the bridge builders, see Dirk J. Struik, *Yankee Science in the Making* and D. B. Steinman, *Builders of the Bridge.*

There is interesting material on the Chicago Columbian Exposition in *The Education of Henry Adams* and in *The Reminiscences* of Augustus St. Gaudens, edited by Homer St. Gaudens. William Walton, *Art and Architecture at the World's Columbian Exposition,* 2 vols., is a complete pictorial record. Biographies of most of the architects who dominated the fair are available: F. L. Olmsted, Jr., and Theodore Kimball, *Frederick Law Olmsted, Landscape Architect,* 2 vols.; Harriet Monroe, *John Wellborn Root;* Alfred H. Granger, *Charles Follen McKim;* Charles Moore, *Daniel Burnham, Planner of Cities,* 2 vols.; C. C. Baldwin, *Stanford White;* and P. B. Wright, *Richard Morris Hunt.*

Montgomery Schuyler's criticism of the architecture of the eighties and nineties can be found—though with difficulty—in his *American Architecture: Studies;* there is a bibliography of his writings in the *Architectural Record* of September, 1914. Russell Sturgis' criticism has never been collected into book form but can be followed in "The Field of Art" department of *Scribner's Magazine* from 1897 to 1909 and in *The Architectural Record* for some of the same years. Lewis Mumford, *The Brown Decades* integrates the architecture of the period with painting and engineering.

The best introduction to Louis Sullivan is through his *Kindergarten Chats,* recently republished and his unfinished *Autobiography of an Idea.* Hugh Morrison has written a biography of him, and there is a good deal about him in Frank Lloyd Wright's *Autobiography.* Both Lewis Mumford and Suzanne LaFollette give generous space in their books to an appreciation of Sullivan's genius. For Wright, see, above all, his *Autobiography,* his miscellaneous speeches in *Frank Lloyd Wright on Architecture,* his Princeton University lectures on *Modern Architecture,* and Henry R. Hitchcock, *In the Nature of Materials: The Buildings of Frank Lloyd Wright.* C. H. Edgell, *The American Architect Today* is a conventional treatment of twentieth-century architecture; Sigfried Giedion, *Space, Time and Architecture* and Claude Bragdon, *Architecture and Democracy* are more sympathetic to the ideas of Sullivan and Wright, as is Larkin above.

CHAPTER XX. *The Twentieth-Century American*

It is difficult to suggest adequate material on this subject, for any interpretation of the twentieth-century American must necessarily be based upon miscellaneous and fragmentary sources—the movies, the radio, newspapers and magazines, imaginative literature, and direct observation. Of more formal accounts, there are the two substantial reports of President Hoover's committees, *Recent Social Trends in the United States,* 2 vols., and *Recent Economic Changes in the United States,* 2 vols., both less illuminating than might have been expected. More valuable is the material in Charles and Mary Beard, *America in Midpassage,* and there is something on the American character in the same authors' more specialized *American Spirit,* an inquiry into the meaning of the concept of civilization in America. Perhaps the best of all interpretations of the modern American character is Denis Brogan, *The American Character.* There are a number of histories of shorter periods that throw some light on the subject of American character and society: F. L. Paxson, *The Post-War Years, 1918–1923;* Preston Slosson, *The Great Crusade and After* and Dixon Wecter, *The Age of the Great Depression,* both in the History of American Life series, cover the period from 1914 to 1941; Broadus Mitchell, *The Depression Years* is primarily an economic study; Charles Merz, *The Dry Decade* is more than a study of Prohibition, and Gilbert Seldes, *The Years of the Locust* more than a study of panic and depression. W. F. Ogburn, ed., *Social Change and the New Deal* emphasizes the impact of government changes upon the structure of society. Of general interpretations, the best are, J. T. Adams, *Our Business Civilization;* Harold Stearns, *America: A Reappraisal;* Margaret Mead, *And Keep Your Powder Dry;* and John Gunther's encyclopedic *Inside U.S.A.*

Particularly valuable are the autobiographies of men and women whose lives spanned the years from the beginning to the middle of the century. Some of the best of these are: *The Autobiography of Lincoln Steffens,* 2 vols.; Hutchins Hapgood, *A Victorian in the Modern World;* Mark Sullivan, *The Education of an American;* Ida Tarbell, *All in the Day's Work;* Frederic Howe, *Confessions of a Reformer;* Gifford Pinchot, *Breaking New Ground;* Edith Wharton, *A Backward Glance;* Cecelia Beaux, *Background with Figures;* Ellen Chase, *A Goodly Heritage;* Oswald G. Villard, *Fighting Years;* and Robert Morss Lovett, *All Our Years.*

Almost equally valuable, though varying greatly in perception, are the observations of foreign, especially English, visitors. Of these, perhaps the best for the period between the wars are: A. Alfred Spender, *Through English Eyes;* J. B. Priestley, *Midnight on the Desert;* R. L. Price, *After Sixty Years,* which contains extracts from the diary of Price's father from 1868; Mary A. Hamilton, *In America Today;* André Siegfried, *America Comes of Age;* and two wartime books, Victor Vinde, *America at War* and Graham Hutton, *Midwest at Noon.*

The literature on manners, customs, attitudes, and prejudices is large but miscellaneous. Of all the books that illuminate this subject, the most valuable are undoubtedly those by Robert and Helen Lynd, *Middletown* and *Middletown in Transition.* A number of similar books were modeled on these classics: Nels Anderson, *Americans,* a study of Burlington, Vermont; Angie Debo, *Prairie City;* James West, *Plainville, U.S.A.,* are good examples. Similar in character but with a lighter touch are David L. Cohn, *The Good Old Days: A History of American Morals and Manners As Seen through the Sears Roebuck Catalogues* and Dixon Wecter, *The Saga of American Society.* For the impact of urbanization, see the somewhat outdated J. V. Thompson, *Urbanization, Its Effects on Government and Society* and Lewis Mumford, *The Culture of Cities* and *Technics and Civilization.*

A substantial literature has grown up around the subject of intolerance. Gustavus Myers, *A History of Bigotry in the United States* is a general work. More specialized are the classic study of the Negro question by Gunnar Myrdal, *An American Dilemma,* 2 vols.; Zacariah Chafee, *Free Speech in the United States;* Morris L. Ernst, *The First Freedom;* Osmond Fraenkel, *Our Civil Liberties;* Howard K. Beale, *Are American Teachers Free?;* Donald Strong, *Organized Anti-Semitism in America, 1929–1940;* Walter Lippmann, *American Inquisitors;* and Maynard Shipley, *The War on Modern Science.* For a general interpretation of the problem of conformity in American society, see H. S. Commager, "Who is Loyal to America?" *Harper's Magazine,* September, 1947.

There is no satisfactory history of American morals but numerous books that, in varying ways, throw some light on this difficult problem. Of these Margaret Mead, *Male and Female* is the most suggestive. Philip Wylie, *Generation of Vipers* is an amusing attack upon the feminization of American society. Charles Merz, *The Dry Decade* tells the story of the breakdown of Prohibition. Alfred C. Kinsey and associates, *Sexual Behavior in the Human Male,* more limited than its title suggests, is the first statistical analysis of American sex attitudes. For the use of leisure, see L. P. Sizer, *The Commercialization of Leisure;* Foster R. Dulles, *America Learns to Play;* and M. M. Davis, *The Exploitation of Pleasure.* There is little that is satisfactory on such institutions as the radio, the movies, or popular literature, but see Lloyd Morris, *Not So Long Ago;* Llewellyn White, *The American Radio;* Francis Chase, *Sound and Fury, an Informal History of Broadcasting;* Edgar Dale, *The Content of the Motion Pictures;* Margaret Thorpe, *America at the Movies;* and L. C. Rosten, *Hollywood.* For American humor, Constance Rourke, *American Humor* and Walter Blair, *Horse Sense in American Humor* are valuable, but the best source is a file of *The New Yorker* magazine. On the steady Americanization of the language, H. L. Mencken, *Supplements One* and *Two* to his classic *American Language* are indispensable. For popular reading, see Frank L. Mott, *Golden Multitudes* and Charles H. Compton, *Who Reads What;* James Hart has under way a study of popular fiction in America. Almost the only civilized treatment of advertising is in David Cohn's curiously named *Love in America.* There has not yet been time to study the impact of war on American society or culture, but see Pendleton Herring, *The Impact of War;* E. S. Corwin, *Total War and the Constitution;* Jack Goodman, ed., *While You Were Away;* and H. S. Commager, *et al., Years of the Modern.*

Index